The Marketing Plan

Second Edition

William A. Cohen, Ph.D.
California State University
Los Angeles

John Wiley & Sons, Inc.,

New York   Chichester   Weinheim   Brisbane   Singapore   Toronto

ACQUISITIONS EDITOR   Ellen Ford
MARKETING MANAGER   Karen Allman
PRODUCTION EDITOR   Edward Winkleman
DESIGNER   Kevin Murphy
ILLUSTRATION COORDINATOR   Anna Melhorn

This book was set in 10/12 Times Roman by Carlisle Communications and printed and bound by Courier/Westford. The cover was printed by Phoenix Color.

Recognizing the importance of preserving what has been written, it is a policy of John Wiley & Sons, Inc. to have books of enduring value published in the United States printed on acid-free paper, and we exert our best efforts to that end.

Library of Congress Cataloging in Publication Data:
Cohen, William A., 1937-
   The marketing plan/William A. Cohen.—2nd ed.
      p.   cm.
   Includes index.

   ISBN 0-471-18033-5 (pbk.   :   alk. paper)
   1. Marketing—Management.   I. Title.
HF5415. 13.C6348 1998
658.8′02—dc21   97-12926
                                                 CIP

Printed in the United States of America

10 9 8 7 6 5 4 3

Preface

This is the era of marketing. Major articles not only in *Business Week,* but also in *Time, Newsweek,* and other popular magazines attest to this fact. Every organization needs marketing to be successful, and the *key* to marketing is the marketing plan. A good marketing plan is the difference between dreams and ideas and organized, tough-minded, financially accurate, bottom-line success.

Sometime after I incorporated marketing plans into the marketing course that I taught, a former student, Robert Schwartz, stopped by to tell me that he was interviewed for an article in *Entrepreneur Magazine.*[1] Robert had started a chain of pizza restaurants. His business was based on a marketing plan he developed in my class. His cash flow was an amazing $48,000 per month. Robert was an undergraduate student. Leon Abjian, a graduate student I taught, sold his marketing plan for $5,000.

A professional consultant had occasion to examine some of the plans prepared by my students. His verdict? The plans were the equivalent of those prepared by himself and other professionals. In his opinion, they were worth $25,000 each! Yet they all were developed by undergraduate and graduate students. Based on this, several former students have gone into the business of preparing marketing plans for businesspeople; some have used their marketing plans to get the funds to start their own businesses; others have used them in corporations where they were employed.

The aim of this book is to give you the knowledge to be able to develop truly outstanding, professional marketing plans. Along with your professor's guidance, this book will explain marketing planning and give you step-by-step procedures to produce a professional plan. It also provides forms that can greatly assist you in your efforts. Actual student plans prepared in the classroom are included. You will see how students adapted the basic ideas in this book and translated them into marketing plans for particular products or services. When you complete the book, you will not only know what to do, but also how and why. You will be able to develop an excellent and professional marketing plan.

Developing a marketing plan is not theoretical. It requires you to work hard, use your imagination, and integrate your knowledge of marketing with other disciplines such as accounting, finance, and management. It is worth the time and effort required. The method described in this book for producing a marketing plan has been action-tested in the classroom and in the real world by thousands of marketing students and professionals. If you work at it steadily over the time allocated, not only will you be successful, you'll have a lot of fun doing it. It works!

William A. Cohen

---

[1] "Entrepreneurship on Campus, A Panel Discussion on Teaching Entrepreneurship," *Entrepreneur Magazine* (November 1984), p. 49.

Acknowledgment

I want to acknowledge and thank the students who contributed sample marketing plans for this edition, as well as the hundreds of others who helped teach me to teach others while developing marketing plans for my classes. Finally, I want to thank Nicole Huynh, who made significant contributions to this edition through both typing and research.

Biographical Sketch

William A. Cohen, Ph.D.

Professor William A. Cohen is Professor of Marketing, Past Chairman of the Marketing Department, and an Institute Director at California State University, Los Angeles. He has also taught at the University of Southern California and Claremont Graduate School.

Among his 33 books translated into 12 languages are *Winning on the Marketing Front, The Entrepreneur and Small Business Marketing Problem Solver, Building a Mail Order Business, The Paranoid Corporation and 8 Other Ways Your Corporation Can Be Crazy* (with Nurit Cohen), *How to Make It Big as a Consultant,* and *The Art of the Leader.* His marketing textbook, *The Practice of Marketing Management* has been adopted by more than 177 universities. His books have been recommended by Mary Kay Ash, Barry Goldwater, Peter F. Drucker, Jagdeth Sheth, numerous CEOs of major corporations, and marketing professors. Professor Cohen is also series editor for the John Wiley Series on Business Strategy.

Professor Cohen has been a consultant to the government and Fortune 500 companies, as well as to numerous small businesses. He is on several boards of directors, government commissions, and editorial advisory boards. He has also served as spokesperson for AT&T, given more than 100 TV, radio, and print interviews, and made hundreds of speeches. He has been quoted or reviewed in *Harvard Business Review, USA Today, Business Week, Fortune, Success, Changing Times, Venture, Chicago Tribune, The Los Angeles Times, The Encyclopedia Britannica,* and many other publications.

He received the Outstanding Professor's Award at California State University, Los Angeles and the Freedoms Foundation at Valley Forge Honor Medal for Excellence in Economic Education. In 1996, he was selected as CSULA Statewide Professor, the first business professor to be given this honor. Professor Cohen has also received numerous awards for excellence in directing consulting activities from the U.S. Small Business Administration.

He has supervised the preparation of more than 1,000 student marketing plans which have won major awards in student competitions and have been successfully implemented by their authors.

Professor Cohen has a B.S. from the United States Military Academy at West Point, an M.B.A. from the University of Chicago, and an M.A. and Ph.D. in management from Claremont Graduate School. He is also a distinguished graduate of the Industrial College of the Armed Forces, National Defense University, and serves as a Major General in the U.S. Air Force Reserve.

Contents

PROLOGUE

THE MARKETING PLAN MYSTIQUE

Not long ago two Harvard Business School students, Mike Wigley and Jerry De La Vega, planned how to promote audio recordings. Their idea was to enable people to order any recording they wanted—right from their own homes. Twelve months later they started their company. David Ishag, another Harvard classmate, joined them. The three entrepreneurs advertised on a cable television network that aired rock 'n' roll videos 24 hours a day. They called their company Hot Rock, Inc. Hot Rock, Inc. received 50,000 inquiries in the first 17 days. Sales grew 10 to 14 percent a month. They expected sales of $6.7 million for the first year. Yet this was no surprise.

Meanwhile, Stouffers Lean Cuisine, a frozen food line, suddenly boosted its market share by more than 30 percent in the $500 million frozen-entree food market. This caught the entire industry by surprise . . . but not those at Stouffers.

The Clorox Company had reached $1 billion in sales but profits were unimpressive. Shortly thereafter, half of the $1 billion revenue disappeared when a key division was sold. Yet only six years later Clorox again hit $1 billion in sales. Moreover, this time profits doubled . . . and Clorox fully expected these figures.

What do these three vastly different types of companies in totally different industries have in common other than their success? The answer is the marketing plan. In each case a marketing plan played a major role in enabling the company to reach its goals and the success it planned. This surprised everyone else, but not those who did it. They had a marketing plan.

THE MARKETING PLAN IS ESSENTIAL FOR EVERY BUSINESS OPERATION

A marketing plan is essential for every business operation and for efficient and effective marketing of any product or service. This is true for a brand new business, or even for marketing a product, service, or product line within a company. Seeking success for any project without the use of a marketing plan is like trying to navigate a ship in bad weather, through stormy waters, while under torpedo attack, and with neither a compass nor a clear idea of where you are going. It does require time to develop a marketing plan. But this is time well spent. It will save you time overall. The marketing plan will allow you to visualize clearly both where you are going and what you want to accomplish along the way. At the same time, a marketing plan details the very important steps required to get you from where you are to where you want to be. An added benefit is that in compiling and developing the marketing plan, you will have thought through how long it will take to accomplish each step and what resources in money, time, and effort you will need. Without a marketing plan, you will not even know when or whether you have reached your objectives.

WHAT A MARKETING PLAN WILL DO FOR YOU

A properly developed marketing plan can accomplish a lot for a relatively small amount of focused effort. A marketing plan will

- act as a road map.
- assist in management control and implementation of strategy.
- inform new participants of their roles in implementing the plan and reaching your objectives.
- assist in helping to obtain resources for implementation.
- stimulate thinking and the better use of limited resources.
- help in the organization and assignment of responsibilities, tasks, and timing.
- help you become aware of problems, opportunities, and threats in the future.

Let's look at each of these benefits in turn.

THE MARKETING PLAN ACTS AS A ROAD MAP

Perhaps the basic purpose of the marketing plan is to act as a road map to tell you how to get from the beginning of the plan to reach your objectives and goals. Like a road map, the plan describes the environment in which you are likely to find yourself along the way. A road map might describe the geographical terrain as well as the type and classification of the various road arteries, times, distances, and available stops for emergencies, gasoline, food, repair, or lodging. In the same fashion the marketing plan will describe the environment of the marketplace including your competitors, politics, laws, regulations, economic and business conditions, state of technology, forecast demand, social and cultural factors, and demographics of the target market, as well as the company's available resources.

THE MARKETING PLAN ASSISTS IN MANAGEMENT CONTROL AND IMPLEMENTATION OF STRATEGY

If you're on a trip, your strategy is the route that you plan to take. Your road map shows it, together with the expected environment. Of course, as you proceed, various problems may arise. You may need to detour due to unplanned circumstances. Perhaps there is road maintenance or severe weather that makes the most direct route or the planned route impossible to use. In fact, it is virtually certain that almost nothing will go exactly as originally planned. Yet, because your road map anticipates potential changes in your environment that may require detours, you can continue toward your destination with ease. In the same way, the marketing plan will allow you to spot and redirect your activities toward alternate paths in order to arrive at your objective with minimum difficulty. You will be able to see clearly the difference between what is happening during the implementation of your strategy and what you had planned to happen. This will give you control of the situation and allow you to take the corrective action necessary to put your project back on track and to keep it on track to reach your final objective.

THE MARKETING PLAN INFORMS NEW PARTICIPANTS OF THEIR ROLES AND FUNCTIONS

Successful implementation of a strategy requires integration of many actions, usually by many different people and departments both inside and outside the organization. Timing is frequently critical. And it is most important that all concerned individuals understand what their responsibilities are as well as how their tasks or actions fit into the overall strategy. Having a marketing plan enables you to describe "the big picture" in detail. It allows everyone to see how their actions fit in with the actions of others. New people may be assigned to activities involving your plan. They, too, can be brought immediately up-to-date regarding their responsibilities, what they must do, and how to adapt to the work of others. Thus, the marketing plan is a document that can be used to inform all participants of your objectives and how these objectives will be done: by whom, with what, and when.

THE MARKETING PLAN PLOTS THE ACQUISITION OF RESOURCES FOR IMPLEMENTATION

You will find that your resources to accomplish any project are far from unlimited. Resources are always limited. This is true whether you are an individual entrepreneur attempting to obtain money from a potential investor or you are employed by a large corporation and seeking resources for your project within the firm. A marketing plan plays an important part in persuading those who have the authority to allocate limited resources—money, people, and other assets—to your project. And with resources scarce, you must convince these individuals that you are going to use capital, goods, and labor in the most effective and efficient manner. You must not only persuade them that your objectives are achievable, but that, despite competition and other potential threats, you will ultimately reach your goals. So, your marketing plan is also a sales tool. Additionally, the marketing plan helps to demonstrate your control over the project from start to finish. It shows that not only can you see the final objective, but that you know what you must do at every point along the way. This includes actions, costs, and alternatives. When you master the project on paper, you're already halfway there. Those who have the resources you need will be more likely to see the potential and give them to you.

THE MARKETING PLAN STIMULATES THINKING AND MAKES BETTER USE OF RESOURCES

Since your resources will always be limited, you must get the maximum results from what you receive. A good marketing plan will help you make the most of what you have—to make one dollar do the work of ten. It will help you build on your strengths and minimize your weaknesses. It will also help you obtain a differential advantage over your competition. You can always do this by economizing where it doesn't count, and concentrating superior resources where it does. This leads to success. As you do the research for your marketing plan and analyze your strategic alternatives your thinking will be stimulated. As the plan unfolds you will change and modify it as new ideas are generated. Eventually you will reach the optimum: a well-organized, well-integrated plan that will make efficient use of the resources available and will assist you in anticipating most opportunities that can help or obstacles that can hinder your progress.

THE MARKETING PLAN ASSIGNS RESPONSIBILITIES, TASKS, AND TIMING

No strategy will ever be better than those who implement it. Therefore timing and the assignment of responsibilities are crucial. A marketing plan clearly outlines these responsibilities so there is no question where they lie. It's also important to schedule all activities to maximize the impact of your strategy while taking full advantage of the environment that is expected to exist at the time of its execution. Hard thinking during development will preclude suboptimization. This occurs when one small element of the plan is optimized to the detriment of the overall project.

Let's say that you are working on a marketing plan for a new personal computer. If the technical details alone are optimized, you may place the bulk of the funds on product development. This allocation may allow you to develop the best computer on the market, but you lack insufficient funds to promote it. You may have a far superior product, but few will be able to buy it because they won't know about it. Because of suboptimization, the product will fail. Yet, a less grandiose technical solution might have satisfied the market and been better than your competition at a lower development cost. Funds would then be available to promote it properly. A good marketing plan will ensure that every task will be assigned in the correct sequence, and that all elements and strategies will be coordinated synergistically to maximize their effect and ensure the completion of the project with the resources available.

Is this important? Consider Zegna, an 85-year-old Italian company that sell men's suits for $1,000 and up. This year, U.S. sales will be $100 million, up 30 percent over last year. In Europe, Zegna's sales are $500 million. That makes the company one of Europe's fastest growing fashion groups. With Zegna, avoiding suboptimization is a major challenge. There are plenty of opportunities to err. Unlike its competitors, Zegna not only puts together its own clothes, but also spins the yarn. Zegna weaves the cotton, cashmere, and wool fabrics, everything that goes into its expensive garments. Not only that, Zegna has its own retail outlets. But according to experts, that's why Zegna is clobbering its competition.[1]

THE MARKETING PLAN PREDICTS PROBLEMS, OPPORTUNITIES, AND THREATS

You may intuitively recognize some of the problems, opportunities, and threats that can occur as you work toward your objectives. Your marketing plan will not only document those of which you are already aware, but will help you identify others that you wouldn't see until you start working on your plan. It will enable you to think strategically and to consider opportunities, problems, and threats that lie in the future. The more analysis and thinking you do as you plan, the more pitfalls you will see. It's far better to note them on paper before you get started rather than when it's too late. These potential problems must never be ignored. Instead, construct your marketing plan to take maximum advantage of the opportunities, come up with solutions to the potential problems, and consider how to avoid the threats.

GETTING IN A COMPETITIVE POSITION BEFORE YOU START

A marketing plan will allow you to jump ahead of your competition even before you begin to execute your plan. You will have systematically thought it through from start to finish. You will already know where the future may lead. On paper, you will have coordinated all efforts to attain a specific objective. You will have developed performance standards for controlling objectives and goals and you will have sharpened your strategy

---

[1]John Rossant, "Is that a Zegna You're Wearing?" *Business Week,* (March 4, 1996), pp. 84–85.

and tactics to a much greater extent than would otherwise have been possible. You will be much better prepared than any of your competitors for sudden developments. You will have anticipated those that are potential problems and will know what to do when they occur. Finally, more than any competitor, you will have a vivid sense of what is going to happen and how to make it happen. Your competitors are going to react, but you will have already acted in anticipation.

TYPES OF MARKETING PLANS

Marketing plans tend to fall into a number of categories for different purposes. The two basic types are the new product and annual marketing plans.

THE NEW PRODUCT PLAN

The new product plan is prepared for a product, service product line, or brand that has not yet been introduced by the firm. It is advisable to develop a completely new product plan even before you start the project. Although the information at this stage may be sketchy, it is still far better to start planning as early as possible before any major resources have been committed. In this way alternatives can be compared and analyzed. Moreover, you will have a general idea of the overall costs and timing of competitive projects. Naturally the marketing plan for a new product will have many more unknowns than the annual marketing plan. This is because the product will have little or no feedback from the marketplace and no track record with your firm. This last point is important, because it is not unusual for products that have achieved successful sales performance with one firm to fall far short of these goals in another. This is frequently due to certain strengths of the first firm that the second firm cannot duplicate and may not even know about.

With a new product plan it is sometimes necessary to make assumptions based on similar products or services that the company has marketed or that have been introduced by other companies. But remember: if you use information based on other companies' experiences, you must assess your ability to duplicate their performance. Other sources of information may be necessary to modify data from other companies' experiences. This will be discussed later in this book. A marketing plan for a new product or service may also include development of the product from scratch. Of course if the product already exists, its technical development as a part of your plan is not needed.

ANNUAL MARKETING PLANS

Annual marketing plans are used for those products, services, and brands that are already in your company's product line. Periodically, preferably once a year, this planning must be formally reviewed. Of course, the plan may be adjusted and modified in the interim as changes occur in the environment or within the company. But the review and annual creation of a new marketing plan for the coming year may help to identify emerging problems, opportunities, and threats that may be overlooked during day-to-day operations and the "fire fighting" associated with the management of an ongoing product or service. Again, however, notice that the plan is for the future; it's how you will get from your present position to some other position at a later time. Therefore, there will still be unknowns, for which information must be forecast, researched, or, in some cases, assumed. Although annual marketing plans are usually prepared for only one year, it is possible to plan for several years and to modify the plan annually. Conversely, product plans generally cover the entire life of the project from initiation to its establishment in the marketplace. Establishment in the marketplace implies that the product is beyond the introductory stage and is growing, it is hoped, at a predicted rate.

SUMMARY

In this chapter we have discussed the importance of the marketing plan in satisfying objectives in the most efficient manner possible. We have noted the main benefits of a marketing plan:

- act as a road map.
- assist in management control and implementation of strategy.
- inform new participants of their roles in implementing the plan and reaching your objectives.
- assist in helping to obtain resources for implementation.
- stimulate thinking and the better use of limited resources.
- help in the organization and assignment of responsibilities, tasks, and timing.
- help you become aware of problems, opportunities, and threats in the future.

Knowledge of the preparation of a marketing plan is not the option of a successful manager of marketing activities—it is a requirement. But beyond that, it is an effective and valuable tool that will enable you to work on a daily basis to accomplish the objectives you have set for the particular project you are going to market.

STEP 1

PLANNING THE DEVELOPMENT OF A MARKETING PLAN

A good marketing plan requires a great deal of information gathered from many sources. It is used to develop marketing strategy and tactics to reach a specific set of objectives and goals. The process is not necessarily difficult, but it does require organization, especially if you are not developing this plan by yourself and are depending on others to assist you or to accomplish parts of the plan. This is frequently true both in the classroom and in the business world. Therefore, it is important before you start to "plan for planning." The time spent will pay dividends later. You will get back more than the time you invest up front.

To prepare for planning you must look first at the total job you are going to do and then organize the work to make sure that everything is done in an efficient manner and nothing is left out. If this is done correctly every element of your plan will come together in a timely fashion. This means that you won't complete any task too early and then have to wait for some other task to be finished before you can continue. It also means that no member of your planning team will be overworked or underworked. To accomplish this you must consider the structure of the marketing plan and all of its elements. Next you must organize your major planning tasks by using a marketing plan action-development schedule. This will give an overview of the entire marketing planning process, including who is going to do what and when each task is scheduled for completion. Managing the process is also important. You'll find some help with that in Appendix D, How to Lead a Team.

THE STRUCTURE OF THE MARKETING PLAN

Every marketing plan should have a planned structure or outline before you start. This ensures that no important information is omitted and that the material is presented in a logical manner. One outline I recommend is shown in the marketing plan outline in Figure 1-1. However, there are other ways to organize a marketing plan that are equally good. You may be required to use a specific outline, or you may be able to use an outline

TABLE OF CONTENTS

Executive Summary (overview of entire plan, including a description of the product or service, the differential advantage, the required investment, and anticipated sales and profits).

I.   Introduction
     What is the product or service? Describe it in detail and explain how it fits into the market.

II. Situational Analysis
     A. The Situational Environs
         1. Demand and demand trends. (What is the forecast demand for the product: Is it growing or declining? Who is the decision maker? The purchase agent? How, when, where, what, and why do they buy?)
         2. Social and cultural factors.
         3. Demographics
         4. Economic and business conditions for this product at this time and in the geographical area selected.
         5. State of technology for this class of product. Is it high-tech state-of-the-art? Are newer products succeeding older ones frequently (short life cycle)? In short, how is technology affecting this product or service?
         6. Politics. Are politics (current or otherwise) in any way affecting the situation for marketing this product?
         7. Laws and regulations. (What laws or regulations are applicable here?)
     B. The Neutral Environs
         1. Financial environment. (How does the availability or unavailability of funds affect the situation?)
         2. Government environment. (Is current legislative action in state, federal, or local government likely to affect marketing of this product or service?)
         3. Media environment. (What's happening in the media? Does current publicity favor this project?)
         4. Special interest environment. (Aside from direct competitors, are any influential groups likely to affect your plans?)
     C. The Competitor Environs
         1. Describe your main competitors, their products, plans, experience, know-how, financial, human, and capital resources, suppliers, and strategy. Do they enjoy the favor with their customers? If so, why? What marketing channels do the competitors use? What are their strengths and weaknesses?
     D. The Company Environs
         1. Describe your products, experience, know-how, financial, human, and capital resources, and suppliers. Do you enjoy the favor of your customers? If so, why? What are your strengths and weaknesses?

III. The Target Market
     Describe your target market segment in detail by using demographics, psychographics, geography, lifestyle, or whatever segmentation is appropriate. Why is this your target market? How large is it?

IV. Problems and Opportunities
     State or restate each opportunity and indicate why it is, in fact, an opportunity.
     State or restate every problem. Indicate what you intend to do about each of them. Clearly state the competitive differential advantage.

V.   Marketing Objectives and Goals
     State precisely the marketing objectives and goals in terms of sales volume, market share, return on investment, or other objectives or goals for your marketing plan and the time needed to achieve each of them.

VI. Marketing Strategy
     Consider alternatives for the overall strategy; for example, for new market penetration a marketer can enter first, early, or late, penetrate vertically or horizontally, and exploit different niche strategies.
     If the marketing strategy is at the grand strategy or strategic marketing management level, a market attractiveness/business capability matrix and product life cycle analysis should also be constructed.

VII. Marketing Tactics*
     State how you will implement the marketing strategy(s) chosen in terms of the product, price, promotion, distribution, and other tactical or environmental variables.

VIII. Implementation and Control
     Calculate the breakeven point and make a breakeven chart for your project. Compute sales projections and cash flows on a monthly basis for a three-year period. Determine start-up costs and a monthly budget, along with the required tasks.

IX. Summary
     Summarize advantages, costs, and profits and restate the differential advantage that your plan offers over the competition and why the plan will succeed.

X.   Appendices
     Include all supporting information that you consider relevant.

*Note under the marketing strategy and tactics sections how your main competitors are likely to respond when you take the action planned and what you will then do to avoid the threats and take advantage of the opportunities.

FIGURE 1-1. Marketing plan outline.

of your choice. What outline you use is unimportant at this point. What is important is that your plan be presented in a logical way with nothing omitted. So, whether you are given a specific outline to follow, or are allowed to develop your own, keep your specific objective for writing the plan in mind.

Let's examine each section of this marketing plan structure in Figure 1-1 in more detail. You will find many sections common to all marketing plans.

THE EXECUTIVE SUMMARY

The first part of the marketing plan structure or outline is the executive summary. It is a synopsis or abstract of the entire plan. It includes a description of the product or service, the differential advantage of your product or service over that of your competitors, the investment needed, and the results you anticipate. These results can be expressed as a return on investment, sales, profits, market share, or in other ways.

The executive summary is especially important if your marketing plan is going to be used to help you to obtain the resources for implementation. Corporate executives are busy. There may well be more than just your marketing plan on which they must make funding decisions. Sometimes several competing marketing plans are submitted simultaneously, but only one is given the green light to proceed. Remember when submitting your marketing plan to a venture capitalist, there will be many competing plans. A venture capitalist receives hundreds of plans every year, but only a few can be funded. Therefore, it is hard to overestimate the importance of your executive overview.

The executive summary is a summary of the entire plan. It may vary in length from a single paragraph to a few pages. From it a busy executive can get a quick overview of the project without reading the entire plan. Therefore, no matter how good the main body of your plan, your executive summary must be well thought out and succinct. It must demonstrate that you know what you're talking about and that your proposal has potential and a reasonable likelihood of success. If not, the executive judging your plan will probably read no further.

Usually the executive summary is one of the last elements to be prepared. This is because it is impossible to summarize accurately until you complete every other part. But even though it is done last, remember that it will appear at the beginning of the plan's documentation and must persuade the reader to read further.

THE TABLE OF CONTENTS

A table of contents sounds rather mundane and you may feel that it is unnecessary. You might be especially inclined to discard the idea if your marketing plan is short. But I assure you that a table of contents is absolutely necessary. It makes no difference whether your marketing plan is only a few pages or a hundred pages in length. It is required, never optional, because of a psychological factor that affects those who will evaluate your marketing plan for approval or disapproval.

If you are using your plan to acquire funds or other resources to implement your project, the table of contents is important because many individuals from many functional disciplines will be sitting on the review board. Some may be experts in the technical area, who will be interested primarily in the technical details of your product or service. Others will be financial experts, who will want to examine your break-even analysis, the financial ratios you have calculated, and other financial information. In fact, every expert tends to look first at his or her own area. Now, if you submit a table of contents, this will be fairly easy to do. The reader will scan the list of subjects and turn to the correct page within a few seconds. If you fail in this regard, the evaluator of your plan will have to search for the information. If you are lucky, he or she will find it anyway. Unfortunately, you won't always be lucky. When many plans must be reviewed, the evaluator may spend only a few minutes or even a few seconds in the search. That's where the psychological factor comes in. If the information can't be found easily, the evaluator may assume it's not there. This not only raises questions of what you don't know, but may also give the competitive edge to a marketing plan done by someone who made the information easier to find.

The need for a table of contents is especially critical when your plan is being submitted to venture capitalists, who put up large sums of money to businesses that already have a track record and a marketing plan for future growth.

You may have heard that venture capitalists look only at business plans. Marketing and business plans are identical, especially in smaller companies and with start-ups and new products. When you are trying to obtain resources from a venture capitalist, or any investor, the two plans are synonymous. Either the business plan must have a heavy marketing emphasis or the marketing plan must include complete financial, manufacturing, and technical data.

Typically, funds are available for investment in fewer than one percent of the plans that are submitted. One venture capitalist told me he receives more than 1,000 marketing plans every month, each of which contains a minimum of 30 pages. Some exceed 100 pages. Under the circumstances, do you think that anyone could actually review all of these plans in great detail? Of course not. Accordingly, this venture capitalist looks first at the executive summary, and, if it appears to be interesting, spot-checks the plan using the table of contents for items of particular interest. If he can't find the information he wants after a few seconds' search, he discards the plan. With so many plans to look at, he just doesn't have the time. In this initial screening most of the plans are dropped, leaving only a few for a more detailed reading and a final decision. So don't forget this mundane tool, and be certain that the contents is an accurate list of all the important topics in your marketing plan.

INTRODUCTION

The introduction is the explanation of the details of your project. Unlike the executive summary, it is not an overview of the project. Its purpose is to give the background of the project and to describe your product or service so that any reader will understand exactly what you are proposing. The introduction can be a fairly large section. After reading it the evaluator should understand what the product or service is and what you propose to do with it.

SITUATIONAL ANALYSIS

The situational analysis contains a vast amount of information and, as the term indicates, is an analysis of the situation that you are facing with the proposed product or service. Because the situational analysis comes from taking a good hard look at your environment, many marketing experts refer to the process as environmental scanning.

I like to approach the situational analysis by dividing the analysis into four categories. I call them the environs of the marketplace. The four categories are situational environs, neutral environs, competitor environs, and company environs. Let's look at each in turn.

Situational Environs. Situational environs include demand and demand trends for your product or service. Is this demand growing, is it declining, or has it leveled off? Are there certain groups in which the demand is growing and others in which demand is declining? Who are the decision makers regarding purchase of the product and who are the purchase agents? Sometimes the decision maker and purchase agent are the same, but often they are not. For example, one family member may be the decision maker with regard to purchasing a certain product, say a brand of beer. But the individual who actually makes the purchase may be another family member. Who influences this decision? How, when, where, what, and why do these potential customers purchase? What are the social and cultural factors? Are demographics of consumers important? If so, maybe you need to discuss educational backgrounds, income, age, and similar factors. What are the economic conditions during the period covered by the marketing plan? Is business good or is it bad? High demand can occur in both a good or bad business climate depending on the product or service offered. What is the state of technology for this class of product? Is your product high-tech state-of-the-art? Are newer products frequently succeeding older ones, thus indicating a shorter product life cycle? In short, how is technology affecting the product or service and the marketing for this product or service? Are politics, current or otherwise, in any way affecting the marketing of this product? What potential dangers or threats do the politics in the situation portend? Or do the politics provide opportunities? What laws or regulations are relevant to the marketing of this product or service?

Neutral Environs. Neutral environs have to do with groups or organizations. Does government have an impact on this project? Is legislation on the state, federal, or local level likely to affect the demand or marketing of the product or service? What's happening in the media? Does current publicity favor your project or does it make any difference? Look at special interest groups. Might they have some impact? Are any influential groups (e.g., consumer organizations) likely to affect your plans for marketing this product or service?

Competitor Environs. Competitor environs are those competing against you. They are important because they are the only elements of the environment that will intentionally act against your interests. In this section of the situational analysis describe in detail your main competitors, the products they offer, their plans, experience, know-how, financial, human, and capital resources, and suppliers. Most important, discuss their current and future strategies. Note whether or not your competitors enjoy favor with their customers, and if so, why. Describe and analyze your competitors' strengths and weaknesses, what marketing channels they use, and anything else that you feel is relevant to the marketing situation as it will exist when you implement your project.

Company Environs. Company environs describe your situation in your company or company-to-be and the resources that you have available. Describe your current products, experience, and know-how, financial, human, and capital resources, suppliers, and other factors as you did environs. Do you enjoy favor with your customers or potential customers, and if so, why? Summarize your strengths and weaknesses as they apply to your project. In many respects this section includes the same items as the competitor environs section.

THE TARGET MARKET

The target market is the next major section in your plan. Describe exactly who your customers are and what, where, when, why, how, how much, and how frequently they buy.

You may think that everyone is a candidate for your product or your service. In a sense this may be true, but some segments of the total market are far more likely candidates than others. If you attempt to serve every single potential customer segment, you cannot satisfy those that are most likely to buy as well as you should. Furthermore, you will dissipate your resources by trying to reach them all. If you pick the most likely target market, or markets, you can devote the maximum amount of money to advertising your product or service in a message that is geared toward your most likely customers.

Remember, the basic concept of strategy is to concentrate your scarce resources at the decisive points. Your target markets represent one application of this concept. You usually cannot be strong everywhere, so you must be strong where it counts, in this case the markets you target.

You should also indicate why the target market you have selected is a better candidate for purchase than others. Of course, you will include the size of each market.

How will you define your target markets? First, in terms of (1) demographics (i.e., such vital statistics as age, income, and education); (2) geography (i.e., their location); (3) psychographics (i.e., how they think); and (4) life-style (i.e., their activities, interests, and opinions). There are of course other ways of describing, and perhaps segmenting your market. Knowing your customers is as important as knowing yourself (the company environs), your competitors (the competitor environs), and the other environs that you have analyzed.

PROBLEMS AND OPPORTUNITIES

The problems and opportunities section is a summary that emphasizes the main points you have already covered in preceding sections. As you put your plan together, developed your situational analysis, and described your target market, you probably implicitly covered many of the problems and opportunities inherent in your situation. Here you should restate them explicitly and list them one by one. Group them first by opportunities, then by problems. Indicate why each is an opportunity or a problem. Also indicate how you intend to take advantage of each opportunity and what you intend to do about each problem.

Many marketing planners are effective in showing how they will take advantage of the opportunities, but they do not explain adequately what they will do about the problems. To get full benefit from your plan you must not only foresee the potential problems and opportunities, but also decide what actions you must take to solve the problems.

This foresight will help you during implementation. It will also favorably impress those who will decide whether to allocate resources for your particular project. In most cases, those who evaluate your plans will know when you omit a problem, and that instantly makes a bad impression. An evaluator will then have one of two perceptions: Maybe you are intentionally omitting a difficult problem because you didn't know what to do about it, or maybe you didn't even recognize that you had a problem! Stating your problems and how you will handle them will give you a decided edge over others who submitted plans but did not take the time or trouble to consider the solutions to potential problems they might face in implementation.

Note that in the strategy and tactics sections, you will find additional potential problems. For example, when you initiate a particular strategy, a competent competitor will not stand idly by and let you take his or her market. Competitor counteractions constitute a potential problem. You'll discuss these counteractions in those sections. You do not have to add these new potential problems and/or opportunities to this section. This is a summary section for your initial scan of your environment.

MARKETING GOALS AND OBJECTIVES

Marketing goals and objectives are accomplishments you intend to achieve with the help of your marketing plan. You have already prepared your reader by your earlier analysis of the target market. In this section you must spell out in detail exactly what you intend to do.

What is the difference between a goal and an objective? An objective is an overall goal. It is more general and may not be quantified. "To establish a product in the marketplace" is an objective. So is "to become the market leader" or "to dominate the market." Goals are quantified. "To sell 10,000 units a year" is a goal. Goals are also quantified in terms of sales, profits, market share, return on investment, or other measurements. There is one major cautionary note here: Don't get trapped into setting objectives or goals that conflict. For example, your ability to capture a stated market share may require lower profits. Make sure that all your goals and objectives fit together. This is done by adjusting and reconfirming your goals and objectives after you have completed the financial portions of your plan.

MARKETING STRATEGY

In this section you will describe what is to be done to reach your objectives and goals. Your strategy may be one of differentiating your product from that of its competitors, of segmenting your total market, of positioning it in relation to other products, of carving out and defending a certain niche, of timing in entering the market, and such. Marketing strategy is a what-to-do section.

One important part of the marketing strategy section that is frequently left out, which you should include is what your main competitors are likely to do when you implement your planned strategy, and how you will take advantage of the opportunities created, solve potential problems, and avoid serious threats. Herein is another excellent opportunity for you to demonstrate what a terrific marketing strategist and planner you are.

MARKETING TACTICS

Just as strategy tells you what you must do to reach your objectives, tactics tell you how you will carry out your strategy. List every action required to implement each of the strategies described in the preceding section and the timing of these actions. These tactical actions are described in terms of what is called the "marketing mix," or the "4 Ps" of marketing: product, price, promotion, and place. Sometimes the 4 Ps are known as strategic variables. However, these variables are really tactical because they are actions taken to accomplish the strategy you developed in the preceding section.

IMPLEMENTATION AND CONTROL

In the implementation and control section you are going to calculate the break-even point and forecast other important information to help control the project once it has been implemented. You are also going to compute sales projections and cash flow on a monthly basis for a three-year period and calculate start-up costs in a monthly budget. After implementation you can use this information to keep the project on track. Thus, if the budget is exceeded you will know where to cut back or to reallocate resources. If sales aren't what they should be, you will know where to focus your attention to realize an improvement.

THE SUMMARY

In the summary you discuss advantages, costs, and profits and clearly state once again the differential advantage that your plan for this product or service offers the competition. The differential or competitive advantage is what you have that your competitors lack. Basically it states why your plan will succeed.

The summary completes your marketing plan outline. You now have an overview of the information that you'll need for your marketing. As you go through this book, forms will be provided to assist in completing every section of the marketing plan that we've talked about. As you complete these forms you will automatically be completing your marketing plan.

Figure 1-2 is a sample marketing plan action development schedule that will assist you in planning to plan. This schedule should reflect your particular situation. It lists the actions that must be taken and shows you where to start and the time needed to complete

Task	1	2	3	4	5	6	7	8	9	10	11	12
Secondary research into demographics, situational factors				↑								
Market research regarding potential demand					↑							
Audit of competitors' and company environs						↑						
Investigation of neutral environs						↑						
Establishment of objective, goals, and overall strategy							↑					
Development and specification of tactics; additional marketing research as required										↑		
Development and calculation of implementation and control information									↑		↑	
Writing and development of marketing plan document												↑

Weeks After Initiation

FIGURE 1-2.   Sample marketing plan action development schedule.

each action. The horizontal line begins when the action is to be initiated and continues until its scheduled completion. An adjusted date is provided by a dashed line; thus as you proceed you can use the action schedule to adjust dates when a certain action was not completed on time and the schedule must be modified. In this way you can develop and coordinate a planning process that reflects your situation and any deadlines you might have for completing your plan.

If you are completing the plan on a team, names can be written within the spaces provided for the tasks to indicate who is responsible for every action. A blank development schedule (Figure 1-3) is provided on page 16 for your use in planning to plan.

KEEPING YOUR MATERIAL ORGANIZED

It is very important to keep your material together to guard against loss and for updating as new data are received. A loose-leaf notebook is a helpful tool. Each section can be marked: executive summary, introduction, situational analysis, target market, problems and opportunities, marketing goals and objectives, marketing strategy, marketing tactics, implementation and control, and summary. As additional information is received in its rough form it can be added to the appropriate section.

SUMMARY

In this chapter you have prepared yourself by planning to plan. You have examined the structure of the outline that will be used for developing your marketing plan, the information required in each of its sections, and a planning form that can be used to help you get organized and work efficiently. Finally, you have seen how to keep your material organized in a simple way by using a loose-leaf notebook.

Task	1	2	3	4	5	6	7	8	9	10	11	12

FIGURE 1-3.   Blank marketing plan action development schedule.

2

STEP 2

SCANNING YOUR ENVIRONMENT

In this chapter you are going to decide what information you need for the introduction and situational analysis sections of your marketing plan and where you can obtain this information.

THE INTRODUCTION

In the introduction you must state what the product or service is, describe it in detail, and note why there is demand for it in the marketplace. To do this accurately and completely you need information that goes beyond product or service attributes and benefits. You must analyze the life cycle for your product or service. Remember, every product and service class passes through a life cycle just as if it were a living thing. The shape of the curve as the product passes through the different stages of its life is called "the product life cycle."

The classic product life cycle is shown in Figure 2-1. Note that its stages are introduction, growth, maturity, and decline. Note also that sales and profits are plotted as a curve that changes shape from stage to stage. Different strategies work better for different stages. This is because conditions in each stage are different. The shape of the curve will have important strategic implications which are needed when you begin to develop a strategy. For now, notice that the sales and profit curves differ. For example, note that profits peak in the growth stage, whereas sales continue to rise and peak in the maturity stage.

You must decide whether your product is in the introductory, growth, maturity, or decline stage. You may think that when a new product is introduced, it is automatically in the introductory stage. If it is sufficiently different from other products or services of its class, maybe it is. When personal computers first came on the market, they were so radically different from the mainframe models used by large corporations that these products were in the introductory stage of their own life cycle.

So this raises an important question. Do you analyze a new product in its own life cycle, or in the life cycle of its class of products or services? The answer: you can gain useful insights in looking at your new product both ways. Which is more important

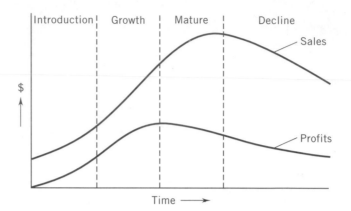

FIGURE 2-1.   Classic product life cycle.

depends on how different your product is from what is already in the marketplace. Let's compare a couple of new products so you can see what I'm talking about.

Take the common, garden-variety marketing textbook. They've been around for a long time. As a class, marketing textbooks are definitely not in the introductory stage. But what if the entire textbook were on a CD ROM? Now you've got a class of new products in the introductory stage of their own product life cycle. That doesn't mean that the textbook doesn't have its own introductory stage also . . . only that it may make sense to consider where this product falls in the product class life cycle as well.

Perhaps your product is new, but its product class is in the growth stage of its life cycle. This could be confirmed if the product class had already been on the market for some time, but sales are still growing. A product that has been in the marketplace for some time and for which sales may still be increasing, but profits are not, is probably in the maturity stage. A typical product might be music recorded on a cassette tape. Finally, the product or service may be in the decline stage. A cigarette lighter might be toward the end of its product class life cycle and in the decline stage.

It may be unwise to introduce a new product that is approaching the end of its product class life. But if your new product could immediately capture most of the declining market, it could still be very profitable.

You should also examine complementary products, which are products that do not directly compete with your product but in some way complement it or are used with it. If your new product is a computer, a complementary product could be a computer disk, peripheral equipment, or furniture built especially for computers. If your new product is a soft drink, complementary products could be the bottle, the bottle cap, or the package.

You should then investigate substitute products, which are products that are substitutes for the product you are introducing. These are not only direct substitutes through similar products made by a competitor, but substitutes in the sense that your target market can get similar benefits from them. If your new product is a video game, your direct substitutes for your product are other video games. But video games are actually a form of entertainment. What other entertainment might your potential customers buy with the money they could spend on your game? When the Wright brothers built the first airplane, no other airplanes existed. Therefore there was only indirect competition from substitute products. What were these substitute products? Some were other means of short-range transportation. Others were probably large luxury items used by the very wealthy. And for the military market, they might have been observation balloons or even horse cavalry.

Now you are ready to describe your product or service: its size, weight, color, shape, the material of which it is made, its function, what it does, and its benefits to potential users.

THE SITUATIONAL ANALYSIS

As we noted in Chapter 1, the situational analysis is an extensive and important part of the marketing plan. On the basis of the situational analysis, you will develop an optimal strategy that you can use to reach your goals and objectives. To make a situational analysis you must answer questions about the environment you are facing. To help you with this challenge, let's go over the questions in Figure 2-2 individually.

TARGET MARKET

The first environmental question under the target market section has to do with location. You will want to describe this location and its special climatic and geographical features. Is it a hot, humid environment? A cold, dry one? A desert? Mountainous area? Oceanfront? Suburban? Urban? Or what? Every climatic or topographical feature should be noted and described in detail.

Now the buyer can be categorized into consumers and organizational buyers. Organizational buyers buy for their organizations rather than for their own consumption. We'll look at consumer buyers first and different ways of describing them.

Cultural, Ethnic, Religious, and Racial Groups. It is important not only to identify the groups that are potential targets for your product or service, but also the size and characteristics of each group.

Years ago, marketers thought that they could maximize their profits by mass marketing. Using this concept, they tried to sell the identical product to everyone. Extensive research and practical experience found this to be an error. It was far more profitable to segment the market according to certain common characteristics and to concentrate on marketing to the particular segments that could be served best. This is consistent with the marketing concept of focusing on the customer rather than on the product. By focusing on characteristics of your customer, you can satisfy his or her needs more easily. This is also consistent with the basic strategic principle of concentrating superior resources at the decisive point.

Obviously it would be difficult to succeed by selling food products containing pork to Jewish or Moslem groups. Also, different groups prefer certain types of products. Have you ever heard of peanut butter soup? In West Africa it is a delicacy. East Asians eat tofu or fermented soybean extract. You may drink only cow's milk, whereas others drink goat's milk. Some Chinese groups drink soybean milk. Certain groups consider insects, monkeys, and dogs culinary delicacies. Food we think of as "normal" would be shunned.

These preferences are crucial for the marketer because they can spell the difference between success or failure. Cultural, ethnic, religious, and racial segmentation of the market is only the tip of the iceberg. As you will see, there are many other ways to segment. All of them will help you satisfy your customers better and more easily.

Social Classes. The next environmental question has to do with social classes. The basic divisions are upper, middle, and lower, but you can categorize them more precisely as lower-lower (unskilled labor), upper-lower (basic wage earners and skilled workers), lower-middle (white-collar salaried), upper-middle (professionals and successful businesspeople), and upper class (the wealthy). Social classes are important as segments because people behave differently even though their income levels may be the same.

Some time ago, researchers surveyed three different social groups which had identical incomes. One group consisted of young attorneys just graduating from law school. They bought the best homes they could afford in prestigious neighborhoods. These homes tended to be fairly small because they couldn't afford large homes in

TARGET MARKET

Geographical location _____

Special climate or topography _____

_____

CONSUMER BUYERS

Cultural, ethnic, religious, or racial groups _____

_____

_____

Social class(es) _____

Reference group(s) _____

Basic demographics: Sex _____ Age range _____

Education _____ Income _____

Household size and description _____

_____

Stage of family life cycle _____

Family work status: Husband _____ Wife _____

Occupation (husband and wife) _____

Decision maker _____ Purchase agent _____

Risk perception: Functional _____ Psychological _____

Physical _____ Social _____ Financial _____

Income for each family member _____

Disposable income _____

Additional descriptions, classifications, and traits of target market _____

_____

_____

Target market wants and needs 1. _____

2. _____ 3. _____

4. _____ 5. _____

Product general description _____

_____

Frequency of usage _____ Traits _____

_____

Marketing factor sensitivity _____

_____

FIGURE 2-2. Situational analysis: Environmental questions for the marketing plan. (Copyright © 1985 by Dr. William A. Cohen. *Note*: This form is based on an earlier form designed by Dr. Benny Barak, then of Baruch College.)

Size of target market _____

Growth trends _____

MEDIA HABITS

	Hours/Week	Category
Television	_____	_____
Radio	_____	_____
Magazines	_____	_____
Newspapers	_____	_____

ORGANIZATIONAL BUYERS

Decision makers _____

_____

_____

_____

Primary motivation of each decision maker _____

_____

_____

_____

_____

_____

Amount of money budgeted for purchase _____

_____

_____

Purchase history _____

_____

_____

_____

_____

_____

Additional descriptions, classifications, and traits of target market _____

_____

_____

Target market wants and needs 1. _____

2. _____   3. _____

4. _____   5. _____

Product general description _____

_____

FIGURE 2-2. *Continued*

Frequency of usage _____ Traits _____

Marketing factor sensitivity _____

_____

_____

Size of target market _____

Growth trends _____

MEDIA HABITS

	Hours/Week	Category
Television	_____	_____
Radio	_____	_____
Magazines	_____	_____
Newspapers	_____	_____

	Number/Year	
Trade shows	_____	_____
Conferences	_____	_____

COMPETITION

Competitor	Products	Market Share	Strategy

FIGURE 2-2. *Continued*

RESOURCES OF THE FIRM

Strengths: 1. _____

2. _____

3. _____

4. _____

5. _____

Weaknesses: 1. _____

2. _____

3. _____

4. _____

5. _____

TECHNOLOGICAL ENVIRONMENT

_____

_____

_____

ECONOMIC ENVIRONMENT

_____

_____

_____

POLITICAL ENVIRONMENT

_____

_____

_____

LEGAL AND REGULATORY ENVIRONMENT

_____

_____

_____

SOCIAL AND CULTURAL ENVIRONMENT

_____

_____

_____

FIGURE 2-2.   *Continued*

OTHER IMPORTANT ENVIRONMENTAL ASPECTS

_____

_____

_____

_____

_____

PROBLEMS/THREATS

1. _____

2. _____

3. _____

4. _____

5. _____

OPPORTUNITIES

1. _____

2. _____

3. _____

4. _____

5. _____

Figure 2-2. *Continued*

prestigious neighborhoods. Next, the researcher called on owners of small businesses whose income was the same as the young attorneys'. Do you think they spent their money in the same way? After all, they were making the same income. However, they didn't buy the same kind of homes at all. These small business owners bought the largest homes, they could afford in average neighborhoods. Finally, the researcher looked at groups in yet another class. Certain workers were longtime employees of large companies and were earning the same income as the small business owners and the young lawyers. This group didn't buy homes in prestige neighborhoods or large homes. Their homes were smaller and in less affluent neighborhoods. Where was their money spent? They bought more expensive automobiles and household appliances (such as larger television sets) than the other two groups. Remember, all three groups had identical incomes.

If this research were conducted today, the findings might be different. Yet some kind of variation in buyer behavior among the social classes is still likely. Therefore this segmentation is important and the identification of the segments, which may constitute your target market, is useful.

Reference Groups. Reference groups are those you turn to for information. They are especially important in the case of a general lack of information. Let's say that you are a member of a trade association that recommends a certain product. When other information is scarce or unavailable, this recommendation can be extremely influential in persuading you to use that product.

A reference group can also be a small number of trusted friends. Thus it is unimportant whether the reference group is large or small—only that you seek its advice when making purchase decisions.

Demographics. The situational analysis question form now asks you to investigate certain fundamental attributes of your potential customers known as demographics. Of what sex is your target market? Are you trying to sell to both male and female or male or female only? What is the primary age range? How well educated are your prospects? Most products appeal primarily to certain demographic segments that can be defined by answering these questions. If your product is an encyclopedia, would it appeal primarily to college or noncollege graduates? In most cases the answer would probably be college graduates. Similarly, certain other types of product or service appeal to individuals with certain levels of education.

How much money does your prospect earn? Can you sell a Rolls-Royce to someone whose annual income is less than $20,000 a year? Unless your prospect is independently wealthy, probably not.

How many people are in the household? Is it headed by a single parent? Male or female? Guardians? How many children are in the family and what are their ages? All of these demographic facts may result in different purchasing behavior.

Like a product, a family has also been described as having a life cycle, but the descriptive terms are different from those of the product life cycle. The family life cycle has been divided into nine stages:

1. The unmarried not living with parents
2. A newly married couple; young with no children
3. A full nest; the youngest child under six
4. A full nest; the youngest child six or older
5. A full nest; an older married couple with dependent children
6. An empty nest; no children at home; head of family in the labor force
7. An empty nest; family head retired
8. A solitary survivor in the labor force
9. A solitary survivor retired

Can you see where different products or services would appeal to each group?

Family Work Status and Occupations. If husband and wife are employed, both occupations should be listed. Or if one or both are retired or the family is receiving public assistance, this is of interest to you as an astute marketer.

Decision Makers and Purchase Agents. Note the spaces on the form in Figure 2-2 for decision maker and purchase agent. The decision maker is the one who actually decides to buy the product; the purchase agent buys it. A woman may prefer a certain brand of dishwasher detergent, but it may be her husband who actually buys the product if he happens to be doing the shopping. The implication is we may have to promote to both spouses for many products.

Consider also those who have influence on the decision maker and purchase agent. Children are subjected to a considerable amount of television advertising for many products, including toys and breakfast cereals. Children may not be decision makers or purchase agents, but their influence on other family members may be significant for your product. Many companies consider the millions of dollars invested in promoting to them as money well spent.

Risk Perception. Risk perception concerns the chance your customer takes in buying a product. Any new product has a certain amount of risk associated with it. There are other types of risk to the customer. Functional risk refers to its dependability, that is, whether it will work. Psychological risks concern the possibility that the buyer may be disappointed or feel cheated if the product proves to be less than expected. Physical risk has to do with damage to the user. Social risk is taken if the buyer feels open to ostracism or ridicule for using the product or service. Finally, there is financial risk. This is the risk of money lost in buying a product that turns out to be worthless.

Risk is calculated as perceived by the customer. It may or may not actually exist in reality. A totally reliable product may be perceived as risky by the potential buyer and a less reliable one as safe. In marketing, the perception is the reality. So if you have a low-risk product perceived as risky, you are going to have to plan for some kind of action.

Income for Each Family Member. In this section of the form additional income that may come from other members of the family is documented. This income is of interest because the total may drastically alter what your prospect can afford and is likely to buy.

Disposable Income. Disposable income is the amount left over after the bills for basic necessities such as food and shelter have been paid. Money left over is disposable income. It can be used for entertainment, a vacation, or luxuries like expensive clothes. The amount of disposable income will vary depending on geographical, cultural, ethnic, religious, and racial considerations.

Additional Descriptions, Classifications, and Traits of the Target Market. This space in the form allows you to describe your potential buyers in any terms that have been omitted previously and that may be peculiar to the particular market you are targeting. For example, one segmentation system which has become extremely popular was developed at the Stanford Research Institute (SRI) in California. Its acronym is VALS, which stands for value and lifestyles. SRI divided consumers into nine different value and lifestyle groups. Other means of categorizing that can give you insights into your target markets can be described in this section.

Target Market Wants and Needs. Wants and needs are both important, but they are not identical. A need is a requirement for basic subsistence, such as ordinary food and shelter. Wants are human desires that are nice to have but not necessary for basic survival. You might want an expensive pair of shoes, but you don't really need them. Satisfying either represents opportunities for the marketer.

You've probably already heard about one of the most important theories of wants and needs. It originated with Abraham Maslow. His theory of human motivation involves a hierarchy of needs, beginning with basic physiological needs and progressing successively to safety or security, the need for love, for esteem or self-respect, and self-actualization. Also at a high level, but not fitting on a direct hierarchy with the others, are two more classes: aesthetic needs and the need to know and understand.

Although there may be some overlap between needs, as one need is satisfied, the next higher need becomes more motivating. The basic physiological need is breathing. If someone suddenly began to choke you and you could no longer breathe, I guarantee you would have no other immediate interest. No marketer offering an attractive product at a competitive price would capture your interest. Your immediate need would be for oxygen!

Once you had regained the ability to breathe, you might then have been interested in the next level, which is safety or security. Would you really be interested in buying an automobile if you didn't know where your next meal was coming from?

You can see how needs are important to the motivation of customers to buy the products or services offered to them. No matter how good our product or service is, if some other major lower-level need has not been satisfied, your target customers may not be interested. In this section of the situational analysis form in Figure 2-2, identify specific target wants and needs that you intend to satisfy with the product or service you offer.

Product Description. The general description here is really an abbreviated version of the more detailed material given in the introduction to the marketing plan. Be certain to note frequency of use; that is, how frequently will the customer use your product or service? Also, write down product traits. What are the attributes of your product or service? These may include price, size, quality, packaging, and service. Finally, you will want to rank the market factor sensitivity; that is, how sensitive are your customers to the traits of your product or service, from the most important to the least?

Size of the Target Market. State the total potential of each target market segment.

Growth Trends. Growth trends describe what is happening to your target market. Is it growing? Is it declining? Has it leveled off? Profits can be made under each of these conditions, but each will require different marketing actions. Therefore you want to know what the trends are for your target market.

MEDIA HABITS

Media habits is a major classification on the form shown in Figure 2-2. It is significant because if you know the habits of your prospects, you will understand how to reach them most efficiently. Consider the basic media including television, radio, newspapers, and magazines. It would be helpful to know how many hours a week are devoted to each category.

ORGANIZATIONAL BUYERS

The basic information you need for organizational buyers is knowing who the decision makers are. With organizations, you must frequently market to more than one individual. Sometimes these decision makers will include engineers and their supervisors, purchase agents, and test and quality assurance groups. Each decision maker may have different motivations. The primary motivation of each decision maker involved in a purchase should be determined and written down on the form.

The Amount of Money Available or Budgeted for the Purchase. Obtain an estimate of the amount of money available for the particular purchase for which the marketing plan is being developed. This is necessary because significant differences in the amount charged lessen the chances of success in marketing the product and at the very least must be explained.

If a group is accustomed to paying $25 per unit in quantities of 1,000 a year, $25,000 will have been budgeted. If a greater amount is to be charged, the decision makers are going to ask why, because this will require an increase in the budget. Even a lower price must be explained lest it be viewed as representing a change to lower quality.

Purchase History. The purchase history of the same or similar products will reveal buying patterns relating to the time of year in which the product was purchased and the quantities ordered.

Additional Industrial Buyer Information. Additional industrial buyer information required is similar to what is needed about the consumer. The exception is media information about trade show and conference attendance.

COMPETITION

Competition is a critical element. It is an intelligent environmental factor that will act against your interests. Pay particular attention when you are targeting a stagnant or a declining market. If you are targeting the same market segment, your competitor can only succeed by taking sales from you. Therefore the more you know about your competition, the better. You should study your competitors, the products they are offering, the share of the market they control, and the strategies they are following. All of this information can be used as you plan your optimal strategy to help you succeed by giving your customers improved service or a better product.

RESOURCES OF THE FIRM

Indicate resources of the firm in terms of strengths and weaknesses. Few organizations are strong in everything. Perhaps you have technical strength like the "high-tech" firms in Silicon Valley. Or perhaps marketing know-how is your forte. Maybe you are strong in financial resources. Just as you have strengths, you have weaknesses. Jot these down on the form as well. Weaknesses don't become strengths by pretending they don't exist.

TECHNOLOGICAL ENVIRONMENT

Sometimes technology changes and expands rapidly. In a single year in the early 1970s, the price of hand-held calculators declined by more than 50 percent. Simultaneously their performance actually increased. Computer technology is still growing by leaps and bounds. The largest memory computers of a few years ago can now be carried around in the pocket.

The technological environment may not be relevant to your particular situation, but if it is, be sure to describe your situation completely.

ECONOMIC ENVIRONMENT

The economic environment involves the economic and business conditions that you will face as you enter the market. It is true that fortunes can be made in recessions and depressions, during inflations, and in periods of economic prosperity. However, the products and services with which you are most likely to be successful in these different economic conditions are not the same. Therefore a description of the economic and business conditions that you are likely to encounter during implementation is necessary.

POLITICAL ENVIRONMENT

The political environment must be examined because of the potential effect that politics may have on your project. There are some countries to which the U.S. government will not permit you to export, just as there are certain products from certain countries that cannot be imported. Japanese imports are of major political interest at this time. So is preventing the unrestricted export of sophisticated weaponry and the knowledge and skills of former Soviet nuclear scientists. Politics affect the marketing of products and services. It is a part of the environment you cannot ignore.

LEGAL AND REGULATORY ENVIRONMENT

The legal and regulatory environment can cause major headaches. One small company invested more than $100,000 in its development of a new bullet-resistant police helmet. Then it discovered that because of product liability the product could not be sold at a profit. Another firm invested thousands of dollars in a new wine cooler on the assumption that the alcoholic beverage tax would be the same whether or not they used another firm's wine to mix with their fruit juice. It wasn't, and the difference in tax made the product unprofitable. Be forewarned: note the impact of the legal and regulatory environment before you complete your marketing plan.

SOCIAL AND CULTURAL ENVIRONMENT

Fifty years ago wearing a bikini on a public beach would have been cause for arrest. Sushi or raw fish has been a popular product in Japan for hundreds of years, yet only a few years ago sushi bars probably would have been unsuccessful in the United States. Today, sushi is extremely popular. Because the timing of an entry into a market may be the dominant factor, a smart marketer investigates the social and cultural environment for a product or service before developing the rest of his or her marketing plan.

OTHER IMPORTANT ENVIRONMENTAL ASPECTS

In this section other important environmental aspects that are peculiar to your product or service not covered previously should be listed and analyzed. An example might be a natural disaster such as a hurricane or an earthquake.

PROBLEMS AND OPPORTUNITIES

The problems and opportunities section of the form is a summary of all that has gone before. You should review your entire environmental situation and restate every problem and opportunity that you can anticipate. Naturally there may be more or less than five problems and five opportunities, so don't be restricted simply because the form provides space only for that number.

Many marketing planners who have no trouble recognizing their opportunities hesitate to discuss their problems. This is a mistake for two reasons. First, it is important to identify the problems clearly to give yourself the opportunity to avoid them once you have begun to develop your strategy. Second, if you have failed to include them and have listed only your opportunities, readers of your plan will suspect that you left them out intentionally or were not smart enough to acknowledge them. They would be more impressed if you described how you propose to overcome them.

SOURCES OF INFORMATION FOR COMPLETING THE ENVIRONMENTAL QUESTIONS FORM

To answer environmental questions you must do research. This research may be primary or secondary. Primary research entails interviews, business surveys, and a personal search for the answers. In secondary research you consult other sources. Secondary research is generally preferable because it is already available. It should be examined before you spend the time and money to do primary research. What are some secondary research sources?

1. *Chambers of Commerce.* Chambers of Commerce have all sorts of demographic information about geographical areas in which you may be interested, including income, education, businesses and their size, and sales volume.
2. *Trade Associations.* Trade associations also have information regarding the background of their members and their industries.
3. *Trade Magazines and Journals.* Trade journals and magazines frequently survey their readership. They also contain articles of interest to you that describe competitive companies, products, strategies, and markets.

4. ***The Small Business Administration.*** The U.S. Small Business Administration was set up to help small business. Whether you own a small business or are a marketing planner in a large company, the studies sponsored can be extremely valuable to anyone doing research in the situational analysis of a marketing plan. The many printed aids supplied include statistics, maps, national market analyses, national directories for use in marketing, basic library reference sources, information on various types of business (including industry average investments and cost), and factors to consider in locating a shopping center.

5. ***Data Bases.*** Data bases are electronic collections of relevant data based on trade journals, newspapers, and many other public or private sources of information. They are accessed by computer, and companies sell the computer time to search the data bases they have available.

6. ***Earlier Studies.*** Earlier marketing studies are sometimes made available to interested companies or individuals. These studies may have cost $40,000 or more when done as primary research. As a consequence, they are expensive—although in effect you are sharing the cost with other companies that purchase the results with you. Several thousand dollars for a short report is not atypical. Nevertheless, if the alternative is to do the entire primary research project yourself, it may be far less expensive to pay the price.

7. ***The* U.S. Industrial Outlook.** Every year the government publishes a document known as the *U.S. Industrial Outlook,* which contains detailed information on the prospects of more than 350 manufacturing and service industries.

8. ***The* Statistical Abstract of the United States.** This abstract is also an annual government publication. It contains a wealth of detailed statistical data involving everything from health to food consumption, to population, public school finances, individual income tax returns, mortgage debt, science and engineering, student numbers, and motor vehicle travel. It is published by the U.S. Department of Commerce, Bureau of the Census.

9. ***The U.S. Department of Commerce.*** If you are interested in export, the U.S. Department of Commerce has numerous sources of information, including amounts exported to foreign countries in the preceding year, major consumers of certain items, and detailed information on doing business in countries around the world. You can find the office of your local U.S. Department of Commerce in the U.S. government listings in your telephone book.

10. ***The U.S. Government.*** The U.S. government has so many sources of information that it is impossible to list them all here. But because so much information is available, and so much of it is free, you would be well advised to see what can be obtained from federal government sources. One recommended source that will give you access to this information is *Information U.S.A.* by Matthew Lesko (Viking, 1983). Another excellent source is the *Entrepreneur and Small Business Problem-Solver, 2nd ed.* by William A. Cohen (Wiley, 1991). An additional listing of secondary-source information is contained in Appendix B of this book.

PRIMARY RESEARCH

In some cases you must do primary research yourself. Minimize the cost as much as possible by thorough planning. Time is also an important factor. Can you complete your primary research in sufficient time to be of use in preparing your marketing plan?

Three basic methods of gathering primary data are face-to-face interviewing and mail and telephone surveying. Each has its advantages and disadvantages; for example, in face-to-face interviewing more detailed information can usually be obtained and the interviewer can use verbal feedback and read body language or facial expressions to probe for answers. But face-to-face interviewing can be costly in time and money. Mail surveys are perhaps the quickest but most impersonal method. Their disadvantages are low return rate and lack of feedback. The telephone is an excellent means of surveying the country in the shortest time. Telephone calls, however, can also be expensive and will provide no visual feedback to your questions.

SUMMARY

In this chapter we explored the environmental questions, the answers to which are necessary to complete the situational analysis of your marketing plan. We have also recorded some of the sources of this information. The information will not be available by the time the marketing planning must be done, in which case you must make the best assumptions possible, based on the information you have already acquired. Don't forget to clearly state the assumptions you have made. You don't want anyone to confuse your assumptions as facts.

Having done the research and situational analysis required and knowing what environment you will face in the marketplace, you are now ready to establish your goals and objectives. We will do so in the next chapter.

CHAPTER 3

STEP 3

ESTABLISHING GOALS AND OBJECTIVES

"Would you tell me, please, which way I ought to go from here?" asked Alice.

"That depends a good deal on where you want to get to," said the cat. "I don't much care where," said Alice.

"Then it doesn't matter which way you go," said the cat.

Lewis Carroll, *Alice's Adventures in Wonderland*

You can't get *there* unless you know where *there* is. This chapter deals with establishing goals and objectives. They are the *there* of your marketing plan. Without them, you haven't got a marketing plan—you have a collection of facts and unrelated ideas.

ESTABLISHING OBJECTIVES

Your objectives answer the question: What are you trying to achieve? The following objectives are typical:

- To establish a product, product line, or brand in the marketplace.
- To rejuvenate a failing product.
- To entrench and protect a market under attack by competitors.
- To introduce a new product.
- To harvest a product that is in the declining stage of its life cycle.
- To introduce a locally successful product nationally or overseas.
- To achieve maximum return on investment with a product or product line.

Normally, the statement of the objective should focus on a single task, but it is possible to have more than one objective or to specify additional conditions as long as they do not conflict with each other. If your objective is to introduce a new product, you might add: "To dominate the market, while achieving maximum sales."

In the same vein your objective might be worded: "To rejuvenate a failing product while maintaining high profitability and with minimum investment."

But in establishing more than one objective, or a main objective with additional conditions, care must be taken to ensure that the objectives do not conflict. It may be desirable to maximize the market share you have been able to capture for a new product and at the same time achieve maximum profitability, but the two may not be achievable simultaneously. Capturing a maximum market share may require a penetration pricing strategy, and the low price and lower margins may result in something far less than maximum profitability. In fact, you may be lucky to reach the break-even point. Therefore, when you establish your objectives and add conditions to them, be certain that there is no conflict and that achievement of one will not make it impossible to achieve another.

Spend the necessary time to make sure that your objective statement is worded correctly and that all important conditions have been incorporated. Even after you have finished with it, however, it will not be complete until you have specified a time by which the objective must be achieved. Ask yourself the question, "By what time?" for every objective that you establish. Let's say that you want to introduce a new product, dominate the market, and build maximum sales. "By what time?" Three months? Six months? Nine months? A year? Longer than that?

If one of your objectives is to harvest a product that is in the decline stage of its product life cycle, how much time will you have? If you are going to introduce a nationally successful product overseas, how long will it take before this introduction can be said to have been made?

Psychologists, time management experts, business researchers, and practitioners all tell us that specifying a time period is extremely important, because this will give you a target on which to focus and a guide that will indicate whether you're on schedule. It will also provide a date toward which everyone involved in the marketing plan can coordinate their efforts.

In 1960 President John F. Kennedy set an objective for the United States. He said, "We're going to have a man on the moon by 1970." Note that he didn't say, "We're going to put a man on the moon sometime." He said, "We're going to put a man on the moon by 1970." In actuality this goal was achieved in 1969. The fact that President Kennedy specified a date was of major significance. It not only helped us to achieve this national objective, it helped us achieve it before the target date set.

George A. Steiner, a man famed for his expertise in strategic planning, recommends 10 criteria to help in developing objectives.[1] Use them as guidelines to ensure that your objectives, whatever they are, will benefit the firm's overall mission:

Suitability. Your objectives must support the enterprise's basic purposes and help to move the company in that direction.

Measurability over Time. Objectives should state clearly what is expected to happen and when so that you can measure them as you proceed.

Feasibility. Your objectives must be feasible. If they cannot be fulfilled, they motivate no one. Be certain that they are realistic and practical even if they are not easy and require considerable effort.

Acceptability. The objectives you set must be acceptable to the people in your organization or to those who may allocate resources to implement your marketing plan. If your objectives are not acceptable, you will not receive the necessary funds. If someone besides yourself is working on the marketing plan and the objectives are not acceptable, you cannot expect to receive the same cooperation.

---

[1]George A. Steiner, *Strategic Planning* (New York: Free Press, 1979), pp. 164–168.

Flexibility. Your objectives should be modifiable in the event of unforeseen contingencies and environmental changes. This does not mean that they should not be fixed, only that, if necessary, they can be adapted to environmental changes.

Motivating. Objectives should motivate those who must work to reach them. If your objectives are either too easy or so difficult that they are impossible to achieve, they will not be motivating. If your objectives are difficult but achievable, they will challenge and motivate others to reach them.

Understandability. Your objectives should be stated in clear, simple language that can be understood by all. If they are not clear, they may be misunderstood and some individuals may unintentionally be working against them. You may also alienate those who allocate resources and capital. Your plan may be halted midway through execution simply because your objectives were not clear to everyone.

Commitment. Make certain that everyone working on the development, planning, selling, and execution of the marketing plan is committed to your objectives. In today's real-life business world, senior managers seek to do this by getting as many managers involved as possible in determining what these objectives should be.

People Participation. Steiner points out that the best results are obtained when those who are responsible for achieving the objectives take some part in setting them. It is vitally important to consult with all who might participate in any way with the execution of the plan. If other staff members are committed to your objectives from the start, you will have much less trouble keeping them on track throughout the implementation of your plan. If you are working on your marketing plan as a team, you will find that ensuring everyone's participation and input will gain commitment to completing the plan. If one or two team members attempt to impose their ideas on the group, the opposite will occur. No matter how brilliant or "right" their ideas, they will be unable to gain the commitment of other team members.

Linkage. Naturally the objectives should be linked with the basic purposes of your organization. They must also be linked with the objectives of other collateral organizations in your firm. They must be consistent with and meet top management objectives. It's no good setting objectives that involve high sales if this runs counter to top management's overall philosophy of serving a small exclusive clientele. Ensure that the objectives you set are linked to other unique requirements of your firm's environment.

After you have decided on the time frame for achieving your objectives, indicate it on the form in Figure 3-1.

GOALS

Goals are the specifics of the objectives. Let's look at one of the objectives we talked about: "Introduce a new product and dominate the market while achieving maximum sales. Time to achieve: one year."

Now the question is this: Does *introduce* mean to distribute it among 500 major retail outlets or at only one? Is maximum sales $100,000 in six months and then $1 million in one year? What are the figures that demonstrate introduction? What exactly do the words in your objectives mean? How about *dominating* the market? Is dominating the market having a market share of 100, 90, or 50 percent? When the market is fragmented, you may dominate it by taking a 25 percent share (or less).

Objectives can also be broken down into smaller intermediate units within the overall time period specified. These shorter-term objectives are also goals. Thus maximum sales may be defined at the end of the period indicated (one year) as well as at shorter intervals, say six months. The same can be done to define *dominating the market.*

Objectives	Time to Achieve
1. _____	_____
2. _____	_____
3. _____	_____
4. _____	_____
5. _____	_____

Goals	Time to Achieve
1. _____	_____
2. _____	_____
3. _____	_____
4. _____	_____
5. _____	_____

Statement of differential advantage

_____

_____

_____

_____

_____

_____

_____

_____

FIGURE 3-1. Objectives, goals, differential advantage statement. (Copyright © 1985 by Dr. William A. Cohen.)

Let's look at another example: "Rejuvenate a failing product with minimum investment while maintaining high profitability."

First, what does *rejuvenate* mean? In this case let's say that it means increasing sales by 30 percent over the preceding year. How about *minimum investment?* Let's say that the maximum amount your company is ready to invest is $100,000. If you think this is the minimum amount that you can get the job done with, then your *minimum investment* may be $100,000. And *high profitability?* Well, profitability is related to the margin; that is, your costs compared with the selling price that was set. Let's say that the definition of high profitability is a margin of 60 percent. You can use this figure to define high profitability.

Again, you must consider the time for achieving these goals. You may want to indicate quarterly sales increases over the preceding year combined with a total sales increase of 30 percent at the end of the coming year. Both final and the intermediate figures are goals.

You can now complete the goals section in Figure 3-1. Specifying your goals and writing them down makes sense. It allows you to concentrate your efforts on achieving what is really important in order to obtain the objectives that were set earlier.

Specificity also affects vision. Vision has to do with the future as the leader or manager sees the outcome of the project. A major study of world-class leaders discovered that groups were far more likely to follow leaders and were much more enthusiastic about doing so when the leaders set specific objectives and goals.[2]

When goals and objectives are made specific, it is much easier to avoid conflict between individuals and groups that must assist in carrying out the tasks necessary to reach them. Also, individuals will work together to coordinate their efforts in a synergistic way. This makes their efforts far more effective than if their actions were simply to achieve movement in a general direction toward a less specific goal.

THE CONCEPT OF COMPETITIVE OR DIFFERENTIAL ADVANTAGE

In all cases, you must direct your efforts toward satisfying the customer by achieving a competitive or differential advantage over your competitors. That's one reason organizations are always striving to improve their services. As they get better and better at what they do, the customer wins by getting better products at lower prices.

Some call this competitive advantage, others differential advantage, and still others use all three words together: "competitive differential advantage." This is unimportant. What is important is what the words stand for. They mean not only that your product or service has one or more advantages, but that these are more important than the advantages your competitors may have.

Also, do you seek one competitive advantage, or can there be more than one? There may be one overriding competitive advantage so significant that others become less important. At times, your statement of competitive advantage may actually encompass a number of advantages over your competitor. The number is less important than the total strength of your advantage or advantages over your competitors.

Include this concept in your marketing plan. You must think about, develop, and find ways to promote your competitive advantage. If you have no competitive advantage you will not succeed. Why should customers buy your product or service if it is identical to a competitor's product with which they are satisfied? Therefore the key question is, "Why should anyone buy from us as opposed to one or more of our competitors?"

Although your objectives and goals focus on what *you* want, the differential competitive advantage focuses on what your customer wants. What is the advantage of the customer buying your product or service? Think this through to determine how the two are linked. Your competitive advantage is derived from an eventual customer benefit.

Let's look at an example of this linkage. Why have so many Americans bought Japanese cars in the past? Americans saw a benefit over American-made cars. It may be stated as "quality at an affordable price," or "value for the price."

This quality was made possible by a combination of factors. First was the notion that much higher quality than had previously been achieved was possible. Also, the Japanese automobile industry was automated to a far greater extent than its American competitors. This meant their labor force was more productive. Finally, the Japanese have a lower cost of labor. Assuming this to be correct, these factors were competitive advantages over American automobile manufacturers. Together they resulted in the benefit of "high quality at an affordable price."

This is not to say that American manufacturers may not also have competitive differential advantages that will eventually result in benefits to customers, which may exceed those currently offered by Japanese companies. As a matter of fact, that is exactly what American manufacturers have been doing in recent years—capitalizing on their own differential advantages to achieve a link to customer benefits.

Competitive advantages can be derived from a number of widely varying factors. A competitive differential advantage could be the ability to buy in quantity from special

---

[2]Warren Bennis and Burt Nanus, *Leaders* (New York: Harper & Row, 1985).

sources not enjoyed by others. The resulting benefit to the customer: low price. There may be a great many Ph.D.'s in your research and development department. The resulting benefit to the customer: advanced state-of-the-art technology. You may own a restaurant for which you have employed the best chef in your entire geographical area. The resulting benefit to the customer: the best gourmet food. Knowledge can also be a competitive differential advantage that will result in customer benefits; for example, marketing know-how translates into better satisfied customer needs.

You can even find competitive advantages in what you might consider disadvantages. When Mercedes-Benz first introduced diesel models, they didn't sell. At that time diesel fuel sold for almost the same price as gasoline. Also, diesel fuel wasn't sold at many gasoline stations, so it was not as convenient to use. Finally, if you've ever heard a diesel engine, you know that it's much louder and noisier than one burning gasoline.

Mercedes-Benz saved the product line by turning these disadvantages into competitive advantages. They promoted the fuel as exotic and exclusive, "not available at every gasoline station." As for the noisy engine? Mercedes-Benz said it was unique, too. "It wasn't like gasoline-burning engines that were so quiet you couldn't even tell if they were running or not. When you start up a diesel engine, you can hear its power." Mercedes-Benz knew that to the wealthy segments at which these products were targeted, uniqueness and exclusivity were major benefits.

Make sure that any competitive advantages have the following characteristics:

They must be real. Wishes will not make it so. Some retail stores claim that their prices are lower than those of all their competitors. Sometimes even a cursory inspection will prove this to be untrue or that they are lower only in certain circumstances or with certain products. Thus their advantage will *not* be translated into a benefit for the customer.

They must be important to the customer. Note that I say *to the customer*, and not *to you*. According to Freeman Gosden, Jr., who was once president of the largest direct response agency in the world, "It's not what you want to sell, but what your customer wants to buy." This principle is directly applicable to the competitive advantage. It's not the competitive advantage that you seek but rather the benefits as the customer sees them.

A major supplier of U.S. Air Force helmets once considered getting into the motorcycle helmet market. This company believed it could make a better protective motorcycle helmet than its competitors because of its experience with pilot helmets—and it did. These more protective helmets, however, were priced approximately 30 percent higher than the earlier top-of-the-line motorcycle helmets. This pricing was not arbitrary, merely based on higher manufacturing costs for a more protective product. Additionally, this expensive helmet was 15 percent heavier than competitive models. Despite all this, the company actually thought it had a competitive edge because of the greater protection. Within a year this manufacturer learned a hard lesson when the product failed. The customer did not want a more protective helmet, at least not to the degree that the customer would pay 30 percent more, and accept a 15 percent weight penalty. When the perception of competitive differential advantage differs between marketer and customer, the customer always wins.

Lee Iacocca says that in 1956, Ford decided that safety was of primary interest to the consumer and emphasized it in all the advertising of its 1956 models. Ford's sales plummeted and the competition won on all fronts. Quickly realizing that he lacked a competitive differential advantage, Iacocca hit on what was really the main issue: ability to purchase the car. The year 1956 was one of mild recession. Therefore Iacocca instituted a policy by which customers could purchase new cars for only $20 down and $56 a month. This made it easier to buy a Ford than competitive cars. Iacocca hit on the correct differential advantage, as perceived by his potential customers. His sales district went from last place to number one in sales.[3]

They must be specific. Whatever your competitive differential advantages, they must be specific, just as objectives and goals must be specific. It is not enough to say, "We're

---

[3]Lee Iacocca, *Iacocca* (New York: Bantam, 1984), p. 39.

the best." The question is, the best what? And why? To the customer nonspecificity translates into mere puffery and is not a competitive differential advantage.

They must be promotable. Whatever your competitive differential advantages are, they must be promotable to the customer. The Edsel was a great failure in the marketplace and is frequently cited as a prime example of poor marketing. Yet Ford did extensive market research to determine what the customer wanted before introducing the Edsel line. This research indicated that power was an important competitive differential advantage. The Edsel was designed to be one of the most powerful cars ever built for its price range. Unfortunately in the same year that the Edsel was introduced a new government regulation limited automobile advertisers from promoting high horsepower engines. As a result this competitive differential advantage, although it existed and may have been desired by the customer, could not be promoted. If you are planning on a specific differential advantage, it is essential that your customer know it; otherwise it might as well not exist.

When you have thought through this challenge, return to Figure 3-1 and enter your statement of competitive differential advantage in the space provided on the form. What do you have that others don't and how does it translate into benefits to your potential customers?

SUMMARY

In this chapter we have examined objectives and goals: objectives being what you are trying to achieve, and goals the specifics of your objectives. In both cases it is very important to indicate the time frame within which these objectives and goals should fall. Remember, there is a sound psychological basis for both specificity and time frame that will help you to organize your efforts. Although your objectives and goals are what *you* want, you must also be aware of what is wanted by your potential customers. Thus you must build and emphasize a concept of competitive differential advantage. This should be something unique that you will have but your competition will not. Otherwise there is no reason for your customers to buy from you, and they won't. And your competitive differential advantages must translate into benefits and satisfaction as perceived by your customers.

Develop strong objectives, goals, and competitive advantages and you will be well on your way to success. You will be in a position to develop strategy to reach your objectives and goals building on the competitive advantages you have formulated.

CHAPTER

4

STEP 4

DEVELOPING MARKETING STRATEGY

The word *strategy* stems from the Greek *strategos,* which means the art of the general. Many of the concepts that we use in marketing strategy evolved from early use in military strategy. The very top level of military strategy is sometimes called grand strategy. It entails many other elements besides that of military force, including economic power and diplomacy. At the next level down is military strategy itself. Military strategy involves all actions taken by military forces up to the point of reaching the battlefield. Finally, according to the military concept of strategy, we have tactics, which are those actions taken on the battlefield. In all cases there are objectives: national objectives that are achieved by grand strategy, military objectives achieved by military strategy, and tactical objectives achieved by tactics. The basis of all strategy is the concentration of superior resources at the decisive point. For example, over the last few years, Procter & Gamble Company adopted a strategy of simplification. It trimmed its product line, slashing items in hair care alone by more than half. It also standardized packaging and promotions worldwide. As one P&G executive said, "There is a real push in the company to do fewer, bigger things." By simplifying, P&G could concentrate resources where it counted. The results? P&G sales grew by a third in five years.[1]

THE STRATEGY PYRAMID

In marketing we have a similar concept. I call it the strategic pyramid (see Figure 4-1). At the very highest level of the pyramid is strategic marketing management (SMM). SMM seeks to achieve the mission of the firm. To do this, SMM decides on what businesses, product lines, and products to pursue. One level down is marketing strategy. This is the strategy you implement in support of the businesses, product lines, and products decided on in SMM.

---

[1]Zachary Schiller, Greg Burns, and Karen L. Miller, "Make it Simple," *BusinessWeek,* (September 9, 1996), pp. 96–104.

FIGURE 4-1. The strategic pyramid.

Let's say that at the corporate or top organizational level a decision had been made to exploit the capability that your company has for manufacturing certain products. This would be an SMM decision. Moving one level down to the marketing strategy level, how might this be accomplished? Penetrating new markets might be one way. Expanding the share of the market that you already have for this product might be another. If you select the option for new market penetration, you might consider a niche strategy, which is a strategy whereby you market to a definable segment that you can dominate. If you have sufficient resources, you might consider a vertical marketing strategy. You would try to control more of the marketing functions between production and selling to the customer. You might also consider entry strategy in which you would weigh the advantages against the disadvantages of being first, early, or late in the market with your new product.

If you decide on a strategy of market share expansion, you might choose product differentiation or market segmentation—that is, you could consider emphasizing a product that is considerably different from other products and go after the entire market. Or you could segment your market into smaller markets and enter each with a slightly different product. You might also consider a limited share expansion versus a general share expansion.

The lowest level in your strategic pyramid is marketing tactics. Tactics are the actions you take to support the marketing strategy decided on at the preceding level. To do this you manipulate certain marketing variables having to do with the product, price, promotion, or distribution. You can manipulate all of these variables, or only one, depending on your overall tactical plan.

Maybe the marketing strategy you decide on is market share expansion. One tactic for accomplishing this may involve modifying your product to increase its performance. It may involve a lower price to make your product more affordable. It may involve increased advertising, or advertising in new media or new media vehicles. Finally, your tactics may include different distribution channels, or more emphasis on the distribution channels you are currently using.

Because resources are always limited, you usually cannot do all of these; therefore you allocate your resources, including your money, time, personnel, facilities, capital goods, and equipment, where they can have the most effect. The resulting tactical mix, known as a marketing mix, is what finally implements the decision that started at the very top of the corporate ladder with the mission of the firm.

Now let's look at the details of making these strategy decisions.

STRATEGIC MARKETING MANAGEMENT

To make the decisions that are necessary for developing strategy at the SMM level and then incorporate them into your marketing plan, you will need a method for deciding to what businesses, product lines, or products the firm should allocate its resources.

To do this, we will use a portfolio matrix and the product life-cycle curve. The portfolio matrix is a box with four cells. The vertical axis represents business strength. The horizontal axis represents market attractiveness. We will locate candidate businesses, product lines, or products in the matrix.

The product life cycle graphically shows what happens to product sales and profits as a new business, product line, or product passes through the introduction, growth, maturity, and decline phases.

Let's look at the four-cell portfolio matrix first.

THE FOUR-CELL PORTFOLIO MATRIX FOR DECISION MAKING IN SMM

The first step in using the four-cell matrix is to decide whether you are going to work with individual products, product lines, or even an entire business. If you have or are developing strategy for only a few products, you will plot their individual product positions in the matrix. If you have several different product lines, you will plot them in the matrix. If you are doing SMM for a large corporation with many businesses, then you will plot businesses in the matrix.

If you are plotting products or product lines, what you plot are called strategic product units (SPUs). If you are working with businesses, you plot strategic business units (SBUs). If you have many different types of products be sure to combine products into product lines, or even product line groupings to form SPUs. Do the same if you have many businesses to form SBUs. This will greatly simplify your work, and it will also enable you to take advantage of economies of scale where possible. To establish SPUs or SBUs, look for similarities in customers served, product lines under a single manager, or products having identical competitors.

Once you have your SPUs established, calculate the values of the SPUs for both business strength and market attractiveness. Now let's see how to do this.

Calculation of SPU Value for Business Strength. The first step in calculating the SPU value for business strength is to list the criteria important to the SPU being analyzed. Typical business strength criteria that may be relevant include:

Current market share	Raw materials cost
Growth rate	Image
Sales effectiveness	Product quality
The proprietary nature of the product	Technological advantages
Price competitiveness	Engineering know-how
Advertising or promotion effectiveness	Personnel resources
Facilities' location or newness	Product synergies
Productivity	Profitability
Experience curve effects	Distribution
Value added	

You may think of even more. The question is, which of these are relevant to you in your situation?

Once you've established which criteria of business strengths are relevant, you establish relative importance weightings. This isn't difficult to establish. Just remember that all the weightings of the different relevant criteria together must total 100 percent.

	Weight × Rating
Engineering know-how	0.40 × 5 pts = 2.00
Size of the organization	0.15 × 2 pts = 0.30
Organizational image	0.30 × 4 pts = 1.20
Productivity	0.15 × 3 pts = 0.45
	Total = 3.95

FIGURE 4-2.   Calculation of SPU value for business strength.

Look at this simple example: Let's say that only four business strength criteria are considered important to you. We will assume that these are engineering know-how, size of your organization, organizational image, and productivity. Now, the question is, what is the relative importance of each of these four criteria to your business strength? After some thought, you decide that the most important by far is engineering know-how. You assign it a relative importance to the whole of 40 percent. You decide that the next most important criterion is organizational image. You give it 30 percent. Next you decide that the size of your organization and productivity are worth about 15 percent each. The addition of 40, 30, 15, and 15 percent equals 100 percent. If they didn't add up, you'd go back and adjust your weightings.

The weightings you establish will be used to rate all of your products, or SPUs against the same criteria. The only thing that will vary is how well each SPU does when measured against each. We'll use a point assignment to do this: 1 point means very weak; 2 points is weak; 3 points means fair. If the SPU looks good on this criterion, we'll give it 4 points if it's strong and 5 points if it's very strong.

Let's say for the specific SPU that you are analyzing you award a point rating of 5 for engineering know-how, 4 for organizational image, 2 for size of the organization, and 3 for productivity. You must now multiply the point rating for this particular SPU by the weightings you have established for the SPU (Figure 4-2) to arrive at a weighted rank for business strength of 3.95. Repeat this process for every SPU you are analyzing on the business strength computation sheet (Figure 4-3). Duplicate this figure and use a separate sheet for each SPU.

Market Attractiveness. Next you are going to calculate market attractiveness to plot along the horizontal axis of your matrix. Typical market attractiveness criteria include:

Size of the market segment	Ease of entry
Growth of the market segment	Life-cycle position
Market pricing	Competitive structure
Strength of demand	Product liability
Vulnerability to inflation and depression	Political considerations
Government regulation	Distribution structure
Availability of raw materials	

Again, you may think of additional market attractiveness factors that are important to your company.

Let's assume that only four marketing attractiveness criteria are considered important. These are the size of the market, the growth rate of the market, the ease of entry, and the life-cycle position. You estimate that the relative importance of the size of the market is 40 percent, growth rate of the market is 30 percent, ease of entry is 25 percent, and life-cycle position, 15 percent.

Business Strength Criteria	Weights	× Rankings	= Weighted Rank
	1.00	× Rank	=

SPU # _____ Date _____

FIGURE 4-3. Business strength computation sheet. (Copyright © 1983 by Dr. William A. Cohen.)

Note that once again the relative importance of all the market attractiveness criteria must equal 100 percent. If it doesn't, we'll go back and reestimate our percentages until it does.

You must rate each market attractiveness criterion for the SPU being analyzed on a scale of 1 point for very unattractive, 2 points for unattractive, 3 points for fair, 4 points for attractive, and 5 points for very attractive.

Let's assume that you assign the following ratings: size of market, 4 points; growth of market, 4 points; ease of entry, 1 point; and life-cycle position, 5 points.

You then calculate the rating for each market attractiveness criterion by multiplying the weight times the point rating. Add it up to find the total (Figure 4-4). Note that the total value is 3.40. Now we repeat the process for each of your SPUs. You can use Figure 4-5 and duplicate it to use a separate sheet for each SPU.

You are now able to plot the location of your SPU on the matrix (Figure 4-6, page 44). Note that in this matrix business strength increases from bottom to top and market attractiveness increases from right to left. The position of the SPU is located at the coordinates of business strength, 3.95 and market attractiveness, 3.40.

	Weight × Rating
Size of market	0.30 × 4 pts = 1.20
Growth of market	0.30 × 4 pts = 1.20
Ease of entry	0.25 × 1 pts = 0.25
Life-cycle position	0.15 × 5 pts = 0.75
	Total = 3.40

FIGURE 4-4.   Calculation of SPU value for market attractiveness.

SPU # _____   Date _____

Market Attractiveness Criteria	Weights	× Rankings	= Weighted Rank
	1.00	× Rank	=

FIGURE 4-5.   Market attractiveness computation sheet. (Copyright © 1983 by Dr. William A. Cohen.)

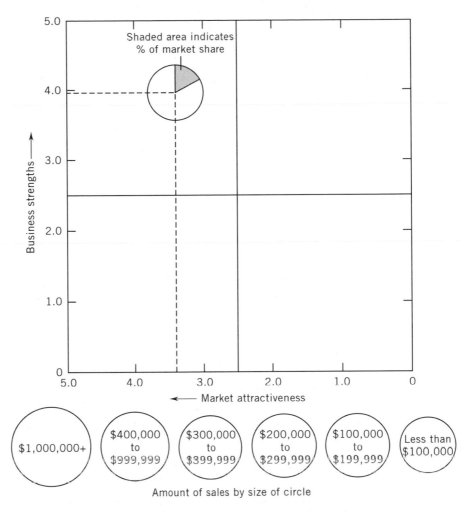

FIGURE 4-6. Matrix showing sales, size of market, and location of SPU: business strength versus market attractiveness.

You can illustrate the amount of current sales for this SPU by the size of the circle illustrated and can indicate the percentage of the market share that this SPU represents with a shaded portion of the circle.

You can plot other SPUs in the same manner (see Figure 4-7, page 46). Each is calculated and compared with the criteria for business strength and market attractiveness, using the same relative importance percentages. Only the point ratings for each market attractiveness or business strength criterion differ. This causes the SPU to be located in different positions in the matrix.

The location of the SPU in the matrix suggests a number of strategic moves. Those in the upper left quadrant imply additional investment priority, which is logical since that quadrant contains SBUs that have attractive markets and for which the firm has considerable business strength. The names for the SPUs in each quadrant come from the names given to the original four-celled matrix designed by the Boston Consulting Group in 1960. The measurements in that matrix were different, but the names still fit. The SPUs in the upper left-hand quadrant are known as *stars*.

SPUs that fall in the upper right-hand quadrant of the matrix imply selective investment. You have the business strength, but the market just isn't all that attractive. Still SPUs can be profitable in this quadrant. SPUs that fall in this quadrant in the matrix are called *question marks* or *problem children*.

The lower left quadrant of the matrix contains SPUs for which you must apply selective investment to move to star status or to manage for earnings. These SPUs, which

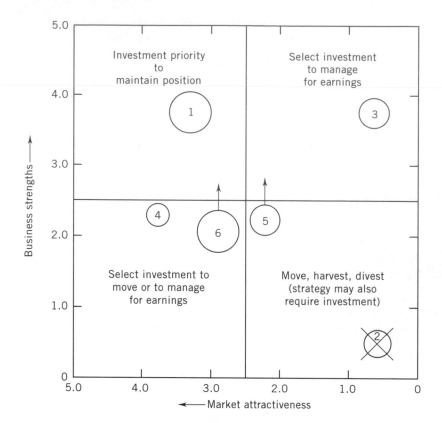

FIGURE 4-7. Planning strategic moves of SPUs on four-cell.

can be moved by increasing your business strength, are known as *cash cows*. That's because if this SPU exists you are already in an attractive market even though your business strength is low. You don't have to use resources to get into the market, yet are benefiting from the market's attractiveness.

Finally you have *dog* SPUs located in the lower right-hand quadrant of the matrix. They can be moved, but usually they are harvested or divested. You don't have the business strength, and why would you want to invest resources to move yourself into a less attractive market? In Figure 4-7, SPU 5 does indicate possible movement into the question mark quadrant. However, note that SPU 5 is a borderline SPU, already close to the star and the question mark quadrants.

If your SPUs are potential ones, it makes little sense to invest in them unless they are stars. The exceptions being if you have more opportunities than resources (rare) and they are close to the star quadrant.

Decisions concerning which SPUs to invest in and possible SPU movements must be made considering other factors—such as sales, percentage of market share, and so on—after the graphic analysis using the four-celled portfolio matrix is complete. SMM is complete only when this has been accomplished.

PRODUCT LIFE-CYCLE ANALYSIS

Each product has a cycle of life that contains different stages: introduction, growth, maturity, and decline. This is called the product life cycle, or PLC. During each stage of the PLC, the product exhibits characteristics and performances that favor the use of different marketing strategies.

There is also an overall trend for products to proceed more rapidly through the PLC. This can be important. The mechanical watch was invented hundreds of years ago and over the centuries proceeded very slowly through its life cycle. Yet over the last 15 years electronic watches have exhibited life cycles that are sometimes measured in months, not years. Electronic watches with features that once sold for several hundred dollars may sell today for less than $50.

Finally, if you can, it is best to maintain a portfolio of products in different stages. You don't want to get caught with all of your products in the maturity or decline stage. You can also have trouble with a large number of products in the introduction stage because of the considerable expense in introducing each new product. With a number of new products in the introduction stage at once there is a heavy negative cash flow. The solution is to know in what stages your products are in the PLC.

THE INTRODUCTORY STAGE

In the introductory stage of the product life cycle the organization experiences high costs due to marketing. Manufacturing is generally involved in short production runs of highly-skilled labor content and there is an overcapacity. These factors lead to high production costs. Furthermore, buyers have not yet been persuaded to purchase the product on a regular basis. Many buyers may be totally unaware of the product. Generally, the only good news in the introductory stage of a new product is that competitors are few or nonexistent. Profits, of course, are also nonexistent or negligible. The basic strategy during this stage is generally to establish market share and to persuade early adopters to buy the product.

GROWTH

In the growth stage the situation begins to change. The product has established itself and is successful. Sales are continuing to increase.

As a result, other companies are attracted and new competitors will probably be entering the market with their own version of the product. Marketing costs are still high, but manufacturing costs are reduced somewhat. An undercapacity develops because of a shift toward mass production. Distribution channels were probably limited in the introductory stage simply because of limited resources, but not anymore. In the growth stage distribution tends to become intensive and multiple channels may be used. All other things considered, profits tend to reach peak levels during this stage because of the increased demand and the fact that most companies take advantage of this demand with high pricing. Strategies followed during the growth stage are new market penetration and market share expansion. Tactical support of these strategies includes product improvement, development of new channels of distribution, and a manipulation of price and quality.

MATURITY

The product in the maturity stage has changed its situation again. Although many competitors may remain from the growth stage, they are now competing for increasingly smaller market shares. As a result the competition heats up and what is known as a shake-out begins to occur. Less efficient competitors go under or withdraw from the market. Buyers who have been purchasing the product exhibit repeat buying, and although sales continue to increase during this stage, profits begin to fall. Manufacturing costs are much lower during this stage, but the increased competition for a smaller market share ultimately forces prices down. This stage encourages a strategy of entrenchment, yet a search for new markets is still possible. Typical tactics include reducing some channels to improve profit margins, low-pricing tactics against weaker competitors, and increasing emphasis on promotion.

DECLINE

In the decline stage, as in the introductory stage, there are few competitors. Buyers who are purchasing the product are now sophisticated and much more selective. Production presents problems once again because there will be an overcapacity caused by reduced demand. Marketing expenditures will probably be reduced. In this stage both profits and sales are declining. At some point this will force a liquidation of inventory. The most logical strategy for the decline stage is some form of withdrawal, although entrenchment may also be followed in selective markets over the short term. Tactics in support of this strategy include reduction of distribution channels to those that are still profitable, low prices, and selective but quick spurts of promotion when rapid liquidation is needed. You've got to consider immediate liquidation versus a slow milking and harvesting of all possible benefits over a period of time. In any case, you must now be prepared for ultimate product removal.

LOCATING THE PRODUCT IN ITS PRODUCT LIFE CYCLE

Before you can analyze the PLC for strategy implications, you've got to locate the product in its life cycle. This requires considerable judgment. Although the general shape of the product life cycle shown in Figure 2-1 is true in many cases, it is not true in all. As a matter of fact many other shapes for product life cycle have been calculated, such as those shown in Figure 4-8 below. So before you can find out what position the product has taken in its life cycle, you must know what the life-cycle shape looks like. To do this, first look at what has happened to the product so far. Use Figure 4-9 to help you do this.

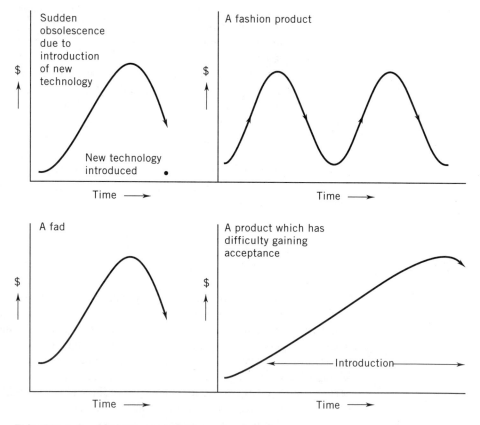

FIGURE 4-8.   Various product life-cycle shapes.

Product _____   Date _____

	Period 1	Period 2	Period 3	Period 4	Trend
Sales					
Profits					
Margins					
Market share					
Prices					

Complete matrix with following information:	Characterize trends as:	
Very low or very small	Declining steeply	↓
Low or small	Declining	↘
Average	Plateau	→
High or large	Ascending	↗
Very high or very large	Ascending steeply	↑

FIGURE 4-9. Historical trend analysis matrix. (Copyright © 1983 by Dr. William A. Cohen.)

Write down the approximate sales, profits, margin, market share, and prices for varying periods over the product's life so far. You don't need exact figures, only whether your sales are high, low, or average or very high or very low. The same is true for profits, margins, and the other elements. You will also want to look at the trends and characterize them as declining steeply, declining, on a plateau, ascending, or ascending steeply.

Next, you will use the form in Figure 4-10 to analyze the recent trends in competitors' product share and their strengths. These can be characterized as very weak, weak, medium, strong, or very strong.

Now you will take a closer look at recent trends in competitive product quality, performance characteristics, shifts in distribution channels, and their relative advantages. Write down this information on the form in Figure 4-11, page 50.

Finally you will accomplish an analysis of your competitors' short-term tactics using Figure 4-12, page 51. Be sure to note the probable meaning of each action.

Leave the analysis of the product and its competition and scan the historical information on product life cycles of similar or related products. Find a product that is similar to the one you are analyzing and determine what happened to it during its introduction, growth, maturity, and decline. Gather as much information as possible regarding the number and strength of competitors, profits, pricing, strategies used, and the length of time in each stage. Use the form in Figure 4-13 (page 52) for this.

With this information turn to Figure 4-14 on page 52, which is a matrix that contains sales and profits on the vertical axis and time in years or months on the horizontal axis. Use the other information to help determine the shape of the curve. Sketch a rough sales curve and a rough profit curve for the similar or related product you have just analyzed.

The next step is to project sales of your current product over the next three to five years, based on information from the first part of your analysis of your own and

Your Product _____   Date _____

Strength code: VW = very weak   M = medium   VS = very strong
                 W = weak   S = strong

Competitor	Market Share	Strength	Products

FIGURE 4-10.   Recent trends of competitor's products, share, and strength. (Copyright © 1983 by Dr. William A. Cohen.)

Your Product _____   Date _____

Company	Product	Quality and Performance Characteristics	Shifts in Distribution Channels	Relative Advantages of Each Competitive Product

FIGURE 4-11.   Recent trends in competitive products. (Copyright © 1983 by Dr. William A. Cohen.)

Your Product _____ Date _____

Competitor	Action	Probable Meaning of Action	Check Most Likely

FIGURE 4-12. Analysis of competitors' short-term tactics. (Copyright © 1983 by Dr. William A. Cohen.)

competing products. You can use the form in Figure 4-15 on page 53 to estimate sales, total direct costs, indirect costs, pretax profits, and profit ratio which is the estimate of total direct costs to pretax profits.

By comparing this information with the historical product information that you have already documented, you can make an estimate of the profitable years that remain for your product. You can plot your product in its PLC using Figure 4-16 on page 53.

Product _____		Similar or Related Product _____		
Product stage	Introduction	Growth	Maturity	Decline
Competition				
Profits				
Sales (units)				
Pricing				
Strategy Used				
Length of Time in Each Stage				

FIGURE 4-13. Developing life cycle of similar or related product. (Copyright © 1983 by Dr. William A. Cohen.)

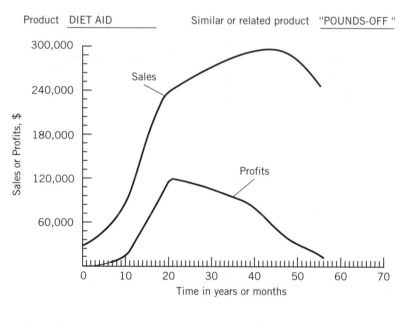

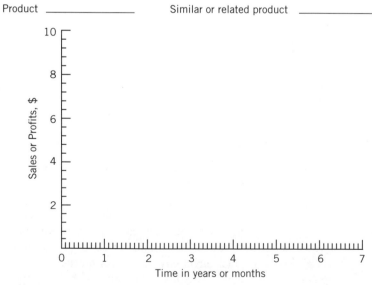

FIGURE 4-14. Life cycle curve of similar or related product. Sketch a rough sales curve and a rough profit curve for a similar or related product. (Copyright © 1983 by Dr. William A. Cohen.)

Product _____ Date _____					
Year	1	2	3	4	5
Estimated sales					
Estimated total direct costs					
Estimated indirect costs					
Estimated pretax profits					
Profit ratio (est. total direct costs to pretax profits)					

FIGURE 4-15. Sales and profit projections. (Copyright © 1983 by Dr. William A. Cohen.)

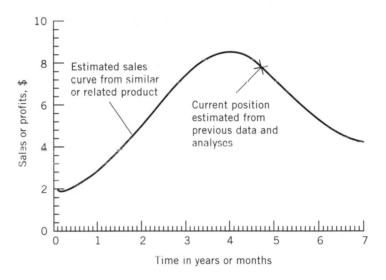

FIGURE 4-16. Position in product life cycle curve (Copyright © 1983 by Dr. William A. Cohen.).

DEVELOPING STRATEGIES FOR THE PRODUCTS IN EACH STATE OF THE PRODUCT LIFE CYCLE

To develop strategies for products in each stage of the product life cycle you must consider industry obsolescence trends, the pace of new product introduction, the average lengths of product life cycles of all the products in your product line, growth and profit objectives, and the general situation you are facing because of the present stage of the product's life cycle. You can use the alternative marketing strategies discussed in the next section. Before you leave the PLC, however, you must understand that changes will sometimes occur that will alter the anticipated shape of the PLC. What can cause this to happen?

A need may disappear. Demand for the buggy whip is close to zero today not because the buggy whip itself was replaced but because the buggy was replaced by the automobile. Thus there was no longer a need for the product. In the same vein, demand for the iron lung, once essential to the breathing of many polio victims, is very low because the disease for which it was most used has been eradicated.

A better, less expensive, or more convenient product may be developed to fill a need. All engineers once carried a device known as a slide rule. This was a mechanical device used for making mathematical and other scientific calculations. The electronic calculator introduced in the early 1970s, replaced hundreds of thousands of slide rules virtually overnight.

A competitive product may, by superior marketing strategy, suddenly gain an advantage. Adam Osbourne's second generation of computers failed and suddenly had its product life cycle terminated not because of technological inferiority but by IBM's superior marketing strategy when it introduced the famous PC.

There may be an intentional change in the shape of the curve by product repositioning, innovation, or extension. Arm and Hammer baking soda was once used only as an additive for home cooking. As the product went into the decline stage, its life was extended by its use as an odor absorbent in refrigerators. In the same way, the DC-10 became an advanced cargo tanker for the Air Force.

Any of these occurrences will cause the anticipated life-cycle curve to change. Under these circumstances, a new marketing plan and marketing strategy must be developed.

ALTERNATIVE STRATEGIES FOR THE MARKETING PLAN

The major alternative strategies that you might pursue are new market penetration, market share expansion, entrenchment, and withdrawal.

NEW MARKET PENETRATION

There are four classes of new market penetration strategy. They may be pursued simultaneously, although they need not be. They involve entry, niche, dimension, and positioning. Let's look at each in turn.

Entry. In new market penetration you can be first, early, or late. A company that chooses a strategy of being first is the first to benefit from its learning curve—that is, as it gains experience in manufacturing and marketing of the product it is using for new market penetration, its cost goes down. This means that as competitors attempt to enter the market, the company that was there first has a cost advantage that can be passed on to the customer in the form of a lower price. Alternatively, the company can use this advantage against competitors by using their higher profits for additional promotion, to establish new channels of distribution, and so forth. Those customers who have been persuaded to buy the first product on the market and whose needs have been satisfied may be reluctant to switch due to inertia. Also, the firm that enters first picks up a certain momentum. Firms that enter later must catch up, and thus the first firm has an advantage. It can continue to innovate to maintain a lead over its competition. The first firm into a market also has an edge in dominating that market.

Yet, being first is not without its risks. As Peter F. Drucker said in his book, *Innovation and Entrepreneurship,* to reap the benefits of being first requires an extreme concentration of effort on a clear-cut goal. Once a firm is successful in entering the marketplace first, it must expend considerable effort to maintain leadership or everything that has been invested will be lost to one of the later-entering competitors. Being first does not automatically ensure victory. This firm must react and react strongly to later-entering competitors to maintain its lead.

A second possibility is that of entering the market early but not first. This early entry may be intentional or unintentional. Perhaps the firm intended to be first but was edged out by another firm. When this happens, the firm that is edged out may suffer all of the disadvantages of being first, but reap none of the advantages. Being early rather than first entry can be advantageous if the firm has sufficient resources to fight the firm ahead of it.

It has somewhat reduced risk because risk in demand, technological obsolescence, and other areas of business have been absorbed by the first entry. Some knowledge will be gained of what works and what does not. This was all paid for by the firm that enters first. Finally, coincident with lower risk, much of the opportunity in the marketplace still exists. It is not a case of a product being in the mature stage of its life cycle, with many competitors fighting for reduced shares, or even of the later growth stages, with many competitors entering the market. This product is usually still in the very early stage of its introduction.

The major disadvantages of being early but not first are the barriers to entry set up by the first entry. Also, the market opportunity may be somewhat reduced. IBM overcame these disadvantages and captured a large share of the market for personal computers even though Apple got there first.

Finally, we have a late entry. Believe it or not, there are a number of advantages to entering the market after it is already established. For example, the fact that earlier entrants are usually committed to the previous direction of their products means that late entrants can include the latest technological improvements without penalty. The Japanese entered the American car market with brand new plants and manufacturing processes that competed against older, established American competitors that were tied to their obsolescent capital equipment and facilities. Late entrants may be able to achieve greater economies of scale because all entrants have a better idea of the actual size and demand of the market and can produce optimal facilities. Late-entry firms may also be able to get better terms from suppliers, employees, or even customers because earlier entrants may be locked into negotiations or fixed ways of doing business. Late entrants will enjoy reduced costs of research and development because they have been borne by earlier competitors. Finally, the late entrant can attack a perceived soft spot in the market, whereas a defending firm may have to defend everywhere.

Of course, a late entrant has some obvious disadvantages. At this stage several competitors have become established in the market and there are reduced opportunities.

Niche. A niche strategy simply means finding a distinguishable market segment, identifiable by size, need, and objective, and to dominate it. You do this by concentrating all resources on fulfilling the needs of this particular niche and no other. This strategy can work because a niche may not be large enough to be worthwhile to larger competitors. This is a real advantage because the organization that practices a niching strategy may be smaller, yet be a king in its niche. It becomes a "big frog" in its chosen small pond. Drucker identified three separate niching strategies: the toll-gate, the specialty skill, and the specialty market.

A company attempting to dominate a particular niche with the toll-gate strategy seeks to establish itself so that potential buyers cannot do without its product. This means that the product must be essential, that the risk of not using it must be greater than the cost of the product, and that the market must be eliminated so that whoever controls the niche preempts others from entrance.

One maker of a small valve needed in all oxygen masks for fliers had strong patents protecting it. Though many companies manufactured oxygen masks, all had to use that particular valve. The niche was too small for other companies to pay the price to get in.

The specialty skill strategy can be used when a company has a particular skill that is lacking in other organizations. A management consultant who has acquired a particular skill in locating venture capital through contacts, knowledge, or other expertise usually has developed a particular niche that others cannot enter.

Then there is the specialty market strategy. This is somewhat akin to the specialty skill strategy; however, rather than a unique skill, it capitalizes on a unique market. One of my students was general manager of a mail order company selling unique products to physicians. The company followed this niche strategy, selling to this specialty market.

Drucker notes that the danger is that the specialty market will become a larger market and therefore more attractive to larger competitors. This is what happened to Osbourne and some of the early computer manufacturers. The market grew rapidly from a limited number of business and professional users. This encouraged larger manufacturers such as IBM to develop strategies that overcame the nicher's leads.

Dimension. Another alternative for new market penetration is vertical versus horizontal expansion. Vertical penetration involves combining two or more stages of the production or marketing processes under a single ownership. Thus a farm that formerly sold its chickens to a food processor buys a processor and sells prepared chickens to a retail store.

In a sense, vertical integration can be a type of niching. It also has the advantage of a narrow focus that can make marketing activities easier and more effective by the concentration of resources in a certain class of market. There may also be advantages in economies of scale of combined operations. One example might be lower transaction costs due to the purchase of a greater supply of raw materials. This could lead to bigger profits.

But vertical market penetration also has its disadvantages. There is a potential loss of specialization due to different management requirements for different types of operation in the vertical integration. Capital investment requirements and higher fixed costs will increase. Methods of management, marketing, and production may have little in common. Raising chickens doesn't require the same skills or equipment as processing them. Instead of an overall net reduced cost there may be an overall increase in costs.

Horizontal expansion means expansion into new markets. The risk here is that the new markets may not be well understood, even though the supplier has a good handle on the product and its marketing. Horizontal expansion may have an additional advantage in greater potential for sales than in vertical integration. It is a workable strategy in those markets that are as yet untapped. It is more difficult when competitors are already established in those markets in which penetration is sought.

Both vertical and horizontal new market penetration require an investment in resources. Therefore an assessment of the investment and the potential payoff, as well as the risks and uncertainties, must be considered before a decision can be made.

Positioning. Positioning refers to the position of the product in relation to those of competing products in the minds of the customers. The position of your product is always important. The position occupied by Rolls-Royce is different from Volkswagen's. A Brooks Brothers suit does not occupy the same position as a suit purchased at K Mart. But there are more subtle differences than these extremes. You should always have a particular position in mind and strive to achieve it with your other marketing strategy objectives.

Sometimes the positioning of the product can be the center of gravity in the whole situation; it should receive emphasis equal to those of entry, niche, and dimension strategy.

MARKET SHARE EXPANSION

There are two basic market share expansion strategies. One is product differentiation versus market segmentation. The other has to do with a limited versus general expansion.

Product Differentiation versus Market Segmentation. Product differentiation and market segmentation are sometimes considered alternatives. Basically, product differentiation promotes product differences to the target market. Market segmentation is a strategy that emphasizes that subgroups of buyers may have common characteristics which can best be served individually.

Although product differentiation and market segmentation can be employed simultaneously, a company usually chooses one or the other. This is due in part to the fact that successful product differentiation results in giving the marketer a horizontal share of a broad and generalized market, whereas successful market segmentation tends to produce

Use product differentiation											Use market segmentation
Emphasis on Promoting Product Differences	Strategy Selection Factors										**Emphasis on Satisfying Market Variations**
Narrow	Size of market										Broad
							Ⓐ		Ⓑ		
	1	2	3	4	5	6	7	8	9	10	
High	Consumer sensitivity to product differences										Low
			Ⓑ				Ⓐ				
	1	2	3	4	5	6	7	8	9	10	
Introduction	Stage of product life cycle										Saturation
							Ⓐ		Ⓑ		
	1	2	3	4	5	6	7	8	9	10	
Commodity	Type of Product										Distinct
	Ⓑ							Ⓐ			
	1	2	3	4	5	6	7	8	9	10	
Few	Number of competitors										Many
		Ⓑ				Ⓐ					
	1	2	3	4	5	6	7	8	9	10	
Product differentiation	Typical competitor strategies										Market segmentation
			Ⓑ	Ⓐ							
	1	2	3	4	5	6	7	8	9	10	

FIGURE 4-17.   Strategy selection chart. Ⓐ—home computers; Ⓑ—salt. Adapted from R. William Kotruba, "The Strategy Selection Chart," *Journal of Marketing* (July 1966), p. 25.

greater sales to the market segments that have been targeted. Both involve coordinating the market with the product offered.

Product differentiation is used to gain greater sales in a large market by differentiating the product so that it is superior to its competition. In market segmentation, a product is optimized for the target markets selected. Because the product is optimal for the market segments, it is superior to its competitors' products in these markets. The strategies may occur simultaneously when two or more competitors target the same segments. Then, both may pursue a product differentiation strategy in addition to market segmentation in the segments in which they are competing.

Varying conditions tend to call for one strategy or the other; for example, marketing scientist R. William Kotruba developed the strategy selection chart shown in Figure 4-17, which illustrates the alternatives that must be considered.

Consider the size of the market. If the market segment served is already small, additional segmentation may not be possible because the financial potential is insufficiently attractive.

In some cases the consumer or buyer may be insensitive to product differences. This would also argue for a market segmentation strategy.

The stage of a product life cycle may also have an effect. As noted earlier, a new product priority is to become established in as large a market segment as possible. This would argue against a market segmentation strategy and for product differentiation.

The type of product may also be important. Oil, butter, salt, and gasoline are commodity products, which means that if these products are differentiated the variation will stand out and can be readily promoted to potential customers.

The number of competitors can affect which strategy is selected. With many competitors in the marketplace it is far more difficult to differentiate the product. Thus market segmentation strategy may be appropriate.

Of course, we must also consider competitive strategies. If many competitors are using the market segmentation strategy, it will be difficult to counter with a product differentiation strategy because attempting to sell to all segments simultaneously means becoming all things to all people. That's a difficult proposition. Your best choice may be to do a little market segmenting of your own and to select your target market, along with your competitors, carefully. On the other hand, if many of your competitors are using a product differentiation strategy, you probably could counter with a market segmentation strategy.

Limited versus General Expansion. Depending on resources, objectives, and the competition, a firm can also initiate a limited or a general market share expansion. More than 100 years ago Confederate General Nathan Bedford Forrest said that strategy was a matter of getting there "furstest with the mostest." Thus a new product intended for introduction on a national basis had better pursue a general market share expansion rather than alert its competitors to its intentions and give them the opportunity to preempt with a general market share expansion of their own.

On the other hand, sometimes limited resources force a company to adopt a limited market share expansion strategy, or perhaps a limited market share expansion into certain areas or segments of the market. This may be because a general expansion is not possible due to the strength of the competition.

ENTRENCHMENT

Entrenchment means digging in. It is not a withdrawal strategy, neither is it one of new market penetration or market share expansion. Entrenchment may be necessary when a product is in its mature or even somewhat declining stage of the life cycle. In any case, the market is no longer expanding. Two different entrenchments are possible: repositioning and direct confrontation.

Repositioning. Repositioning means changing the position of your product in the mind of the buyer relative to competitive products. A repositioning strategy means that you will no longer position the product where it was before, but will position it somewhere else.

Some years ago a successful men's aftershave called Hai Karate was introduced. After several years of successful sales, the market contracted. There was a general shake-out, after which few competitors were left. Hai Karate was positioned first as a brand of aftershave that was more expensive than older brands like Old Spice, Aqua Velva, and Mennen, but less expensive than the prestige brands. When the market collapsed, marketing strategy options included withdrawal and entrenchment. One alternative for entrenchment was to reposition. The product could be repositioned as a cheap brand with a lower image than that of the older brands or as a prestige brand. In this case the brand survived by being repositioned against Old Spice and other similar brands.

Did you know that Marlboro, the macho man's cigarette, was once a woman's cigarette and that Parliament, repositioned as a cigarette for all classes, was once a prestige cigarette, the Rolls-Royce of its product category?

The advantage of repositioning is finding a position in which competition is less or can be overcome more easily. Disadvantages include the cost of repositioning, promotion to make the consumer aware of the new position of the brand in relation to its competitors, and possibly repackaging and establishing new distribution channels.

Direct Confrontation. Direct confrontation means that you're going to fight it out toe-to-toe against the competition. Obviously this strategy should never be attempted unless you are certain you are going to win. Usually it is used when you have superior resources or the know-how to use your resources more effectively than your competitors.

Reentrenchment by a direct confrontation is actually a power strategy. If your competitors are more powerful, then you shouldn't attempt it.

WITHDRAWAL

Withdrawal means that you are going to take this product out of the market. The only question is when and how. The mildest type of withdrawal is risk reduction, in which you don't withdraw the entire product or service from all geographical areas, but merely try to limit the risk of profit loss.

Going up the scale, you may consider harvesting, which implies an eventual total withdrawal but at a planned rate. You will harvest this particular product for maximum profits even as you are withdrawing from the marketplace.

Finally there is liquidation or sell-out. In liquidation you are leaving the marketplace immediately. This strategy is adopted when there are no advantages to harvesting over a period of time and an immediate use can be found for the resources that you gained by getting out of the marketplace at once. Repositioning can also be a part of this strategy. Certain alternative marketing strategies tend to be more effective at different stages of the product life cycle. This is shown in Figure 4-18. A summary of the alternative strategies is contained in Figure 4-19.

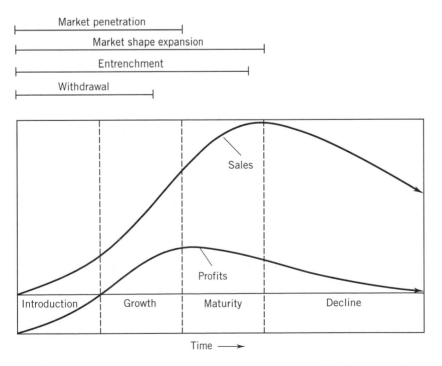

FIGURE 4-18. The product life cycle with alternative marketing strategies implied at each stage.

I. New Market Penetration
  A. Entry
    1. First
    2. Early
    3. Late
  B. Niche
    1. Toll gate
    2. Specialty skill
    3. Specialty market
  C. Dimension
    1. Vertical
    2. Horizontal
  D. Positioning

II. Market Share Expansion
  A. Product differentiation versus market segmentation
  B. Limited versus general expansion
  C. Repositioning

III. Entrenchment
  A. Direct confrontation
  B. Repositioning

IV. Withdrawal
  A. Harvesting
  B. Risk reduction
  C. Liquidation
  D. Repositioning

FIGURE 4-19.   Marketing strategies.

SUMMARY

In this chapter you've seen the three different levels of strategy. These are strategic marketing management, marketing strategy, and marketing tactics. We examined ways of developing SMM strategies by the use of a four-cell portfolio matrix that measures factors having to do with business strengths and marketing attractiveness. We looked at developing marketing strategies using the product life cycle. We also considered other alternative marketing strategies. These included new market penetration, market share expansion, entrenchment, and withdrawal. In preparing your market plan, it is helpful to indicate exactly what strategies you plan to use to meet the goals and objectives set. You will implement your strategies with the tactics that are discussed in Chapter 5.

CHAPTER 5

STEP 5

DEVELOPING MARKETING TACTICS

Tactics tell you how to implement the strategy you have developed. There are two general classes of tactics. The first includes marketing variables that you can control fairly easily. The second involves manipulating marketplace environs. Let's look at each in turn.

MANIPULATING THE CONTROLLABLE VARIABLES

Professor E. Jerome McCarthy in Michigan conceptualized many controllable tactics under only four categories, each beginning with the letter "p": product, price, promotion, and place. These four categories of controllable marketing variables are known as "the four Ps."

PRODUCT

There are three basic things that can be done with any product. It can be introduced into the marketplace, it can be modified or changed, and it can be withdrawn. Each alternative can be the best in different conditions.

A product may be introduced into the market to support a strategy of new market penetration. A tactic of product withdrawal may also support the same strategy. This is because the resources that were used to market the withdrawn product can be put to use elsewhere.

A product can also be changed or modified to alter the shape of the product's life cycle. When a product has been effectively rejuvenated in this fashion, there are a number of benefits. Goodwill toward the product and product awareness that is already established are retained. As a consequence, promotional costs for introducing and familiarizing consumers with a brand new product are unnecessary.

Other actions can be taken that will also affect your ability to implement a marketing strategy. These actions include decisions related to product quality, branding, and packaging.

Research has shown that product quality not only affects the image and the price that can be charged but also the product's profitability. This does not necessarily mean that the highest quality product is desired by customers in all instances. Rather that for a particular class of product or service, customers want the highest quality that they can get.

That is where some marketers make a mistake. Within their class, they reduce quality to lower production costs. They think that this increases profitability. This is incorrect. The customer wants the best that he or she can get for the money, and will reward marketers that provide it.

You must also analyze the situation carefully. During a depression or recession, when money is short, less expensive products are generally expected to be more successful. This isn't always true. When the United States sank into depression in 1929, cigar smokers proclaimed, "What this country needs is a good 5-cent cigar." A company selling premium cigars was started right in the middle of the depression. It grew into a multimillion-dollar company while many makers of 5-cent cigars failed.

Branded products are much more expensive than products that are not branded. You may have heard of Chiquita bananas and Sunkist oranges and Dole pineapples. But have you heard of TomAhtoes? TomAhtoes sell at about 30 percent per pound more than unbranded tomatoes. Clearly this is an exclusive brand.

Higher profit margins are only one reason for branding a product. Another is image and identification. Once a product's name has been planted in the mind of the consumer, it can be as important as any functional aspect of the product.

In general, there are four branding possibilities:

1. A company can use a new brand with a product or service in a category that is completely new to the company.

2. A company can introduce a new brand in a category in which the firm is already selling products.

3. A company can use a line-extension tactic in which the company's brand name is used to cover a new product as well as others already in the product line.

4. A firm can adopt a franchise extension in which a brand name familiar to the consumer is applied to products in a category that the firm has never marketed.

A new get-well card in Hallmark's line of greeting cards or a new ice cream flavor are examples of line extension, whereas franchise extension may include Ivory shampoo and conditioner developed from Ivory soap.

There are advantages and disadvantages to each of these tactics. A brand-line extension attempts to capitalize on some of the company's valuable assets in the form of goodwill, brand name, and brand awareness. The expectation is that a synergistic effect will help to promote the old and new products under the same label.

There are disadvantages to brand extension in some situations. An inexpensive Cadillac may increase sales over the short run for individuals who wish to own a prestige car but do not wish to pay a lot of money for it. Over the long run this tactic may cause the loss of buyers in Cadillac's traditional market segment of affluent consumers because Cadillac's high-priced, exclusive brand image would be less distinct. In the extreme, using a brand name for such items as Cadillac greeting cards or Cadillac gasoline could destroy the old brand name with no gain to the new product.

Packaging is important to protect the product, to help promote it, and to make it stand out when displayed among many other products. In a recent year more than 5,000 new items appeared on grocery shelves. In this new product clutter, many experts have shown that simple repackaging can increase brand identification and awareness significantly.

PRICE

Three basic pricing tactics may be followed in introducing a new product: penetration pricing, meet-the-competition pricing, and price skimming.

Penetration pricing involves entering the market with a low price that will capture as large a share of the market as possible. The lower price is emphasized as a competitive differential advantage over the competition. Once the product is well established in the marketplace, the price may be raised to be level with or even higher than the competition.

When the Nissan was introduced to the United States as a sports car under the Datsun brand name in the early 1970s, it carried a low price compared with similar sports cars. Then, as the market responded and the car became an established brand, the price was slowly raised. Today it is on the high end of the price scale for its product class.

Of course, low price tactics may always be introduced in support of an overall strategy. Some years ago Procter and Gamble reduced its supermarket specials and replaced these promotional tactics by setting lower list prices on all its products. Retailers weren't pleased, because they lost income due to the loss of discounts and special deals. They responded by cutting back on purchases. However, customers bought more at the lower prices, and P&G has held steady or increased volume market-share for 38 months in a row.[1]

Meet-the-competition pricing involves introducing a product or service at about the same level as that of its competitors. If this tactic is used, you must differentiate your product in some other way. Some marketers that adopt this tactic offer higher quality or better service. Some bundle the product with several other products or benefits to increase the overall value. An entertainment system containing a TV, an AM–FM stereo, and a CD player may be priced at the price sum of the individual components. The bundling into a system provides a differential advantage. If you do not offer some competitive advantage, there is no reason for a consumer to switch from a competitive product or service.

Price skimming involves pricing a new product relatively high. Skimming is frequently done when the product or service is first in the marketplace. Computers, when first introduced, were frequently priced high. This was not only because of the cost of components and labor, but also because competition was almost nonexistent.

As competitors enter the market the price is usually reduced to meet their lower prices or to make it more difficult for them to enter the market. Moreover, additional financial resources have been accumulated because of the higher profit margin. These resources can be used to fight the competition with other tactics. A company that used the skimming tactic can spend more on promotion when competitors enter the market, and it can open additional channels of distribution.

The price can also be raised in the face of competition, however. Marketing genius Joe Cossman introduced a plastic-hose, lawn-sprinkling device, which consisted of a single flexible plastic tube containing many holes. Although highly innovative, this product was easy to copy and manufacture and could not be protected by patent.

Even though the first season's market was all his, Cossman knew that competition would enter the following year at a lower price. Cossman's tactics were creative. He raised his recommended selling price and decreased the wholesale price to the retailer. Because of the larger margins offered to the retailers, Cossman shut out his competitors and maintained a market share through a second season with a higher retail price.

Other Tactical Pricing Tactics. You should also give consideration to other pricing tactics. There is always the alternative of promotional versus baseline pricing. P&G decided on lower baseline prices as we saw earlier. The question is should you introduce a lower price to promote the product or maintain a standard price? Promotional pricing can increase sales. However, you've got to make certain that your customers aren't confused by the two prices. If your customers are led to believe that the promotional price is your standard price, you're in trouble. It will be difficult to sell at the baseline price once the promotional period has ended.

Various psychological pricing tactics are also useful and should be considered. Have you ever wondered why numbers such as $3.99 and $6.98 are used in selling products

---

[1]Zachary Schiller, Greg Burns, and Karen L. Miller, "Make It Simple," *Business Week* (September 9, 1996), p. 96.

rather than $4.00 and $7.00? Psychologists have discovered that $3.99 is frequently seen as $3.00 rather than $4.00, and $6.98 as $6.00 rather than $7.00.

There are other important psychological considerations. At relatively low prices, a 10 percent difference may be perceived as significant by a potential buyer or prospect. So dropping your price 10 percent can make a real difference in sales. But with a higher priced product, a 10 percent difference may have no impact whatsoever. So dropping a $1 product to 90 cents makes a difference. But knocking off $3 from a product selling for $30.00 makes no difference. Yet the $3 is 30 times the 10-cent reduction! A 10 percent price difference is simply not perceived by the prospect as significant at higher prices.

Any markdowns must be examined from your customer viewpoint. The way to do this is to make certain that the premarkdown price is perceived as a real value for the product. You might even explain why it is in your promotion before you reveal the markdown price. Then a markdown will increase sales and the baseline price can also be restored more easily if that is your plan.

You must also consider discount pricing. Most buyers expect that the greater the quantity purchased, the lower the price. This expectation is so pervasive that if you do not discount on larger quantities, you must have valid reasons that are acceptable to the buyer.

Finally, never forget the psychological aspect of pricing's effect on image. A high price denotes an expensive image and a low price, a cheaper one. The same is true of quality. In situations where buyers must make a choice among products, many will pick the most expensive one. Buyers may feel that this increases their chances of getting a higher quality product.

PLACE

Place has to do with channel and distribution tactics to support. There are six basic channel alternatives to consider:

1. Direct or indirect channels
2. Single or multiple channels
3. Length of channel
4. Type of intermediaries
5. Number of distributors at each level
6. Which intermediaries to use

A direct channel means selling directly to the consumer. Perishables may spoil if they must pass through many channels. Specialty products may require a great deal of explanation and demonstration that can best be done by the manufacturer.

Sometimes the limited resources of a smaller firm may prohibit the use of a direct channel, especially when a large number of customers are widely scattered. But selling directly to these customers or organizational buyers is so lucrative that larger firms may choose this alternative as well.

The use of indirect channels includes retailers, wholesalers, industrial supply houses, manufacturer's representatives and agents. The fact that your profit margin on each item is far lower when sold through these intermediaries may be outweighed by the fact that you can reach many more customers than would otherwise be the case. Thus your overall profit could be much greater than if you attempted to sell direct.

The choice of multiple channels means working more than one simultaneously. Because an additional channel would seem to involve more outlets for sales and more chance for selling, you may wonder why multiple channels are not always selected. There are several reasons. First, additional channels cost more, and this additional capital may not be available to you. Small companies with limited resources sometimes start with a single channel and expand to a greater number as more money becomes available. The same is true regarding where to distribute. A company may begin distribution locally and later expand to national distribution as more capital becomes available.

Interchannel rivalry is another reason for not always using multiple channels. Let's say you sell to retail outlets. These outlets will not be enthusiastic about your selling to other channels, particularly discount houses. Similarly, a mail order catalog house won't want to see its product in retail stores and vice versa. But even if you decide to operate with multiple channels, you should recognize that one or more channels may not push your product aggressively. A channel could even boycott your product and refuse to handle it. Veterinarians did this to the Upjohn Company many years ago when Upjohn refused to grant them exclusive use of a drug intended to cure an illness in cattle. Eventually, the company was forced to create a special product exclusively for veterinarians.

The length of the channel is based on the number of intermediaries along a single line of distribution. You don't have to sell to a retailer. You can sell to a wholesale distributor who, in turn, sells to a retailer. But your channel could be even longer. You can employ an agent or sell to a jobber who sells to a wholesaler. There is no single answer to the length of a channel. Factors to be considered include your strength as a manufacturer, the average order size, the geographic concentration of customers, seasonality of sales, geographical distance from producer to market, and the perishability of the product.

Types of intermediaries to use must also be considered. A wholesaler may be desirable when greater distribution is required over a larger area. When this is unnecessary, retailers may be preferred. A small company with limited resources may choose to work with manufacturers' representatives or agents who do not take title to the goods even though their profitability would be far greater with a sales force of their own. Why? To recruit, train, and maintain a sales force is expensive and requires a lot of other resources. As noted earlier, many small companies lack these resources. Also, established manufacturers rep resentatives and agents who take a percentage of the sales price may also have the contacts and know-how to sell the product better than you could, at least in the near term.

You also need to decide on the number of distributors at each level of distribution. More distributors at each level are needed when the unit value of the product is low, the product is purchased frequently, the technical complexity of the product is high, service requirements and inventory investment are high, product differentiation is significant, the total market potential is high, geographic concentration is low, the manufacturer's current market share is high, competition is intense, and the effect on the customer's production process due to lack of availability is significant. When these factors are absent, you'll need fewer distributors at each level.

The selection of specific intermediaries does not depend only on their track records, although this certainly is a major consideration. You must also consider the market segment served, how well the intermediary knows and understands this market, how you and the intermediary fit together in policy, strategy, and image, and whether you and the distributor understand the roles each of you play in marketing the product.

Place tactics also require decisions in regard to physical distribution of the product. These include what physical distribution services are needed, how they should be provided, and what resources are required. Warehousing, packaging for transportation, the form of transportation, and distribution points must be considered. These all involve serious trade-offs among alternatives. Only in this way can you develop the best tactical "place" decisions.

PROMOTION

Most marketers divide promotion into additional categories of face-to-face selling, sales promotion, advertising, and publicity. Face-to-face selling requires decisions having to do with your own sales force or using the services of an agent to sell for you. We may have considered this decision previously under distribution. If so, you don't need to repeat your analysis. But if you haven't considered the alternatives, now is the time.

This decision can be especially important in the early stages of a firm's growth, when limited resources may argue against investing large sums to operate your own sales force.

Sometimes you must weigh this means of promotion against others. Never forget that you have limited resources for implementing your marketing plan. So you must weigh face-to-face selling against other ways of gaining sales.

The advantages of personal selling over other promotional methods include:

More flexibility (your salesperson can tailor the sales presentation to fit a customer's needs, behavior, and motives in special situations)

Immediate feedback from the customer (this will let you know when your appeal isn't working and must be adjusted)

Instant receipts for sales

Additional services to be rendered at the time of the sales call

Flexible time to make the sale

In developing tactics for face-to-face selling, decisions must be made regarding recruitment, compensation, and training of your sales force, the allocation of exclusive or nonexclusive sales territories, and, perhaps most important, motivation of your sales-people to maximum performance.

Use of Sales Promotion Tactics. Sales promotion is one of the hottest areas of the promotional tactic variable. Companies spend more than $60 billion annually on this tactic. And no wonder . . . it can be extremely effective in boosting sales. A single display at the front of a store can increase a product's sales 600 percent.

Sales promotion techniques can involve sampling, coupons, trade allowances, price quantity promotion, premiums, contests and sweepstakes, refund offers, bonus packs, stamp and continuity plans, point-of-purchase displays, and participation in trade shows. Naturally, each of these options has a cost associated with it. Therefore testing is essential to determine which work best in different situations. It is unlikely that any firm would be strong enough financially to employ all or even most of these techniques simultaneously. Therefore resources should be concentrated where they will have the greatest payback in implementing the mix of sales promotion tactics selected.

Sales promotion tactics are especially useful for new product introduction and during periods of high competition, when additional stimulation is necessary to increase sales.

Advertising and Publicity Tactics. Advertising and publicity tactics are usually required. Why? Because no matter how good the product or service, there will be no sales if the potential buyer or prospect has never heard of it. So your main objective is to make the product or service known to the market and to present it in its most favorable light in comparison with competitive products.

Some marketers think that advertising and publicity works automatically and should be used in every marketing situation. This simply is not true. For one thing, it can be extremely expensive. No company has unlimited resources to spend in advertising everywhere simultaneously just as no firm has unlimited resources to spend on executing many tactics, such as both low price and very high quality, simultaneously. In some cases advertising may be only marginally beneficial. In others, it may not work at all.

Cigarette advertising on television and radio came to an end on January 2, 1971. Although many cigarette manufacturers claimed that sales would drop drastically, sales over the next few years actually increased without this advertising. The forced move from radio and television uncovered the amazing fact that other types of advertising were more effective. Some TV and radio advertising may have been hurting sales. Too much advertising by different manufacturers was probably canceling out the value of each others' promotion.

Publicity is sometimes touted as free advertising, with the added advantage of greater credibility because promotion seems to come from a third party. But publicity costs money. Even a simple release involves preparation and mailing costs.

Some years ago, the promotion of a science fiction book, *Battlefield Earth,* by L. Ron Hubbard, cost a staggering $750,000. Therefore, although it definitely makes sense to consider a publicity campaign in addition to advertising, it is not "free" in the true sense of the word.

One final point about advertising and publicity: Advertising can never force a consumer to buy products or services that are not really wanted or are believed to have low value. Even though various governmental and nongovernmental regulatory agencies forbid misleading and inaccurate advertising, the product or service must live up to its advertising or publicity claims or customers will not buy it again. Even raising the expectations of the consumer by too much hype may cause a product to be returned or ignored in the future, even though it has technically met all the claims in its advertising.

Five key issues will determine whether your use of advertising and publicity will be successful:

1. Where to spend
2. How much to spend
3. When to spend
4. What to say
5. How to measure results

The answers to these questions depend on your overall advertising and publicity objectives, your target market, and certain broad alternatives for reaching the advertising objective.

The broad alternative objectives you should consider are to stimulate primary demand for the product or service; to introduce unknown or new advantages or attributes; to alter the assessed importance of an existing product or service attribute; to alter the perception of a product or service; or to change the perception of competing products. Keep focused on what you are trying to accomplish.

In advertising, *media* refers to TV, radio, print, or whatever carries your message; *vehicle* is the particular TV channel and spot, magazine, or newspaper. In every case you must not only outline the cost of advertising in the media and vehicles chosen but also the expected benefits. These benefits should be quantified by sales or market share increases over a specific time period. In other words, an acceptable publicity or advertising objective would be to sell 500,000 units in three months or to capture one percent of the market in six months. Only in this way can you reconcile costs and benefits or determine whether results have met your expectations in your advertising and publicity tactical campaign.

Note the similarity in describing these benefits and objectives for your marketing plan.

MANIPULATING MARKETPLACE ENVIRONS

For many years manipulating the environs for marketing tactics was largely ignored. Of course, it was recognized that demand, social and cultural factors, state of the technology, and politics and laws could be influenced. In general, however, marketing experts felt that it was far easier and less demanding for firms to attempt to manipulate the variables of product, price, promotion, and place. Thus environmental variables were assumed to be uncontrollable.

More recently the possibility of changing the context in which the organization operates, in terms of constraints on the marketing function and limits on the marketing organization, were investigated. Researchers found that these conditions can be used effectively and less expensively than was imagined.

The bottom line is that you should consider environmental marketing tactics as a possible alternative. Consider a company engaging in a private legal battle with a competitor on the grounds of deceptive advertising, or efforts to lobby for a particular political action before Congress to ensure a more favorable business environment or to limit competition. Two marketing scientists, Carl P. Zeithaml and Valerie A. Zeithaml, did a great deal of work in this field and prepared a framework for environmental management tactics. Their division of these tactics into independent, cooperative, and strategic subcategories is shown in Figure 5-1.

Environmental Management Tactic	Definition	Examples
	Independent Tactics	
Competitive aggression	Focal organization exploits a distinctive competence or improves internal efficiency of resources for competitive advantage.	Product differentiation. Aggressive pricing. Comparative advertising.
Competitive pacification	Independent action to improve relations with competitors	Helping competitors find raw materials. Advertising campaigns which promote entire industry. Price umbrellas.
Public relations	Establishing and maintaining favorable images in the minds of those making up the environment.	Corporate advertising campaigns.
Voluntary action	Voluntary management of and commitment to various interest groups, causes, and social problems.	McGraw-Hill efforts to prevent sexist stereotypes. 3M's energy conservation program.
Dependence development	Creating or modifying relationships such that external groups become dependent on the focal organization.	Raising switching costs for suppliers. Production of critical defense-related commodities. Providing vital information to regulators.
Legal action	Company engages in private legal battle with competitor on antitrust, deceptive advertising, or other grounds.	Private antitrust suits brought against competitors.
Political action	Efforts to influence elected representatives to create a more favorable business environment or limit competition.	Corporate constituency programs. Issue advertising. Direct lobbying.
Smoothing	Attempting to resolve irregular demand.	Telephone company's lower weekend rates. Inexpensive airline fares on off-peak times.
Demarketing	Attempts to discourage customers in general or a certain class of customers in particular, on either a temporary or a permanent basis.	Shorter hours of operation by gasoline service stations.
	Cooperative Tactics	
Implicit cooperation	Patterned, predictable, and coordinated behaviors.	Price leadership.
Contracting	Negotiation of an agreement between the organization and another group to exchange goods, services, information, patterns, etc.	Contractual vertical and horizontal marketing systems.
Co-optation	Process of absorbing new elements into the leadership or policymaking structure of an organization as a means of averting threats to its stability of existence.	Consumer representatives, women, and bankers on boards of directors.
Coalition	Two or more groups coalesce and act jointly with respect to some set of issues for some period of time.	Industry association. Political initiatives of the Business Roundtable and the U.S. Chamber of Commerce

Figure 5-1.   A framework of environmental management strategies. From "Environmental Management: Revising the Markets Perspective," by Carl P. Zeithaml and Valerie A. Zeithaml, *Journal of Marketing* (Spring 1984), pp. 50–57. Used with permission.

Environmental Management Tactic	Definition	Examples
	Strategic Maneuvering	
Domain selection	Entering industries or markets with limited competition or regulation coupled with ample suppliers and customers; entering high growth markets.	IBM's entry into the personal computer market. Miller Brewing Company's entry into the light beer market.
Diversification	Investing in different types of businesses, manufacturing different types of products, vertical integration, or geographic expansion to reduce dependence on single product, service, market, or technology.	Marriott's investment in different forms of restaurants. General Electric's wide product mix.
Merger and acquisition	Combining two or more firms into a single enterprise; gaining possession of an ongoing enterprise.	Merger between Pan American and National Airlines. Philip Morris's acquisition of Miller Beer.

Figure 5-1. *Continued*

TACTICAL QUESTIONS FOR THE MARKETING PLAN

The form contained in Figure 5-2 (pages 70–73) includes questions in each of the areas discussed in this chapter—product, price, promotion, and place as well as in the use of the marketing environs to develop tactics. Completing this form will assist you in considering the trade-offs to develop powerful marketing tactics for your marketing plan.

SUMMARY

In this chapter you have learned how to develop marketing tactics to implement the strategies that you selected in Chapter 4. Marketing tactics have to do with your manipulation of product, price, promotion, and place and the marketing environs. In Chapter 6 you will learn how to determine the total potential available for any given market, and to forecast sales that will result from the strategy and tactics that you selected.

PRODUCT

Product description _____

_____

_____

Life cycle stage _____

Characteristics of stage _____

_____

_____

_____

Complementary products   1. _____ 2. _____

3. _____ 4. _____ 5. _____

Substitute products   1. _____ 2. _____

3. _____ 4. _____ 5. _____

Package: Message _____

Size _____ Shape _____ Color _____

Function _____ Material _____

Brand: Name _____

Type of branding _____

Forecast sales volume _____

Forecast production volume _____

_____

Basic product strategy _____

_____

_____

PRICE

Objectives 1. _____ 2. _____

3. _____ 4. _____

Basic per unit cost of acquisition _____

Other relevant costs _____

_____

_____

_____

_____

FIGURE 5-2.   Tactical questions for the marketing plan. (Copyright © 1985 by Dr. William A. Cohen. Note: This form is based on an earlier form designed by Dr. Benny Barak, then of Baruch College.)

Discount policy _____

_____

_____

Pricing strategy _____

_____

_____

Unit pricing _____

_____

_____

Forecast revenue _____

Forecast profit _____

DISTRIBUTION

Channels to be used and timing _____

_____

_____

_____

Alternative strategies: Push/pull _____

Intensive/selective/exclusive _____

PROMOTION

Positioning _____

_____

Advertising: Objectives 1. _____

2. _____ 3. _____

Campaign theme _____

_____

Copy theme _____

_____

_____

_____

Graphics and layout_____

_____

_____

_____

FIGURE 5-2.   *Continued*

Media plan	Description	Length/size	Freq/dates	Cost
Newspapers	_____	_____	_____	_____
	_____	_____	_____	_____
	_____	_____	_____	_____
Magazines	_____	_____	_____	_____
	_____	_____	_____	_____
	_____	_____	_____	_____
Television	_____	_____	_____	_____
	_____	_____	_____	_____
	_____	_____	_____	_____
Radio	_____	_____	_____	_____
	_____	_____	_____	_____
	_____	_____	_____	_____
Other	_____	_____	_____	_____
	_____	_____	_____	_____
	_____	_____	_____	_____

Budget for advertising _____

Publicity: Objectives 1. _____ 2. _____

3. _____ 4. _____

Action/cost/timing

Description of action	Timing	Cost
_____	_____	_____
_____	_____	_____
_____	_____	_____
_____	_____	_____
_____	_____	_____
_____	_____	_____
_____	_____	_____
_____	_____	_____
_____	_____	_____
_____	_____	_____
_____	_____	_____

Budget for publicity _____

Personal selling: Objectives 1. _____

2. _____ 3. _____

_____

FIGURE 5-2. *Continued*

Sales force size and type _____

_____

_____

Sales territories _____

_____

_____

Method of compensation _____

_____

_____

Budget for personal selling _____

Sales promotion: Objectives 1. _____

2. _____   3. _____

Methods and costs

_____

Method	Timing	Cost
_____	_____	_____
_____	_____	_____
_____	_____	_____
_____	_____	_____
_____	_____	_____
_____	_____	_____
_____	_____	_____

Budget for sales promotion _____

Summary of overall goals/costs/time to achieve of project

Goals 1. _____   2. _____

3. _____   4. _____

Overall cost _____ Timing _____

_____

_____

_____

_____

FIGURE 5-2. *Continued*

STEP 6

FORECASTING FOR YOUR MARKETING PLAN

When you forecast, you attempt to predict the future. To a significant extent you will do this by analyzing the past. Of course, this does not necessarily mean that whatever happened in the past will continue to happen in the future, but it is here that the process of forecasting begins. By forecasting you will be able to establish more accurate goals and objectives for your marketing plan. But forecasting does even more for you. It will help you to do all of the following:

- Determine markets for your products
- Plan corporate strategy
- Develop sales quotas
- Determine whether salespeople are needed and how many
- Decide on distribution channels
- Price products or services
- Analyze products and product potential in different markets
- Decide on product features
- Determine profit and sales potential for products
- Determine advertising and sales promotion budgets
- Determine the potential benefits of various elements of marketing tactics.

So sales forecasting involves decisions made in all sections of your marketing plan. As you will see as you proceed, forecasting may involve some guesswork and a great deal of managerial judgment. Nevertheless, even guesswork becomes far more valuable when supported by facts and careful analysis.

If you simply pull facts out of thin air and construct your marketing plan based on them without a logical method of proceeding, many of your basic assumptions are as likely to be wrong as right. Succeeding under these conditions would be largely a matter of luck.

In this chapter you will learn how to optimize your hunches through forecasting techniques. This will make the figures in your marketing plan far more credible. It will also greatly increase your chance of success should you actually implement your plan.

THE DIFFERENCE BETWEEN MARKET POTENTIAL, SALES POTENTIAL, AND SALES FORECAST

Market potential, sales potential, and **sales forecast** all mean different things. *Market potential* refers to the total potential sales for a product or service or any group of products being considered for a certain geographical area or designated market, over a specific period. Market potential relates to the total capacity of that market to absorb everything that an entire industry may produce, whether airline travel, light bulbs, or motorcycle helmets.

Let's say that there are 1 million new motorcyclists every year, and that 1 million old motorcycle helmets wear out every year and must be discarded. The market potential for motorcycle helmets in the United States is 2 million helmets every year. If helmets sell for $100 each, that would be a market potential of $200 million a year.

Sales potential refers to the ability of the market to absorb or purchase the output of a single company in that industry, presumably yours. Thus, if you are a motorcycle helmet manufacturer, the ability of the market to purchase that output might be only $50 million, even though the market potential is $200 million.

The term *sales forecast* refers to the actual sales you predict your firm will realize in this market in a single year. In using our motorcycle helmet example, perhaps your sales forecast will be only $20 million, even though the market potential is $200 million for the entire industry and the sales potential $50 million for your company.

Why the difference? Why can't you reach the full market potential in sales? Sales potential may not exceed market potential because of your production capacity. You can produce only $50 million in helmets, not $200 million.

There may be many reasons for not trying to achieve 100 percent of the sales potential of which you are capable. Perhaps selling to the entire market would require more money than you have available for your marketing campaign.

Maybe the return on your investment to reach your full sales potential is insufficient to make this a worthwhile objective. To achieve 100 percent of anything requires consideration of the law of diminishing returns. This means that the marginal cost of each additional percentage point becomes greater and greater as you try to achieve the full sales potential. Therefore it may be wiser to stop at 90, 80, or even 70 percent of your sales potential because the significantly higher costs of achieving those final percentage points to get to 100 percent make the goal less desirable. There may be far better uses for your resources because the return on each dollar you invest elsewhere may be greater.

Finally, there may be some other reason that will discourage you from achieving 100 percent. Maybe competition is particularly strong. Perhaps there is an unfavorable factor in the marketing environment, such as the law that requires cyclists to wear helmets in your state being repealed.

Nevertheless, we must know the market potential and sales potential before we can calculate our sales forecast.

FINDING MARKET POTENTIAL

Sometimes it is possible to find the market potential for a specific product through research already done by someone else. Such research may have been previously accomplished by the U.S. government, a trade association, or an industry magazine. At other times it is necessary to derive the market potential for your products by using a chain of information. This latter method is called a chain ratio and involves connecting many related facts to arrive at the total market potential you are seeking.

Some years ago, I wanted to explore the market potential for body armor used by foreign military forces for an export project. Because at that time only a few countries used this equipment, this number had to be determined by a chain ratio method.

First, I calculated the number of units of body armor used by U.S. military forces. I used a government publication called the *Commerce Business Daily,* which lists contracts awarded for most government purchases. An average number of body armor units per year was derived from a look at purchases over several years.

Next I researched the size of the U.S. Army during that period. From the total annual sales of body armor to the U.S. Army and the average size of the ground forces during the same period, a ratio of body armor units per soldier could be developed.

Then, I consulted the *Almanac of World Military Power,* which listed the strength of military forces for all countries. Because the body armor was an export military item, the sale of it is controlled by the U.S. government. Therefore only those countries for which sales were likely to be approved by the U.S. government were included.

I added the figures for each country and calculated the total. Next, I took the ratio of body armor units per soldier developed earlier from U.S. data and applied it to this figure. The result was a total market potential of military body armor for export from the United States to foreign armies.

Note that this was not the sales potential for the sale of body armor by any single company for this market, nor was it a forecast of what body armor would be sold. It was the market potential for sales from the United States.

Here's another example. Let's say that a dance studio wishes to know the market potential for dance students in its geographical area. The first step would be to note the total population in the area served by the studio. If the area has a 5-mile circumference, then you will want to know its population. These population figures can be obtained from the census surveys of the Department of Commerce. Sometimes your local Chamber of Commerce may have this information or surveys may have been done by local or state governments.

Once you have the population, the next step is to arrive at the per capita expenditure for dance lessons. Again, government statistics may be helpful. Industry associations of dance studios may be able to provide this information. You might also look for trade magazines having to do with professional dance and studio management. Naturally you must be sure that the geographical information furnished corresponds closely with the geographical area you are analyzing. Per capita expenditure can differ greatly, depending on the region of the country, its culture and climate, and the attitudes and interests of its people.

If you multiply the population in the 5-mile area by the per capita expenditure for dance lessons, you will end up with a total annual expenditure.

As you can see, the market potential for any product or class of product or service can be determined by doing a little detective work. Think about how you might get the market potential which is not available directly by linking other available information.

THE INDEX METHOD OF CALCULATING MARKET POTENTIAL

An alternate way of calculating market potential is by the use of indices that have already been constructed from surveys and basic economic data. One example is the survey published by *Sales and Marketing Magazine.* This magazine publishes a survey of buying power indices every year. They develop commercial indices by combining estimates of population, income, and retail sales. This results in a positive indicator of consumer data demand according to regions of the U.S. Bureau of Census by state, by its organized system of metro areas by counties, or even by cities with larger populations. The resulting buying power index (BPI) is multiplied by national sales figures to obtain the market potential for any local area.

Let's say that you sell a certain brand of national television but only in the local area in your own city store. From the manufacturer you learn that 10 million units are sold every year. Now you want to calculate the market potential for your city. You take the listed BPI and multiply it by 10 million. The answer is the market potential for your city. The *Sales and Marketing Magazine's* methodology also permits you to calculate the market potential with a custom BPI depending on demographics of your target market and your geographical area.

The BPI can also be used as a relative indicator to compare the potential buying power of the market you have targeted for your product. You can calculate a custom BPI for each market targeted.

Once you have the market potential, you can calculate sales potential by deciding how much of this market potential "belongs" to your firm. With no competition perhaps it's all yours. But, again, you must consider your capacity for satisfying the entire market. Once you have sales potential, you can turn to forecasting.

BOTTOM-UP AND TOP-DOWN SALES FORECASTING

There are two basic ways to forecast sales: the bottom-up and top-down methods. With the bottom-up method the sequence is to break up the market into segments and forecast each separately. You sum the sales forecast in each segment for the total sales forecast. Typical ways of doing this are by sales-force composites, industry surveys, and intention-to-buy surveys. We'll look at each of these later in the chapter.

To accomplish top-down forecasting the sales potential for the entire market is estimated, sales quotas are developed, and a sales forecast is constructed. Typical methods used in top-down surveys are executive judgment, trend projections, a moving average, regression, exponential smoothing, and leading indicators. Let's look at each of these forecasting methods first.

EXECUTIVE JUDGMENT

Executive judgment is known by a variety of names including "jury of executive opinion," "managerial judgment," and even "gut feeling." With this method you just ask executives who have the expertise. This could be many individuals or one single person who may be responsible for the program. This method of forecasting is fairly easy to use, but it is not without its risks. All experts have differing biases and differing opinions.

To overcome individual bias, some unusual methods have evolved. Perhaps the best known is the Delphi method. Experts are assembled and their opinions asked. Instead of stating their opinion verbally, they are written down anonymously, along with the reasons behind it. A facilitator analyzes the results, and calculates the range of answers, the frequency of each answer, the average, and indicates the reasons given. This summary is returned to the group of experts. A second round is then conducted and the same questions are asked. This process may be repeated several times until a group consensus emerges to result in the final forecast.

This method is effective because it enables expert opinion and reasoning to be shared without many of the psychological "hang-ups" of a public debate or alteration of opinion. It eliminates many psychological barriers inherent in roundtable discussions that might block legitimate input, like relative power. The Delphi method has been a useful and accurate method of using executive judgment in forecasting.

SALES-FORCE COMPOSITE

A sales-force composite can be obtained by assigning each of your salespeople the duty of forecasting sales potential for a particular territory. These territorial estimates are then summed to arrive at an overall forecast. The dangers in obtaining a forecast this way are based on the possibility that customers may not be entirely truthful in giving information to the salesperson. Also, the salesperson may overstate or understate the area's potential.

Why would a salesperson do this? Perhaps fear of being assigned sales quotas that are difficult to reach may cause the potential to be understated. Or the salesperson may overstate the potential to prevent the area from being eliminated.

If you have a new business, you may not be able to use this method because you haven't got a sales force.

TREND PROJECTIONS

A trend projection in its simplest form is an analysis of what has already happened, extended into the future. Your recorded observations of past sales may reveal that they have increased on an average of 10 percent every year. A simple trend projection would assume that sales will increase by 10 percent for the coming year as well.

If sales two years ago were $100,000 and last year, $300,000, and you projected the trend into the future by percentage, you would estimate $900,000 for next year. You might also estimate an increase in sales in absolute terms. If you did, you would estimate an increase of $200,000 each year. So next year's sales would be $500,000. Which type of linear project to use depends on your circumstances. You need to find out why you achieved the previous increase. If the reason can be related more to a percentage, then that's the way to do your trend analysis projection. If not, maybe an absolute dollar increase will provide a more accurate forecast.

A moving average is a more sophisticated trend projection. With this approach the assumption is made that the future will be an average of past performance rather than a linear projection. This minimizes the danger of a random event or element that could create a major impact on the forecast and cause it to be in error. Maybe a salesperson made a huge, unexpected sale.

I met a young real estate salesman who sold an $18 million property three months after he started in the business. He was even written up in the local newspapers. It would have been unwise for his organization to create a sales forecast for the following year without some consideration that this type of event was unlikely to be repeated.

What can we do to take care of unusual events like this? Let's see what would happen to our forecast using a moving average. The average of $100,000 and $300,000 for two years is $200,000—you would forecast $200,000 for the coming year. The moving average is simply summing up the sales in a number of periods and dividing by that number.

Which is the "correct" method of trend projection? Well, that's what makes marketing and forecasting so much fun. There isn't a correct method. You've got to consider other factors to help you decide which is correct for your situation.

Again, if you have no track record, you can't use this method.

INDUSTRY SURVEY

In the industry survey method you survey companies that make up the industry for a particular product or service. The industry survey method has some of the characteristics of the bottom-up method, rather than the top-down, and some of the advantages and disadvantages of executive opinion and sales-force composites. Representatives of companies may give inaccurate answers.

One thing you can do to minimize this is to make certain you talk to the right people. Some employees who want to help may not have access to accurate information, but will try to give you some answer anyway. At other times, companies consider information highly proprietary. On occasions, however, you can collect useful information or you may obtain useful data from industry associations or trade magazines.

Naturally, no one is going to do your forecasting for you, but you may be able to obtain information regarding the norm for salespeople in the industry and geographical area you're interested in. You then apply this or similar information to work out your forecast.

REGRESSION ANALYSES

A regression analysis may be linear or it may have to do with multiple regression. With linear regression, relationships between sales and a single independent variable are developed to forecast sales data. With multiple regression, relationships between sales and a number of independent variables are used. Computer programs are available to assist you in doing these calculations.

Sales predictions are made by estimating the values for independent variables and incorporating them into the multiple regression equation. Thus, if a relationship can be found among various independent variables—for example, units of computers sold, number of males between the ages of 36 and 55, average family income, rate of inflation, and per capita years of education—a multiple regression equation based on this information can be developed to predict sales for the coming year.

INTENTION-TO-BUY SURVEY

An intention-to-buy survey is done before the introduction of a new product or service or for the purchase of any product or service for some future period. The main problem with these surveys is that individuals may not always give accurate information regarding their intention to buy products or services in the future. So what's new? you may ask. What is it this time?

Inaccurate responses may be due to an inadequate explanation, a misunderstanding on the part of the respondent, or to other psychological factors, such as the individual's unwillingness to offend or a desire to respond in a socially acceptable way.

Face-to-face surveys regarding sexually explicit reading matter frequently indicate almost no intent to purchase. Yet, if *Playboy* magazine can be used as an example, this is a multimillion-dollar business with a large number of readers and subscribers.

Also, there is something about actually making the purchase that distinguishes it from intending to do so. The respondent may have really believed he or she would buy if the product were available. When it comes to the moment of truth, however, there may be reasons the respondent never thought of to interfere with the sale.

EXPONENTIAL SMOOTHING

Exponential smoothing is a timed series approach similar to the moving average method of trend analysis. Instead of a constant set of weights for the observations, however, an exponentially increasing set of weights is used to give the more recent values more weight than the older values.

This is exponential smoothing in its most basic form. More sophisticated models include adjustments for factors such as trend, seasonal patterns, and such. Forecasting techniques based on exponential smoothing are available on various computer programs, so you don't need to be a mathematical wizard. Just put the disk in your computer and follow the directions.

LEADING INDICATORS

Leading indicators to predict recessions and recoveries are used by the National Bureau of Economic Research. Typical leading indicators reported by this bureau include the prices of 500 common stocks, new orders for durable goods, an index of net business formation, corporate profits after taxes, industrial material prices, and changing consumer installment credit.

The problem of sales forecasting with these leading indicators is in relating them to specific products or services. When relationships are found, a multiregression model can be constructed. In fact, leading indicators are incorporated into some computer programs available for forecasting.

You can make rudimentary guesses based on leading economic indicators and apply them to your forecast. Frequently this will have as good a chance of being correct as an expensive computer model.

WHICH METHOD TO USE

Some methods are more popular in forecasting than others. A survey of 175 firms conducted some time ago indicated that the jury of executive opinion and sales-force composite were the two most popular. This is shown in Figure 6-1. Another study, which confirms that the executive opinion method is still the most popular, found that the two quantitative methods, time series smoothing and regressional analysis, were in second and third place, respectively, with sales-force composite following.

Consideration of a sales forecasting method for your particular situation and for your marketing plan should not be based merely on popularity of the method, but on situational factors that affect you. These factors include the resources that you have available, the time available, accuracy required, your estimation of the accuracy that can be attained by different methods available to your sales force, your customers, the individuals surveyed, and the cost of the forecast. Thus your judgment in choosing a sales forecasting method, or a combination of methods, is of primary importance.

Alvin Toffler, author of *Future Shock* and *The Third Wave,* probably said it best: "You can use all the quantitative data you can get, but you still have to distrust it and use your own intelligence and judgment."

YOU NEED MORE INFORMATION FOR YOUR FORECAST

Forecasting sales alone is insufficient. You must also forecast the costs involved and when they occur. This is done with a project development schedule, a break-even analysis, a balance sheet, a projected profit and loss statement, and cash-flow projections. Let's look at each in turn.

Method	Regular Use (%)	Occasional Use (%)	Never Used (%)
Jury of executive opinion	52	16	5
Sales force composite	48	15	9
Trend projections	28	16	12
Moving average	24	15	15
Industry survey	22	20	16
Regression	17	13	24
Intention-to-buy survey	15	17	23
Exponential smoothing	13	13	26
Leading indicators	12	16	24

FIGURE 6-1. Utilization of sales forecasting methods by 175 firms. Adapted from Douglas J. Dalrymple, "Sales Forecasting Methods and Accuracy," *Business Horizons, 18* (December 1975), p. 71.

THE PROJECT DEVELOPMENT SCHEDULE

The project development schedule, or PDS, is shown in Figure 6-2. It lists every task necessary to implement the project and the money spent during each period. These periods can be months or, in the case of the example indicated, weeks. Note that you don't need to know the exact date you will begin in order to develop an accurate PDS. All you need to do is describe the timing as "weeks or months after project initiation." If many different departments or individuals are involved, you can include them all to see who is doing what. By incorporating the amount of money spent by each, you can determine the amount spent by each department, amount spent for each task, and when money is needed for each task.

The project development schedule shows your entire plan financially and graphically. It will reveal problems in timing, financing, and coordination before you start. Once you begin to implement the plan, it will help you to monitor and control the project.

THE BREAK-EVEN ANALYSIS

A break-even analysis is used for evaluating relationships among sales revenues, fixed costs, and variable costs. The break-even point is the point at which the sales from a number of units sold cover costs of developing, producing, and selling the product. Prior to this point, you will be losing money. Beyond it you will make money. This is an excellent means for helping you forecast both the success of the product and what you need to succeed before the project is actually initiated, because it will tell you the following:

- How many units you must sell in order to start making money.
- How much profit you will make at any given level of sales.
- How changing your price will affect profitability.
- How cost increases or reductions at different levels of sales will affect profitability.

Combining your sales forecasts with break-even analysis will tell you how long it will take you to reach breakeven.

To accomplish a break-even analysis, separate the cost associated with your project into two categories: fixed costs and variable costs.

Fixed costs are those expenses associated with the project that you would have to pay whether you sold one unit or 10,000 units or, for that matter, whether you sold any units at all.

If you need to rent a building to implement your project and the owner of the building charges you $50,000, then this would be a fixed cost. You would have to pay the $50,000 whether you sold no units or millions of units. Research and development costs for a project or a product are also considered fixed costs. You have to spend this money whether or not you sell any of the product.

Variable costs are those that vary directly with the number of units you sell. If postage for mailing your product to a customer is $1.00, then $1.00 is a variable cost. If you sell 10 units, then your postage is 10 times $1.00, or $10.00. If you sell 100 units, your total variable costs for postage would be 100 times $1.00, or $100.00.

It is sometimes difficult to decide whether to consider costs as fixed or variable, and there may not be a single correct answer. Use sound judgment, along with the advice of financial or accounting experts if they are available. As a general guideline, if there is a direct relationship between cost and number of units sold, consider the cost as variable. If you cannot find such a relationship, consider the cost fixed. The total cost of your project will always equal the sum of the fixed costs plus the variable costs.

Here's an example of an item that you are going to sell for $10.00. How much profit would you realize if you sold 1,000 units?

Task	\multicolumn{12}{c}{Months After Project Initiation}
	1	2	3	4	5	6	7	8	9	10	11	12
Manufacture of units for test manufacturing	$5,000 →											
Initial advertisement in test area	$10,000	$10,000	$10,000 →									
Shipment of units in test market area	$300	$200 →										
Analysis of test		$500	$700	$200 →								
Manufacture of units— 1st year				$5,000	$10,000	$10,000	$10,000	$10,000 →				
Phase I advertising and publicity				$10,000	$30,000	$30,000	$15,000 →					
Shipment of units					$1,000	$1,000	$1,000	$1,000	$500 →			
Phase II advertising								$10,000	$10,000	$5,000	$5,000	$5,000 →

FIGURE 6-2. Project development schedule.

Fixed Costs

Utility expense at $100 per month for 36 months	$3600
Telephone at $200 per year for three years	600
Product development costs	1000
Rental expense	2500
Total fixed costs	$7700

Variable Costs

Cost of product	$1.00 per unit
Cost of postage and packaging	0.50 per unit
Cost of advertising	3.00 per unit
Total variable costs	$4.50 per unit

To calculate the break-even point, start with the equation for profit. Total profit equals the number of units sold times the price at which we are selling them, less the number of units sold multiplied by the total variable cost, less the total fixed cost.

If P stands for profit, and p for price, and U equals the number of units sold, V equals variable costs, and F equals fixed costs, then our equation becomes

$$P = (U \times p) - (U \times V) - F$$

You can simplify this to

$$P = U (p - V) - F$$

Substituting the values given in your example, you have

$$P = \$1000 (\$10 - \$4.50) - \$7700$$
$$= \$5500 - \$7700 = -\$2200.$$

The significance of the minus is that instead of making a profit at the particular number of units you have estimated, you have lost $2200.

If you want to know how many units you must sell in order to reach the break-even point, you can again use the equation for profit:

$$P = U (p - V) - F$$

Since profit at the break-even point is by definition zero, you can transpose terms and let $P = 0$. Then the break-even point equals F divided by p − V.

Because you know that $F = \$7700$, $p = \$10.00$, and $V = \$4.50$, the break-even point must equal $7700 divided by $10.00 − $4.50. That's $7700/5.50 or 1400 units.

This means that if you don't change price or reduce expenses, you must sell 1,400 units of the product before you can start making money.

You can calculate this graphically by using the chart in Figure 6-3. A break-even chart has an advantage over using the break-even equation. It shows you the relationship between profits and sales volume graphically, therefore making it easier for you to see how cost and other factors affect the results.

Even though there are advantages to break-even analysis, keep in mind that there are some limitations. First, break-even analysis shows profit at various levels of sales but does not show the return for our investment and other measures of financial efficiency. Because there are always alternative uses for a firm's financial resources, it is impossible to compare return on investment solely on the basis of break-even analysis. Also,

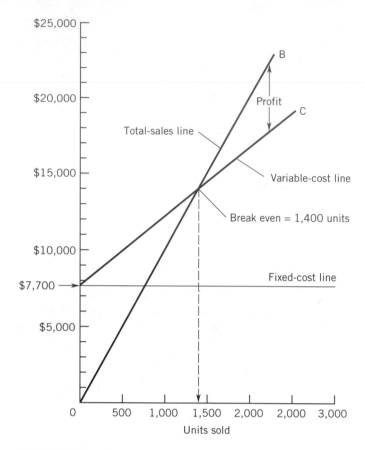

FIGURE 6-3.   Break-even analysis chart.

break-even analysis does not allow you to examine the cash flow. One way to compare investment or capital budgeting alternatives is to consider the value of the cash flows over a period of time and to discount the cost of capital by an appropriate percentage. You can't do this with a break-even analysis alone because the time to reach the various levels of sales is not indicated.

Despite these shortcomings, break-even analysis is a useful technique that should always be included as a part of your marketing plan.

THE BALANCE SHEET, PROJECTED PROFIT AND LOSS STATEMENT, AND CASH-FLOW PROJECTIONS

A balance sheet is usually calculated for businesses but it can also be calculated for a project. Basically, it consists of financial snapshots of two or more different points in your project. Most people select start-up and at least one other important milestone in the project.

In Figure 6-4, a balance sheet form is shown for Year 1 and Year 2. You calculate current assets, fixed assets, other assets, current liabilities, and long-term liabilities to arrive at a total net worth.

The projected profit and loss statement is shown in Figure 6-5. It is broken down on a monthly basis. Document total net sales, the cost of sales, and gross profit. Also note controllable expenses and fixed expenses and develop a net profit or loss before taxes for every month. This may be done only for a single year or it can be done for up to five years into the future, depending on the project.

The profit and loss statement along with the cash-flow projections in Figure 6-6 will show what happens between balance sheets. The latter displays cash, income, and

BALANCE SHEET

	Year 1	Year 2
Current Assets		
Cash		
Accounts receivable		
Inventory		
Fixed Assets		
Real estate		
Fixtures and equipment		
Vehicles		
Other Assets		
Licenses		
Goodwill		
Total Assets		
Current Liabilities		
Notes payable (due within 1 year)		
Accounts payable		
Accrued expenses		
Taxes owed		
Long-Term Liabilities		
Notes payable (due after 1 year)		
Other		
Total Liabilities		
Net Worth (Assets minus Liabilities)		

Total Liabilities plus Net Worth Should Equal Assets

FIGURE 6-4. Balance sheet.

PROJECTED PROFIT AND LOSS STATEMENT

	Month 1	Month 2	Month 3	Month 4	Month 5	Month 6	Month 7	Month 8	Month 9	Month 10	Month 11	Month 12
Total Net Sales												
Cost of sales												
Gross profit												
Controllable expenses: salaries												
Payroll taxes												
Security												
Advertising												
Automobile												
Dues and subscriptions												
Legal and accounting												
Office supplies												
Telephone												
Utilities												
Miscellaneous												
Total Controllable Expenses												
Fixed expenses: depreciation												
Insurance												
Rent												
Taxes and licenses												
Loan payments												
Total Fixed Expenses												
Total Expenses												
Net profit (loss) (before taxes)												

FIGURE 6-5.   Projected profit and loss statement.

CASH-FLOW PROJECTIONS

	Start-up or prior to loan	Month 1	Month 2	Month 3	Month 4	Month 5	Month 6	Month 7	Month 8	Month 9	Month 10	Month 11	Month 12	TOTAL
Cash (beginning of month)														
Cash on hand														
Cash in bank														
Cash in investments														
Total Cash														
Income (during month): Cash sales														
Credit sales payments														
Investment income														
Loans														
Other cash income														
Total income														
Total Cash and Income														
Expenses (during month): Inventory or new material														
Wages (including owner's)														
Taxes														
Equipment expense														
Overhead														
Selling expense														
Transportation														
Loan repayment														
Other cash expenses														
Total Expenses														
Cash Flow Excess (end of month)														
Cash Flow Cumulative (monthly)														

FIGURE 6-6. Cash-flow projections.

expenses on a monthly basis from start-up. Do these for the same number of years that you did the profit and loss statement.

A cash-flow projection shows the availability of cash on a monthly basis. If you need additional cash to keep your project going, it will show when the money will be needed. Obviously this will not only be of great interest to you, but also to your potential investors or company finance officers. They will want to know not only how much is needed, but when.

SUMMARY

In this chapter you have seen how to forecast everything you need for your marketing plan. You have seen how to calculate market potential, sales potential, and sales forecasts. You have seen how to forecast costs to develop a project development schedule with costs recorded periodically as needed, how to complete a break-even chart to determine how many units you need to sell to be profitable, how to determine how much money you made at any level of units sold, how to complete a balance sheet that indicates the status of your project at the end of various periods of time, and how to calculate a profit and loss statement and cash-flow projections on a monthly basis.

No marketing plan can be implemented without financial resources. The forecasts discussed in this chapter will enable you to determine what financial resources are necessary, as well as the benefits that will accrue as a result of investing these resources.

You are now in a position to calculate important financial ratios and to use them to help determine how efficient your plan is and how beneficial it is to the firm compared with other alternatives. Knowledge of these financial ratios will help you to obtain resources from those in authority in your company or from outside lenders. They will add tremendous credibility to your plan. We will learn how to calculate them in the next chapter.

CHAPTER 7

STEP 7

CALCULATING IMPORTANT FINANCIAL RATIOS FOR YOUR MARKETING PLAN

The financial ratios in this chapter will help provide the information so that you, or others, can compare your plan with competing plans on a financial basis. They will enable you to gain a better understanding of the financial efficiency of your plan and will help you to win support for your project. To do this you analyze your planned figures. If you implement your marketing plan, you can analyze what is actually happening partly by use of these financial ratios.

Some of these ratios are used primarily to measure the financial condition of an entire business, rather than a single project. However, with many marketing plans, especially start-ups, the project and the business are the same. You must decide which ratios are applicable to your situation and which are not.

MEASURES OF LIQUIDITY

Liquidity is the ability to use the money available. In general, the more liquid, the better the state of financial health. The ratios intended to measure liquidity will tell you whether you have enough cash on hand, plus assets that can be readily turned into cash, to pay debts that may fall due during any given period.

THE CURRENT RATIO

The current ratio is possibly the best-known measure of financial health. It answers this question: Does your business have sufficient current assets to meet current debts with a margin of safety for possible losses due to uncollectible accounts receivable and other factors?

BALANCE SHEET   December 31, 19 ____

Current assets:
Cash	$ 35,000.00	
Accounts receivable	55,000.00	
Inventory	60,000.00	
Temporary investments	3,000.00	
Prepaid expenses	2,000.00	
Total current assets		$155,000.00

Fixed assets:
Machinery and equipment	$ 35,000.00	
Buildings	42,000.00	
Land	40,000.00	
Total fixed assets		$117,000.00

Other assets:
None		
Total other assets		0
Total assets		$272,000.00

Current liabilities
Accounts payable	$ 36,000.00	
Notes payable	44,000.00	
Current portion of long-term notes	4,000.00	
Interest payable	1,000.00	
Taxes payable	3,000.00	
Accrued payroll	2,000.00	
Total current liabilities		$ 90,000.00

Long-term liabilities:
Notes payable	$ 25,000.00	
Total long-term liabilities		$ 25,000.00

Equity:
Owner's equity	$115,000.00	
Total equity		$115,000.00
Total liabilities and equity		$272,000.00

FIGURE 7-1.   Sample balance sheet for the XYZ Company.

The current ratio is computed by using information on your balance sheet. Divide current assets by current liabilities. Look at the sample balance sheet in Figure 7-1. Current assets are $155,000 and current liabilities are $90,000; $155,000 divided by $90,000 equals a current ratio of 1.7.

Is 1.7 a "good" current ratio? You cannot determine this from the numerical value of 1.7 by itself. There is a popular rule of thumb which says that you want a current ratio of at least 2.0. However, a desirable current ratio very much depends on your business and the specific characteristics of your current assets and liabilities. That's why a comparison with other current ratios is a better indication. I'll give you sources for this information in the "Sources of Ratio Analyses from All Industries" section later in the chapter.

If after analysis and comparison you decide that your current ratio is too low, you may be able to raise it by the following actions:

1. Increase your current assets by new equity contributions.

2. Try converting noncurrent assets into current assets.

3. Pay some of your debts.

4. Increase your current assets from loans or other types of borrowing which have a maturity of at least a year in the future.

5. Put some of the profits back into the business.

THE ACID TEST, OR "QUICK," RATIO

The acid test, or "quick," ratio is also a measurement of liquidity. You calculate this ratio as follows: cash plus government securities plus receivables divided by current liabilities.

The company shown in Figure 7-1 has no government securities. Therefore the numerator of this figure becomes $35,000 cash plus $55,000 in accounts receivable, or $90,000. This is divided by current liabilities on the same balance sheet of $90,000 to result in an acid test ratio of 1.0.

The quick ratio concentrates on liquid assets whose values are definite and well known. So the quick ratio answers this question: If all your sales revenue disappears tomorrow, can you meet current obligations with your cash or quick funds on hand? Usually an acid test ratio of approximately 1.0 is considered satisfactory. However, you must also make this decision conditional on the following:

1. There should be nothing to slow up the collection of your accounts receivable.

2. The receipt of accounts receivable collections should not trail the due schedule for paying your current liabilities. In checking out this timing, you should consider payment of your creditors sufficiently early to take advantage of any discounts which are offered.

If these two conditions are not met, then you will need an acid test ratio higher than 1.0. It is a mistake to believe that the current or the acid test ratio should always be as high as possible. Only those from whom you have borrowed money would agree. Naturally, they are interested in the greatest possible safety of their loan. However, you do not want to have large sums of money lying idle and not earning you additional profits. If you do have idle cash balances and receivables and inventories that are out of proportion to your needs, you should reduce them.

Be conservative enough to keep a safety pad and yet bold enough to take advantage of the fact that you have these resources that can be used to earn additional profits. Before deciding on the right amount of liquidity you should consider the next two ratios: average collection period and inventory turnover.

AVERAGE COLLECTION PERIOD

The average collection period is the number of days that sales are tied up in accounts receivable. This number can be calculated by using your profit and loss statement or income statement as shown in Figure 7-2. Divide net sales by the days in your accounting period.

In Figure 7-2 net sales are $1,035,000, and your accounting period 365 days. This equals $2,836. This is the average sales per day in the accounting period.

Next, look at your accounts receivable which you obtained from the balance sheet, Figure 7-1. Accounts receivable are $55,000. Divide $55,000 by the average sales per day in the accounting period; $55,000 divided by $2,836 equals 19.

The result (19) is the average number of days sales are tied up in receivables. It is also your average collection period.

This tells you how promptly your accounts are being collected, considering whatever credit terms you are extending. It also provides other important insights. First, the quality of your accounts and notes receivable—that is, whether or not you are really getting paid promptly. It also shows you how good a job your credit department is doing in collecting these accounts.

Now the question is whether the figure of 19 days is good or not good. A rule of thumb says the average collection period should not exceed one and one-third times the credit terms offered. Therefore, if you offer terms of 30 days to pay and the average collection period is only 19 days, you are doing very well. On the other hand, anything in excess of 40 days ($1\frac{1}{3} \times 30 = 40$) would indicate a problem.

For the year ended December 31, 19___

INCOME STATEMENT			
Sales or revenue		$1,040,000.00	
Less returns and allowances:		5,000.00	
Net sales			$1,035,000.00
Cost of sales:			
Beginning inventory, Jan. 1, 19 ___		250,000.00	
Merchandise purchases	500,000.00		
Cost of goods available for sale		750,000.00	
Less ending inventory, Dec. 31, 19 ___		225,000.00	
Total cost of goods sold			525,000.00
Gross profit			$ 510,000.00
Operating expenses:			
Selling and general and administrative			
Salaries and wages		180,000.00	
Advertising		200,000.00	
Rent		10,000.00	
Utilities		5,000.00	
Other expenses		10,000.00	
Total operating expenses			405,000.00
Total operating income			$ 105,000.00
Other revenue and expenses			0
Pretax income			$ 105,000.00
Taxes on income		50,000.00	
Income after taxes but before extraordinary gain or loss			$ 55,000.00
Extraordinary gain or loss			0
Net income (or loss)			$ 55,000.00

FIGURE 7-2.   Sample income statement for the XYZ Company.

INVENTORY TURNOVER

Inventory turnover will show you how rapidly your merchandise is moving. It will also show you how much capital you have tied up in inventory to support the level of your company's operations for the period that you are analyzing. For your marketing plan, you can analyze planned inventory turnover.

To calculate inventory turnover, simply divide the cost of goods sold that you obtain from your income statement by your average inventory.

From Figure 7-2, your income profit and loss statement, the cost of goods sold equals $525,000. You cannot calculate your average inventory from Figure 7-1. You only know that for the period for which the inventory is stated, it equals $60,000. Let's assume that the previous balance sheet indicated that your inventory was $50,000. Then the average inventory for the two periods would be $60,000 plus $50,000 divided by 2, or $55,000.

Now, let's see what inventory turnover is: Cost of goods sold of $525,000 divided by average inventory of $55,000 equals 9.5.

This means that you turned your inventory 9.5 times during the year. Put another way, through your business operations you used up merchandise that total 9.5 times the average inventory investment. Under most circumstances, a higher inventory turnover is preferable, because it means that you are able to operate with a relatively small sum of money invested in this inventory.

Another implication is that your inventory is the right inventory. You know this because it is salable and has not been in stock too long. But even here you must consider that too high a figure may signify a problem. Very high inventory turnover may mean that you have inventory shortages. Inventory shortages soon lead to customer dissatisfaction, which may mean a loss of customers to the competition in the long run.

Is 9.5 a satisfactory inventory turnover or not? Again, the desirable rate depends on your business, your industry, your method of valuing inventories, and numerous other factors that are unique to your situation. Once again, it is helpful to study and compare your turnover rate with that of similar businesses of your size in your industry. After you have been in operation for some time and have a track record, past experiences with inventory turnover will indicate what is good and what is not with less reliance on industry comparisons.

Of course, you can analyze specific inventory turnover for different products or even groups of products or product lines in your marketing plan. This will show you which items are doing well and which are not.

You may also prepare turnover analyses for much more frequent periods than a year. Even monthly or weekly periods may be necessary or required for perishable items or items that become obsolete very quickly. You will learn to reorder "hot" items well in advance and be aware of the items you should not order. You will also know which items you must order before their value goes down to a point at which you can no longer sell them.

PROFITABILITY MEASURES

Measures of profitability are essential if you are to know how much money you are making, whether you are making as much as you can, or whether you are realizing any profit at all. Five different ratios will assist you in determining this. These are the asset earning power, return on owner's equity, net profit on sales, investment turnover and, finally, return on investment (ROI).

ASSET EARNING POWER

Asset earning power is determined by the ratio of earnings before interest and taxes to total assets. From the income statement in Figure 7-2 we can see that total operating profit or income is $105,000. Total assets from the balance sheet, Figure 7-1, are $272,000; $105,000 divided by $272,000 equals 0.39, or 39 percent.

RETURN ON THE OWNER'S EQUITY

Return on the owner's equity shows the return that you received in exchange for your investment in your business. To compute this ratio you will usually use the average equity for 12 months. If this isn't available, use the average of figures from two different balance sheets, your latest and the one before.

Return on the owner's equity equals net profit divided by equity. Net profit from Figure 7-2 is $55,000. Equity from Figure 7-1 is $115,000. Assuming the equity from the period before is also $115,000, use this as an average. Therefore, return on the owner's equity equals $55,000 divided by $115,000. That equals 0.48, or 48 percent.

You can calculate a similar ratio by using tangible net worth in lieu of equity. Tangible net worth equals equity less any intangible assets, such as patents owned and goodwill. If no intangible assets exist, the two will be equal.

NET PROFIT ON SALES

The net profit on sales ratio measures the difference between what you take in and what you spend in the process of doing business. Again, net profit was determined to be $55,000. Net sales from Figure 7-2 are $1,035,000. Therefore net profit on sales equals 0.053, or 5.3 percent. This means that for every dollar of sales, the company has earned a profit of 5.3 cents.

The net profit on sales ratio depends mainly on operating costs and pricing policies. If this figure goes down, it could be because you have lowered prices or it could be because costs have been increasing while prices have remained stable.

Compare this ratio with those from other similar businesses. Also consider trends over a period of time. By comparing net profit on sales ratios for individual products, you will know which products or product lines need additional emphasis and which should be eliminated.

INVESTMENT TURNOVER

The ratio of investment turnover is annual net sales to total assets. In this case net sales of $1,035,000 divided by total assets of $272,000 from Figure 7-1 equals 3.8.

Once again, compare this ratio with those of other similar businesses and watch for trends.

RETURN ON INVESTMENT (ROI)

ROI is a great way of measuring profitability of your investment or proposed investment. There are several different ways of calculating return on investment.

One simple way is to take net profit and divide it by total assets. In this case (Figure 7-1) the net profit equals $55,000. Total assets are $272,000. Therefore, $55,000 divided by $272,000 equals 0.20, or 20 percent.

You want the highest net profit for the smallest amount of total assets invested. You can use this rate of return on investment for intercompany and interindustry comparisons, as well as pricing costs, inventory, and investment decisions, and many other measurements of efficiency and profitability. No matter how you use it, always be sure that you are consistent in making your comparisons—that is, be sure that you use the same definitions of net profit and assets invested.

Here are some additional measures of profitability using ROI:

1. *Rate of Earnings on Total Capital Employed Equals Net Income Plus Interest and Taxes Divided by Total Liabilities and Capital.* This ratio serves as an index of productivity of capital as well as a measure of earning power in operating efficiency.

2. *Rate of Earnings on Invested Capital Equals Net Income Plus Income Taxes Divided by Proprietary Equity and Fixed Liabilities.* This ratio is used as a measure of earning power of the borrowed invested capital.

3. *Rate of Earnings on Proprietary Equity Equals Net Income Divided by Total Capital Including Surplus Reserves.* This ratio is used as a measure of the yield on the owner's investment.

4. *Rate of Earnings on Stock Equity Equals Net Income Divided by Total Capital Including Surplus Reserves.* This ratio is used as a measure of the attractiveness of common stock as an investment.

5. *Rate of Dividends on Common Stock Equity Equals Common Stock Dividends Divided by Common Stock Equity.* This ratio is used to indicate the desirability of common stock as a source of income.

6. *Rate of Dividends on Common Stock Equity Equals Common Stock Dividend per Share Divided by Market Value per Share of Common Stock.* This ratio is used as a measure of the current yield on investment in a particular stock.

SOURCES OF RATIO ANALYSES FROM ALL INDUSTRIES

In order to compare your business with other businesses in your industry it is necessary to obtain pertinent data on other businesses. The following are sources of this information:

1. *Dun & Bradstreet, Inc., Business Information Systems, 99 Church Street, New York, NY 10007.* This firm publishes key business ratios on 125 lines annually. Copies can be obtained free upon request.

2. *Accounting Corporation of America, 1929 First Avenue, San Diego, CA 92101.* This organization publishes *Parameter of Small Businesses,* which classifies its operating ratios for various industry groups on the basis of gross volume.

3. *National Cash Register Company, Marketing Services Department, Dayton, OH 45409.* This firm publishes *Expenses in Retail Businesses,* which examines the cost of operations in more than 50 kinds of businesses obtained from primary sources, most of which are trade associations.

4. *Robert Morris Associates, Philadelphia National Bank Building, Philadelphia, PA 19107.* Robert Morris has developed and published ratio studies for more than 225 lines of business.

5. *The Small Business Administration.* The SBA has a series of reports that provide expenses as a percentage of sales for many industries. Although the reports do not provide strict ratio information, a comparison of percentage expenses will be very useful for your financial management.

6. *Trade Associations.* Many national trade associations publish ratio studies, including the following:

Air-Conditioning & Refrigeration Wholesalers, 22371 Newman Avenue, Dearborn, MI 48124

Air Transport Association of America, 1000 Connecticut Avenue NW, Washington, DC 20036

American Bankers Association, 90 Park Avenue, New York, NY 10016

American Book Publishers Council, One Park Avenue, New York, NY 10016

American Booksellers Association, 175 Fifth Avenue, New York, NY 10010

American Carpet Institute, 350 Fifth Avenue, New York, NY 10001

American Electric Association, 16223 Meyers Street, Detroit, MI 48235

American Institute of Laundering, Doris and Chicago Avenues, Joliet, IL 60433

American Institute of Supply Associations, 1505 22nd Street NW, Washington, DC 20037

American Meat Institute, 59 East Van Buren Street, Chicago, IL 60605

American Paper Institute, 260 Madison Avenue, New York, NY 10016

American Society of Association Executives, 2000 K Street NW, Washington, DC 20006

American Supply Association, 222 Merchandise Mart Plaza, Chicago, IL 60601

Automotive Service Industry Association, 230 North Michigan Avenue, Chicago, IL 60601

Bowling Proprietors' Association of America, Inc., West Higgins Road, Hoffman Estates, IL 60172

Florists' Telegraph Delivery Association, 900 West Lafayette Boulevard, Detroit, MI 48226

Food Service Equipment Industry, Inc., 332 South Michigan Avenue, Chicago, IL 60604

Laundry and Cleaners Allied Trades Association, 1180 Raymond Boulevard, Newark, NJ 07102

Material Handling Equipment Distributors Association, 20 North Wacker Drive, Chicago, IL 60616

Mechanical Contractors Association of America, 666 Third Avenue, Suite 1464, New York, NY 10017

Menswear Retailers of America, 390 National Press Building, Washington, DC 20004

Motor and Equipment Manufacturers Association, 250 West 57th Street, New York, NY 10019

National-American Wholesale Lumber Association, 180 Madison Avenue, New York, NY 10016

National Appliance and Radio-TV Dealers Association, 1319 Merchandise Mart, Chicago, IL 60654

National Association of Accountants, 525 Park Avenue, New York, NY 10022

National Association of Building Owners and Managers, 134 South LaSalle Street, Chicago, IL 60603

National Association of Electrical Distributors, 600 Madison Avenue, New York, NY 10022

National Association of Food Chains, 1725 I Street NW, Washington, DC 20006

National Association of Furniture Manufacturers, 666 North Lake Shore Drive, Chicago, IL 60611

National Association of Insurance Agents, 96 Fulton Street, New York, NY 10038

National Association of Music Merchants, Inc., 222 West Adams Street, Chicago, IL 60606

National Association of Plastic Distributors, 2217 Tribune Tower, Chicago, IL 60611

National Association of Retail Grocers of the United States, 360 North Michigan Avenue, Chicago, IL 60601

National Association of Textile and Apparel Wholesalers, 350 Fifth Avenue, New York, NY 10001

National Association of Tobacco Distributors, 360 Lexington Avenue, New York, NY 10017

National Automatic Merchandising Association, Seven South Dearborn Street, Chicago, IL 60603

National Beer Wholesalers' Association of America, 6310 North Cicero Avenue, Chicago, IL 60646

National Builders' Hardware Association, 1290 Avenue of the Americas, New York, NY 10019

National Electrical Contractors Association, 1200 18th Street NW, Washington, DC 20036

National Electrical Manufacturers Association, 155 East 44th Street, New York, NY 10017

National Farm and Power Equipment Dealers Association, 2340 Hampton Avenue, St. Louis, MO 63130

National Home Furnishing Association, 1150 Merchandise Mart, Chicago, IL 60654

National Kitchen Cabinet Association, 918 Commonwealth Building, 674 South 4th Street, Louisville, KY 40204

National Lumber and Building Material Dealers Association, Ring Building, Washington, DC 20036

National Machine Tool Builders Association, 2071 East 102nd Street, Cleveland, OH 44106

National Office Products Association, Investment Building, 1511 K Street NW, Washington, DC 20015

National Oil Jobbers Council, 1001 Connecticut Avenue NW, Washington, DC 20036

National Paper Box Manufacturers Association, 121 North Broad Street, Suite 910, Philadelphia, PA 19107

National Paper Trade Association, 220 East 42nd Street, New York, NY 10017

National Parking Association, 1101 17th Street NW, Washington, DC 20036

National Restaurant Association, 1530 North Lake Shore Drive, Chicago, IL 60610

National Retail Furniture Association, 1150 Merchandise Mart Plaza, Chicago, IL 60654

National Retail Hardware Association, 964 North Pennsylvania Avenue, Indianapolis, IN 46204

National Retail Merchants Association, 100 West 31st Street, New York, NY 10001

National Shoe Retailers Association, 200 Madison Avenue, New York, NY 10016

National Sporting Goods Association, 23 East Jackson Boulevard, Chicago, IL 60604

National Stationery and Office Equipment Association, Investment Building, 1511 K Street NW, Washington, DC 20005

National Tire Dealers and Retreaders Association, 1343 L Street NW, Washington, DC 20005

National Wholesale Druggists' Association, 220 East 42nd Street, New York, NY 10017

National Wholesale Hardware Association, 1900 Arch Street, Philadelphia, PA 19103

National Wholesale Jewelers Association, 1900 Arch Street, Philadelphia, PA 19103

North American Heating & Airconditioning Wholesalers Association, 1200 West 5th Avenue, Columbus, OH 43212

Optical Wholesalers Association, 222 West Adams Street, Chicago, IL 60606

Paint and Wallpaper Association of America, 7935 Clayton Road, St. Louis, MO 63117

Petroleum Equipment Institute, 525 Dowell Building, Tulsa, OK 74114

Printing Industries of America, 711 14th Street NW, Washington, DC 20005

Robert Morris Associates, Philadelphia National Bank Building, Philadelphia, PA 19107

Scientific Apparatus Makers Associates, 20 North Wacker Drive, Chicago, IL 60606

Shoe Service Institute of America, 222 West Adams Street, Chicago, IL 60606

Super Market Institute, Inc., 200 East Ontario Street, Chicago, IL 60611

United Fresh Fruit and Vegetable Association, 777 14th Street NW, Washington, DC 20005

United States Wholesale Grocers' Association, 1511 K Street NW, Washington, DC 20005

Urban Land Institute, 1200 18th Street NW, Washington, DC 20036

Wine and Spirits Wholesalers of America, 319 North Fourth Street, St. Louis, MO 63102

SUMMARY

In this chapter we've looked at many financial ratios that can be used to measure the financial efficiency of what we plan to do. These ratios can be used by comparing our planned figures with alternative approaches, and also by comparing our planned ratios with others that are published for the same industry. If your marketing plan is implemented, you will want to return to this chapter to use actual rather than planned information. In this way the ratios enable us to monitor our implementation and to make adjustments as we proceed.

Now we have all the information needed to put together an outstanding presentation of your marketing plan. You'll see how to do that in the next chapter.

CHAPTER 8

STEP 8

PRESENTING THE MARKETING PLAN

By the time you have reached this chapter you should have all the information necessary to put together a first-rate marketing plan. But now you have another hurdle. You've done all necessary research and assembled your material. You've completed the situational analysis and scanned your environment. You've established goals and objectives and developed marketing strategy and tactics. You've peered into the future and forecasted sales and costs. You've developed extensive financial information and measured its efficiency. Now it is important not to trip up. You must present your marketing plan to those who have the authority to approve it or give you the resources necessary to implement it. You need to do this in the most professional manner possible. The purpose of this chapter is to show you how to do this.

THE MARKETING PLAN AS A PRODUCT

Your marketing plan is a sales document. But, it is also a product representing your concept for the project or business. It must be as professional a product as you can make it. There is an old saying, "You can't judge a book by its cover." It may be true, but it is irrelevant. A professional-looking plan has a far better chance of success than one that is highly creative with accurate information, but put together in a haphazard fashion with grammatical or spelling errors. So, your marketing plan must look as good as it is. If it does, the psychological advantage is yours. The reader will proceed from the premise that your plan is accurate and that you know what you are talking about.

On the other hand, if your marketing plan doesn't look professional, the contents must overcome a significant negative bias. Let's see what you can do to make your plan look more professional.

The first thing is to have your plan typed by one person. That way the printing will have a consistent style and format throughout the document. It should be neat and free from typographical errors and obvious corrections. In this day of computerization, this should pose no problem.

A standardized method of typing and collating the different sections of the plan should be used. Which method you choose is usually not critical, unless specified by whoever has asked you to prepare the plan. Standardization also means a consistent way of presenting footnotes, bibliography, and so forth. Several different style manuals are available. Pick one and stick with it.

Sometimes, when several different people work on a single marketing plan, different sections of the plan are assigned to each of the participants. Although there is nothing inherently wrong with this, one individual should be assigned the task of assembling the overall product to ensure that its writing, styling, typing, and formatting are consistent. If one coordinator is not assigned, it is not unusual to find sections that do not fit together.

It is sad to report, but I have seen a conclusion in one section nullified by a statement in another section. I have also seen terminology that is inconsistent within different sections.

If the typing or printing is done by different individuals, the marketing plan may have an inconsistent appearance due to different styles of type, darkness of imprint, margins, fonts, and paper. This guarantees a shoddy-looking product, so don't let this happen to you!

Illustrations and charts should be included as a part of your marketing plan. You must never, however, include illustrations or any unnecessary information merely to pad the marketing plan and make it appear more substantial. Information that may distract from the presentation can be added as an appendix. The survey form used to gather research might be an example. But even information in the appendix should be necessary and relevant and not added simply to increase the size of the document.

There is no minimum length for a marketing plan. Many venture capitalists prefer shorter plans, say 50 pages or less. This is because they review so many marketing and business plans that they prefer to have the essential facts in the plan and to request additional information only if needed. This is usually not the case if you are preparing the marketing plan in the classroom, someone else is paying you to prepare it, or you are preparing it as a member of a large corporation. In these cases it is best to ensure that all the information is available right from the start. This will require at least 50 pages and maybe more.

Make your plan long enough to tell your entire story, always considering what your readers will want to know. If you need more pages to cover essential information, use them. On the other hand, if you have covered all the information you think is necessary for your reader, then stop. Don't pad.

The final point to consider is binding. Some excellent plans are typed neatly and compiled with accurate and complete information, yet they still fail to present a professional appearance simply because a cheap binding is used. What amazes me is how easy and inexpensive it is to get a top-of-the-line binding. Yet many fail to get it for their plans.

Hardcover binding (bound like a book) is available from many printers for less than $10. One cautionary note: In their enthusiasm, one of my student teams got their marketing plan bound in leather to the tune of $70! I don't recommend needless expense, even for a professional plan.

If you are unable to obtain hardcover binding, consider spiral binding. A mechanical means of doing rapid spiral binding is available at many printers. Check the Yellow Pages of your telephone book for additional sources. Again, the point here is to make your marketing plan look as professional as possible. Your marketing plan should be good and it should look good.

THE FORMAL PRESENTATION

In most cases, simply preparing the marketing plan is insufficient. You must also make a formal presentation of your marketing plan to someone else. This may be to individuals who may be interested in funding your plan or to higher management in your company who must give the approval to implement it. Your professor may ask you to make a formal presentation of your plan in the classroom.

In all cases you must first consider the object of your presentation. Usually the object of a marketing plan is to persuade management or investors to allocate money to enable you to implement your project. Remember that no one is going to give you money for your plan unless they are convinced that it will succeed and will make money for them.

What will these people want to know? They'll want to know how much money can be made, how much money will be needed from them and when, how long it will be before they will get their money back, exactly what you will do with the money, and why your project will succeed. Therefore, although the outline of your marketing plan can be used as described in preceding chapters, some minor changes may be needed to maximize the impact of your presentation.

Here is one outline for a formal presentation:

I. *Introduction.* In the introduction you cover the information in your executive summary, including the opportunity and why it exists, the money to be made, the money that's needed, and some brief financial information, such as return on investment, to support the extent of the opportunity as you see it.

II. *Why You Will Succeed.* In this section you will cover your situational analysis and environmental scanning and the research you did to support it. You conclude the section with problems, opportunities, and threats, as well as the project's goals and objectives. Finally, you spell out your differential competitive advantage. The essential message in this part of the presentation is why you will succeed even though others may fail.

III. *Strategy and Tactics.* In this section you will cover the strategy you are going to follow as well as the tactics used to implement that strategy.

IV. *Forecast and Financial Information.* In this section you will discuss your forecast, project development schedule, profit and loss statement, and financial ratios and data. This section will contain a detailed description of what you need and when you need it. Sometimes, because of the limited time available for the presentation, you may have to refine this section and present only the main points. The important financial information, however, should always be available so that in the question-and-answer session that follows, you can provide any additional data that may be required.

V. *Conclusion.* In this final part of your formal presentation you will restate the opportunity and why you will succeed with it, the money that is required, and the expected return on the investment. You told 'em. Now tell 'em what you told 'em.

PREPARING FOR YOUR PRESENTATION

Your first step in preparing for your presentation is obtaining the answers to several important questions. These include the time and date of your presentation, where it is to be held, the time allowed, who the audience is, who is in the audience, and the purpose of your presentation. You should also think about the audience's attitude, their knowledge and preconceived notions, and anything that requires particular care. After getting this information, you can write down the main points to cover.

In most cases, the purpose of presenting your marketing plan will be to obtain resources. This holds true whether you are an entrepreneur presenting a marketing plan to the loan officer of a bank, a venture capitalist, or someone else who is going to lend you money, or whether you are a member of a company and have been asked to prepare a plan as a potential investment. The exception is a plan that you have prepared as a consultant to an entrepreneur or larger corporation interested in implementing it. In this case your main object is to demonstrate that you have done your job by preparing a plan that your client can use to obtain resources and eventually to implement.

Think through and write down the answers to these questions, because they can affect what you are going to cover and how you are going to do it.

Your next step is to make an outline of your main and supporting points. To develop this outline you need not follow the outline of the written marketing plan report. Remember that you may wish to change your order in presenting different elements depending on your audience and their backgrounds, interests, and concerns. With different audiences, different sections or topics must be emphasized. If the audience is primarily financial, don't omit any financial information from your presentation. On the contrary, you should emphasize it.

On the other hand, an engineering audience will probably be more interested in the technical aspects of your product, its manufacture, and so forth. Some financial data can be excluded in order to allow time to include more technical information. Now, you are probably doing this for your marketing class at the direction of your marketing professor. Need I say what emphasis your plan should have?

Remember, the purpose for developing a special outline is to allow you to make the maximum use of the available time and to have the maximum impact. The following technique is sometimes useful in helping you prepare your outline and its supporting points. Obtain a number of 3 × 5-inch file cards and, without stopping to think, write down everything you think should be emphasized in your presentation, one item to a card. Don't try to coordinate or organize anything at this point. If you have statistics that you think should be included, or anecdotes, quotes, or even jokes, write each on a separate card.

Once you have written down as many ideas as you can, begin to organize the cards into your main points and supporting points. Statistics will be supporting points to some main points. So will anecdotes, jokes, and quotes. By using this system you will soon have a stack of cards for each major element of your presentation. They will automatically be organized in a logical fashion.

After you complete your presentation by arranging your ideas using these cards, you can prepare a complete written outline. Notice that this is a flexible system. You can move cards around, as well as add cards and points to your presentation as new ideas occur.

Note that I have not said to write a speech. Your presentation should never be written out word-for-word. If you do, you will probably present it that way. Marketing plan speeches are dull and boring. You want your marketing plan presentation to reflect the work, the accuracy, and the potential it represents for whoever implements it. But above all, you want it to be exciting. This cannot be done with a written speech. So leave your presentation as an outline.

Once you have completed your outline you can begin planning for your visual aids.

PLANNING FOR VISUAL AIDS

Visual aids can greatly enhance the impact of your presentation and should always be used in making a presentation of a marketing plan. Your basic options are the use of 35-mm slides, overhead transparencies, charts, handouts, videos, computer presentations, or chalkboards. All have their advantages and disadvantages. Let's look at each of them.

Slides (35-mm). A 35-mm projector and 35-mm slides are easy to carry around. Furthermore, the slides can be done in color, look quite professional, can be manipulated by the presenter, and yield an extremely professional experience. The disadvantages are the lead time to prepare the slides, the cost, and the difficulty of changing a particular slide once it has been developed. New systems are now available by which 35-mm slides are constructed by computer and then enhanced, in color or otherwise, rapidly and at relatively low cost per unit. However, the equipment costs several thousand dollars. This system will not be readily available to everyone.

Overhead Transparencies. Overhead transparencies are as portable as 35-mm slides. Most of these projectors are heavier, more cumbersome, and less transportable, although some models available today are as portable and only slightly larger than slide projectors. There is a lead time associated with the preparation of overhead transparencies, if you have them done professionally. If camera-ready artwork is available, however, duplicating machines located at many printing shops can make instant overhead transparencies from your camera-ready copy. Also, desktop publishing programs available for many computers allow you to make your own professional quality transparencies. Another advantage of an overhead transparency is that you can write on it as you talk. As a result, you can also make changes in the transparency if required. This cannot be done with a 35-mm slide. Although you can talk and operate a projector with overhead transparencies at the same time, this is more difficult than with a 35-mm projector since the latter can be operated remotely.

Videos. A videotape presentation allows a lot of flexibility and can add interest to your presentation. However, there are drawbacks. First, don't get so carried away with your presentation on film that you make the video your entire presentation, unless this has been requested. Practice with the tape to ensure the timing fits with the rest of your presentation. Of course, a television and video cassette player or other means to show your video must be available. Most presenters work with equipment furnished by someone else. Frequently, the first time they see the equipment is when they make their presentation. As a result, presenters often struggle with getting unfamiliar equipment to work. This distracts from your presentation and can irritate your audience.

Computer Presentations. The state-of-the-art of computer technology has advanced to the point where some very sophisticated multimedia presentations can be easily developed and used with a portable computer and a device linking it to an overhead projector. Here again, there is a danger of getting carried away with sound effects and visuals possibilities. While entertaining, this can distract from your basic purpose in making the presentation. Again, be careful of equipment. Practice with the actual equipment you will use. I have seen presenters begin speaking only to discover that the equipment available is not compatible with what they have put together and that no one can see the presentation except in complete darkness, under which conditions they cannot see their notes. Veteran presenters of multimedia always have standard overheads as backup.

Handouts. Handouts are easy to make. They can be reproduced in quantity, even in color if required. Handouts can be changed and new information substituted for the old. But handouts suffer from two major disadvantages. First, if the information is extensive and the audience large, a considerable amount of material must be carried around and distributed. Second, audiences may read ahead in your handout and miss the points you are covering. At the same time, a dramatic sequence of events that you've built into your presentation may be spoiled as the audience reads ahead to your "punch line." Handouts that are exact duplicates of transparencies or multimedia programs are excellent backup should some electronic means fail. They are also useful when members of the audience ask for copies of your transparencies.

Charts. Charts can be the flip variety or they can be large cardboard or plastic devices that are used in conjunction with your other visual aids. Charts are much less portable than 35-mm slides, transparencies, or handouts. One advantage of charts, however, is that if you have an artistic bent you can prepare them on your own and thus need not allow as much lead time as with professionally prepared overhead transparencies or 35-mm slides. This places them in the same category as handouts as far as this particular attribute goes. However, if you do prepare your own charts, it is important that it *not* be done the night before. You need to allow enough time to check them for accuracy, typographical errors, and so forth. If you do them the night before, you are almost certain to make errors.

Chalkboards. Chalkboards, or plastic boards on which you can write with colored pencils, can also be useful during presentations. The major disadvantage is that you cannot prepare your material ahead of time. In this case, the advantage is also the disadvantage, for there is much more drama and spontaneity in having your audience see the point you wish to get across as you write it. However, there are usually so many disadvantages with chalkboards that, at best, they can be used only as an adjunct to your other systems. Among these disadvantages are: they are not readily transportable, the material is not permanent, you cannot use the material to jog your memory (an advantage with all four other visual systems), and chalkboards may not always be available where you give your presentation.

Whatever system of visual aids you plan on, you should prepare your visual aids immediately, even before you begin to practice for the first time, and not wait until the last moment. I recommend that you attempt a presentation in the time you have been allocated at least once. When you are reasonably confident that your presentation will not change in its major points, have your visual aids constructed. One reason is the long lead time, which is always a lot longer than you think it will be. Also, you want to allow yourself time to proofread the material that has been prepared by someone else.

After having given hundreds of presentations using all of these methods, I have found that in 90 percent of the cases there will be typographical errors. If your visual aids are prepared at the last minute, you may find that insufficient time is available to correct the errors. So once you know what you want on your visual aids, have them made at once. You can practice with dummy visual aids while the real ones are being prepared.

Use of Products as Visual Aids. Sometimes the product that is the subject of your marketing plan is available. These products can be very useful for adding interest to your presentation. If you use products as part of your visual aids, make sure they are relevant. If your product is interesting and the particular twist or unique advantage in your product is worth seeing, then it's worth showing. On the other hand, if your marketing plan concerns a product that everyone is familiar with, don't use it as a visual aid unless there is some unique aspect that should be seen or demonstrated. Do something else with the time you have available.

To summarize our discussion on visual aids, I'd like you to consider the following points as you prepare for your presentation.

Make sure you use aids that contain material that is easy to read, without too much information on each. They must make an impact on the audience and reinforce what you say, or make what you say more easily understood. If there is too much information in a single view, your audience may get lost. If the type is too small, your audience will not be able to read what you have prepared.

Even your pointing techniques may be important. If you are going to use a pointer, be careful not to turn your body when you use it so as not to cut off the view of someone in your audience. The best way to avoid this is to follow this rule: If you are standing to the right of the view of your presentation, have the pointer in your left hand. This will keep you from turning your back on the audience and cutting off the view of audience members who are to your right front. Conversely, if you are standing to the left of the view, use the pointer in your right hand. In this way, you will not turn your back and block the view of audience members who are on your left front.

Keep your visual aids covered until you use them. Displaying many visual aids simultaneously only causes distractions. It may cause your audience to become more interested in your visuals than in you. So show only one visual at a time.

THE PRACTICE SEQUENCE

I want to emphasize that you must never memorize anything. If you try to memorize your presentation, you may forget it. Memorization simply isn't necessary. Nor is it necessary to read your presentation. Believe me when I tell you, I learned this lesson the hard way.

As a young Air Force officer, I was once asked to make a presentation to 300 science and math teachers on space navigation, a topic which greatly interested me at the time. I prepared superb 35-mm full-color slides and spent considerable time writing and honing a one-hour speech. I wrote down every single word. I memorized this speech perfectly, word for word, and coordinated it with my excellent multicolor slides.

When the day came I looked out at 300 science and math teachers, gulped once, and could barely remember my name. After several awkward attempts to try to remember the speech I thought I had memorized perfectly, I reached in my pocket and read my speech word for word.

What a mistake! Hours of work wasted unnecessarily for a boring speech. After all, I knew the subject matter. By simply flipping through my slides, I could have talked to my audience and told them about each. That really was all that was required for an excellent presentation.

The same is true for you. To give an outstanding presentation of your marketing plan, you don't have to memorize anything. You don't have to bore your audience to death by reading a speech, either. You know your subject better than anyone else. Once you are prepared, just going through your presentation as you use your visuals to support what you say will enable you to communicate with your audience for maximum impact. In this way, you can give an outstanding presentation.

If your visual aids are complete while you practice, use them during your practice. If not, write the content of your visual aids on 8 × 10½-inch sheets of paper and practice with them. You can use the cards you prepared earlier to help remember the main points. I recommend going through your presentation three times and making adjustments as necessary in order to complete the presentation and get your points across in the time you have been allotted.

If you use cards to supplement what you have displayed on your visual aids to help you remember the main points, do not write more than a few words on the cards. If you do, you will read them. And once you begin to read your cards, you will probably continue to read them. Then you are back to reading a speech. So write just a few words on each and use them only as cues. Of course, the same is true of the visual aids. They should be sparsely worded for maximum impact. Simply look at the visual aid and describe it to your audience.

As I fine-tune my presentations, I may add statistics, I may take out a point here or add one there, and I may modify other parts of what I originally intended to discuss. One element is fixed: I concentrate on staying within whatever time constraints have been given me. Time is crucial.

THE IMPORTANCE OF CONTROLLING YOUR TIME

You must always control your time, and practice within as well as give your presentation in the allotted time. This is true whether you are making a 15-minute presentation or one lasting several hours. Why is this so? The individuals in your audience, no matter how critical and important they feel your presentation will be to them, allot a certain amount of time for it in their schedules. If you exceed this time, even by a few minutes, you will make it more difficult, even impossible, to achieve the objective of your presentation. If you exceed your allotted time by only a few minutes, it may be annoying. If you go over by more than that, this could set up a negative reaction due to its impact on the schedules of those in the audience.

Let me give you a couple of examples to illustrate just how important controlling your time can be. A few years ago a large aerospace corporation was competing for a major government contract with the Air Force. Fifty representatives from the Air Force flew in to receive what was to be a full day's presentation to end no later than 4:00 P.M. The presentation, however, was not well planned by the presenters. By 3:30 P.M. it was clear their full presentation could not be completed as planned within the allotted time. The audience was not given a choice. The presenters forged ahead, determined to cover every single one of their overhead transparencies. The presentation was completed more than an hour late. As a result, most of these government representatives had to reschedule their return flights. While the presentation was sufficiently important that these representatives listened to the full presentation, they were definitely unhappy with the poor planning on the part of the prospective contractor. Maybe this was only one factor among many, but this company did not win the contract.

Mistakes like this in time control are not limited to industry. One practice generally followed in hiring university professors is to require the candidate to make a presentation to the department. Typically this presentation is on the candidate's research. This presentation is critical because the membership of the department has a say in whether or not to hire the candidate.

Several years ago, a major university reviewed the credentials of a candidate who had graduated from a well-known university. This individual's background was so outstanding that the members of the department were in favor of hiring the candidate even before he made his face-to-face appearance.

They asked the candidate to limit his presentation to 25 minutes due to the prior commitments of his audience. All 14 members of this department listened attentively as the candidate began. His presentation was interesting and relevant. However, 25 minutes after he started he was still speaking. At 30 minutes professors in the audience began to fidget; several had other meetings scheduled. A few had classes and excused themselves. Thirty-five minutes went by, then 40. The candidate finally concluded after 45 minutes.

Despite all this, the candidate was hired as a professor by the institution involved, but even though he had interviewed for a position leading to tenure and promotion, because of just 20 minutes he was offered only a one-year appointment. After one year, he might be considered for the original position that was offered. Twenty minutes cost this professor one year in time toward a promotion to the next rank, including pay, allowances, and other fringe benefits.

The lesson is clear. Ask if there is a certain time allotted for your presentation. If there is, do not exceed this time. Practice to make sure that you stay within the time limit. Give yourself a slight pad. And when you make your presentation, control your time.

Once you have practiced three times and have good control over your presentation, I recommend that you do the presentation twice more, only this time in front of other people—a spouse, friend, brother, sister, or whomever. The important thing is that we are not looking for a pat on the back but for a real critique. This includes the answers to a number of questions:

Should I talk louder or softer?

Did I use eye contact?

Did I talk in a conversational fashion, or did I simply start reading from my cards or visual aids?

Did I have a good opener that grabbed the interest of my audience?

Did I close my presentation with impact?

Did I use supporting matter such as anecdotes or statistics?

Was there something particular I said that was liked?

Something not liked?

If available, were my visual aids written large enough, and could they be read? Do they need to be changed or improved in some way?

Was there anything in my presentation that was unclear, and, if so, how could I make it understandable?

Are there any other points or comments or advice that may be relevant?

QUESTIONS AND ANSWERS AND HOW TO PREPARE FOR THEM

Questions and answers are going to be a part of every marketing plan presentation you make. The first thing you must do is prepare ahead of time. Research has shown that approximately 85 percent of the questions asked can actually be anticipated. So once you have prepared your presentation, think about what questions might be asked by your audience, and prepare for them. You might also have your practice audience ask questions, both to test your responses and your ability to think on your feet.

Next have your facts, figures, quotes—all of this information—available. Many astute presenters who cannot fit all the information they would like into their presentation due to time restrictions have other visual aids ready and waiting. That way when this information is requested, it can be immediately used to good advantage.

An example might be financial information such as cash flow on a monthly basis. You may not have time to cover this in your formal presentation, but it would be advisable to have an overhead transparency or some other visual aid available so that when you are asked a question about these details, you can immediately use it. This will not only demonstrate your knowledge, but your preparation for any eventuality.

Remember to keep cool in the face of an embarrassing question, or one you may not be able to answer. I recommend a four-step procedure in answering questions. First, restate the question that has been asked. This ensures that the entire audience has heard the question and that you understand it. It also gives you additional time to think about your answer. Second, state your position or your answer to the question. Third, state the supporting reasons for your position. Finally, restate your position to make it clear to everyone.

In general, keep your answers brief. If you know the individual who asked the question, use his or her name. If the individual is right and you are wrong about something, admit it. Or, if you don't know something, admit that also. Simply say, "I don't know." Of course, if every other answer is, "I don't know," your audience will feel that you have not done a good job of preparing or are not knowledgeable about the marketing plan or your material.

Never get sidetracked or argue with someone who has asked a question. Always be tactful, even with individuals who attack you or your position. Harshly correcting a questioner can turn other members of your audience against you even if they agree with your point of view. This is because the audience may be members of the same firm or group. Also, they may resent the manner of your response to an innocent question, even if it is not tactfully asked.

USE OF THE MENTAL VISUALIZATION TECHNIQUE

I've always worried about speeches before I made them. As I lay in bed thinking about what I was to do the next day, I would go over the entire speech in my mind. I automatically rehearsed it again and again. On January 13, 1982, *The Wall Street Journal* published an article entitled "Why Do Some People Out-Perform Others?" It mentioned a psychologist by the name of Charles Garfield who had investigated top performance among business executives. Garfield said that he was most surprised by a trait that he called mental rehearsal, which had caught on as a popular concept in sports. According to Garfield, top chief executives would imagine every aspect and feeling of a future presentation, including a successful ending, while less effective executives would prepare their facts and the presentation agendas, but not their psyches.

Now I teach this technique to others to help them prepare for presentations, and they report outstanding success with it. All that is necessary is to take a few minutes before falling asleep the night before your presentation. Visualize everything from greeting your host and your audience to going through your presentation to a successful conclusion. Visualize your conclusion in detail, with smiles and vigorous applause. Repeat this process again and again, each time with a favorable conclusion. You will find that you can go through an entire hour's presentation in a few seconds, and thus you can have as many as 30 or more repetitions of success even before you go before your audience to make your presentation for the first time.

I believe this technique has several benefits. First, because you visualize a success again and again, you come to expect that success and, more frequently than not, that is exactly what you will receive. Second, mental rehearsal tends to eliminate excessive nervousness. All of us may be slightly nervous when we make a presentation, and this is probably good. If we weren't nervous at all, we probably would come across as rather dull and uninteresting. But too much nervousness can cause us to stumble, and may make our audience uncomfortable as well. With mental visualization, you have made your presentation so many times before that when you stand and look at your audience, the sting is gone. It is "old hat." After all, didn't you make the same presentation before the same audience 30 or more times the night before?

I highly recommend that you try this technique. From my own experience and the experience of many others, I know that it will work wonders in helping you to present your marketing plan in an interesting, confident way.

THE KEYS TO SUCCESS FOR MARKETING PLAN PRESENTATIONS

The number-one key for making your marketing plan presentation a success is to be enthusiastic about your project. If you aren't enthusiastic, you certainly cannot expect anyone else to be. What happens when you don't have a great deal of enthusiasm for a project? Perhaps it was not your idea at all. In the classroom, it is your professor who decides that you must make this presentation. At work, it is probably your boss who instructed you to prepare this marketing plan presentation for top management. It really doesn't make any difference. My recommendation is that if you really aren't interested in the project, then you must act; you must pretend to be interested. This is crucial.

Whenever I discuss acting or pretending, I think about the movie *Patton*. George C. Scott played the famous World War II general. In one scene depicting an event during the Battle of the Bulge, things were not going well for American forces. General Patton suddenly turned to an aide and exclaimed, "If any of our commanders retreat, shoot them!" The aide was shocked. In disbelief, he asked, "You really don't mean that?" Patton answered, "It really is not important whether you know whether I really mean it or not. It's only important that I know." In other words, Patton was acting.

It turns out that Patton was a tremendous actor. I know this for a fact because Patton's diaries have been published. During World War I, Patton was 29 years old and the commander of the first U.S. tank forces in France. He wrote to his wife, saying, "Every day I practice in front of a mirror looking mean." He called this his "war face." Patton felt that his mean-looking "war face" saved lives, because it meant his men were more afraid of him than they were of the enemy.

But Patton isn't the only one who recommends acting in order to achieve success. Mary Kay Ash developed a $100 million cosmetic company, and to her salespeople, she recommends, "Fake it till you make it." In other words, until you actually have a good day, pretend you're already having one. Or, until you have success, pretend that you are already achieving it. If you do this, if you pretend to be enthusiastic about your product and your project even though you are not, I promise you that this enthusiasm is contagious, and that your audience will be enthusiastic as well.

You must dress professionally. You represent your marketing plan, and appearance does count. As pointed out previously, although you may not be able to judge a book by its cover, psychologically people will do so. The same goes for your presentation. If you have any doubts about how to dress, consult the most famous book on this subject, *Dress for Success* by John T. Molloy. Another important book is *Power Dressing* by Victoria Seitz, a professor at California State University–San Bernardino. I highly recommend both of these books.

If you have any kind of test to do, or something that must work as a part of your presentation for your marketing plan, it is wise that you practice this test fully, and not just go through the motions.

Several years ago, a Navy project engineer made a presentation about an important Navy project. When Navy aviators must eject from aircraft over water, they have a serious problem in getting rid of their parachutes once in the water. The normal procedure is to climb into a small, one-person life raft. The raft is attached to a nylon line attached to the parachute harness, which extends 15 feet below the pilot. It opens automatically at ejection.

The pilot must climb into the raft while wearing heavy flight equipment, including boots, helmet, and survival gear. Obviously this is difficult. Worse, the parachute canopy can fill with water. But even if it doesn't, its water-soaked weight may drag the aviator straight down to the bottom.

The Navy teaches its aviators to use an emergency release to get rid of the parachute canopy just as their feet hit the water. Naturally, most pilots cheat a little in case the quick release gets stuck. They actually start dumping their "chute" a few feet before they hit.

There is a serious problem, however. Because the ocean appears flat, it is very difficult to judge height. As a result, many aviators think they are a few feet above the water and release their parachutes while they are still several hundred feet in the air. This practice can be dangerous.

In order to overcome this problem, the Navy developed a special squib. This is a light explosive charge that automatically releases the canopy when a sensor attached to the life raft contacts water. Remember, it hangs 15 feet below the pilot and so comes in contact with the water first. In this way, the parachute is jettisoned safely without endangering the pilot.

The Navy project manager did an outstanding job of presenting. His presentation included films of how the system worked, 35-mm slides, and handouts illustrating the project. For the grand finale, he donned a parachute himself and held up a jar of seawater. He told his audience of several hundred that he would introduce the sensor into the seawater. He told them that they would hear a loud crack as the squib exploded, and that the parachute canopy trailing behind the harness he had donned would immediately separate.

The audience prepared themselves, some holding their hands over their ears, and others waiting expectantly for the loud report of the exploding squib. The presenter inserted the probe into the seawater with high drama. There was a deafening silence. Nothing happened. He extracted the sensor and inserted it again, and again, and again. Nothing happened. Finally, red-faced as the audience began to snicker, he examined the harness. He discovered that someone had forgotten to replace a discharged battery. With no current there was nothing to ignite the squib.

Here was an important and outstanding presentation ruined by a demonstration that went awry. It was a mistake that could have been avoided if a full demonstration had been done during the practice stage.

Throughout your presentation you should try to establish empathy with your audience. You can do this by being friendly and maintaining eye contact. Remember, the audience is not your enemy. Enjoy yourself, and think of yourself as the host of your presentation.

The presentation and your written marketing plan report go together. They support one another, and will support your achieving whatever objectives you have set.

SUMMARY

In this chapter we have seen that presenting the marketing plan has two main elements: the written report and the formal presentation. This is not the frosting on the cake. Both are necessary for success. You will be successful by focusing on preparation and ensuring that your plan is presented with a high degree of professionalism.

With professionalism, your excellent content will be supported by an excellent package. I hope that you have learned that professional is not accidental. If you implement the techniques outlined, you cannot miss. In the classroom, your professionalism in presenting your plan will lead to a high grade. In the "real world" it will help you obtain the resources necessary to implement your marketing plan. You may not implement your plan in the classroom, but when you graduate and begin to use your marketing skills, you will. You are now ready to see how this is done in the next chapter.

CHAPTER

9

STEP 9

IMPLEMENTATION

Regardless of how good your marketing plan is, or how well you have presented it, once you have received the go-ahead you must actually carry out the actions you have planned. Implementation is the final stage in the marketing planning process. During implementation, you can and should use your plan to help you. But the execution of your plan is not automatic. Your plan is not a light switch which, simply turned on, automatically completes every task, tactic, and strategy in exactly the manner you planned. To implement your marketing plan successfully, you must exercise control to ensure that you will reach your planned objectives and goals. To accomplish this you must monitor the implementation of your plan on a periodic basis. Use your project development schedule and measure planned resource allocations against those actually used, along with the time frame in which they were to be used. Measure expected results against actual results. Calculate your financial ratios.

Once implementation has been initiated, things never go exactly as planned. This may be because your planning was not perfect (and what planning ever is?), or it may be because of a change of one or more marketplace environs. Perhaps your competition responded in a way that you never expected. All of this is normal. It simply means that you must make adjustments to get back on track to achieve the objectives and goals you have set.

Conceptually, certain actions are always required in implementation:

1. If you are the person responsible for the plan's implementation, or some subsection of the plan, take complete responsibility for implementation. This does not only mean responsibility for initiating the actions contained in the plan but responsibility for reaching the goals and objectives contained in the plan.

2. Track all tasks, tactics, and strategies and measure what is planned against what actually happens. Make adjustments as required and do not blindly continue any action simply because it is in your plan.

3. Track the changes in the environs as the implementation of your marketing plan progresses. Changes will sometimes tell you that actions planned for the future should not be taken, or should be altered. And just as an ounce of prevention is worth a pound of cure, an ounce of change taken now may be well worth a pound of change at a later date, when a foreseeable or predictable threat grows and causes a major problem in implementation.

No marketing plan, regardless of how good it is, with brilliant strategies and clever tactics, can succeed without being implemented. You cannot achieve your objectives by implementing a poor marketing plan. But you cannot achieve your objectives by poorly implementing a good marketing plan either.

Therefore I wish you the development of an outstanding marketing plan. And if you implement it, I wish you an outstanding implementation as well.

APPENDIX

SAMPLE MARKETING PLANS

The following marketing plans were done by students as a part of regular courses in marketing. They range from plans for entrepreneurial start-ups to plans for a division of a large corporation. They involve different products and varied services. They were accomplished by teams consisting solely of marketing majors, and mixed teams from other disciplines. They were done by students taking the entry-level undergraduate course in marketing, and students at the graduate level. They were developed by native-born American students, and mixed teams of American and foreign students. One plan was done by two students from Singapore.

These students sometimes used different approaches. They applied the concepts and techniques of marketing to develop the best plans they could. These plans are not perfect . . . but they are good.

My purpose in including them is to show you what can be done as well as to give you some new ideas. Sometimes the students used a different approach than you might want to use. They saw things differently than you might today. They came up with different solutions to what might even be different problems than you may find. This is true even if you were to develop a plan for the identical product and industry. I hope their efforts will challenge and motivate you to develop the most professional marketing plan that you can. Because only by stretching to your limits can you grow to your potential for mastering this important marketing skill.

A1

EXCEL AIRE

Developed by
ROSE SIMON
JOHN IEZZA
CARLTON SKERRETT
ANGEL CAMARGO, AND
DANIELLE DENSON

Contents

EXECUTIVE SUMMARY

Excel Aire is about providing nonscheduled convenient, fast, safe, efficient, professional, and comfortable air flight services to the top executives of the Greater Western Region of the United States.

We will be the "new kids on the block" starting January 1997 when we launch our new charter services stationed at the Santa Monica Airport, 3100 Donald Douglas Loop North, Santa Monica CA 90405.

We chose this location because of the convenience and accessibility it provides our target customers. Located at the Santa Monica Airport, in the heart of the Los Angeles area, Excel Aire will be within 15 minutes of all main business and entertainment areas of Los Angeles . . . just where we want to be.

In launching this new charter service, we are in need of at least $3,890,916 capital for the first year just to run the operation. We will be providing you with the financial analysis to give you a fuller picture of this charter operation.

We at Excel Aire are excited about this new venture, as we are confident that the service that we are about to offer is one that is nonexistent in the market today. Excel Aire offers service-personalized service. We fully stand by our motto when we say "Your need is our service."

INTRODUCTION

There are several important reasons why one would choose a charter service. First, chartering saves time, otherwise lost by inflexible schedules. Second, it compresses time so that an hour-long out-of-town transaction does not require an overnight stay. Third, it expands time so that overall productivity is greater. Excel Aire will offer this and more, not to mention the intangible benefits to executives such as comfort, convenience, and prestige.

Ground service is another reason why Excel Aire should be your first choice in air charter. We will offer the finest in service and safety at a price that is highly competitive within the business jet community. Our personalized service extends from the moment you call our office, to the air and back down to the ground because "Your need is our service" at Excel Aire. We provide hotel reservations, taxi/car/limo service, personal services (laundry, dry cleaning, etc .) because we want to make life easier for you.

Our top priority at Excel Aire is customer satisfaction, and our only means of achieving it is through employee commitment, reliability, speed of service, and excellent customer service. We will attempt to accomplish this specifically through our personalized, custom-tailored ground service.

SITUATION ANALYSIS

There are several areas of concern in the situation analysis process—the technological environment, the neutral environment, the company environment, and the competitor environment. The following is an analysis of each of these areas.

Company Environment

Company environment analysis is composed of three areas: (1) financial resources, (2) human resources, and (3) experience and expertise. Research is extremely important as this information becomes the backbone of the company's operation.

Financial Resources. In trying to assess the financial resources aspect of this project, our company has in hand a capital of $500,000 to assure a solid start-up of the business. This figure is based on a $100,000 outlay of each of the five owners. We are additionally seeking a loan for the additional funds needed (see *Financial Summary Sheets*) This total capital pool will encompass all anticipated expenses; both fixed and variable.

Human Resources. Human resources is another aspect of the company environment that needs research. This area of the business encompasses not only the who but also the what. The who of the human resources is the personnel who will make up the corporation. This is where the different functions of the organization are drawn out. The what of human resource has to do with the kind of training and any continuing education necessary to carry out the proposed functions or responsibilities each personnel will hold.

Human resources is also the area where a company determines its objectives, formulates policies, and plans programs and procedures to attain these objectives. This is also where a budget that will serve as a short-range plan of operations to meet the objectives is developed.

Excel Aire's personnel will consist of a president, a vice-president/director of marketing, director of flight operations/chief pilot, and a director of maintenance (provided by FBO, thus no cost to Excel Aire). We will be contracting our captains and flight crews.

The President will be responsible for the entire operation of the corporation and for coordination of all departmental activities to ensure a smooth functioning operation.

The Vice-President will be the Chief Financial Officer, responsible for accounting to ensure a smooth financial operation. This person will also be the Marketing Director for sales and customer service to ensure that our service is at the best possible standard we can offer.

The Director of Flight Operations will be responsible for the entire flight operations and for coordinating all flight activities. This person will also be the Chief Pilot and will be responsible for the management of the corporation's policies and compliance with laws, rates, requirements, and regulations governing air taxi (135) operations as applicable to the corporation under its charter and certificate. He will also be responsible for the supervision and scheduling of pilot personnel and aircraft as well as act as liaison between the FAA and the corporation for all matters pertaining to air taxi operations.

The Director of Maintenance is provided by the FBO (Flight Based Operation) and is responsible for the planning, organizing, and scheduling of maintenance and inspections. He is responsible for the maintenance records and the proper distribution of same. He will also act as liaison between the corporation and the FAA on maintenance matters. As mentioned earlier, he is paid by the FBO.

Our financial statements in the Appendix will show how the salaries of these employees fit in with our operational costs.

Experience and Expertise. All officers of the corporation must have at least a bachelor's degree in business administration. All flight officers must have a high school diploma and have completed aviation school plus proper FAA certification. A captain must have a commercial license, an instructor rating, a multiengine rating, and an airline transport pilot certificate. A copilot must possess all of the above requirements except the airline transport pilot certificate. In addition, a captain needs 1,500 hours of total flight hours in order to be eligible and a copilot must meet a minimum of 50 to 100 total flight hours in type to be considered to fly any of Excel Aire's airplanes.

Continuing education is required annually to renew certificates. FAA-approved doctors administer medical certification biannually.

Competitive Environment

Our company's competition is based on price and promotion. Though competition is very strong, chartering services are promoting lower rates rather than quality service. The price range for charting a plane is very tight, within a couple of hundred dollars of each other. Most chartering services fly worldwide, giving them a broader market to deal with. With a broader market, they have to provide a wider range of services to capture market share.

Very few chartering services have a one-line fleet of planes to provide their services. For example, one chartering service has 54 planes ranging from turboprops to jet airplanes. A high number of planes is very costly, which will cut into profits. The average number of planes that our competitors have to provide for their services has a mean of 13 with a standard deviation of 2 that range in variety. Our company is focusing on capturing a niche with a one-line fleet that will provide safety, quality, and service that none of our competitors are stressing.

Through extensive studies on our competitors' environment, chartering services are aiming for the same strategy. They are providing a wide range of service upon request. Through a telephone survey, when we asked about a specific service that they provide, such as full entertainment systems on the plane, that causes the chartering price to increase. This study concluded that the more a client requests, the more that client pays. Very few chartering services provide quality service as a standard policy. Our company standards are focusing on safety, quality, price, and service.

A weak area of our competition is the lack of services being provided on the ground. Although most chartering services provide ground transportation and hotel reservation services, they are not being stressed as a standard service. No personal services are being provided to help ease the pressure from traveling due to rushed time. In addition, incentives are not being offered to clients to encourage them to use the chartering services. Our company plans to use a flying incentive to capture market share.

Most of our competition is based out of Santa Monica Airport, Van Nuy Airport, Burbank Airport, and Los Angeles Airport. The reasons for this is the FAA requirements. The noises that the older planes create limit the flights in and out of Long Beach Airport. Our company chose Santa Monica Airport because of the location and its accessibility to the Greater Los Angeles Airport. Our choice of fleet is the new Citations, which utilize modern technology to produce less noise to meet FAA requirements.

All of our competitors promote their business through several sources. The number-one way is through direct mail. In addition, companies advertise through magazines, newspapers, and phone books.

Neutral Environment

Legal Aspects of Regulations. The impact of regulations and CONTLOS upon the aviation business must be taken into consideration when conducting business operations. Recognizing this impact or influence and taking any required action is an important aspect of successful management.

Regulations are frequently associated with change that threatens the psychological, social, and economic aspects of the manager's world. To cope with regulations and change, there are some guidelines that might help establish a favorable viewpoint. Successful handling of regulations is facilitated by the creation and maintenance of an effective reports system that fits the needs of the individual business.

There are two broad categories of regulations that influence an aviation business: (1) regulations dealing with aviation operations and (2) regulations dealing with the business aspects of the organization. Aviation operations are regulated by the FAA, NTSB, and other federal, state, and local agencies. They cover flight regulations, personnel, support activities, safety, and security programs. The normal business activities are influenced by the regulatory aspects of federal and state taxes and the myriad controls and guidelines contained in the statutes, legislation, and guidelines covering unemployment compensation, Social Security, wage and hour administration, lessees, legal field, OSHA, insurance, licenses and permits, price, regulation, competition safeguards, consumer credit, advertising, and equipment regulations.

Rules and Regulations. In charter operations, the company is selling air transportation to meet a customer's specific need. The aircraft, with our crew members, is provided to the customer according to agreement for exclusive use. In complying with Part 135 and other pertinent regulations, the company must ensure the following:

1. The receipt of an air taxi/commercial operator (ATCO) operating certificate.

2. A current manual for the use and guidance of flight, ground operations, and maintenance personnel in conducting operations.

3. Procedures for locating each flight for which an FAA flight plan is not filed.

4. Exclusive use of at least one aircraft that meets the requirements of the operations specifications.

5. Qualified air crew personnel with appropriate and current certificates and the necessary recency experience.

6. Maintenance of required records and submission of mechanical reliability reports.

7. Compliance with the operating rules prescribed in FAR Parts 91 and 135, including:

    Airworthiness check

    Area limitations on operations

Available operating information for pilots

Passenger briefing

Oxygen requirements

Night operations

Fuel requirements, VFR and IFR

VFR operations (Visual Flight Rules)

IFR operations (Instrument Flight Rules)

These requirements reflect only a summary of the pertinent sections of Part 135. Refer to Federal Aviation Regulations for complete details of the requirements.

Insurance. The typical aviation business is faced with many problems, but of special importance is the concern of insurance. The four general categories of insurance have been classified as (1) loss or damage to property, (2) bodily injury and property damage liability, (3) business interruptions and losses resulting from fire and other damages to the premises, and (4) death or disability of key executives. Insurance protection should be considered for those areas found in any business as well as in those areas which are unique to the aviation field. It is important to consider active risk reduction as a key element of risk management.

The actual quotes for our insurance needs can be found in the Appendix.

Technological Environment

Aircraft Acquisition Analysis. A major decision that had to be made was how we were going to acquire our aircraft fleet. Some of the objectives that were of concern were cost, tax advantage, and profitability. Our options were owning the aircraft or leasing them. In order to aid us in our decision, we compiled a comparison analysis and it follows.

Company-Owned Aircraft.

Advantages: Optimum utility, convenience and safety, tax benefits.

Disadvantages: Can be inflexible if the company is not getting the hourly utilization expected, or purchased the wrong aircraft and must dispose of it.

Leasing.

Advantages:

1. *Conservation of Working Capital.* A big advantage of leasing is that it conserves working capital while allowing all the benefits of aircraft ownership. In a lease agreement, the leasing company acquires the aircraft at a specific request of the lessee with the lessee making the decision regarding the options, modifications, and price. At that point, the lessee signs a contract to lease a plane over a period of time for a specified monthly payment. With the exception of a possible advance payment of between one and five months, there is no other down payment. The down payment customary in other methods is saved, and that amount of working capital is available for other purposes.

2. *Tax Saving.* In financing an aircraft, only the interest portion of the monthly payment is a deductible expense. In addition, the company would depreciate that asset. In a lease situation, the entire lease payment is a deductible expense, effectively a straightline write-off of the asset over the term of the lease.

3. **Preservation of Credit Line.** A lease is generally not considered debt on the balance sheet. Keeping the additional debt off the balance sheets allows a higher availability of debt through normal banking transactions for other needs.

4. **Flexibility.** No assets are required to refinance or liquidate before upgrading equipment. Leasing makes it easier to upgrade and time acquisitions with market and company growth.

Disadvantages:

1. **No Equity, No Asset.** A leased aircraft cannot be shown on the balance sheets as an asset since it is not considered a debt. During the term of the lease, the lessee usually cannot own the airplane or have equity in it.

2. **Extra Cost.** The main disadvantage of leasing is the extra cost over an outright purchase, including the interest rate and the profit to the lessor.

3. **Limited Flight Time.** In a leased aircraft, the lessor usually has the right to the use of the aircraft. This could somehow lessen the effectiveness of the charter business, cutting into the availability of the aircraft and into profitability.

In view of the preceding findings, Excel Aire has opted to lease its aircraft because it is the most sensible option at this time. We will, however, evaluate the circumstances again in the future since we plan to expand both our line of business and our target market. We will also continuously analyze our hourly plane usage to determine the affinity of each plane to the end user.

TARGET MARKET

We will be utilizing a concentration strategy to determine our segmentation. We are aware that cost will prohibit many people from utilizing our services, and know that we must target our promotion with that in mind.

Geographic Segmentation

Based on Fortune 500 April 1994 listing of the location of the top 500 sales-producing companies in America, 44 corporations are based in California. More than half of these are located in Southern California. Likewise, the Southern California Business Directory's listing of the state's top 100 companies in California boasts over a 50 percent concentration in Southern California. Santa Monica Airport is a midway point accessible to San Diego or the Greater Los Angeles Area. Los Angeles is the second largest metropolitan area in the country and is ranked as having the fourth busiest airport in the country. This leaves many business travelers wasting additional time in preparation which could easily be eliminated with charter service.

Demographic Segmentation

We will be targeting the high-level executives within the top sales-producing companies, who have the authority to charter aircraft services. Our demographic research is based on a study by G. R. Bassiry and R. Hrair Dekmejian for *Business Horizons* magazine (May–June 1990). The average profile of a CEO is a 59-year-old male having a bachelor's degree, coming from middle/lower middle class socioeconomic background. He has served in the military and receives an average annual compensation package of $1,599,000. Although we will be targeting executives other than just CEOs, we find this information to be crucial in establishing our promotion and distribution tactics.

Psychographic Segmentation

Through the initiation of primary research interviewing 25 executive managers who have traveled at least three times in the last year on business, certain demands became apparent. Every person interviewed stated service to be in the top four most important categories when it comes to air travel. When asked to be more specific, frequently required services included limousine service, quality food service, secretarial services, laundering and dry-cleaning services, and business equipment availability.

MARKETING OBJECTIVES AND GOALS

Excel Aire is an exciting venture. Our primary business objective is to provide outstanding jet transportation with the finest service and safety. We feel our clientele would be willing to make a commitment to our company if they felt they were truly getting something they could not get elsewhere without additional expense.

Our projected financial objectives are to increase revenue at a 10% annual rate over the next three years. We are looking to gain a 10% market share. We are also concerned with keeping a low debt-equity ratio. Our control over costs and marketing objectives can be more consistent with what the five owners want when there are not shareholders to satisfy.

In terms of business expansion, we are looking to expand not only our product, but also our geographic target market. Within the next year, we plan to add a Citation 10 to the fleet to handle long-distance charters, and ideally double the existing fleet over the next three years. Our geographic expansion attainments will be a longer process depending on the growth of the company. However, we are looking at San Francisco, Dallas, and Orlando as sights for future Excel Aire locations.

MARKETING TACTICS

Promotion

Through extensive research of the competition's promotional tactics as well as consideration of financial control, the following is a promotional plan designed to establish Excel Aire as a company with an outstanding reputation and profit margin.

Distribution Materials. Our Appendix includes samples of the competitors' distribution materials. We are planning to use the same quality in printing and graphics except we will be utilizing our five key owners' skills in desktop publishing to do our own layouts. This allows for at least a 28 percent reduction of printing costs. The following are rates quoted by an independent printing company based on the assumption that the materials are already laid out.

Brochures—8½ by 11 trifold color cardstock brochures:

1–100	=	$0.99 each
100–500	=	$0.78 each
501–1000	=	$0.57 each
1001 & up	=	$0.36 each

Using the assumption of printing 2,000 to start, our cost would be $720 for the brochures. Our primary use of these brochures is to provide an introduction to the business community in a mass mailing, utilizing mailing lists, and data collected on the top 100 companies in sales in Southern California, and Fortune 5OO's issue of the top 500 companies each year. In-depth booklets—9 x 12 notebook with a pocket containing 8½ x 11 inch stationery with our company logo and an in-depth description of our company and the services available:

Stationery costs—8½ by 11 with company logo:

1–100	=	$0.06 each
101–250	–	$0.05 each
251–500	=	$0.04 each
501 & up	=	$0.035 each

Booklet style color folder with a pocket to hold stationery:

1–100	=	$4.99 each
101–200	=	$4.62 each
201 300	=	$4.25 each
301–400	=	$3.83 each
401–500	=	$3.46 each
501–750	=	$3.09 each
750 & up	=	$2.72 each

Using the assumption of printing 1,000 booklets to start, our costs would be $2,720 for the booklets and $3,500 for 10 pieces of stationery in each booklet, for a total cost of $5,720.

We would also print up an additional 5,000 pieces of stationery for business correspondence at a cost of $1,750. Business cards are also a cost factor at $50 per 1,000.

We would start with this level of business supplies and closely monitor the flow to determine our future needs. Thus, our overall start-up costs for printing will be $8,240.

Distribution Methods. As previously stated in our competition environment, most companies utilize a direct mail approach. Our target market allows us to be quite specific in our approach. We will utilize direct mail as follows:

We will compile lists from the following sources:

1. Listing of the top 100 companies in sales in Southern California Business Directory.

2. Listing of the top 500 companies in America from Fortune 500's annual listing. We will not only send information to the companies based in Southern California (44), but also any company that has a sizable office in the area.

3. Listing of all executives working for the major motion picture and television studios based in California.

4. Listing of all CEOs for all companies based in Southern California from the D&B (Dun and Bradstreet).

Our postage cost will be approximately $580 for an initial mailing of 2,000 brochures. It is our intention to utilize our owners to compile these lists, thus saving the recurring fee of renting lists repeatedly each time we want to do a mailing.

Advertising

Our advertising strategy is to establish that Excel Aire is responsible in providing solutions for the customers' needs without charging a premium for them. We are looking to appeal directly to business travelers whose time is so valuable, they don't have enough flexibility with a commercial carrier. The following is our logo, which will be used in association with any promotional materials:

◆ Excel Aire ◆

Your Need Is Our Service!

The following are rates for advertising in the kind of magazines we would be able to reach our target market with:

Forbes Magazine	Full Page 1 × rate	=	$33,840
Black and White	2/3 Page 1 × rate	=	$24,360
Non Bleed	1/2 Page 1 × rate	=	$19,970
	1/3 Page 1 × rate	=	$12,860
Fortune Magazine	Full Page 1 × rate	=	$37,130
Black and White	1/2 Page 1 × rate	=	$21,910
	1/3 Page 1 × rate	=	$14,110
Business Week	Full Page 1 × rate	=	$40,700
Black and White	2/3 Page 1 × rate	=	$30,520
Non Bleed	1/2 Page 1 × rate	=	$25,440
	1/3 Page 1 × rate	=	$16,280

Wall Street Journal (Western Region)

Black and White	1/2 Page 1 × rate	=	$14,003.76
	1/3 Page 1 × rate	=	$ 9,335.84
	1/4 Page 1 × rate	=	$ 7,001.88
	1/8 Page 1 × rate	=	$ 3,500.94

Delta Sky Magazine (using a destination rate)

Black and White	Full Page 1 × rate	=	$19,343
	2/3 Page 1 × rate	=	$14,355
	1/2 Page 1 × rate	=	$11,468
	1/3 Page 1 × rate	=	$ 8,618

All costs quoted are based on a one-time rate. Each magazine has different levels of multirating, and this definitely factors into our decision as to where we will advertise.

Based on the preceding quotes, we have decided on a concentration in the Western Region *Wall Street Journal.* By running our advertisement at least 10 times, we will discount our rates by 5 percent. We will take ⅛ of a page for a price of $3,325.89 per ad with a total cost of $33,258.93. We are also going to advertise in the *Delta Sky Magazine.* During our primary research of business travelers, Delta Airlines was mentioned in approximately 84 percent of our surveys. We will take a ⅓ page ad using a three-time discount rate of $10,920 for a total cost of $32,760.

Our intention is to begin advertising with these sources, but with revenue coming in, we will expand into the other quoted magazines in a conservative but deliberate manner.

Product

We have decided to use the Citation Jets for our charter service for several reasons which are highlighted in our Comparison Chart of Optional Planes. Since the beginning of the jet era, Citations have had a tradition of producing the most efficient and cost-effective light jets. At a time when the industry is seeing a decrease in manufacturers, Citation has been producing a new line of jets. They provide more options in price, size, and category; and they represent the most impressive combination of efficiency, performance, and reliability in light jets.

From the new lineup, we have chosen the Citation Jet, Citation V, and the Citation VII. These airplanes meet many of today's tough regulations, and have very low acquisition costs in comparison to others in their class.

Each jet has outstanding fuel efficiency that is a high priority in the time of rising costs. Each provides the lowest cost of operation of any comparable new aircraft available. Every Citation is backed by a large dedicated support organization, with service centers around the country.

Through much deliberation over which kinds of aircraft would best suit our marketing and business needs, we decided to use the Citation Series of aircraft for these additional reasons.

1. Fleet unification allows for our flight operators to interchange much more effectively between planes.

2. The Citations are using some of the most current technology available, thus concurring with the FAA's newest regulations including those on noise.

3. The planes can be leased directly from Citation, Inc., allowing us to be in control of our specification needs.

The Comparison Chart (Table A1.1) shows the features of our particular choice of Citations at this point. We based our selection on trying to create a good mix of size, speed, distance capability, number of seats, and cost effectiveness.

Services Available. Aside from the regular flight services most charter companies provide, we at Excel Aire strive to be different. We are building our company on the motto "Your need is our service," and we fully intend to deliver. The following list is a sample of some of the services our primary research indicated people would be interested in using if there was no additional premium:

1. Limousine service

2. Quality food service

Table A1.1 Comparison Chart of Optional Planes

	Citation Jet	King Air	Citation V	Lear Jet	Citation VII	Challenger
Seats	6-6	6-7	9-13	10	8-13	10-19
Price	3.2 million	2.1 million	4.4 million	4.6 million	7.6 million	10 million
Power plant	2 William	2 P&W	2 P&W	2 Gorrett	2 Gorrett	2 GE CF-34-319
Fuel Capacity	3,070	2,573	5,771	6,198	7,384	17,900
Gross weight	10,100	10,100	16,100	18,500	22,650	44,750
Empty weight	5,730	6,634	8,827	10,119	11,686	25,760
Useful load	4,370	3,526	7,273	8,381	10,964	18,990
Cruise speed	322 @ 41,000	247 @ 16,000	370 @ 45,000	4254 @ 43,000	424 @ 45,000	424 @ 41,000
Fuel flow	489/72	592/88	860/127	990/148	1,145/170	1,737/255
Max endurance	5.6 hrs. @ 41,000	7.1 hrs. @ 29,000	5.7 hrs. @ 45,000	5.5 hrs. @ 43,000	5.8 hrs. @ 47,000	3.8 hrs. @ 41,000
Takeoff distance	3,080'	2,710'	3,160'	4,972'	4,690'	5,875'
Landing distance	2,800'	2,290'	2,870'	3,075'	3,000'	3,300'
Rate of climb	3,450 fps	2,005 fps	3,684 fps	4,340 fps	4,000 fps	4,259 fps
Engine out roc	1,070	494	1,180	1,280	990	1,207
Max optg. weight	41,000	29,000	45,000	45,000	51,000	41,000
Ceiling	26,500	13,100	31,100	25,000	23,000	26,500
Stall speed	78 mph	78 mph	85 mph	96 mph	98 mph	103 mph
Landing Configuration	77 mph	80 mph	85 mph	110 mph	98 mph	116 mph

3. Secretarial services

4. Laundry services

5. Dry-cleaning services

6. Business equipment on airplane

7. Hotel reservations services

We will specify the equipment needed for the Citation in our lease agreement, and utilize our staff to provide any of the other services mentioned.

Price

Please refer to the Appendix for an outline of charges for each aircraft. We based our decisions on establishing a price on competitive information as well as our break-even needs.

Distribution

Excel Aire chose Santa Monica Airport to house its air charter business simply because of the accessibility of the location to our target clientele.

We have contracted a 15,000-square-foot facility with Gunnell Aviation. They are a step beyond the classic definition of an FBO (Fixed Base Operator). As Excel Aire's FBO, Gunnell Aviation will greet, fuel, store, and care for our fleet of aircraft where, for over 30 years, highly individualized service to demanding clientele has stood above all else.

Gunnell Aviation has fine-tuned an approach to FBO service that matches professionalism with instinct, detail with thoroughness, not to mention complete service with individual need. The following amenities lured us to Gunnell Aviation:
Full-service FBO with 30 years of service

- Corporate and executive hangars
- World-class museum and art gallery
- Premier gourmet restaurant, The DC3
- Commonwealth limousine
- Avis rental car site
- Complete line of aviation services

At Excel Aire, we feel that the more sophisticated our distributor, the better our clients will be served. For Excel Aire's clients, Gunnell Aviation also boasts such conveniences as:

- Luxurious lobby area
- Fully appointed conference room
- 24-hour ground support services
- Private offices and meeting rooms
- Full telecommunication (telephone, fax, pager, portable phones)
- Complimentary message services

These additional amenities, however, will mean nothing if not fully supported by the commitment that our clients' flight safety is our first priority. This is more reason that

Excel Aire has chosen to be a part of the Gunnell Aviation family, because from minor maintenance services to major inspections, from aircraft parts sales to a fully equipped avionics department, Gunnell Aviation guarantees that each aircraft performs at its peak—on demand and at a moment's notice—because our clients' safety is our primary concern.

Furthermore, we chose Gunnell Aviation because of their high profile, their commitment to their clients. Gunnell Aviation gives Excel Aire the edge needed to operate the finest air charter service in Southern California due to a common goal we share, and that is "Customer Satisfaction." We selected Santa Monica Airport because of its dedication to first-class general aviation. We selected Santa Monica because of its proximity to the important business and entertainment centers of Los Angeles. What this means to our clients is complete convenience without sacrifice.

PROBLEMS/SOLUTIONS

Aviation managers are faced with many problems, some of which are more critical than others to the continued longevity and success of the business. Among the more critical problem areas are insurance, leases, and legal matters. The manager's recognizing these problem areas, possessing the capability to deal with them, and initiating positive action for achievement in each area will be necessary to the success of our aviation business.

Insurance

Risk is a part of doing business. Risk management is a part of the manager's job of directing the business. In running Excel Aire, few risks can be eliminated completely, although some can be reduced by safe operating procedures, thorough personnel training, and good equipment. Some risks can be transferred through the purchase of insurance. Some risks will be assumed by the business. Knowing what kind of insurance to carry and how much to purchase are important aspects of good risk management.

The average aviation business has considerable investment in buildings, furnishings, and inventory. These investments should be protected against fire and other perils such as smoke, windstorm, hail, civil commotion, explosion, and damage by aircraft or motor vehicles.

Liability Exposure

There are four types of liability exposure:

1. Employer's liability and worker's compensation
2. Liability to nonemployees
3. Automobile liability
4. Professional liability

1. Under common law as well as workers' compensation laws, an employer is liable for injury to employees at work caused by his failure to provide safe tools and working conditions, hire competent fellow workers, or warn employees of an existing danger.

2. Nonemployee liability, general liability, or third-party liability is insurance for any kind of bodily injury to nonemployees except that caused by automobiles and professional malpractice. This includes customers, pedestrians, delivery people, the public at large, and may extend to trespassers or other outsiders even when the manager exercised "reasonable care."

3. Cars and trucks are a serious source of liability. This is encountered primarily in vehicles owned by the business, but can be experienced under the doctrine of agency when the employee is operating his own or someone else's car in the course of employment. In this instance, the business could be held vicariously liable for injuries and property damage caused by the employee. If customary or convenient for an employee to operate his own car while on company business, the business is well advised to acquire nonownership automobile liability insurance.

4. Our hiring policies will assure a minimization of professional risk pursuant to professional malpractice as well as proper certification. We are also establishing a check system for all procedures required in proper flight operation.

Legal Affairs

Eventually, the company will be faced with legal problems. In view of this possibility, it is highly desirable that the organization have a sound legal foundation and that the services of a competent lawyer be available for assistance when needed. Although legal services are myriad, the following represent possibilities:

1. Establishing, maintaining, or changing the correct legal form of organization.

2. Preparing contracts, deeds, and other legal documents.

3. Determining legal liability in accident cases involving company personnel, vehicles, or premises.

4. Interpreting the regulations of governmental agencies such as the Internal Revenue Service, the FAA, and the Wage and Hour Law.

5. Conducting all necessary litigation such as those associated with damage suits and contractual problems.

6. Legal assistance necessary in obtaining and executing specific technical or exacting contracts.

7. Maintaining the correct legal position when dealing with employees or unions on labor relations problems.

SUMMARY

Based on the findings of this research, we are confident that Excel Aire will be a successful operation and will find its way to the top of the industry given what we have to offer and our deep commitment to the needs of our clients.

We fully stand behind our product, that is our "personalized service" both in the air and on the ground. Our commitment to providing the finest jet transportation which focuses on a convenient, fast, safe, efficient, professional, and comfortable air flight service is the essence of our business and that is our promise to our customers. We mean it when we say "Your need is our service!"

REFERENCES

Magazines

Popkin, J. "Charters Are Cheaper, Most of the Time"; *U.S. News and World Report;* February 26, 1990
Collins, R. "The Citation Turns 20," *AOPA Pilot,* September 1992
Lacagnina, M. "Golden Eagle"; *AOPA Pilot,* August 1993
General. "Fortune 500 Listing for 1992," *Fortune Magazine,* April 1992
Bassiry, C. & Dekmejian, R. "Corporate Elite, A CEO's Profile," *Business Horizons Magazine,* January, 1991

Business Publications

Southern California Business Directory, 1992
Dun and Bradstreet CEO's Listings, 1992
ADPA's Aviation USA, 1992

Books

Pride/Ferrell. *Marketing,* 8th Edition
Richardson, J. D. and Rodwell, J. F. *Essentials of Aviation Management,* 3rd Edition
Wells, A. and Chadbourne, B. *General Aviation Marketing,* 1987

Interviews

Barton, Gault S. President of Premiere Air
Buell, Brian. Property Manager, Gunnell Aviation
Caridi, Penny, Underwriter, Aviation West Brokers
Duggan, James. Charter Dispatcher, Zephyr Aviation
Goode, Ken. Credit Representative, Cessna Finance Corporation
Griffith, Shawn. Chief Pilot, Argosy Airlines
Higares, Chris. Service Scheduler, Cessna Aircraft Company
Hiney, Richard C. Underwriter, USAIG
Krebs, Tisha. Office Manager, Civic Helicopters
Lefezar, Mark. Vice President, Avjet Aviation
Shoody, Jonathon. Service Person, KINKO'S Desktop Publishing
Rizzi, Wayne J. Director of Marketing, Premier Air
Simon, Michael. Flight Officer, Premier Air

APPENDIX A1-A

Insurance Information

UNITED STATES AVIATION UNDERWRITERS
  Incorporated

Code	Description	Exposure	Rate	Est. Premium
8810	Clerical President Payroll Max	$59,800.00	.98	$ 586.00
8742	Outside Sales (V.P.)	50,000.00	1.40	700.00
7424	Flight Crew	88,060.00	7.23	6,367.00

Employers Liability Increased Limits—Minimum Fee   150.00
(1,000,000.00/1,000,000.00/1,000,000.00)

CA User Fund Assessment 7,803.00 @ .00126   10.00
CA Fraud Investigation Surcharge 7,803.00 @ .000548   4.00

ESTIMATED ANNUAL PREMIUM $7,817.00

Rates are subject to change without prior notice.

Rooo, with tho abovo figuroc projoctod for your projoct (which aro only ostimatos) tho total promium would be $92,537.00.

We would also require all pilots to attend formal simulator based recurrent training every six months. For an idea on this price, you can call Flight Safety International in Long Beach. Explain your project and I am sure they would be glad to help (213-420-7660).

I hope this is of help to your project. Remember that these estimates are only an idea. We are in a hardening market and expect the rates to continually go up.

Please, call if I can help anymore.

Best Regards,

Richard C. Hiney

RCH/mad

APPENDIX A1-B

Sample Job Order

◆ Excel Aire ◆
Your Need Is Our Service!

Trip Planning Form
24 Hour Reservation Line
(818) 752-2009

Today's Date: _____   Confirmation #:_____

Hotel code: _____

Itinerary: (Please include any requested stop-overs, drop-offs, or overnights)

_____

_____

Date of Travel: _____

Time of Travel: _____

Number of Passengers: _____

Departure Location: (If other than Santa Monica Airport)

_____

Amount and Type of Luggage (i.e., Golf Clubs, Skiing Equipment, etc.)

_____

Passenger Name: _____

Contact Name and Phone #: _____

Form of Payment: _____

Special Catering Requests: _____

_____

Notes: _____

_____

_____

_____

(*Note:* Copies of this form may serve as original)

APPENDIX A1-C

Interview Questionnaire

Name of Interviewer: _____   Date: _____

Name of Interviewee: _____   Company: _____

Number of times you travel for business in 1 year: _____

Typical service used (commercial or charter): _____

Which companies? _____

Please rate the following factors you consider when choosing an air travel service on a scale from 1 (most important) to 10 (least important):

Cost: _____

Location of airport: _____

Pilot: _____

Competition incentives: _____

Flexibility of schedule: _____

Services available: _____

Plane type: _____

Staff: _____

Ground handling: _____

Safety records: _____

What specific services do you ever require when traveling?

_____

_____

_____

What rules does your company enforce when it comes to chartering an airplane?

_____

_____

_____

Other comments:

_____

_____

_____

APPENDIX A1-D

Citation Jet

$1250/hr

Leg Num	From Apt	To Apts	Tru Crs	Dist nmi	Fuel Stop	ETE Hrs + Min	Allow Load Pounds	Fuel Burn
1	SMO	DAL	8	1,082	0	3 + 12	1,306	2,744
2	DAL	SMO	280	1,082	1	4.33	843	3,960
Subtotals				2,164		7.8 Hrs		6,704
Flight time charges								$ 9,750
0.0 Individual standby hour(s)								0
1 Overnight(s) (Include 1 day's standby each)								300
Extra items								0
10% tax								1,005
Totals				2,164		7.8 Hrs		$11,055

DAL Love Field—Dallas TX
SMO Excel Aire—310-222-1325

APPENDIX A1-E

Monthly Break-even Point

Break-even point computed as average for all three planes:

	Price per hour
Citation jet	1,250
Citation V	2,700
Citation VII	3,300
Total divided by 3 = avg. price/hr	2,417

Average break-even point for all three planes in hours:

$$\text{Break-even} = \frac{FC}{S} - VC = \frac{213,021}{1,710} = 125$$

FC = 213,021
Sale (avg.) = 2,417
VC = 95507/135 = 707

Average break-even point in sales:

$$\text{Break-even} = \frac{FC}{1} - \frac{VC}{S} = \frac{213,021}{.70} = \$304,316$$

Note: 45 hours were used as a base for variable cost expenses; 135 hours were divided into the variable cost to get a unit cost of $707.

APPENDIX A1-F

Expense Breakdown per Month Basis

Expenses
Fixed costs:
Leases:

Citation Jet	$37,333	
Citation V	51,333	
Citation VII	88,666	$177,332
Office rental		6,000
Insurance		7,753
Hanger rental		6,000
Other expenses		1,500
Advertising (printing costs)		687
Officers salaries (3)		13,749
Total Fixed Costs		$213,021
Variable costs:		
Crew salaries (3)		5,355
Fuel		54,000
Maintenance reserves		27,000
Routine maintenance		900
Other variable expenses		1,500
Transportation expenses		1,250
Advertising expenses		5,502
Total Variable Costs		95,507
Total Fixed and Variable Costs		$308,528

APPENDIX A1-G

Break-even Analysis

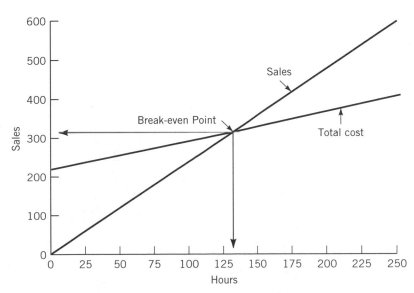

APPENDIX A1-H

A Four-Year Projection of Earnings before Interest and Taxes
on a 10% Growth Rate per Year

	Year 0	Year 1	Year 2	Year 3	Year 4
Sales	$ 3,651,792.00	$ 4,016,971.00	$ 4,418,669.00	$ 4,860,535.00	$ 5,346,589.00
Variable costs	(1,095,540.00)	(1,205,094.00)	(1,325,603.00)	(1,458,164.00)	(1,603,980.00)
Contribution margin	2,556,252.00	2,811,877.00	3,093,066.00	3,402,371.00	3,742,609.00
Fixed costs	(2,556,252.00)	(2,556,252.00)	(2,556,252.00)	(2,556,252.00)	(2,556,252.00)
Earnings before interest and taxes	$ 0.00	$ 255,625.00	$ 536,814.00	$ 846,119.00	$ 1,186,357.00

APPENDIX A1-I

Graph Showing a 10% Growth Rate per Year

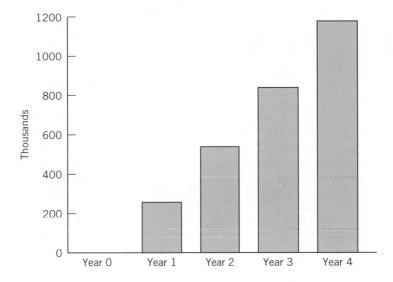

APPENDIX A1-J

Ranking of Busiest Metropolitan Areas

		1980 Census	1985 Projection	Percent Change 1980–85
1	Dallas-Fort Worth, TX	3,885	4,334	11.0%
2	Los Angeles-Anaheim-Riverdale, CA	14,532	16,090	10.5
3	Seattle-Tacoma, WA	2,559	2,811	9.8
4	Portland-Vancouver, OR-WA	1,478	1,586	7.3
5	San Francisco-Oakland-San Jose, CA	6,253	6,679	6.8
6	Philadelphia-Wilmington-Trenton, PA-NJ-DE-MD	5,899	6,254	6.0
7	Hartford-New Britain-Middletown, CT	1,086	1,151	6.0
8	Chicago-Gary-Lake County, IL-IN-WI	8,066	8,417	4.4
9	Denver-Boulder, CO	1,848	1,928	4.3
10	Cincinnati-Hamilton, OH-KY-IN	1,744	1,817	4.2
11	Miami-Fort Lauderdale, FL	3,193	3,301	3.4
12	New York-Northern New Jersey-Long Island, NY-NJ-CT	18,067	18,272	1.0
13	Houston-Galveston-Brazoria, TX	3,711	3,715	0.1
14	Cleveland-Akron-Lorain, OH	2,760	2,747	−0.5
15	Detroit-Ann Arbor, MI	4,665	4,626	−0.8
16	Milwaukee-Racine, WI	1,097	1,586	−1.3
17	Pittsburgh-Beaver Valley, PA	2,243	2,153	−4.0
18	Buffalo-Niagara Falls, NY	1,189	1,139	−4.2
19	Boston-Lawrence-Salem, MA-NH	4,172	3,779	−0.4
20	Providence-Pawtucket-Fall River, RI-MA	1,142	944	−17.3

Note: Consolidated Metropolitan Statistical Areas, ranked by percent change 1980–85, population in thousands.

Source: Census Bureau, Equifax Marketing Decision Systems.

APPENDIX A1-K

The Busiest Airports

Chicago is the third most populous metropolitan area, but it has the country's busiest airport. Almost one-quarter of all airline passengers board in one of the top five airports.

Rank	Airport	Passengers	Percent
1	Chicago (O'Hare), IL	25,664,266	6.0%
2	Dallas/Ft. Worth (Regional), TX	22,623,065	5.3
3	Atlanta, GA	20,397,697	4.8
4	Los Angeles, CA	18,583,292	4.3
5	San Francisco, CA	13,326,085	3.1
6	Denver (Stapleton), CO	12,320,246	2.9
7	New York (La Guardia), NY	10,839,833	2.5
8	Phoenix, AZ	10,166,095	2.4
9	New York (John F. Kennedy), NY	10,081,490	2.3
10	Newark, NJ	9,822,491	2.3
11	Detroit (Wayne County), MI	9,739,265	2.3
12	Boston (Logan), MA	9,661,258	2.2
13	St. Louis, MO	9,396,335	2.2
14	Honolulu, Oahu, HI	8,943,521	2.1
15	Miami, FL	8,591,936	2.0
16	Minneapolis/St. Paul, MN	8,469,115	2.0
17	Pittsburgh, PA	7,940,962	1.8
18	Orlando, FL	7,373,449	1.7
19	Seattle-Tacoma, WA	7,059,777	1.6
20	Houston (Intercontinental), TX	7,039,001	1.6
21	Las Vegas (McCarran), NV	7,026,900	1.6
22	Charlotte, NC	6,903,482	1.6
23	Washington (National), DC	6,895,563	1.6
24	Philadelphia, PA	6,247,289	1.5
25	San Diego, CA	5,317,177	1.2
	Total U.S.	429,654,602	100.0%

Note: Total revenue passengers enplaned annually for the 25 busiest airports and the United States, and percent of passengers enplaned in the United States, 1989.

Source: Airport Activity Statistics of Certificated Route Air Carriers, FAA, 1989.

APPENDIX A1-L

Excel Aire Salary Breakdown 1994

Title	Annual Salary
President	$ 75,000.00
Vice president/marketing	50,000.00
Chief pilot	40,000.00
Total Officers' Salaries	$165,000.00
Contract Employees	
2 Captains	
($20 p/hr @ 45 hrs p/mth × 2)	$ 21,600.00
3 Co-pilots	
($13 p/hr @ 45 hrs p/mth × 3)	21,060.00
1 Attendant	
($10 p/hr @ 45 hrs p/mth)	5,400.00
Total Contract Salaries	$ 48,060.00
Total Annual Salaries	$213,060.00

A2

MARKETING PLAN FOR PROFESSIONAL FITNESS

Developed by
IAIN MOZOOMBAR

Contents

EXECUTIVE SUMMARY

Professional Fitness will be an upscale health club located in the City of San Marino, California, and will be targeted at the over-40 age group. This club will offer state-of-the-art equipment and facilities. The aerobic room of Professional Fitness will be soundproofed to ensure that nonaerobic class participants can work out or relax with minimum discomfort. The club will be equipped with high-end weight resistance machines, exercise bicycles, stair climbers, treadmills, cross-country ski machines, satin-finished dumbbells and barbells, and a sauna in both the male and female locker rooms. The club will also provide child-care for members when they work out and will also house a health bar, pro shop, and an attractive members' lounge.

The decision to target the over-40 market was made so as to capitalize on the ongoing transition of the health club industry from an industry that primarily targeted the under-30 market, to one that focuses on the over-40, and family market. Currently, an increased emphasis is being placed on enhancing the quality of life for seniors through the use of specially designed weight training programs. Researchers have found these programs to be very effective in battling the physical and mental deterioration of the body as one moves into the "golden years."

The main differential advantage offered by Professional Fitness will be the unmatched level of personal service and pampering that will be extended to the clients. The aging of the American population, an increased health awareness, and the lack of another such upscale, over-40 facility in the primary trading area of the club will also contribute to the success of the club. The club is expected to have a potential market of 58,258 people. These potential clients will be geographically located from San Marino and the surrounding cities of Pasadena, South Pasadena, Arcadia, Alhambra, Monterey Park, Glendale, and La Canada Flintridge.

The start-up costs for the club are estimated to be $1,274,055. The club will charge an initiation fee of $675 and monthly dues of $75. This pricing strategy is conservatively expected to attract 1,200 clients in the first year, 1,800 in the second, and 2,300 by the end of the third year. The club will offer a limited membership of 2,500 people. The expected return on investment will be 15.1 percent in year one, 22.8 percent in year two, and 33.1 percent in year three. The club will break even with 1,096 members and is expected to achieve this within the first year. The estimated dollar gross sales figure for the first year is $1,371,040.31 and this is expected to increase to $2,570,343.27 by the end of the third year.

INTRODUCTION

Statement of Purpose

The purpose of this marketing plan is to document the credibility and feasibility of opening an upscale, health club in the City of San Marino, California—Professional Fitness. This upscale club will offer a soundproofed aerobic room, state-of-the-art weight stations, exercise bicycles, stair climbers, treadmills, cross-country ski exercisers, free weights, a sauna in both locker rooms, massage facilities, health bar, pro shop, an upscale member lounge, and a child-care center.

Background

Over the past decade, numerous varieties of health clubs have popped up all over America. Every major city has at least one major health club specializing in total body fitness. The booming movie industry in Southern California has played a major role in making California the most health-conscious state in the country. Southern California's climate and long summer days coupled with mild winters encourage an outdoor-oriented lifestyle. Be it trekking, sun tanning, biking, competitive sports, or just plain "loafing," Southern Californians want to look their best, hence the sprouting of fitness-oriented clubs all over the Southland.

The American Medical Association (AMA) has also placed a stronger emphasis on health and fitness for the aging population (40 and above) over the past five years. This factor has also played a great part in the health club boom. Other factors will be discussed in more detail in the environmental analysis sections.

Scope

This marketing plan will include an analysis of the situation, neutral, competitor, and company environments; the target market to be reached; opportunities and threats faced by Professional Fitness; marketing objectives, strategy, and tactics; financial implementation and control.

Limitations/Delimitations

A time constraint requiring the entire business plan to be completed within 10 weeks causes the content and detail of the business plan to be narrowed in focus.

Methods

This business plan consists of applied research since the strategies and tactics of this plan are going to be used by the owners and management of Professional Fitness to gain a competitive edge over its competitors. The data for the plan are collected mainly through secondary research and financial data are based on calculated estimates. Some of the results and conclusions used in the competitor analysis section were collected via a questionnaire instrument.

Assumptions

It is assumed that the economic environment of the primary trading area remains constant and also that the current low interest rate will prevail. It is also assumed that the current lifestyle trends of Southern Californians remain unchanged and that the viable fitness-oriented market segment continues to grow at the same rate.

Preview

SITUATIONAL ANALYSIS

The Situational Environment

The situational environment for Professional Fitness is to be analyzed using the following format:

1. Demand and demand trends

2. Social and cultural factors

3. Demographics

4. Economic and business conditions

5. State of technology for fitness equipment

6. Laws and regulations

Demand and Demand Trends. There are many factors that are affecting the demand for an upscale health club in San Marino. One of the most important factors is the life cycle of the health club industry. This industry grew at an increasing and phenomenal rate from the late 1970s to about 1989; since then, the industry is growing, however at a decreasing rate. On the product life-cycle chart, as illustrated in Figure A2-1, the industry would roughly be at point A.

According to *Club Industry,* a trade publication, from 1982 to 1987, the industry grew at the rate of up to 15 percent a year.[1] In 1987, there were an estimated 10,000 clubs around the country. Also, in 1987, an estimated 30 million Americans had memberships to at least one health club, up from 20 million in 1982.[2] These clubs ranged from aerobics-only to multipurpose facilities. In 1988, consumer spending on health clubs, massages, and the like, increased to a record high of 25 percent over 1987 and became the fastest growing category in personal care.[3]

---

[1]Laura Loro, "Health Clubs Stretch Markets," *Advertising Age,* May 16, 1988: 38.
[2]Dennis Rodkin, "Health Clubs Sweat the Details in Ads," *Advertising Age,* Dec. 3, 1989: 39.
[3]Vivian Brownstein, "Consumers Will Help the Economy Stay in Shape Next Year," *Fortune,* Oct. 23, 1989: 32.

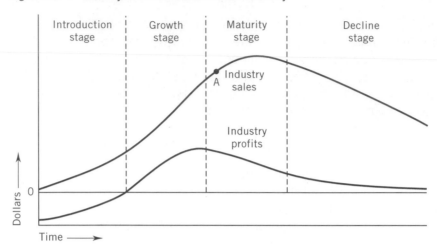

Figure A2-1   Life Cycle of the Health Club Industry

In 1989, there were an estimated 30,000 clubs all over the country, thanks to a slew of company-owned fitness clubs. These company-owned clubs ranged from a basic weight room with a few free weights and machines, where employees would work out during their lunch break, to comprehensive athletic facilities, like that of corporate giants AT&T, Saatchi & Saatchi Advertising, and Tenneco.[4]

In 1990, an industry estimate by *Club Industry,* showed that there were just under 33,000 clubs in the country, an increase of less than 10 percent.[5] Also, in 1990, Americans spent $5.3 billion on health club memberships and $1.73 billion on exercise equipment.[6]

The slight slowdown in the industry has been due in part to the recession which has been plaguing the United States since the middle of 1990. Investment and real estate loans have become increasingly difficult to obtain. The collapse of the savings and loan industry has also caused banks and investors to become more tightfisted.

Consumers of health club memberships are also becoming much more selective and educated in choosing a health club. This is due in part to the large number of clubs available, and also to the natural progression of any industry as it moves into the maturity stage of its life cycle. The industry has now become so competitive that a large number of clubs not emphasizing personal service and custom-tailored fitness programs have gone bankrupt. In fact, Mare Onigman, the editor of *Club Industry,* admitted that the battle is usually fought and won on the service side and that an increasing number of clubs are "servicing the daylights out of members" just to stay in business.[7]

Social and Cultural Factors. Since the 1970s, health clubs have been a very popular way to meet people of the opposite sex and to make new friends. In fact, at one point in the mid-1970s, coed gyms began to take the place of singles bars! Over the past four years, health clubs that had initially focused only on the young adult market, and those that primarily marketed breathtaking physiques have seen their market shrink dramatically due to the aging of the baby boomers. According to the Census Bureau, the number of people between the ages of 18 and 34 is projected to shrink by 11 percent during the

[4]Brian O'Reily, "New Truths about Staying Healthy," *Fortune,* Sept. 25, 1989: 58.
[5]"Health Clubs Cool Down," *Club Industry,* March 1991: 17.
[6]Eleanor Branch, "Making Your Fitness Their Business," *Black Enterprise,* Sept. 1991: 83.
[7]Loro, p. 28.

1990s.[8] The executive director of the Association of Quality Clubs (AQC), John McCarthy, stated that the industry was in a phase of major transition, from being one that focused primarily on the under-30 market, to an industry that focuses on the corporate market, families, and the 40-plus group.[9] This shift is not away from the aerobically toned baby boomers, but rather it is aimed toward improved health at all ages.

In a recent study of the 40-plus market, the AQC found that nearly 50 percent of those surveyed exercised at least three times a week, and nearly 75 percent of the respondents stated that they had become more concerned about their health. But, interestingly enough, only 10 percent of those surveyed belonged to a health club.[10]

In fact, advertisers are starting to recognize that ads featuring well-built, male Chippendale dancers and sexy, shapely, 22-year-old female models are scaring away millions of potential male and female customers who cannot expect to look that way. Thus, clubs like the Health & Tennis chain, are featuring an increasing number of older celebrities such as Cher, Victoria Principal, and Farrah Fawcett in their advertisements as they seem more credible to potential members.[11]

The new buzz word for health clubs is now wellness. Since the emphasis has now been shifted to the older age groups, many health clubs are evolving into comprehensive health centers, that are as concerned with the emotional and medical well-being of their members as they are with flabby thighs and love handles. This transformation has occurred as the consumer of the 1990s is, in general, demanding that clubs be concerned with the whole person.[12] Thus, most upscale clubs now offer seminars in stress management, nutrition, and smoking cessation. Some of these clubs are even affiliating with physicians, cardiologists, and plastic surgeons to provide medical services for their clients.

Over the past three years, an increasing number of executive women have started weight training. Women, who for years have dedicated themselves to slimmer thighs and flatter stomachs, have finally acknowledged the need for upper-body strength. For example, Darcy Troy, a Yale graduate and investment banker, said it was "the coolest thing. . . one minute, nothing. Next minute, muscles."[13] These women have found that upper-body strength improves posture, protects against backache and bone loss, and improves confidence.

This increase in the number of serious women weight trainers has given rise to a new kind of health club—women-only clubs. In addition to the normal aerobic floors and other amenities, these clubs usually have specially designed weight machines and poundages that are geared toward a woman's frame size and strength capabilities. This phenomenon, according to *Club Industry* magazine features editor, Dan Tobin, is because women who were in their early 20s during the heyday of the fitness boom in the early 1980s, are now in their early-to-mid-30s and are now less interested in joining a health club for social reasons.[14]

Finally, it seems to be currently chic to be able to remain fit, healthy, and physically strong during the "golden years," that is, ages 60 and beyond. A survey conducted by the Gallup Organization for the *American Health* magazine showed that the most rapidly growing segment of fitness enthusiasts is aged 50 or older. This segment increased by 46 percent from 1984 to 1986.[15]

---

[8]Judith Waldrop, "Feeling Good," *American Demographics,* May 1990: 6.
[9]Rodkin, p. 38.
[10]"Health Clubs Look Beyond the Baby Boomers," *Changing Times,* Feb. 1990: 95.
[11]Loro, p. 28.
[12]Janice M. Horowitz, "From Workouts to Wellness," *Time,* July 30, 1990: 64.
[13]Dorothy Schefer, "The New Body Building," *Vogue,* May 1989: 368.
[14]Laura Broadwell, "Girls Just Wanna Work Out," *Women's Sports & Fitness,* Sept. 1990: 47.
[15]Waldrop, p. 6

Table A2-1 Selected Population Breakdown

	Total Population	White	%	Black	%	Asian	%
San Marino	12,959	8,559	66.1	32	0.3	4,189	32.3
Pasadena	137,501	79,312	57.6	25,064	18.2	11,593	8.4
South Pasadena	23,936	16,711	69.8	745	3.1	5,086	21.3
Arcadia	48,277	34,512	71.5	374	0.8	11,321	23.5
Glendale	180,038	133,270	74.0	2,334	1.3	25,453	14.1
Alhambra	82,106	33,498	40.8	1,643	2.0	31,313	38.1
Monterey Park	60,738	16,245	26.7	374	0.6	34,898	57.5
La Canada Flintridge	19,378	16,645	85.9	81	0.4	2,397	12.4

Source: U.S. Census Bureau, 1990 Population and Housing Census.

Table A2-2 Age Groups and Median Age of Residents

	Aged 25–44	Aged 45–54	Aged 55–59	Aged 60–64	Median Age
San Marino	2,996	2,097	782	742	41.4
Pasadena	48,124	12,339	4,859	4,910	32.7
South Pasadena	9,157	2,764	1,046	959	35.0
Arcadia	12,793	9,848	4,865	4,217	38.9
Glendale	64,075	19,397	7,820	7,614	34.3
Alhambra	29,346	7,119	2,907	3,093	32.1
Monterey Park	18,982	5,870	3,007	3,113	33.9
La Canada Flintridge	4,837	3,110	1,161	982	40.8

Source: U.S. Census Bureau, 1990 Population and Housing Census.

A 43-question health survey was administered by *New Choices* magazine in June 1989 and one-half of the 5,600 subscribers who responded to the survey were aged 63 or older. Eighty percent of the respondents took at least one step to improve their health in 1989. The most popular methods included regular exercise and a good diet—low in fat, high in fiber, and plenty of fresh fruits and vegetables. Almost one-quarter (24 percent) of the respondents attend exercise regardless of their actual chronological age.[16] In general, the respondents were determined to take advantage of their capacity to live healthier and longer than ever before.

Demographics. Selected demographics for San Marino and surrounding cities are shown in Tables A2-1 and A2-2. These demographics include population breakdown, size of the respective age groups, and the median age of the population. These statistics will be used later to help determine the target market for Professional Fitness.

Economic and Business Conditions. As mentioned in the subsection on demand trends, the United States has been in a recession since the middle of 1990. This recession is unlike most other recessions in that it has hit white-collar workers as hard or harder than the blue-collar workers. Southern California has been hit especially hard this time around due to the large reductions in defense and aerospace spending. Within the past two years, more than one million jobs have disappeared in California.

---

[16]Carin Rubenstein, "Here's to Your Health," *New Choices for the Best Years,* Jan. 1990: 37–38.

The business section of the *Los Angeles Times* recently reported that 220,000 jobs have been lost per month over the past six months. The level of the consumer confidence index has also decreased to a level of 46.3, its lowest level since December 1974.[17] This monthly index measures how consumers feel about the economy and its future prospects, and its low level indicates that the consumer may not be willing to spend enough to pull the economy out of its tailspin.

Although the index of consumer spending is not inspiring, economic data obtained from the months of January and February 1992 indicate that a national recovery is underway. These indicators show that consumers are not acting as depressed as they feel, the real estate segment is responding to lower financing costs, car sales have picked up slightly, and the industrial sectors seem to be gaining back a portion of their lost momentum.[18]

Despite the recession, the cities of San Marino and Pasadena are doing quite well. A comparison of the 1990 and 1991 *Survey of Buying Power* published annually by the *Sales and Marketing Management* magazine, shows that in Pasadena the percentage of households with an effective buying income (EBI) of $50,000 or greater increased from 25.9 percent in 1990 to 28.5 percent in 1991. The group with an EBI of $35,000 to $49,999 also increased from 14.7 percent to 15.5 percent during this period of time. This increase in the percentage of households with an EBI of $35,000 and over is also seen in Arcadia, Alhambra, Glendale, and Monterey Park. In all these cities, the percentage increase in households with an EBI of $50,000 and over is significantly greater than the percentage increase of the $35,000 to $49,999 group for 1990 to 1991. Thus, the business conditions for the primary trading area of Professional Fitness are very encouraging.

State of Technology. The fitness equipment that is to be installed in Professional Fitness requires very little maintenance. Weight-resistance machines such as Cybex, Nautilus, David, and Flex require simple maintenance consisting of oiling and cleaning the cables and cams. Due to the low humidity in this area, rust would not be a worrisome factor. The spring-loaded mat that is to be used for aerobic classes would most likely require replacement every three to five years, depending on the level of usage. The saunas also require very little maintenance. The treated wood used in the construction of the saunas has to be inspected yearly and additional treatment or replacement of the panels might be needed.

Laws and Regulations. For zoning purposes, the city of San Marino falls within the C-1 commercial zone. Health clubs are considered establishments that possess "characteristics of such unique and special form as to make impractical an advance classification of permitted or prohibited use in the C-1 zone."[19] Thus, each establishment has to apply for a conditional use permit on an individual basis. City Hall officials gave guaranteed assurance that the required permits and business licenses for an upscale health club could be easily obtained. The required permits also include a building and safety inspection permit and a fire and health safety permit. These licenses and permits would cost approximately $1,730.

A separate conditional use permit is also required for any renovations of the leased site in excess of 20 percent of its value, over the period of five years. Approval for the renovation or remodeling plans shall be granted within 30 days of the application.

---

[17]Michael Mandel, "Bummed-Out in America," *Business Week,* March 16, 1992: 34.
[18]James C. Cooper and Kathleen Madigan, "Cross Your Fingers, Knock Wood: That May Be a Recovery Out There," *Business Week,* March 16, 1992: 31.
[19]Los Angeles County City Ordinance, Article III—C-1 Commercial Zone, Sect. 23.14 (C), p. 220.

Landscaping the exterior of the building and screening of parking spaces need the approval of the Planning Commission. Parking spaces that use concrete surfacing or asphalt placed on soil treated with weed control require further approval by the city.

The Neutral Environment

The neutral environment is to be analyzed using the following four categories:

1. Financial environments

2. Government environments

3. Media environments

4. Special interest environments

Financial Environments. Interest rates have currently dropped to their lowest levels in more than 15 years. The prime rate reported in the March 16, 1992, issue of *Business Week* index is 6.50 percent. Banks and other traditional lending institutions have vastly curtailed new business and other capital investment loans. Venture capitalists are currently also very careful about where they invest their money. However, good projects with minimal risks are still being funded, providing investors with competitive returns.

Funds needed to finance Professional Fitness can be obtained from either of three banks in the Pasadena area: Citizen's Bank, First Interstate Bank, or Bank of America. In general, these institutions quoted rates of 1 to 4 percent above prime for an unsecured, 8-year business loan amount of $375,000. The actual rate, be it prime-plus-one or prime-plus-four depends on the credit standings of the business lender. There is also a 1- to 2-point closing cost depending on the type of loan (secured or unsecured) and financial institution chosen. Funds from venture capitalists can also be sought at a competitive rate of 14 percent APR.

Government Environments. Initially, in 1985, the Federal Trade Commission (FTC), the government "watchdog" for unscrupulous consumer trade practices, decided not to issue industry-wide rules that would have regulated health clubs. The FTC based their 1985 decision on the fact that the pervasiveness of fraud and abuse cases was not occurring nationwide. Thus, the FTC decided to act on a case-by-case basis.[20]

Since 1988, an increasing number of complaints lodged against numerous health clubs have also caused the FTC to step in and close down a large number of clubs. These complaints have ranged from "hard-sell" sales techniques and misleading contracts to deceptive advertisement. A large number of health clubs have been sued by patrons charging that serious injuries were caused by unskilled instructors and poor equipment maintenance.[21]

Many states including California have now legislated formal regulations concerning the operation of health clubs and spas.[22] In general, the regulations mandate the following:

- A "cooling-off" period, during which a consumer can obtain a full refund of the paid membership fee. California law mandates this period to be 3 business days.

- A limit on the length of contract period. Some states forbid lifetime contracts.

---

[20]Margaret Engel, "Beware of Fitness Club Contracts," *Glamour,* Aug. 1987: 92.
[21]Walecia Konrad, "Health Clubs: Exercise Caution," *Business Week,* June 6, 1988: 142.
[22]"Is Your Health Club Healthy?" *Changing Times,* Sept. 1989: 116.

- Cancellation rights for members, in the event that the club relocates or that the member becomes disabled.

- A surety bond amount ranging from as low as $50,000 in several states to as high as $200,000 in Maryland to cover losses in the event that the club folds. California legislates a bond amount of $100,000.

Media Environments. Over the past three years, there has been increasing coverage in such media as documentaries, magazines, and research journals on fitness for the older population; on the positive effects of weight-bearing exercises on bone density, and on the importance of good nutrition. This attention has resulted in positive publicity for the health club industry. The health club industry has received some bad publicity through lawsuits brought about by unsatisfied members and the closing of unscrupulous clubs by the FTC.

A widely publicized experiment performed by Tufts University researchers on nursing home participants aged between 86 and 96 yielded extremely positive and conclusive results. The participants, most of whom suffered from either arthritis, hypertension, or heart disease, were put on a weight-training program to strengthen their legs. After only two months on the program, all the participants either doubled, tripled, or even quadrupled their leg strength. Two of the participants had even gained enough leg strength to discard their canes![23]

Medical researchers have also found the best way to prevent the onset of osteoporosis in women is to develop maximum bone mass prior to bone loss. In the past, women have largely avoided strength training and have preferred to stick with aerobic toning only, because of a perceived social stigma attached to developing muscle mass. Researchers have found that strength training, especially in women, can have an extremely beneficial effect on bone strength and density, and are thus stressing the importance of a specially designed strength training program for women.[24]

In addition to regular physical activity, the importance of a diet low in saturated fat and high in fiber, fruit, and vegetables is also currently stressed in a variety of media.[25]

Special Interest Environments. Three influential special interest groups include the American College of Sports Medicine, the National Health Club Association of Quality Clubs, and the Institute for Aerobics Research.

In 1978, the *American College of Sports Medicine* (ACSM) equated fitness with aerobic exercise and recommended aerobic exercise three to five days weekly for 15 to 60 minutes for all healthy adults. Due to current proven research on the benefits of strength training, these 1978 guidelines were revised in 1990 to include a twice-weekly routine of 8 to 10 different weight-bearing exercises to strengthen the legs, back, and chest—in addition to the three to five weekly aerobic workouts.[26] The ACSM also certifies instructors in preventive and rehabilitative health and fitness. This revised recommendation of the ACSM serves as a great opportunity for the health club industry to expand its market.

The *National Health Club Association* (NHCA) is primarily a "trade union" for health clubs nationwide. It costs $180 in yearly dues. There are currently over 2,000 privately owned clubs in the NHCA. Some of the benefits include SBA loan assistance, health insurance plans for owners and staff, group liability insurance plans, sales training seminars, and management workshops.

---

[23]Vic Sussman, "Muscle Bound," *U.S. News and World Report,* May 20, 1991: 88.
[24]Kenneth H. Cooper, M.D., "Fighting Back Against Bone Loss," *The Saturday Evening Post,* March 1991: 32.
[25]Susan Zarrow, "The New Diet Priorities," *Prevention,* Sept. 1991: 36.
[26]Cooper, p. 32.

The *Association of Quality Clubs* (AQC) assures that its member clubs adhere to a strict code of ethics. Affiliation with the AQC ensures club members that the club has attained a certain level of service and competence. Currently, there are approximately 1,550 clubs nationwide affiliated with the AQC. Most of these are upscale clubs that offer members seminars in weight reduction, stress management, and proper nutrition.

The *Institute of Aerobic Research* is the primary agency that certifies aerobic-class instructors. Certifications are available for physical fitness specialists and group exercise leaders.

The Competitor Environment

Professional Fitness has three main competitors. These health clubs are all located in the neighboring city of Pasadena. These clubs consist of the following:

1. Brignole Health and Fitness

2. Pasadena Athletic Club

3. World Gym, Pasadena

Brignole Health and Fitness. This health club is located on De Lacey Street in Pasadena. It has been in operation since 1985. This club will be the *primary competitor* of Professional Fitness. Brignole's offers a spring-loaded aerobic mat in the aerobics room; eight Lifecycles and Stairmasters; one tanning bed; a weight room consisting of Flex resistance machines and free weights, dumbbells ranging from 3 to 125 pounds; two squat cages, for intense thigh exercises (squats); a snack bar; and pro shop.

This club primarily targets the under 40, "yuppie" market and plans to merge with Sports Connection in the near future. This club is also going to be relocated to a larger facility, possibly in another neighboring city. Although the club is touted to be operated and owned by Mr. Doug Brignole, a top amateur bodybuilder from 1986 to 1988, this is not true. Brignole's is actually owned by a group of seven investors. These actual owners employ Mr. Brignole as the manager and pay him in addition to his salary, a small royalty to use his name for the club. Mr. Brignole has no formal marketing, management, or financial background and was once employed as a waiter in a Pasadena restaurant.

The annual membership fees have increased from $330 in 1987 to $550 presently with no initiation fee. The membership fee includes a personal training program and two free workouts with a trainer. The turnover at Brignole's is approximately 25 to 30 percent annually. Currently, the club boasts a membership of about 2,800 members.

Brignole's enjoys an enviable reputation with the members attending its aerobic classes and this can be considered as its greatest strength. Most aerobic instructors who teach at Brignole's are certified by the Institute of Aerobic Research and have won at least one award in nationwide or regional aerobic contests. Brignole Health and Fitness also offers child-care services (at no charge for the first hour) to its members.

Brignole's has three major weaknesses: untrained weight-lifting instructors, poor service attitudes, and poorly maintained weight-lifting equipment.

All of the instructors at Brignole's are male and none of them are certified by any reputable agency; most of them are not even certified. These instructors are able to spot a person during a lift, but have very little knowledge of the mechanics of proper form for the lift. The manager and the instructors also have a poor service attitude. They tend to give more personal service to female members who dress fashionably and are young, affluent, and attractive than to the average member, male or female. In other words, the level of personal service given to members is biased.

Finally, Brignole's has managed to turn away about half of its serious bodybuilders over the past five years, due to its poorly maintained and outdated equipment. In 1989 it promised its members that most of the weight-resistance machines would be given a complete overhaul and updated. This promise was never fulfilled through 1991.

Pasadena Athletic Club. This club has been in operation for almost 20 years, opening in 1973; it is located on Walnut Street in Pasadena. This club would not be in direct competition with Professional Fitness because it concentrates on a different market segment. It offers purely aerobic-oriented amenities and does not have a weight-training room. The club offers 3 tennis courts, 6 racquetball courts, an Olympic-sized pool, an indoor basketball court, sauna and dry-steam rooms, and a Jacuzzi. It also offers aerobic classes throughout the day.

A nonrefundable, nontransferable, one-time initiation fee of $400 is charged for families and $300 for singles. The monthly membership dues for family membership is $65 and $43 for singles. This fee includes unlimited usage of the facilities that operate from 6 A.M. to 11 P.M. on weekdays and from 7 A.M. to 10 P.M. on weekends. There is presently a 13-month waiting period for membership at this club for new members. The total number of memberships is currently limited to 2,500.

Pasadena Athletic Club is primarily a family-oriented club as opposed to a singles club as are most health clubs. An informal survey at the club showed that members were very satisfied with the personal service that they received and the amenities available.

The strengths of Pasadena Athletic Club include personable service, a great variety of different amenities, and long operating hours, even on the weekends. Weaknesses include a lack of instructors and pool safety personnel, a long waiting period for membership, and the unavailability of child-care services.

World Gym, Pasadena. This is a hard-core weight-lifting and bodybuilding gymnasium located on Altedena Drive in Pasadena. Although this club only opened on September 28, 1991, it already boasts a membership of about 1,200 members. Membership fees are $389 annually with no initiation fee. The club is open from 5:30 A.M. to 11 P.M. on weekdays and 7 A.M. to 7 P.M. on weekends.

World Gym has a land area of 10,000 square feet and does not have an aerobics room. The club offers state-of-the-art weight-lifting and bodybuilding equipment, including Cybex and Flex weight-resistance machines. It also has 10 Lifecycles, 8 Stairmasters, 2 treadmills, and an extensive variety of dumbbells, barbells, and weight racks. This club would not also be in direct competition with Professional Fitness as it targets primarily serious weight lifters and the under-40 market.

An effectiveness study was carried out on World Gym, Pasadena, in November 1991. A questionnaire (see Appendix) was used to gauge the level of satisfaction of its members with regard to the gym's offerings in terms of price, personnel, and equipment.[27] In general, the members were very satisfied with the level of service and equipment offered by the club. Almost one-third of the members were over 40 and three-quarters of the members lived within a six-mile radius of the club. There is also a three-to-one ratio of male to female members.

Strengths of World Gym include long operating hours, very personable owners and management, great equipment and training atmosphere. Its weaknesses include not having a formal marketing plan, no planned specific target market of its members and also, a lack of a specific and directed promotion campaign.

---

[27]Iain Mozoomdar, "A Study to Determine the Effectiveness of World Gym, Pasadena" (unpublished), Nov. 1991.

The Company Environment

Professional Fitness is to be positioned as an upscale health club in the city of San Marino. It will offer state-of-the-art weight-resistance machines, exercise bicycles, stair climbers, treadmills, cross-country ski simulators, saunas, and aerobic area.

The club will also provide child-care facilities with no time limit as long as the member is working out on the premises. The club will also offer the services of a licensed, professional masseuse at a subsidized rate. The pro shop will carry fashionable workout gear targeted at the over-40 market. The snack bar will carry healthy food items, such as yogurt, low-fat cottage cheese, protein and fruit shakes, sandwiches and the like, that are low in fat, sugar, and cholesterol and generally abide by the guidelines put forth by the American Heart Association (AHA).

The club is to be managed by a certified physical fitness specialist. He or she would preferably have a degree in physical education from an accredited university and a minimum of two years' experience in managing an upscale health club. Marketing, management, and financial consultants will be used when necessary. All aerobic or weight instructors and personal trainers must be certified by a reputable certification agency such as the American College of Sports Medicine or the Institute of Aerobic Research. At least one staff, trained and certified by the American Red Cross in CPR, will be present at all times. The club will also periodically conduct seminars on stress reduction, nutrition, and time management, with emphasis on the over-40 population. Seminars in yoga and meditation will also be offered. The club will limit its membership to 2,500 people. Ideally, this figure will be obtained within the span of three years.

The club is to be financed by a limited partnership of six partners. The cost of each partnership unit is $150,000. Each partner is guaranteed a sum of $1,500 per month with additional income distributions based on yearly gross sales figures. Additional financing would come from either an unsecured, eight-year business loan from a traditional lending institution or from a group of venture capitalists with a guaranteed return of 14 percent APR.

The strengths of Professional Fitness include a superior service attitude; knowledgeable, trained, and dedicated staff; and a nonthreatening and comfortable training atmosphere.

The weaknesses of Professional Fitness include the lack of a management consultant and a financial consultant on the permanent staff, the nonavailability of an Olympic-sized pool and Jacuzzi, a possible waiting period needed for new members after three years, and the difficulty of finding land needed for expansion of the club in San Marino, if necessary.

THE TARGET MARKET

Professional Fitness is to be located in the city of San Marino, California. There are two main reasons for choosing this city for the location of Professional Fitness.

The city of San Marino has, for the past two decades, been perceived to be a rich, upper-class town. This perception of San Marino is perfect for the positioning of Professional Fitness. This is to be positioned as an upscale health club and should thus be located in an upper-class neighborhood. According to the latest census results available with per capita income statistics (1988), the per capita income for San Marino for the period of 1979 to 1987 increased 68.5 percent, from $21,485 to $36,196. The per capita income for Beverly Hills in 1987 was $36,690, only 1.4 percent higher than San Marino. These figures clearly confirm that the perceived wealth of San Marino residents is not without foundation. San Marino is chosen also because it is surrounded by affluent cities such as Pasadena, South Pasadena, and Arcadia.

Assuming that the per capita income increases at the rate of 8.5 percent a year, the per capita income in 1991 for San Marino residents should be around $46,233. This health club is thus going to target executives who earn at least $40,000 annually.

As mentioned in the section on competitor environment, a study on the effectiveness of World Gym, Pasadena, revealed that although one-half of their members were above 30 years old, surprisingly, about one-third of their members were over 40. This finding proves that there is a viable market segment of older consumers. This finding is also in agreement with a large amount of published literature as mentioned in Section I. Thus, Professional Fitness will target clients from the over-40 age groups.

The clientele of Professional Fitness will be targeted toward individual consumers and corporate consumers. This club will not, however, entice groups of executives from a particular firm using special group rate discounts. Group rate discounts will damage the image of Professional Fitness as being an upscale club.

Geographically, the clientele is to be targeted from the primary areas of San Marino, Pasadena, South Pasadena, and Arcadia. Secondary areas to be targeted include Alhambra and Monterey Park to the south, Glendale to the east, and La Canada Flintridge to the west. This geographic targeting is immensely important, because the previous study on World Gym showed that over 75 percent of their clientele lived within a six-mile radius of the gymnasium. Another study conducted by the American Service Finance company in 1989 also showed that 80 percent of a club's members come from within a 15-minute drive radius.[28]

The ethnic groups to be targeted include Caucasians, Asians, and blacks. The highest earning ethnic group are Asians. Historically, a large majority of executive health club patrons have been Caucasians. American-born Chinese and other Asians have assimilated the American fitness lifestyle and patronize executive health clubs with the same frequency as the Caucasians. Over the past decade, an increasing number of black executives are beginning to patronize upscale health clubs. This could be due to the fact that, as an ethnic group, their income has also been steadily increasing over the same period of time.

From the population and age breakdowns in Section 1, there are approximately 139,206 people aged 40 and over, and are either Caucasian, Asian, or black in the target market. From the percentages quoted by the 1991 Survey of Buying Power, there are on average 46.5 percent of the people with an effective buying income of $35,000 or over in San Marino and the surrounding seven cities. Thus the market potential for Professional Fitness consists of 64,731 people. According to the survey by the Association of Quality Clubs (Section I), only about 10 percent of them belong to a health-club-penetrated market. Thus, conservatively, Professional Fitness will have an *effective target market* of approximately 58,258 *people*. This is a conservative estimate, as people aged 65 and over were not included.

In summary, the typical customer profile of Professional Fitness shall include:

- Age group: 40 and over
- Income: $40,000 and over annually
- Sex: Male or female
- Education: College graduates
- Occupation: White-collar workers—executives, or retirees

---

[28]"American Service Finance Renewal Study (1989)," *National Health Club Association,* 1991 (reprinted with permission).

- Family life cycle: Full nest III, empty nest I, and empty nest II[29]
- VALS Scale: Achievers or Experientials[30]
- Benefits sought: Prestige, quality, and service
- Location: San Marino, Pasadena, South Pasadena, Arcadia, Alhambra, Monterey Park, Glendale, and La Canada Flintridge

OPPORTUNITIES AND THREATS

Opportunities

Professional Fitness is presented with the following opportunities:

- There are at present no upscale health clubs specializing in aerobic and weight training in San Marino.
- There are no clubs in the immediate vicinity that specialize in providing upscale exercise facilities for the over-40 segment.
- Current research by the AMA and the ACSM prove that weight training is beneficial for all ages, regardless of sex and physical condition.
- Only 10 percent of people over 40 belong to a health club.
- The current demographic shift of the American population is projected to cause the 18-to-34 age group to shrink 11 percent during the 1990s.

First, since there are presently no upscale health clubs in San Marino, Professional Fitness would be able to position itself easily in the market without facing stiff competition and entry barriers from other upscale club providers. The club would also be able to maintain an effective physical and psychological separation between itself and its three main competitors in Pasadena.

Second, there is no club in the primary trading area of Professional Fitness that specializes in clients aged 40 and over. This relatively untapped niche presents new and profitable market opportunities for the maturing health club industry. This segment also has special needs that can be adequately fulfilled by Professional Fitness. Some of the special requirements include the hiring of older instructors, specialized programs to serve the mature consumer, the "extra" personal service, or pampering expected by the older consumer, and so on.

Third, current medical research, as mentioned in Section I, also helps to educate and motivate the older consumer. This club presents the opportunity for older consumers in the primary trading area to enhance the quality of their life, and to enter the golden years armed with the necessary physical strength to combat painful and debilitating diseases such as arthritis and osteoporosis.

Fourth, since a survey conducted by the Association of Quality Clubs showed that only 10 percent of people aged 40 and over belong to a health club, there is a viable and reachable market segment for the club.

Finally, the aging population also ensures that the over-40 market will expand in the 1990s and into the year 2000. Thus, the effective target market will increase beyond the estimated 58,258 people.

---

[29]Philip Kotler, *Marketing Management* (Englewood Cliffs, NJ: Prentice-Hall, 1991), 7th ed., p. 171.
[30]Ibid., p. 173.

Threats

Threats faced by Professional Fitness include the following:

- Increased federal, state, or city regulations
- Lawsuits against the club
- Entry of new competitors
- Decline in the overall health club industry

First, increased regulations could potentially affect the profit motive of the club. The management of the club has to be alert for changes in the legal environment—environment scanning—and do their utmost to adapt to it.

Second, if lawsuits are brought against the club by members, the club will try to settle out of court to avoid excessive negative publicity. Ideally, this situation can be completely avoided through the use of qualified and trained personnel, and well-maintained equipment.

The last two threats—entry of new competitors and a decline in the industry—are inevitable. Professional Fitness will thus strive to maintain the goodwill of its customers through exceptional personal service and dedication. The club will also fiercely defend its position as an upscale club to enhance its prestigious appeal.

MARKETING OBJECTIVES AND GOALS

Mission Statement

Professional Fitness will provide an exceptional level of personal service and state-of-the-art equipment to our clients while maintaining a return of investment of 15 percent in the first year of operation. All of our clients and customers will be treated equally and with utmost respect regardless of race, sex, or religious preferences. Business operations will be conducted in a legal, ethical, and safe manner as described by federal laws, California state laws, and all applicable county and city ordinances.

Objectives of the Firm

- Establish a limited partnership under the laws of the state of California
- Achieve and maintain a return on investment of 20 percent by the end of year 2
- Break even within 18 months
- Achieve a minimum market share of 3.5 percent by year 3
- Achieve a minimum average sales volume of 100 memberships per month in year 1
- Achieve $1,300,000 in sales by the end of year 1
- Achieve $2,000,000 in sales by the end of year 2

MARKETING STRATEGY

As mentioned earlier, the health club industry's growth has slowed down from approximately 15 percent annually to just under 10 percent. Thus, although the industry is still growing, its sales are increasing at a decreasing rate, and it has thus reached the maturity stage of its life cycle. The industry has, until recently, been focusing primarily on the 18-to-34 age group.

Professional Fitness is to pursue a *market-nicher strategy.* It is also going to be positioned as a quality/price specialist—high-quality equipment and impeccable service, high-price end of the industry; and an end-user specialist—over-40 segment. This strategy is very attractive to Professional Fitness due to its relatively limited capital resources. Niche marketing has also proven to be successful for firms in mature industries. An ideal market niche has the following characteristics:

- Sufficient growth potential
- Sufficient size and buying power
- Negligible interest to major competitors

In addition, the "nicher" firm needs to have the capacity and resources available to serve the niche effectively, and be able to defend its position through built-up customer goodwill.[31]

As was explained in the previous sections, the over-40 segment has sufficient growth potential, size, and buying power. Also, the three competitors of Professional Fitness are currently not pursuing this segment. This club will be specifically designed to provide the manpower and resources needed to serve the segment and protect its position through built-up goodwill.

Since the industry is in its maturity phase, this club will be designed also to effectively serve the early majority and to compete in a monopolistic competition-based market structure. Thus, product differentiation is crucial for the long-term survival of the club and will be discussed in detail in the next section.

Professional Fitness will also try to increase its market penetration by encouraging the adoption of individual, tailor-made programs of weight training and aerobic classes that enhance the quality and preservation of life as the consumer ages, in place of other generic aerobic activities such as jogging, tennis, or golf. Hence, joining Professional Fitness will be a wiser and more educated choice than an upscale athletic or racket club, such as the Pasadena Athletic Club.

This strategy would most likely evoke a defensive response from Pasadena Athletic Club (PAC) and other such facilities. Due to its business experience, PAC might try to engage in price competition and attempt to use the superb-value strategy—offering high quality at a low price. While this strategy would be effective with a majority of products, health club consumers in Pasadena and its neighboring cities are typically upscale customers with relatively inelastic price sensitivities. Thus offering a lower price would most likely damage PAC's prestige factor and in effect, possibly lower its market share instead of increasing it.

Due to this customer profile and price inelasticity, Professional Fitness will not compete in price competition, rather it will defend its competitive position by enhancing the prestige and exclusiveness of the club; in short—"snob appeal." The level of personal service, ambience, and state-of-the-art technology will be emphasized.

MARKETING TACTICS

The market-nicher strategy of Professional Fitness is to be implemented using the four tactical variables of:

1. Product   **3.** Promotion

2. Price   **4.** Distribution

---

[31]Ibid., pp. 395–396.

Product

The heart of Professional Fitness is its personable stuff and state-of-the-art equipment. This subsection is to be discussed using the following categories:

1. Equipment and facilities

2. Staff

3. Hours of operation

Equipment and Facilities. One of the objectives of this club is to promote "health club addiction." This can be achieved in part by the offering of state-of-the-art equipment and excellent facilities. Weight-resistance machines made by Cybex, David, Flex, and Nautilus will be offered. Satin-finished barbells and dumbbells will be purchased from Ironman Inc. The saunas will be made by an American leader in the field—Hex Equipment. Standard and recumbent type exercise bicycles will be offered, and purchased from Universal Inc. and Nautilus, respectively. The stair climbers will also be purchased from Universal Inc. Treadmills will be ordered from Quinton Fitness Equipment, known for its attractive state-of-the-art machines. Finally, cross-country ski exercisers that promote superior total-body aerobic workouts will be purchased from NordicTrack. Three massage tables will also be provided, along with the services of a professional masseuse at a special club rate for members.

Cybex weight machines come in an attractive white finish. The workmanship on these machines is superb, and they are designed according to stringent engineering standards. These machines offer a high degree of safety, reliability, and durability as well as a state of the art appearance. In addition, Cybex machines offer an unparalleled degree of smoothness through their range of movement, and are ideal for people with joint stiffness or prior injuries. These machines are also angled correctly so as to lessen the chance of injury due to bad posture during a lift.

A unique feature of David weight machines is that, in addition to standard models, the company offers an extensive line of equipment designed primarily for women. These machines have lighter poundages and are designed for people that stand under 5 feet 7 inches. David machines are extensively used by women-only clubs all over the country. Professional Fitness will purchase some of these specially designed weight machines to cater to the needs of its female members and older members.

Flex and Nautilus machines are both attractively designed in blue or gray finishes. Both these companies offer state-of-the-art equipment that is functional, durable, and upscale. These companies also include a lifetime warranty on their machines and free scheduled maintenance by factory personnel for a period of two years. These machines also provide extremely smooth operation throughout their range of motion.

All the preceding machines use sealed ball bearings that help prolong the life of the machines by sealing out dirt and other environmental contaminants. These machines will also enhance the upscale appearance of the club.

The saunas made by Hex Equipment feature high-quality treated wood. Wood treatment is of utmost importance in the construction of the sauna, and the company prides itself in having the "best-treated wood in America." These saunas also feature individually adjustable heat controls located inside each sauna. This feature is also extremely useful in the prevention of heatstroke and dizziness. Most saunas are controlled externally and its occupants have no mechanical control over the interior temperature except to manually open the door when the heat becomes overbearing.

The standard and recumbent exercise bicycles made by Universal and Nautilus feature state-of-the-art technology and appearance. These machines are made for heavy commercial use. Recumbent bicycles are ideal for older members because they provide more comfortable seats that follow the natural curvature of the spine and thus offer better lower lumbar support. These machines also provide attractive computer controls and intensity level readouts.

Like its exercise bicycle, stair climbers offered by Universal also provide intensity readouts and a computer-controlled hydraulic stepping mechanism that is designed not to overly stress knees and ankles. NordicTrack's cross-country ski machines also provide smooth operation that reduces harmful stress on the joints. Finally, treadmills offered by Quinton Fitness are used in exclusive corporate clubs nationwide and also in NASA's astronaut training facility. They also feature a state-of-the-art appearance and technology.

The aerobic room will be partitioned off from the weight-training section of the club. A state-of-the-art sound system will be offered and a custom-made, spring-loaded mat will be ordered to lessen the intensity of impact on the knee joints. This room will be soundproofed to ensure maximum comfort for other members not attending aerobic classes. This would also enhance the prestigious appeal of the club.

Professional Fitness will also provide a child-care center staffed by certified child-care professionals. This center is to be used by members while they are working out. No time limits shall be imposed on the members.

A health bar serving foods low in fat, sugar, and cholesterol, and high in fiber will also be offered. This bar will serve low-fat yogurt, sherbet, protein shakes, and other such foods. Fresh juices and sandwiches will also be served.

A professional masseuse will also be available at a special club rate for members. Sixty-minute massages usually cost between $45 and $80. The club hopes to negotiate a price of $30 to $35 for its members.

The pro shop will feature the latest workout fashions targeted at the over-40 market. The member lounge will offer a large-screen television, laser disc player, videocassette recorder, and comfortable sofas for members. Members will be encouraged to use the lounge for informal business meetings and social purposes.

Staff. As mentioned in the subsection on company environment, Professional Fitness will only employ certified fitness personnel. The hired fitness personnel will be trained to provide exceptional personal service and formulate correct, custom-tailored exercise programs for the clientele. The club is to be managed by a physical fitness specialist. He or she must have a degree in physical fitness from an accredited university and at least two years' experience managing an upscale health club.

The manager will report to the board of directors, comprising the six partners. The manager will be given full authority to implement any training program for the fitness instructors employed by the club. Although the manager will also be given the autonomy to manage the club as he or she sees fit, the manager needs to report on the progress of any improvement plans or staff training schedule to the board of directors monthly. The board of directors will intervene only when it feels that the ongoing plans or training programs are contrary to the prestigious and sophisticated image and positioning of the club.

The manager will be paid an annual salary of $30,000 initially. A salary increase based on a good performance appraisal is possible after nine months. The manager will also receive additional monetary incentives if the club performs well financially after the first year of operation. The other employees will be started at a rate of $10 per hour based on a standard 40-hour week. This basic rate will be raised to $11 in the second year of the club's operations. Standard overtime pay will also be given. This rate will be one and one-half times hourly wage for weekdays and two times hourly wage for nonscheduled weekends. Employees will be required to work on some weekends.

Employees will be instructed in personal service, operating procedures, and personal hygiene. The club will also provide uniforms to the staff. Laundry and dry-cleaning expenses will be the responsibility of the employee.

Hours of Operation. The club will be open seven days a week, from 5 A.M. to 11 P.M. on weekdays (Monday to Friday) and 7 A.M. to 10 P.M. on weekends. These hours are determined based on the research done on World Gym, Pasadena.

Price

Professional Fitness is to be priced as an upscale club. The use of a premium pricing strategy will be employed—high price and high quality. This strategy is very viable in the health club market in this geographic area due to the relatively inelastic price sensitivities of the upscale consumer.

As mentioned in the subsection on competitor environment, PAC is the only fitness club in the immediate area that charges an initiation fee. Their initiation fee is $300 and the monthly dues are $43 for single members, and $400 initiation and $65 monthly dues for families. This strategy has worked well for PAC as it has been pursuing good-value strategy—low price coupled with medium-quality product.

Professional Fitness will charge members a $675 initiation fee and monthly dues of $75. It will have a maximum membership of 2,500. This price range is justified because the club is to be positioned to promote and enhance a country club atmosphere and ambience. The club would not price itself out of the market with this price either, since exclusive clubs in Los Angeles charge as much as $2,000 in initiation fees.

The club expects to attract 1,200 members in its first year, 1,800 in the second, and 2,300 in the third year with this price. This is a conservative estimate, since World Gym, Pasadena boasts a membership of 1,200 members in just 5½ months of operation.

Monthly expected cash flows, pro forma income statements, and balance sheets for a period of 36 months using this estimate will be shown in the next section—"Control and Implementation."

Various membership scenarios follow:

- Optimistic

    Year 1: 1,600 members
    Year 2: 2,100 members
    Year 3: 2,500 members

- Conservative

    Year 1: 1,200 members
    Year 2: 1,800 members
    Year 3: 2,300 members

- Pessimistic

    Year 1: 900 members
    Year 2: 1,500 members
    Year 3: 2,000 members

Promotion

The promotion campaign that is to be used to launch Professional Fitness will be divided into two segments:

1. Precommercialization phase including the Grand Opening

2. Regular promotional mix for the first two years of operation

Precommercialization Phase. The promotional campaign that is to be used in this phase is to last a period of 13 weeks. The Grand Opening, which is to last an entire week, occurs in the last week of this phase. The promotional budget for this entire phase is $100,000. The promotion mix that is to be used includes direct mail, print and radio media advertising, sales promotion, and publicity. The advertising platform will be designed to emphasize the high degree of personal service and the exclusive "country club" ambience of the club, the importance of improving the quality of life as one ages, and the benefits of feeling younger instead of looking younger. These issues will be the central theme for all the components of the promotion mix.

Direct mail will be used to reach corporate customers. This campaign will start at week 1 and continue through the grand opening. Color brochures will be sent out to selected businesses in all eight cities, especially in Glendale, Pasadena, and La Canada Flintridge, at the rate of 250 per week.

Print advertising and spot-radio advertising will be used. Advertisements will be placed in the *Los Angeles* magazine; the *Star News,* the Pasadena daily newspaper; and the Southern California Community newspapers for the cities of San Marino, Alhambra, Monterey Park, South Pasadena, and Arcadia. The *Los Angeles* magazine is chosen because it has readership of over 1 million upscale consumers, 70 percent of whom are over 35. This magazine also has the capability of offering a four-color display advertisement instead of black and white. The *Star News* has a readership of around 45,000 in the Pasadena, San Marino, and South Pasadena areas and about one-half of them are aged 40 and over. The Southern California Community Newspapers are weekly papers published every Thursday, and can be custom designed to reach the targeted cities previously mentioned. These papers have a readership of around 73,000, half of which are businesses.

Spot radio will also be used to target older audiences. KKGO 105.1 FM is the only classical music station in Los Angeles and has a listenership of 550,000 people spanning Ventura to San Bernardino counties. The station states that more than 80 percent of its audience are upscale consumers, aged 35 and over. Advertisements will also be placed on K-BIG 104.3 FM. This station boasts a listenership of more than 1 million weekly; about 40 percent of them are aged between 35 and 54.

Publicity releases will also be issued to various news stations. The publicity campaign will promote a cause-related marketing plan. A $25 donation will be given to either the Green Peace ecological movement or the Los Angeles Mission for every new member who joins Professional Fitness. The donation will be made quarterly. This campaign will also help the club's corporate social image and standing in the community.

The Grand Opening will take place on the last week of the phase—the thirteenth week. This event will be designed to last for an entire week. During the Grand Opening, the public relations personnel from the Los Angeles Mission and Green Peace will be invited to give promotional talks on their respective organizations. This event is also expected to attract fitness celebrities such as Arnold Schwarzenegger, Lou Ferrigno, and others. Snacks and entertainment will also be provided.

Sales promotion, in the form of a sweepstakes, will also be used during the Grand Opening. A five-day/four-night cruise for two to either Mexico or Hawaii will be offered daily throughout the seven days. The Grand Opening will last from Sunday to Saturday the following week.

The cost breakdown of this precommercial campaign and Grand Opening is shown in Table A2-3 and Figure A2-2. A Gnatt chart for the implementation of this campaign is shown in Table A2-4.

Table A2-3 Promotion Campaign for Precommercialization Phase and Grand Opening

Direct Mail
  $4.00 per mailing × 3,250 mailings $13,000.00

Print Advertising
  Newspapers
    Star News
      6 × ½-page ads @ $1,770.75   10,624.50
    Southern California Community Newspapers (SCCN)
      6 × ½-page ads @ $1,315.20 (Thursdays)   7,891.20
  Magazines
    Los Angeles
      3 × 4-color, ½-page ads @ $4,800 (monthly)   14,400.00

Radio Advertising
  KKGO 105.1 FM - Classical
    3 months × 48 spots/month @ $125 per 30-seconds   18,000.00
  K-BIG 104.3 FM
    3 months × 48, 30-second spots/month @ $5,000   15,000.00

Sales Promotion
  7 × 5-day/4-night cruise for two to Mexico/Hawaii
  @@$1,000—awarded during Grand Opening   7,000.00

Grand Opening
  7 days × $500 per day   3,500.00

Subtotal $ 89,415.70
Outside services—ad agency and miscellaneous   10,584.30
Total $100,000.00

Figure A2-2   Precommercialization Promotion Mix Costs Allocation

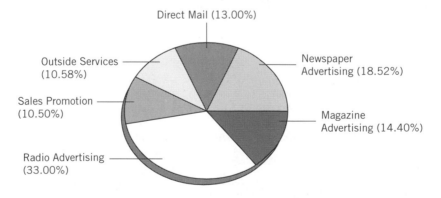

Regular Promotion Mix. The cost of the promotion mix for the first three years of operation amounts to $108,000 yearly, or $9,000 per month. This mix is identical to that of the precommercialization phase, with the exception of times and frequency of advertising. For example, ads will be placed in the Los Angeles magazine every other month—six times per year. Sweepstakes will be offered only once a year, on the yearly anniversary of the club. The costs of this regular promotion mix are shown in Table A2-5 and Figure A2-3 and a Gnatt chart for its implementation is shown in Table A2-6.

Table A2-4 Gnatt Chart for Precommercialization Promotion Mix

PROMOTION	WEEK												
	1	2	3	4	5	6	7	8	9	10	11	12	13
Direct Mail	▨	▨											
Star News			▨		▨		▨		▨		▨		▨
SCCN		▨		▨		▨		▨					
L.A. Magazine				▨				▨				▨	
KKGO 105.1 FM		▨	▨	▨	▨	▨	▨	▨	▨				
K-BIG 104.3 FM		▨	▨	▨	▨	▨	▨	▨	▨	▨	▨	▨	▨
Sweepstakes													▨

Table A2-5 Promotion Campaign for Year 1 to Year 3 of Professional Fitness

Direct Mail
  $4.00 per mailing × 1,200 mailings $ 4,800.00

Print Advertising
  Newspapers
    Star News (2 times per month for 6 months)
      12 × ¼-page ads @ $881.60   10,579.20
    Southern California Community Newspapers (SCCN)
      26 × ¼-page ads @ $621.30 (Thursdays)   16,153.80
  Magazines
    Los Angeles
      6 months × 4-color, ½-page ads @ $4,515   27,090.00

Radio Advertising
  KKGO 105.1 FM-Classical
    6 months × 24 spots/month @ $125 per 30-seconds   18,000.00
  K-BIG 104.3 FM
    6 months × 24, 30-second spots/month @ $2,500   15,000.00

Sales Promotion
  1 × 2-week cruise for two to Europe
  @$4,500—awarded during Anniversary Party   4,500.00

Anniversary Party (AP)
  1 × $3,500 per event   3,500.00

Subtotal $ 99,623.00
Outside services—ad agency and miscellaneous   8,377.00

Total $108,000.00

Figure A2-3   Regular Promotion Mix Costs Allocation

Direct Mail (4.44%)
Outside Services (7.76%)
Sales Promotion (7.41%)
Newspaper Advertising (24.75%)
Magazine Advertising (25.08%)
Radio Advertising (30.56%)

Table A2-6 Gnatt Chart for Promotion Mix of Year 1 to Year 3

PROMOTION	MONTH											
	1	2	3	4	5	6	7	8	9	10	11	12
Direct Mail	▓	▓	▓	▓	▓	▓	▓	▓	▓	▓	▓	▓
Star News	▓		▓		▓		▓		▓		▓	
SCCN			▓		▓		▓		▓		▓	
L.A. Magazine			▓		▓		▓		▓		▓	
KKGO 105.1 FM	▓		▓		▓		▓		▓		▓	
K-BIG 104.3 FM	▓		▓		▓		▓		▓		▓	
Sweepstakes	▓											

Distribution

Professional Fitness is a direct service facility. Thus, to promote the upscale and sophisticated image that the club desires, the interior of the facility has to be decorated accordingly.

The interior of the club is to be designed using a subdued color scheme of a combination of pastel blue, pale green, pink, and ivory, since these colors tend to be preferred by educated people, and also seem to sell well throughout the country.[32]

---

[32]Marshall E. Reddick, *Entrepreneurship* (Los Angeles: California State University, Los Angeles, 1990), p. 143.

The furniture and lighting fixtures will have an upscale appearance and complement the rest of the club's decor. The aim is to provide a facility that is conducive to upscale consumers. Furthermore, towels and other essential toiletries will be also provided for the clients.

If this club is extremely profitable after three years, there is a possibility that the club might start an upscale health club franchise. This move will only take place after the Board of Directors incorporates the company, thus obtaining the rights to issue stock and sell bonds.

CONTROL AND IMPLEMENTATION

Start-Up Costs

The start-up cost for Professional Fitness is shown in Table A2-7. The total start-up cost is $1,274,055. Thus, a bank loan of $374,055 will be required. With the prevailing low interest rate, the assumption is that an unsecured, 8-year business loan is obtainable at a rate of prime plus two, that is, 8.5 percent. This assumed rate will be used in all future interest calculations.

The outlay required for the precommercialization promotional campaign and Grand Opening is calculated as part of start-up and fixed costs.

Break-Even Analysis

Since Professional Fitness makes a donation of $25 to charity for every new member who joins the club, the effective initiation fee is $650. The yearly dues for each member amount to $900 ($75 × 12). Thus, each new member pays an effective total of $1,550 for the first year of membership. Most of this fee represents fixed cost, the only variable

Table A2-7 Start-Up Costs

Remodeling and Equipment	
Equipment and furniture	$ 400,000
Remodeling and air-conditioning/heating system	675,000
Computer system	10,000
Inventory and supplies	15,000
Advertising	
Precommercialization promotion campaign	100,000
Deposits and Other Fees	
Lease of 12,000 square feet @ $1.20 per sq. ft..	
3 months prepaid lease + last month + 1 month security deposit	72,000
Utilities deposit	325
Legal fees	
Fire and health safety, city permits, and business license	1,730
Total Start-Up Costs	$1,274,055
Partners' equity	(900,000)
Loan Amount	$ 374,055

Figure A2-4

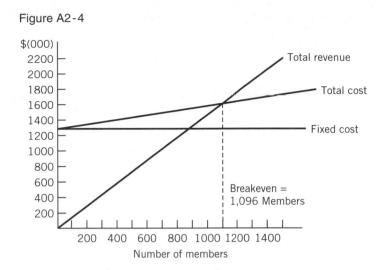

amount being staff salaries. Out of each new member's $1,550 approximately 25 percent goes toward staff salaries. Thus:

Break-even volume = Fixed cost/Price − Variable cost
= $1,274,055/($1,550 − $387.5)
= 1,096 members (see Figure A2-4).

Pro Forma Monthly Cash Flows

Pro forma monthly cash flows have been computed for 36 months (Table A2-8a to A2-8f). The health club industry in Southern California is relatively constant except for the months of January and May. There is usually an increase over normal membership numbers during these two months. In January, many people get very motivated about their New Year's resolutions to lose weight, and hence an increase in membership to health clubs. In May, people want to trim down before the summer months actually arrive so that they can fit into the previous year's swimsuits! For the rest of the year, the demand is relatively constant.

The following assumptions are made in the monthly cash-flow calculations:

- The club is to open on November 1, 199X. This is done so that the club gets two whole months to smooth out initial "kinks," before January arrives.
- The conservative membership assumption is used: 1,200 members in year 1; 1,800 in year 2: 2,300 in year 3.
- There is a constant level of memberships sold in year 1 for every month except for January and May. There will be 90 memberships sold every month for 10 months, and 150 memberships each month in January and May.
- Interest paid on the 8-year $374,055 loan amounts to $5,383.45 monthly at 8.5 percent APR. Monthly lease payments amount to $14,400. This lease payment starts on month 4, because there was three months' prepaid rent.
- In year 2, the club gets a 70 percent renewal rate and 30 percent of year 1's members drop out. An assumption made is that the club loses this 30 percent of year 1's members at a constant monthly rate. For example, by the end of year 2, the club will have 0.7 × 1,200 = 840 members who signed up in year 1. The 360 members who dropped out did so at a rate of 30 members a month. In order to have

Table A2-8a Pro Forma Monthly Cash Flow for Professional Fitness for Month 1 to Month 6

	1	2	3	4	5	6
REVENUES						
Initiation Fees	$58,500.00	$58,500.00	$ 97,500.00	$58,500.00	$58,500.00	$ 58,500.00
Monthly Dues	6,750.00	13,500.00	20,250.00	31,500.00	38,250.00	45,000.00
Total Revenues	$65,250.00	$72,000.00	$117,750.00	$90,000.00	$96,750.00	$103,500.00
EXPENSES						
Salaries	$27,140.00	$27,140.00	$ 27,140.00	$37,700.00	$37,700.00	$ 37,700.00
Rent	0.00	0.00	0.00	14,400.00	14,400.00	14,400.00
Advertising	9,000.00	9,000.00	9,000.00	9,000.00	9,000.00	9,000.00
Maintenance	1,500.00	1,500.00	1,500.00	1,500.00	1,500.00	1,500.00
Administration	1,000.00	1,000.00	1,000.00	1,000.00	1,000.00	1,000.00
Supplies	1,000.00	1,000.00	1,000.00	1,000.00	1,000.00	1,000.00
Insurance	3,000.00	3,000.00	3,000.00	3,000.00	3,000.00	3,000.00
Utilities	2,500.00	2,500.00	2,500.00	2,750.00	2,750.00	2,750.00
Depreciation	6,833.33	6,833.33	6,833.33	6,833.33	6,833.33	6,833.33
Loan Interest	5,383.45	5,383.45	5,383.45	5,383.45	5,383.45	5,383.45
Outside Services	5,000.00	5,000.00	5,000.00	5,000.00	5,000.00	5,000.00
Total Expenses	$62,356.78	$62,356.78	$ 62,356.78	$87,566.78	$87,566.78	$ 87,566.78
NET PROFIT (LOSS)	**$ 2,893.22**	**$ 9,643.22**	**$ 55,393.22**	**$ 2,433.22**	**$ 9,183.22**	**$ 15,933.22**

Table A2-8b Pro Forma Monthly Cash Flow for Professional Fitness for Month 7 to Month 12

	7	8	9	10	11	12
REVENUES						
Initiation Fees	$ 97,500.00	$ 58,500.00	$ 58,500.00	$ 58,500.00	$ 58,500.00	$ 58,500.00
Monthly Dues	51,750.00	63,000.00	69,750.00	76,500.00	82,500.00	90,000.00
Total Revenues	$149,250.00	$121,500.00	$128,250.00	$135,000.00	$141,000.00	$148,500.00
EXPENSES						
Salaries	$ 37,700.00	$ 37,700.00	$ 37,700.00	$ 45,240.00	$ 45,240.00	$ 45,240.00
Rent	14,400.00	14,400.00	14,400.00	14,400.00	14,400.00	14,400.00
Advertising	9,000.00	9,000.00	9,000.00	9,000.00	9,000.00	9,000.00
Maintenance	1,500.00	1,500.00	1,500.00	1,500.00	1,500.00	1,500.00
Administration	1,500.00	1,500.00	1,500.00	1,500.00	1,500.00	1,500.00
Supplies	1,500.00	1,500.00	1,500.00	1,500.00	1,500.00	1,500.00
Insurance	3,000.00	3,000.00	3,000.00	3,000.00	3,000.00	3,000.00
Utilities	3,000.00	3,000.00	3,000.00	3,000.00	3,000.00	3,000.00
Depreciation	6,833.33	6,833.33	6,833.33	6,833.33	6,833.33	6,833.33
Loan Interest	5,383.45	5,383.45	5,383.45	5,383.45	5,383.45	5,383.45
Outside Services	5,000.00	5,000.00	5,000.00	5,000.00	5,000.00	5,000.00
Total Expenses	$ 88,816.78	$ 88,816.78	$ 88,816.78	$ 96,356.78	$ 96,356.78	$ 96,356.78
NET PROFIT (LOSS)	**$ 60,433.22**	**$ 32,683.22**	**$ 39,433.22**	**$ 38,643.22**	**$ 44,643.22**	**$ 52,143.22**

Table A2-8c Pro Forma Monthly Cash Flow for Professional Fitness for Month 13 to Month 18

	13	14	15	16	17	18
REVENUES						
Initiation Fees	$ 48,750.00	$ 48,750.00	$ 68,250.00	$ 48,750.00	$ 48,750.00	$ 48,750.00
Monthly Dues	93,375.00	96,750.00	102,375.00	105,750.00	109,125.00	112,500.00
Total Revenues	$142,125.00	$145,500.00	$170,625.00	$154,500.00	$157,875.00	$161,250.00
EXPENSES						
Salaries	$ 57,772.00	$ 57,772.00	$ 57,772.00	$ 63,580.00	$ 63,580.00	$ 63,580.00
Rent	14,400.00	14,400.00	14,400.00	14,400.00	14,400.00	14,400.00
Advertising	9,000.00	9,000.00	9,000.00	9,000.00	9,000.00	9,000.00
Maintenance	1,500.00	1,500.00	1,500.00	1,500.00	1,500.00	1,500.00
Administration	2,000.00	2,000.00	2,000.00	2,000.00	2,000.00	2,000.00
Supplies	2,000.00	2,000.00	2,000.00	2,000.00	2,000.00	2,000.00
Insurance	3,500.00	3,500.00	3,500.00	3,500.00	3,500.00	3,500.00
Utilities	3,250.00	3,250.00	3,250.00	3,250.00	3,250.00	3,250.00
Depreciation	6,833.33	6,833.33	6,833.33	6,833.33	6,833.33	6,833.33
Loan Interest	5,756.85	5,756.85	5,756.85	5,756.85	5,756.85	5,756.85
Outside Services	5,000.00	5,000.00	5,000.00	5,000.00	5,000.00	5,000.00
Total Expenses	$111,012.18	$111,012.18	$111,012.18	$116,820.18	$116,820.18	$116,820.18
NET PROFIT (LOSS)	**$ 31,112.82**	**$ 34,487.82**	**$ 59,612.82**	**$ 37,679.82**	**$ 41,054.82**	**$ 44,429.82**

Table A2-8d Pro Forma Monthly Cash Flow for Professional Fitness for Month 19 to Month 24

	19	20	21	22	23	24
REVENUES						
Initiation Fees	$ 68,250.00	$ 48,750.00	$ 48,750.00	$ 48,750.00	$ 48,750.00	$ 48,750.00
Monthly Dues	118,125.00	121,500.00	124,875.00	128,250.00	131,625.00	135,000.00
Total Revenues	$186,375.00	$170,250.00	$173,625.00	$177,000.00	$180,375.00	$183,750.00
EXPENSES						
Salaries	$ 69,388.00	$ 69,388.00	$ 69,388.00	$ 75,696.00	$ 75,696.00	$ 75,696.00
Rent	14,400.00	14,400.00	14,400.00	14,400.00	14,400.00	14,400.00
Advertising	9,000.00	9,000.00	9,000.00	9,000.00	9,000.00	9,000.00
Maintenance	1,500.00	1,500.00	1,500.00	1,500.00	1,500.00	1,500.00
Administration	2,250.00	2,250.00	2,250.00	2,250.00	2,250.00	2,250.00
Supplies	2,250.00	2,250.00	2,250.00	2,250.00	2,250.00	2,250.00
Insurance	3,500.00	3,500.00	3,500.00	3,500.00	3,500.00	3,500.00
Utilities	3,500.00	3,500.00	3,500.00	3,500.00	3,500.00	3,500.00
Depreciation	6,833.33	6,833.33	6,833.33	6,833.33	6,833.33	6,833.33
Loan Interest	5,756.85	5,756.85	5,756.85	5,756.85	5,756.85	5,756.85
Outside Services	6,000.00	6,000.00	6,000.00	6,000.00	6,000.00	6,000.00
Total Expenses	$124,378.18	$124,378.18	$124,378.18	$130,686.18	$130,686.18	$130,686.18
NET PROFIT (LOSS)	**$ 61,996.82**	**$ 45,871.82**	**$ 49,246.82**	**$ 46,313.82**	**$ 49,688.82**	**$ 53,063.82**

Table A2-8e Pro Forma Monthly Cash Flow for Professional Fitness for Month 25 to Month 30

	25	26	27	28	29	30
REVENUES						
Initiation Fees	$ 52,000.00	$ 52,000.00	$ 78,000.00	$ 52,000.00	$ 52,000.00	$ 52,000.00
Monthly Dues	137,625.00	140,250.00	145,875.00	148,500.00	151,125.00	153,750.00
Total Revenues	$189,625.00	$192,250.00	$223,875.00	$200,500.00	$203,125.00	$205,750.00
EXPENSES						
Salaries	$ 85,676.00	$ 85,676.00	$ 85,676.00	$ 85,676.00	$ 85,676.00	$ 85,676.00
Rent	14,400.00	14,400.00	14,400.00	14,400.00	14,400.00	14,400.00
Advertising	9,000.00	9,000.00	9,000.00	9,000.00	9,000.00	9,000.00
Maintenance	1,500.00	1,500.00	1,500.00	1,500.00	1,500.00	1,500.00
Administration	2,250.00	2,250.00	2,250.00	2,400.00	2,400.00	2,400.00
Supplies	2,250.00	2,250.00	2,250.00	2,400.00	2,400.00	2,400.00
Insurance	4,000.00	4,000.00	4,000.00	4,000.00	4,000.00	4,000.00
Utilities	3,750.00	3,750.00	3,750.00	3,750.00	3,750.00	3,750.00
Depreciation	6,833.33	6,833.33	6,833.33	6,833.33	6,833.33	6,833.33
Loan Interest	5,756.85	5,756.85	5,756.85	5,756.85	5,756.85	5,756.85
Outside Services	6,000.00	6,000.00	6,000.00	6,000.00	6,000.00	6,000.00
Total Expenses	$141,416.18	$141,416.18	$141,416.18	$141,716.18	$141,716.18	$141,716.18
NET PROFIT (LOSS)	**$ 48,208.82**	**$ 50,833.82**	**$ 82,458.82**	**$ 58,783.82**	**$ 61,408.82**	**$ 64,033.82**

Table A2-8f Pro Forma Monthly Cash Flow for Professional Fitness for Month 31 to Month 36

	31	32	33	34	35	36
REVENUES						
Initiation Fees	$ 78,000.00	$ 52,000.00	$ 52,000.00	$ 52,000.00	$ 52,000.00	$ 52,000.00
Monthly Dues	159,375.00	162,000.00	164,625.00	167,250.00	169,875.00	172,500.00
Total Revenues	$237,375.00	$214,000.00	$216,625.00	$219,250.00	$221,875.00	$224,500.00
EXPENSES						
Salaries	$ 95,356.00	$ 95,356.00	$ 95,356.00	$ 95,356.00	$ 95,356.00	$ 95,356.00
Rent	14,400.00	14,400.00	14,400.00	14,400.00	14,400.00	14,400.00
Advertising	9,000.00	9,000.00	9,000.00	9,000.00	9,000.00	9,000.00
Maintenance	1,500.00	1,500.00	1,500.00	1,500.00	1,500.00	1,500.00
Administration	2,400.00	2,400.00	2,400.00	2,400.00	2,400.00	2,400.00
Supplies	2,400.00	2,400.00	2,400.00	2,400.00	2,400.00	2,400.00
Insurance	4,000.00	4,000.00	4,000.00	4,000.00	4,000.00	4,000.00
Utilities	3,900.00	3,900.00	3,900.00	3,900.00	3,900.00	3,900.00
Depreciation	6,833.33	6,833.33	6,833.33	6,833.33	6,833.33	6,833.33
Loan Interest	5,756.85	5,756.85	5,756.85	5,756.85	5,756.85	5,756.85
Outside Services	6,000.00	6,000.00	6,000.00	6,000.00	6,000.00	6,000.00
Total Expenses	$151,546.18	$151,546.18	$151,546.18	$151,546.18	$151,546.18	$151,546.18
NET PROFIT (LOSS)	**$ 85,828.82**	**$ 62,453.82**	**$ 65,078.82**	**$ 67,703.82**	**$ 70,328.82**	**$ 72,953.82**

1,800 members by end of the year 2, 960 new members signed in year 2. The new members joined the club at the constant rate of 75 per month for 10 months and 105 members each in January and May. Thus, at the end of year 2, the club will have 840 members in their second year and 960 new members in their first year. This same 70 percent retention/30 percent loss is also used in year 3.

- A second manager is hired in year 2. The club is also assumed to maintain a staff-to-client ratio of 50 to 1. Thus, by the end of the second year, the club will employ 36 staff to service the expected 1,800 members.

Pro Forma Income Statements

Pro forma income statements have also been prepared for the period of three years (Tables A2-9, A2-10, and A2-11). The interest income reported on this statement is calculated based on two equal deposits into a 90-day money market fund paying an interest of 5 percent APR. The deposits are made in the beginning of the second period—month 4, and on day 1 of the fourth period of year 1—month 10. It is assumed that the interest income is paid on October 31 of each year.

Table A2-9 Pro Forma Income Statement for Professional Fitness for Year 1 Ended October 31, 199X

REVENUES	
Initiation Fees	$ 780,000.00
Monthly Dues	588,750.00
Interest Income	2,290.31
Total Revenues	$1,371,040.31
EXPENSES	
Salaries	$ 443,340.00
Payroll Taxes (10%)	44,334.00
Rent	129,600.00
Advertising	108,000.00
Maintenance	18,000.00
Administration	15,000.00
Supplies	15,000.00
Insurance	36,000.00
Utilities	33,750.00
Depreciation	81,999.96
Loan Interest	64,601.40
Outside Services	60,000.00
Total Expenses	$1,049,625.36
Profit Before Taxes	$ 321,414.95
Taxes (40%)	128,565.98
NET INCOME	**$ 192,848.97**

In summary, the pro forma income statement shows a net income after taxes of:

- $192,848.97 for year 1
- $290,249.37 for year 2
- $421,829.95 for year 3

Return on Investment (ROI)

The return on investment—ROI—can be calculated from the income statements. The fixed assets cost $1,274.055. Thus from the income statements, it can be seen that:

- ROI in year 1 = $192,848.97/$1,274,055 = 15.1%
- ROI in year 2 = $290,249.37/$1,274,055 = 22.8%
- ROI in year 3 = $421,829.95/$1,274,055 = 33.1%

Table A2-10 Pro Forma Income Statement for Professional Fitness for Year 2 Ended October 31, 199X

REVENUES

Initiation Fees	$ 624,000.00
Monthly Dues	1,379,250.00
Interest Income	9,119.91
Total Revenues	**$2,012,369.91**

EXPENSES

Salaries	$ 799,308.00
Payroll Taxes (10%)	79,930.80
Rent	172,800.00
Advertising	108,000.00
Maintenance	18,000.00
Administration	25,500.00
Supplies	25,500.00
Insurance	42,000.00
Utilities	40,500.00
Depreciation	81,999.96
Loan Interest	69,082.20
Outside Services	66,000.00
Total Expenses	**$1,528,620.96**
Profit Before Taxes	$ 483,748.95
Taxes (40%)	193,499.58
NET INCOME	**$ 290,249.37**

Pro Forma Balance Sheets

The pro forma balance sheets for Professional Fitness are shown in Tables A2-12, A2-13, and A2-14. The depreciation on fitness and office equipment was calculated using the straight-line method over a period of five years. The estimated total assets of the club during its first three years of operation are:

- Year 1: $1,015,474.78
- Year 2: $1,047,390.29
- Year 3: $1,159,708.53

Table A2-11 Pro Forma Income Statement for Professional Fitness for Year 3 Ended October 31, 199X

REVENUES

Initiation Fees	$ 676,000.00
Monthly Dues	1,872,750.00
Interest Income	21,593.27
Total Revenues	$2,570,343.27

EXPENSES

Salaries	$1,086,192.00
Payroll Taxes (10%)	108,619.20
Rent	172,800.00
Advertising	108,000.00
Maintenance	18,000.00
Administration	28,350.00
Supplies	28,350.00
Insurance	48,000.00
Utilities	45,900.00
Depreciation	81,999.96
Loan Interest	69,082.20
Outside Services	72,000.00
Total Expenses	$1,867,293.36
Profit Before Taxes	$ 703,049.91
Taxes (40%)	281,219.96
NET INCOME	**$ 421,829.95**

Table A2-12 Pro Forma Balance Sheet for Professional Fitness for Year 1—October 31, 199X

ASSETS

CURRENT ASSETS

Cash	$ 15,000.00	
Short-term Investments	122,474.78	
Merchandise Inventory	5,000.00	
Office Supplies	5,000.00	
Total Current Assets		$ 147,474.78

BUILDING & EQUIPMENT

Building	$675,000.00		
Less Accumulated Depreciation	135,000.00	$540,000.00	
Fitness Equipment	$400,000.00		
Less Accumulated Depreciation	80,000.00	320,000.00	
Office Equipment	$ 10,000.00		
Less Accumulated Depreciation	2,000.00	8,000.00	
Total Building & Equipment			868,000.00
Total Assets			**$1,015,474.78**

LIABILITIES

CURRENT LIABILITIES

Salaries Payable	$ 45,240.00		
Account Payable	3,000.00		
Total Current Liabilities		48,240.00	
Total Liabilities			$ 48,240.00

PARTNER'S EQUITY

CONTRIBUTED CAPITAL

6 Partnership units at $150,000 per unit	$900,000.00		
Total Contributed Capital		$900,000.00	
RETAINED EARNINGS		67,234.78	
Total Partners' Equity			967,234.78
Total Liabilities and Partners' Equity			**$1,015,474.78**

Table A2-13 Pro Forma Balance Sheet for Professional Fitness for Year 2—October 31, 199X

ASSETS

CURRENT ASSETS

Cash	$ 25,000.00	
Short-term Investments	361,390.29	
Merchandise Inventory	5,000.00	
Office Supplies	5,000.00	
Total Current Assets		$ 396,390.29

BUILDING & EQUIPMENT

Building	$675,000.00		
Less Accumulated Depreciation	270,000.00	$405,000.00	
Fitness Equipment	$400,000.00		
Less Accumulated Depreciation	160,000.00	240,000.00	
Office Equipment	$ 10,000.00		
Less Accumulated Depreciation	4,000.00	6,000.00	
Total Building & Equipment			651,000.00
Total Assets			**$1,047,390.29**

LIABILITIES

CURRENT LIABILITIES

Salaries Payable	$ 75,696.00	
Account Payable	3,500.00	
Total Current Liabilities		79,196.00
Total Liabilities		$ 79,196.00

PARTNERS' EQUITY

CONTRIBUTED CAPITAL

6 Partnership units at $150,000 per unit	$900,000.00	
Total Contributed Capital		$900,000.00
RETAINED EARNINGS		68,194.29
Total Partners' Equity		968,194.29
Total Liabilities and Partners' Equity		**$1,047,390.29**

Table A2-14 Pro Forma Balance Sheet for Professional Fitness for Year 3—October 31, 199X

ASSETS

CURRENT ASSETS

Cash	$ 35,000.00	
Short-term Investments	680,708.53	
Merchandise Inventory	5,000.00	
Office Supplies	5,000.00	
Total Current Assets		$ 725,708.53

BUILDING & EQUIPMENT

Building	$675,000.00		
Less Accumulated Depreciation	405,000.00	$270,000.00	
Fitness Equipment	$400,000.00		
Less Accumulated Depreciation	240,000.00	160,000.00	
Office Equipment	$ 10,000.00		
Less Accumulated Depreciation	6,000.00	4,000.00	
Total Building & Equipment			434,000.00
Total Assets			**$1,159,708.53**

LIABILITIES

CURRENT LIABILITIES

Salaries Payable	$ 95,356.00	
Account Payable	3,900.00	
Total Current Liabilities	99,256.00	
Total Liabilities		$ 99,256.00

PARTNERS' EQUITY

CONTRIBUTED CAPITAL

6 Partnership units at $150,000 per unit	$900,000.00	
Total Contributed Capital	$900,000.00	

RETAINED EARNINGS

	160,452.53	
Total Partners' Equity		1,060,452.53
Total Liabilities and Partners' Equity		**$1,159,708.53**

SUMMARY

Professional Fitness is to be located in the city of San Marino, California. It will be the first upscale weight training and aerobic facility in the city. The club will cater to the over-40 age group and will pride itself in offering an exceptional level of personal service to its members. This will be complemented by the offering of state-of-the-art fitness equipment. Equipment to be offered includes high-end weight resistance machines, exercise bicycles, stair climbers, treadmills, cross-country ski machines, a soundproofed aerobic room with a custom-designed, spring-loaded aerobic mat, satin-finished dumbbells and barbells, and a sauna in both the male and female locker rooms. The club will provide child-care facilities for members while they work out, and house a health bar, pro shop, and an upscale members' lounge.

The total start-up costs will be $1,274.055. Members will be charged an initiation fee of $675 and monthly dues of $75. At this price, the club will break even with 1,096 members. The club expects conservatively to attract 1,200 members in its first year, 1,800 in the second year, and 2,300 in the third year of operation. A 15.1 percent return on investment can be expected in the first year, 22.8 percent in the second, and 33.1 percent in the third. A positive monthly cash flow is obtained every month for the first three years of operation. Promotional expenses amount to $9,000 per month for the first three years of operation. This expense is to be viewed by the club as an investment for the future.

Professional Fitness will succeed due to the following differential advantages:

- None of the club's three major competitors are presently specifically targeting the over-40 market.

- There are currently no upscale weight training and aerobic clubs in San Marino.

- The level of service that will be offered by the club will be unmatched by any of its competitors.

- The aging of the American population will ensure that the potential market for Professional Fitness will increase in the future.

- Fees will be acceptable because of the relatively inelastic price sensitivities of upscale fitness consumers in the trading zone of the club.

- The increased emphasis on improving the quality of life for older people and the widely publicized benefits of weight-training programs for seniors will also ensure the success of the club.

BIBLIOGRAPHY

"American Service Finance Renewal Study (1989)," *National Health Club Association,* 1991 (reprinted with permission).

Branch, Eleanor. "Making Your Fitness Their Business," *Black Enterprise,* Sept. 1991:83–90.

Broadwell, Laura. "Girls Just Wanna Work Out," *Women's Sports & Fitness,* Sept. 1990:45–48.

Brownstein, Vivian. "Consumers Will Help the Economy Stay in Shape Next Year," *Fortune,* Oct. 23, 1989:31–32.

Cooper, James C., and Madigan, Kathleen. "Cross Your Fingers, Knock Wood: That May Be a Recovery Out There," *Business Week,* March 16, 1992:31.

Cooper, Kenneth H., M.D. "Fighting Back Against Bone Loss," *The Saturday Evening Post,* March 1991:32–36.

Engel, Margaret. "Beware of Fitness Club Contracts," *Glamour,* Aug. 1987:92.

"Health Clubs Cool Down," *Club Industry,* March 1991:17–18.

"Health Clubs Look Beyond the Baby Boomers," *Changing Times,* Feb. 1990:95.

Horowitz, Janice M. "From Workouts to Wellness," *Time,* July 30, 1990:64.

"Is Your Health Club Healthy?" *Changing Times,* Sept. 1989:116–118.

Konrad, Walecia. "Health Clubs: Exercise Caution," *Business Week,* June 6, 1988:142–143.

Kotler, Philip. *Marketing Management* (Englewood Cliffs, NJ: Prentice Hall, 1991), 7th ed., pp. 171–173, 395–396.

Loro, Laura. "Health Clubs Stretch Markets," *Advertising Age,* May 16, 1988:28.

Los Angeles County City Ordinance, Article III—C-1 Commercial Zone, Sect. 23.14 (C), p. 220.

Mandel, Michael J. "Bummed-Out in America," *Business Week,* March 16, 1992:34–35.

Mozoomdar, Iain. "A Study to Determine the Effectiveness of World Gym, Pasadena" (unpublished), Nov. 1991.

O'Reily, Brian. "New Truths about Staying Healthy," *Fortune,* Sept. 25, 1989:57–66.

Reddick, Marshall E. *Entrepreneurship* (Los Angeles: California State University, Los Angeles, 1990), p. 143.

Rodkin, Dennis. "Health Clubs Sweat the Details in Ads," *Advertising Age,* Dec. 3, 1989:38–39.

Rubenstein, Carin. "Here's to Your Health," *New Choices for the Best Years,* Jan. 1990:35–39.

Schefer, Dorothy. "The New Body Building," *Vogue,* May 1989:368.

Sussman, Vic. "Muscle Bound," *U.S. News and World Report,* May 20, 1991:85–88.

Waldrop, Judith. "Feeling Good," *American Demographics,* May 1990:6.

Zarrow, Susan. "The New Diet Priorities," *Prevention,* Sept. 1991:33–36, 118–120.

APPENDIX A2-A

Questionnaire

A study is being conducted to help us run the gym more effectively. Please answer the questions honestly as we would like to know how you guys/gals *REALLY* feel! Thank you for your help.

1. Sex: _____ Male _____ Female

2. Age: a. Under 21   b. 21−25   c. 26−30   d. 31−35   e. 36−40   f. Over 40 HANG IN THERE!

3. I have to travel _____ to get to the gym.

   a. 0−3 miles b. 4−6 miles c. 7−10 miles d. 11−15 miles e. 16−20 miles f. Over 20 miles

4. I joined this gym because: (Check ALL that apply)

   a. the equipment is great!

   b. I want to get buffed! (or more attractive, for you gals/guys out there!)

   c. it is close to where I live or work.

   d. my friends joined and encouraged me to join too.

   e. of the abundance of attractive men/women! AT LEAST YOU WERE HONEST!

   f. the hours are very convenient.

   g. the training atmosphere is great!

   h. the membership fee was cheap/reasonable.

   i. Other: _____

5. I feel that the membership fee as compared to other similarly equipped gyms is:

   a. Cheap   b. A bargain!   c. Reasonable   d. Expensive   e. Exorbitant

6. I usually train (per week): a. 1−2X   b. 3X   c. 4X   d. 5X   e. 6−7X ANIMAL!!!

7. I usually train: a. Before 8 a.m.   b. 9−Noon c. 1−3 p.m.   d. 4−7 p.m.   e. After 7 p.m.

8. I find the informational and teaching capabilities of the gym instructors to be:

   a. Excellent!   b. Good   c. Average   d. Poor   e. Ineffective   f. Never needed one!

9. I use the following equipment: (*Check # of times per week* for EACH equipment) THANKS!

		1X	2X	3X	4X	5−7X	Never (0X)
a.	Bench presses (Flat or Incline)	____	____	____	____	____	_____
b.	Squat rack or leg press machine	____	____	____	____	____	_____
c.	Leg extension or curl machines	____	____	____	____	____	_____
d.	Weight stations/Assisted chin-up	____	____	____	____	____	_____
e.	Lower abs machine/Crunch board	____	____	____	____	____	_____
f.	Stairmaster	____	____	____	____	____	_____
g.	Lifecycle	____	____	____	____	____	_____
h.	Treadmill	____	____	____	____	____	_____

10. For my purposes, the quantity and poundages of the free weights are:

    a. Sufficient   b. Insufficient   c. Don't use free weights so don't care!

11. I would like to see the following equipment added in the future:
    (Check *ALL* that apply! - Better more than less!)

    a. _____ Additional squat rack/free weights/benches/bars (any type) Specify:_____

    b. _____ Other machines   Specify:_____

    c. _____ There is NO NEED for more equipment. *Are you serious? Really?*

12. I feel that the shower facilities are:

    a. Excellent! b. Above average   c. Average   d. Below average   e. Venice Beach is cleaner!!

LKJ CONSTRUCTION COMPANY MARKETING PLAN FOR ENTRY INTO THE HEALTHCARE CONSTRUCTION SECTOR

Developed by
ANDREW G. MCINTYRE

EXECUTIVE SUMMARY

The aging of America along with the boom in healthcare construction has created the opportunity for the LKJ Construction Company's Structural division to enter this new market segment. Healthcare is almost recession-proof and the time is right for LKJ to enter a market in which the six largest contractors control only 38 percent.

Healthcare construction was $2.1 billion in 1991, and is expected to grow at about 5 percent a year. Based on the projected growth, it should reach $2.4 billion by 1994. LKJ's objective will be to control 1 percent of the market by 1994. With the average fee in this market 2.5 percent, LKJ's profit will be at least $600,000. The initial cost to enter this market will be approximately $443,000 in the first year, but should reduce drastically in subsequent years as LKJ starts the actual building.

Although LKJ has very limited healthcare construction experience (mainly renovations), its reputation for producing top quality work should be to its advantage. The writer has no doubt that the opportunities which the market now possesses, as well as a commitment by top management, will help establish a niche for LKJ in this ever-growing market.

Contents

INTRODUCTION

The healthcare construction field is cluttered with different types of medical facilities. There are seven basic classes and within each class four different types. While LKJ is interested in building mainly large-scale facilities, outpatient clinics and rehabilitation centers are not out of the question.

The need for medical facilities will not reduce in the near future. Although medical science has been able to prolong life, older people will need more medical attention. LKJ will have to position itself so that it can be ready to take on different types of facilities.

Projection for this marketing plan can only be made on a conceptual basis, because it is hard to determine what the actual product will look like. The structural dimensions of most buildings are the same (e.g., plumbing, concrete, steel)—it is the design that will make them different.

SITUATIONAL ANALYSIS

The Situational Environment

Demographics. The aging of America has brought on the need for more healthcare facilities. It has been predicted that by the year 2040, one out of every five Americans will be 65 years and older. Currently, 12 percent of the population in California is 65 years and older,[1] and if the national average is any predictor, that percentage is expected to rise as new medicines and technology prolong the lives of the populace. An aging population translates into a healthier populace, but it also translates into more healthcare facilities.

Economic Conditions. Despite a downturn in the construction industry overall in 1991, construction in the medical field showed a 5 percent increase in growth in the United States (U.S.).[2] In California, where 9 percent of the nation's hospitals are located, the growth in this field has been no exception. The healthcare construction market was estimated at $2.1 billion in 1991,[3] and if it grows by the same 5 percent, will reach $2.2 billion in 1992.

Healthcare facilities on the increase do not only include the traditional long-term care hospitals. Currently more popular are hospital-based outpatient clinics, free-standing outpatient hospitals, rehabilitation and psychiatric hospitals, and retirement homes with healthcare facilities. For the purposes of this marketing plan, however, all facilities will be termed "hospitals."

Demographers predict that California will be in need of approximately 50,000 new hospital beds in the next 10 years. The need for such additional facilities is highlighted by Los Angeles County USC Medical Center's recent plan to build a $1.4 billion expansion.[4]

This industry is also helped by the ever-changing medical technology that requires alterations or renovations of existing structures to accommodate new medical equipment. Though this marketing plan is concentrating on new hospital construction, it is worth noting that in 1991, 67 percent of all hospital construction activity involved expansions.[5]

Politics. Recent anti-Japanese sentiments aired in the Los Angeles area could have some effects on the industry. If the Los Angeles City Council gets its way and imposes a local content requirement in all publicly funded projects, this might drive up the cost of new construction. Less competition could lead to more costs and fewer hospitals willing to expand or to undergo new construction.

Laws and Regulations. In 1971, the Office of Statewide Health Planning and Development (OSHPD), assumed responsibility for developing and administering a uniform code for the construction of all healthcare facilities. OSHPD was formed out of the need to build better hospital structures after the devastating 1971 Sylmar earthquake. Prior to its inception, the enormous damage done to hospitals during earthquakes was a direct result of poor construction techniques.

---

[1]James S. Fay, editor, *California Almanac. 5th Edition* (Santa Barbara, CA: Pacific Data Resources, 1991), p. 20.
[2]Jude Shiver Jr., "Developers Find a Cure in Health Care," *Los Angeles Times,* September 7, 1991, Section D, p. 4.
[3]"California Construction Review," *Construction Industry Research Board,* January 9, 1992, p. 10.
[4]Benjamin M. Cole, "County Med" Still Dwarfs Other Hospitals," *Los Angeles Business Journal,* April 29, 1991, p. 25.
[5]Elizabeth Gardner, "Healthcare Construction Survives Ailing Economy," *Modern Healthcare,* March 11, 1991, p. 28.

The Uniform Building Code (UBC) was designed to standardize the building requirements in the medical sector and create a "level playing field" for all general contractors. All contractors intending to do any building in this field had to first get certification from the OSHPD before bidding on any hospital work.

The Neutral Environment

Financial Environments. Apart from the growing need for hospitals in California, one of the reasons for growth in hospital buildings is the fact that this funding has not been slowed by the recent credit crunch in the rest of the building industry. Most public hospitals are funded by revenue bonds issued by local healthcare agencies. Private hospitals, on the other hand, have access to long-term corporate financing.[6] Consider that the largest private hospital chain in the United States, National Medical Enterprises, Inc. (NME), has $914 million in retained earnings in 1991, a 30 percent increase over 1990![7]

Industry will come from the federal government in the form of national health insurance. The call for a national health plan for the United States will definitely change the funding for the industry, because it would be subject to the gerrymandering of political representatives. Centrally planned oversight as to the number and quality of local hospitals will hamper the current growth in California and divert funding to other parts of the country.

Special Interests Environments. Special interests will become a problem only if national health insurance becomes a reality. If this idea picks up steam, it will pit the construction industry (as it relates to medical facilities) and the American Medical Association against the civil libertarians. It is currently politically more correct to expound the virtues of national health insurance. However, no one knows the full impact or the cost of such a plan, so it is somewhat nebulous at the moment.

Though architects have no control over the decisions of the OSHPD, they definitely influence its decisions indirectly. Architects frequently develop master plans for large institutions which have to file with OSHPD. OSHPD would have to consider these plans when planning on a statewide basis for future facilities. The principal architects in California that specialize in the healthcare industry are:

1. Henningson, Durham and Richardson, Inc., AIA
   2415 Campus Drive
   Irvine, CA 92715
   (714) 476-0336
   HDR is considered the nation's number one healthcare architect. It employs more than 1,300 people in 23 offices nationwide, with four major design centers in Omaha, Nebraska; Alexandria, Virginia; Dallas, Texas; and Irvine, California. Seventy-five percent of HDR's business comes from medical facilities and they have completed over $10 billion since its inception. It is a full-service firm, offering both architectural and engineering services.

2. Bobrow/Thomas and Associates, AIA
   1001 Westwood Boulevard
   Los Angeles, CA 90024
   (213) 208-7017

---

[6]Shiver Jr., p. 4
[7]National Medical Enterprises, Inc. 1991 Annual Report, Consolidated Balance Sheet, p. 29.

Ninety percent of Bobrow/Thomas's business comes from this industry and it is considered a leader in healthcare facilities design. It employs 60 people, all in one Los Angeles office; it offers no in-house engineering services.

3. HMC Group, AIA
   500 East "E" Street
   Ontario, CA 91764
   (714) 983-9623
   This 174-person firm gets 85 percent of its income from the healthcare industry. It offers general architecture services, as well as interior designing and planning. Engineering services are offered through consultants.

4. Stichler Design Group, Inc., AIA
   9245 Skypark Court, Suite 200
   San Diego, CA 92123
   (619) 565-4440
   Eighty to 90 percent of Stichler's practice is made up of medical facilities. They employ about 60 architects and are a full-service firm, offering both structural and mechanical engineering services in-house.

The Competitor Environment

LKJ has identified seven general contractors that will provide the strongest competition in this arena. Of the seven, only one, The Turner Corporation, is a publicly traded company. Therefore, comparisons of financial information will be done based on Turner's financial statements, as well as industry standards. On the other companies, comparisons will be made based on the percentage change in the volume of business.

1. The Turner Corporation
   1055 W. 7th Street
   Los Angeles, CA 90017
   (213) 683-1430

Turner is the largest construction company in the United States and is also the largest builder of healthcare facilities (even though this accounted for only 14 percent of their total volume in 1990). The company is well known in the industry and has a proven track record of quality work. It has 38 offices and subsidiaries in 16 states (6 in California), as well as 3 overseas. In 1990 its value of new contracts secured in the healthcare field was $999.4 million in total assets ($47.2 million in liquid assets), and $22.5 million in retained earnings. Turner actually showed a loss of $10.8 in 1990, but this was due to a $21 million reserve that was set up against a real estate joint venture.

Turner intends to aggressively pursue the healthcare market in coming years, as evidenced by the increase in new contracts. It currently controls about 12.5 percent of the Californian healthcare construction sector, with a volume (i.e., value of completed work) of $325 million in 1990. This figure increased 14 percent over the 1989 amount.

Turner's experience in this field is second only to McCarthy Construction Company, with 88 years combined project manager experience (110 managers), compared to 126 McCarthy (60 managers). By being the largest construction company in the United States, it has the advantage of name recognition and the distinction of completing highly visible projects (e.g., the 75-story First Interstate Building in downtown Los Angeles and the Kaiser Permanente Primary Care in Fontana).

Any weakness that Turner has would be that it does not concentrate on any one sector of the construction industry. Even though it is the leader in almost all sectors, it does not overly dominate these sectors and could be subject to strong competition directed at just one sector.

2. M.H. Golden Construction Company
   440 E. Huntington Drive, Suite 103
   Arcadia, CA 91006
   (818) 446-7595

This company has approximately 8 percent of the market. It has an annual volume of $300 million, of which $210 million is medical facilities construction. However it only has six project managers with 10 years' experience in healthcare construction.

3. Kitchell Contractors
   26 Executive Park, Suite 100
   Irvine, CA 92714
   (714) 261-1227

Kitchell averages about $180 million in healthcare construction yearly. No figures are available for 1991, but in 1990 it did about $125 million worth of business. It controls about 6 percent of the healthcare market in California with a team of 56 project managers having 40 years' total experience.

4. McCarthy Construction Company
   2 Park Plaza, Suite 1200
   Irvine, CA 92714
   (714) 474-9999

Healthcare projects currently account for 65 percent of McCarthy's business. The company completed five hospitals in 1991, including the $110 million Pomona Valley Hospital Center. Its total volume nationwide was $355 million and it earned fees of $18.4 million. McCarthy averages about $71 million in volume in California, which translates into earned fees of about $3.7 million, guaranteeing it a 4 percent share of the market. Though the square footage it completed nationwide fell by 15 percent, volume (which determines the fee) rose by 8 percent.

McCarthy has the advantage of having the most experienced project managers in this field—126 years of combined experience. It can only be assumed that given the current growth in the industry, and the increase in its fees, that McCarthy is doing well financially.

5. Pozzo Construction Company
   2890 Rowena Avenue
   Los Angeles, CA 90039

Approximately 80 percent of Pozzo's $100 million annual volume is devoted to healthcare construction in California. It does almost no hard bidding, preferring to negotiate "guaranteed maximum" contracts (GMP). It currently has about 3 to 4 percent of the California market. No information is available at this time regarding its project management experience.

6. Robert E. McKee, Inc.
   4701 San Fernando Road
   Los Angeles, CA 90039
   (818) 240-6270

This firm has averaged about $78 million in volume over the last three years. Healthcare makes up approximately 30 percent of its total business, and it currently enjoys about 3 percent of the California market. REM has a very experienced management team, consisting of 42 managers with 65 years of experience.

The unavailability of adequate financial data on all except Turner, leads the writer to make assumptions based on volume and growth in the marketplace. (Turner is the only publicly-held company of all of the above general contractors. This the exception rather than the rule in the construction industry. General contractors rarely divulge any kind of financial information on themselves. Some even go as far as refusing to acknowledge, for example, the total square footage of a building that they have completed, even though this might be public knowledge.) The fact that this kind of construction is somewhat specialized, companies like the ones mentioned, which have developed a niche, should be doing quite well. Bearing in mind that commercial construction is the cornerstone of the market, the overall financial picture for these companies might be gloomy.

The Company Environment

LKJ is one of the top 20 general contractors in the United States (based on volume), and one of the top 10 in California, with total assets in excess of $118 million. The following statements of operations and balance sheets will shed some light on the financial performance of LKJ between 1989 and 1990:

Statements of Operations
(Years ending December 31)

	1990	1989
Contract Revenues	$ 490,085,876	$ 422,208,233
Contract Costs	(481,179,608)	(407,737,924)
Gross Profit	8,906,268	14,470,309
General & Admin. Expenses	(13,609,199)	(15,406,596)
Operating Loss	(4,702,931)	(936,287)
Other Income (Expense):		
Interest Income	1,389,078	1,257,270
Interest Expense	(185,135)	(208,226)
EBIT	(3,498,988)	112,757
Income Tax Benefit	1,455,697	165,977
Net Earnings (Loss)	$ (2,043,291)	$ 278,734

Balance Sheets

Assets	1990	1989
Current Assets:		
Cash	$ 15,989,030	$ 18,007,924
S/term Investments	5,301,685	3,300,000
Receivable	86,256,685	91,846,833
Unbilled Contract Revenue	2,494,003	1,621,302
Prepaid Expenses/Deposits	459,016	1,474,240
Deferred Income Taxes	667,580	
		172,693
Total Current Assets	111,168,275	116,422,992
Property & Equipment (net)	3,942,510	4,264,296
Real Estate Investments (net)	1,855,668	1,902,583
Deferred Income Taxes	337,692	548,123
Cash Surrender Value of Officers' Life Insurance	949,147	1,335,938
Total Assets	$ 118,253,292	$ 124,472,932

Liabilities and Stockholders' Equity

Current Liabilities:		
Payables	$ 85,984,329	$ 85,431,370
Deferred Revenue	11,485,902	13,043,927
Accrued Liabilities	5,167,425	5,976,139
Deferred comp. (current)	120,471	120,471
Long-term Debt (current)	526,399	1,653,383
Total Current Liab.	103,284,526	106,225,290
Long-term Debt:		
Real Estate Investments	2,259,455	2,298,867
Other	159,175	366,226
Deferred Compensation	1,468,498	1,486,656
Stockholders' Equity:		
Capital Stock: $2.50 par value.		
Authorized: 1,000,000 shares.		
Outstanding:		
215,712 shares in 1990		
233,292 shares in 1989	581,880	625,830
Additional Paid-in Capital	3,445,319	3,528,372
Retained Earnings	8,966,383	11,929,522
	12,993,582	16,083,724
Notes Receivable	(1,911,944)	(1,985,831)
Total S/holders' Equity	11,081,638	14,097,893
	$118,253,292	$124,473,932

Though total volume increased by 16 percent in 1990 from $422 to $490 million, net profits fell dramatically from $279,000 in 1989, to a loss of just over $2 million in 1990. LKJ still remains to have a good liquidity base with $21 million in liquid assets and retained earnings of $9 million. A measure of LKJ's financial strength can be done by comparing the financial ratios of LKJ with Turner and the industry standards:

Financial Ratios	LKJ	Turner	Industry
Quick ratio	1.04	1.03	1.1
Current ratio	1.08	1.05	1.3
Debt to Equity	7.73	9.25	3.2
Revenue to Equity	44.55	91.12	3.2
Days in Accounts Receivable	64.24	60.83	46.3
Profit Margin	−0.42%	−3.6%	0.25%
Return on Assets	−1.68%	−1.53%	3.1%
Return on Equity	−18.1%	−33.33%	13.1%
Earnings per share	−9.47	−2.41	N/A
Percentage change in volume	22.50%	8.5%	19.9%

LKJ's financial position compares variably with Turner's. Obviously Turner's size and its public trading status gives it a more favorable revenue to equity ratio. However, LKJ grew at more than twice the rate of Turner, with a 22.5 percent increase in volume.

The main reason for the 800 percent drop in net profit to −0.42 percent was that office and hotel construction, which are a large part of LKJ's business, fell off drastically in 1990. There was almost a complete halt to any new construction (apart from healthcare) in California caused by lack of long-term capital financing. Compounding the problem was the collapse of the savings and loan industry, which placed more restrictions on the issuance of new credit, leading to the cancellation of many developer-sponsored prospects. The fact that LKJ had $11.5 million deferred in revenue also did not help matters any. Some of the ongoing projects ran into financial problems and even some of the completed ones were tied up in litigation because of the owners' inability to pay for change order work. So, the receipt of these tied-up funds would definitely have made the financial statements look a lot better. However, over the last four years LKJ has averaged $995,000 in net profits.

LKJ has a reputation in California for delivering prospects before schedule and for the high level of professionalism in its project teams. It is one of the oldest firms in the country, going back almost 100 years, and so has wide name recognition, especially on the West Coast. LKJ has 18 project managers with total experience of 76 years, making it one of the most experienced firms in the industry. Its ability to take on GMP and cost-plus (hard-bid) jobs and still provide the owner with savings in either case, points to LKJ's dedicated project team.

One of the good things about the current recession is that LKJ has been able to do serious manpower evaluations. The company has pared down to two-thirds its pre-recessionary size, and in the process has become more efficient by removing duplicated functions and streamlining and decentralizing divisional operations. LKJ's other strengths include: (a) a good safety/risk management record, (b) a wide subcontractor base, (c) good bonding ability, and (d) an Interiors and an Industrial division.

LKJ's proven track record in the commercial sector is beyond reproach, but lack of experience in the healthcare construction sector points to a number of weaknesses: (a) though LKJ has done some remodeling and renovation in this sector, it has not undergone any large-scale hospital projects; (b) its project management has only 10 years' experience in this industry from previous firms; (c) LKJ has no previous experience of any kind in building or renovating OSHPD-mandated facilities; (d) LKJ does not have a working (or personal) relationship with any of the architects or developers in healthcare building design, and/or construction; and (e) it has inadequate information on its competitors' strengths and weaknesses.

TARGET MARKET

The healthcare construction market in California is estimated at $2 billion a year and is expected to grow by 5 percent in 1991 to $2.1 billion. The six previously named competitors have approximately 38 percent of the market, and with no one dominant player controlling the remaining 62 percent, the opportunity exists for strides to be made here. In these recessionary times this market is ideal for a number of reasons: (a) healthcare is probably the only industry that is recession-proof with huge positive growth every year; (b) by the turn of the century one-fifth of the population will be 65 years or older, so there is a constant need for more medical facilities; (c) other areas of nonresidential construction are in a slump because of the current credit squeeze; and (d) residential construction is not a viable alternative, since LKJ has no intention of getting into this highly regulated and volatile market.

OPPORUNITIES AND PROBLEMS

Opportunities

LKJ's attempt to enter the healthcare sector of the construction industry is prompted by a number of prevailing circumstances:

a. The healthcare industry is probably the only one that is practically recession-proof. With a conservative projection of 5 percent growth, new construction of medical facilities will definitely be on the rise.

b. The 65 years and older segment of the population is the fastest growing age group. By the turn of the century, it will make up 20 percent of the California population. Even though medical science has helped to prolong life these days, an older population will also mean more people getting sick.

c. The current growth of big hospital chains and their plans for expansion (e.g., NME), has signaled these companies' confidence in the future growth of the industry. Also, USC Medical's $2 billion expansion confirms the government's realization that there is an urgent need for additional facilities.

d. The current trend, especially by the baby-boomers, of preventive medical care, means outpatient care facilities will be in demand. Health maintenance organizations (HMOs), such as Maxicare and Kaiser Permanente, that stress preventive medicine, have been more popular in the workplace than the traditional personal doctor.

e. The possible enactment of a national health plan could lead to more facilities being built, since more people could afford to go to the doctor than before.

f. In the midst of a recession is the best time to plan strategies for the inevitable recovery. LKJ has the opportunity to place itself in a good position to take advantage of the work that will be offered soon.

Problems

LKJ will encounter some problems that could threaten its success in the healthcare construction industry:

a. The firms that dominate this sector are well-known and all have a proven track record in healthcare construction and experienced project teams. LKJ's job will be to start actively networking with the subcontractors, general contractors, architects, developers, government agencies, and the medical establishment, so that its name can be recognized. A good place to start would be with companies that LKJ has done work for before, that are in the healthcare field, or have related companies in the field.

b. A total commitment will be needed from the top management to recruit a project team with experience in healthcare construction. LKJ could try to establish liaisons with other companies in the field and maybe try to recruit some of their personnel. Getting a good project manager, for example, who has worked for Turner or Kitchell, would lend much needed credibility to the LKJ team during negotiations.

c. LKJ needs to implement a training program to acquaint its team(s) on the OSHPD regulations and requirements for healthcare construction. In the past LKJ has been dedicated to the ongoing training of its personnel, and this should be no exception.

d. There has been an increase in the number of non-union competitors in the industry. Since LKJ has only unionized employees, its bargaining position for most of its trade costs is dictated by outside forces. LKJ would have to stress its high level of expertise to overcome the possible trend away from unionized trades.

e. Healthcare construction is inherently riskier due to the possible handling of toxic/ hazardous materials. This would definitely increase workers compensation coverage and possibly LKJ's excess liability coverage. A rigorous training program on the kinds of toxic materials that might be encountered, along with LKJ's outstanding safety record, should be able to alleviate these concerns.

f. The construction industry as a whole has become very litigious. The healthcare sector is no exception and is subject to more of this because of its very technical nature and the various interest groups that have to be appeased. LKJ will have to try to increase its bonding ability in order to counter any future legal action.

MARKETING OBJECTIVES AND GOALS

LKJ's primary objective is for its Structural division to have 1 percent of the healthcare construction market by 1994. This is a very conservative figure given the growth in the industry and the fact that more than 60 percent of the sector is shared by small contractors. At a growth rate of 5 percent, this translates into a volume of $24 million, assuming a $2.4 billion market ($2.2 billion in 1992, growing at 5 percent per annum). The average fee for this kind of construction is 2.5 percent,[8] making LKJ's potential fee approximately $600,000 (net profit). Once LKJ has a project, any shortfall in the projected fee could be made up by scheduling changes, additional cost savings, or change-order increased scope. Based on Marshall's Valuation system (standard for the industry), the average hospital is 100,000 square feet in area.[9] At an average of $90 per square foot,[10] the typical hospital costs $9 million. Given a 52-week construction target, LKJ would have to successfully bid and complete 2.7 hospitals by 1994 to accomplish its primary objective. LKJ has a historical success rate of 10 percent on jobs bid. This new venture into healthcare construction suggests a lower than usual rate of about 5 percent. This means that LKJ will have to bid at least 50 jobs to accomplish its goal of two guaranteed prospects. Based on the writer's initial assumption, LKJ's construction of medical facilities will also include outpatient centers and such, but for simpler calculations hospitals are being used. Figures were derived by taking averages of the least to the most complicated structures. (Bear in mind that these conservative estimates are based on 1991 valuations, and will definitely increase in the future.)

MARKETING STRATEGIES AND TACTICS

To accomplish its goal of 1 percent in the healthcare construction market by 1994, LKJ has adopted the strategies and tactics listed in Table A3–1. Under the section "Elements/Tasks," the first line of each subsection indicates the strategies that LKJ will

---

[8]Personal interview with Terry Hoffman, Architect and Vice President, HMC Group, Ontario, CA, February 28, 1992.
[9]Marshall Valuation Service (Marshall & Swift, June 1989), Section 15, p. 21.
[10]Marshall, Section 15, p. 20.

pursue (bold letters). The tactics for achieving these strategies are listed below with the probable start and completion dates. Those without end dates will be ongoing, whether or not LKJ gets a project. This action plan is only for a year, but represents the tasks that are going to be done on into 1994 and beyond.

1. The optimization of revenues will be accomplished by the use of historical data as the base and improving upon the various financial ratios. A reduction in operational costs would lead to more cash flow available to pursue the healthcare objective. A careful monitoring of the progress against projected cash flow will determine if the strategy is paying off. A lean and cash-rich company will be more likely to be awarded a contract than not.

2. LKJ's current market resource capabilities are lacking in the area of healthcare construction. All necessary resources will have to come to bear in information-gathering activities. Information obtained through LKJ's own market intelligence will have to be constantly reviewed and adjusted to reflect current industry situations. While industrial espionage is not being advocated, LKJ must do everything legally possible to catch up to its competitors.

3. LKJ's current market resources are centered in the Business Development department. The business manager will be in a better position to determine what the labor requirements are going to be and how proposals will be presented to top management. A total commitment from top management will be needed to ensure that the proper market resources are given to see the project through and carry on into the future. This will be a learning process for LKJ that will put it behind the competition, but the company can only learn from this so that it will eventually find its niche in the industry.

4. Network activities will be one of the more important strategies in developing LKJ's business contacts. The healthcare field is very clannish and likes to do business with people they know. By sending representatives to various conventions and seminars, not necessarily on healthcare construction alone, but also on changing technology and other areas, LKJ will be lending credibility to its desire to be included in the "clan." These affairs will also be perfect opportunities to find out about LKJ's competitors. The camaraderie that often develops at these affairs can lead to interesting information which LKJ would otherwise not be privy to. LKJ can also use these opportunities to pass the word around of its interest in the field. LKJ will have to learn "how to swim with the sharks," to get as much information as possible without giving up too much.

5. Though LKJ is already a member of the Association of General Contractors (AGC), its professional affiliations stop there. LKJ will have to expand its professional associations by joining more national, state, and local bodies. Its market intelligence should also reveal what are the particular associations that its competitors are involved in that are directly related to the healthcare construction industry.

6. Though LKJ has one of the best images in the construction industry, a strategic public relations campaign could only further enhance this image. Making special announcements or contributing to industry digests will help keep the LKJ name in the forefront. The in-house newsletter that was discontinued three years ago should be also revitalized. After establishing relationships with architects and/or developers, the newsletter could be sent out to these principals so that LKJ will be kept in mind. LKJ could also consider trying to advertise more in the healthcare magazines or even in the magazines of some of its biggest competitors, such as Turner.

7. In developing leads that will eventually secure LKJ a hospital project, all members of the team are required to exhaust their industry contacts. Information that is acquired through networking or public media is essential to the success of this strategy. Every lead should be viewed as the catalyst that might land LKJ the project. Business relationships developed from strategies 4 and 5 are important in increasing the number of leads. Being persistent with follow-ups will verify LKJ's interest in growing within this sector.

8. Manpower monitoring will be on track when the project team is assembled. The search for the right people has to be started as soon as possible and completed in about six months. Two prospect managers should be recruited initially from the outside to start building the team. Project engineers and field staff will be recruited internally. Personnel training will not be specific to healthcare construction, but will include LKJ's project management, scheduling, and estimating systems. Full knowledge of the company's management information system (20/20) will be necessary to be able to run job/labor cost and other variance reports.

9. The final strategy of securing probable jobs will not be based on the historical success rate of 10 percent. Being new to this industry requires a more realistic rate of 5 percent of total proposals submitted. By the time this stage is reached, LKJ's healthcare team will have been familiar with the UBCs and OSHPD regulations governing the industry. However, the real success of this strategy will depend on the preconstruction work that will be done to accomplish it. Competitive estimating and accurate scheduling are the two things that could make up for LKJ's lack of experience in this area. Also, LKJ's willingness to use value engineering (e.g., substituting a more expensive material with a cheaper, yet equally reliable one), could endear it to the prospective client, especially in these recessionary times. These preconstruction services are especially important in "hard bid" projects (usually public works) where the competition is very fierce. Though historically, LKJ has preferred negotiated contracts, the nature of healthcare construction does not lend itself to such contracts. LKJ will have to learn the knack of these different bidding processes. Such versatility will enhance LKJ's marketability and broaden its scope even further within the industry.

IMPLEMENTATION AND CONTROL

The construction industry is not like the typical manufacturing concern, where projected sales of the number of units produced can be translated into a simple break-even chart. While the company could be working on more than one project at any given time, each project would be considered a single unit in the manufacturing sense of the word. Each project has its own timetable and own resources contributing to its success. The writer will assume that due to LKJ's lack of healthcare experience and knowledgeable project managers, it will only take on one healthcare project at a time.

Also differentiating the construction from manufacturing is the way that the prospect is financed. While the preliminary marketing strategies will be paid by LKJ, once the project is ready to begin, LKJ will not be putting any of its own money up front. Financing of the prospect is the concern of the developer(s), and LKJ's sole concern is the scheduled completion of the project and, if possible, with some savings.

Whatever the cost of the project, LKJ's fee will be 2.5 percent of that figure. The fee is LKJ's net profit, since all operational costs would have already been included in the cost of the project when the original proposal was made. Therefore, LKJ will only break even if it loses all of its fee. This could happen if LKJ did unauthorized work outside the scope of the contract without the owner's approval. No contractor is in business to break even. While reaching the break-even point in a manufacturing firm would bode well for that company's management, such a scenario in the construction industry could result in that project manager being fired. The following statements will show the cost of the initial marketing campaign to get into healthcare, as well as the general conditions' breakdown and cash-flow statements for LKJ's anticipated project. Marketing costs will obviously be reduced when LKJ gets into the market, since more of this cost will be absorbed by the Interiors and Industrial divisions and/or passed on to the prospective owners. The figures are based on the average spent on these activities over the last four years. Figures are marked up by 20 percent to reflect inflation and the added expense of entering a new market segment. The general conditions' costs ($762,799) are distributed among the various trades within the cash-flow schedule to arrive at the $9 million. The number of weeks/months each general condition item will last is stipulated. This cost is directly related to LKJ (as the others would be subcontracted), and is where any potential cost savings/overruns would come from.

The cash-flow schedule (Figure A3–1) shows the estimated cost over the life of the project (in this case, one year), and the times of completion (striped bars), and the actual cost and time completed (plain bars). The percentages below the bar chart shows the actual work completed. In this chart the project would be ahead of schedule, since $2.4 million worth of work has been completed, as opposed to the estimated $2.115 expected.

This project would yield a fee of $225,000 (2.5 percent of $9 million) for LKJ. The fee is not included in the distribution of the trades, since better interpretation of trade costs can be done without this markup. So in reality the total cost of the building is $9.225 million, provided that LKJ does nothing to relinquish part or all of its fee.

Projected First-Year Costs

Marketing Research	$115,000
Networking Activities	5,500
Professional Associations	8,300
Public Relations	44,800
Manpower Monitoring:	
Project Managers	170,400
Team Training	13,000
Pre-construction Services:	
Estimating	62,700
Scheduling	24,000
Total first-year cost	$443,700

Table A3-1   LKJ's MARKETING STRATEGIES & TACTICS

ELEMENTS/TASKS	JAN	FEB	MAR	APR	MAY	JUN	JUL	AUG	SEP	OCT	NOV	DEC	JAN
(Quarter reviews)	1ST QUARTER REVIEW ▲			2ND QUARTER REVIEW ▲			3RD QUARTER REVIEW ▲			4TH QUARTER REVIEW ▲			▲
1. REVENUE													
1.1 HISTORIC PREVIOUS YEAR	├────												──→
1.2 PROJECTED FUTURE YEAR	├────												──→
2. MARKET RESEARCH													
2.1 FY PREPARATION	├────			┤									
2.2 UPDATES/ADJUSTMENTS (QRTLY)				X			X			X			X
2.3 MARKET INTELLIGENCE	├────												──→
3. MARKETING RESOURCES													
3.1 LABOR	├────												──→
3.2 PROPOSALS	├────						┬						
3.3 SUPPORT MATERIAL (DIVISIONAL)	├────			┤									
3.4 DISPLAYS	├────			┤									
4. NETWORKING ACTIVITIES													
4.1 CONVENTIONS	├────					X			X			X	──→
4.2 CONFERENCES/SEMINARS	├────		X			X		X				X	──→
4.3 REGIONAL MEETINGS	├────		X	X			X	X				X	──→
4.4 LOCAL MEETINGS	├────	X	X	X	X	X	X		X	X	X	X	X ──→
4.5 CONTACT ACTIVITIES	├────	X	X	X	X	X	X		X	X	X	X	X ──→

NOTES

——X—— SPECIFIC EVENT
├———— ACTIVITY STARTS
————┤ ACTIVITY ENDS
————→ ONGOING ACTIVITY

Table A3-1 LKJ's MARKETING STRATEGIES & TACTICS

ELEMENTS/TASKS	FY 1992 JAN	FEB	MAR	◄1ST QUARTER REVIEW► APR	MAY	JUN	◄2ND QUARTER REVIEW► JUL	AUG	SEP	◄3RD QUARTER REVIEW► OCT	NOV	DEC	◄4TH QUARTER REVIEW► JAN FY 1993
5. PROFESSIONAL ASSOCIATIONS													
5.1 NATIONAL	⊢				X								↑
5.2 STATE	⊢	X	X	X	X		X	X		X	X	X	↑
5.3 LOCAL	⊢	X	X	X	X	X	X	X	X	X	X	X	↑
5.4 SECTOR SPECIFIC (NON-REGIONAL)	⊢	X		X			X			X		X	↑
6. PUBLIC RELATIONS ACTIVITIES													
6.1 ANNOUNCEMENTS	⊢		X						X				↑
6.2 MAGAZINE ARTICLES	⊢												↑
6.3 NEWSLETTERS	⊢	X	X	X	X	X	X		X	X	X	X	↑
6.4 SPECIAL PUBLICATIONS	⊢											X	↑
7. LEADS DEVELOPMENT													
7.1 INFO FORMAT/TRACKING SYSTEMS	⊢												↑
7.2 COLD CALL LEADS	⊢												↑
7.3 NETWORK LEADS	⊢												↑
7.4 PUBLISHED LEADS	⊢												↑
7.5 INVENTORY REVIEW	⊢												↑
INTERVIEWS SCHEDULED													
PROPOSALS SUBMITTED													
SPEC./TARGETED LEADS													
GEN. TRACKING LEADS													
8. MANPOWER MONITORING													
8.1 HIRE PROJECT MANAGERS	⊢				⊣								↑
8.2 TRAIN PROJECT TEAM					⊢								↑
9. SECURE PROBABLE JOBS													
9.1 OSHPD CERTIFICATION										⊣			
9.2 PRE-CONSTRUCTION SERVICES					⊢			⊣					↑
9.3 SUBMIT PROPOSALS					⊢								↑

NOTES

—X— SPECIFIC EVENT
⊢—— ACTIVITY STARTS
——⊣ ACTIVITY ENDS
——↑ ONGOING ACTIVITY

APPENDIX A3-A

LKJ MEDICAL BUILDING

PROJECT DATA	MAJOR QUANTITIES
PROJECT :	
TYPE OF PROJECT :	
LOCATION :	
OWNER :	
ARCHITECT / ENG. :	
BID DATE :	
CONTRACT TIME :	
LIQ. DAMAGES :	
ESTIMATED CONST. TIME: 12 MONTHS	APPROXIMATE COST......$

SWINERTON & WALBERG   PROJECT :
GENERAL CONDITIONS WORK SHEET   LOCATION :
PRINT DATE: 02/26/92   OWNER   :   PRICED BY:

DESCRIPTION	QTY	UN	MATERIAL		LABOR		EQUIP. / SUBCONTRAC		GRAND
			UNIT	TOTAL	UNIT	TOTAL	UNIT	TOTAL	TOTAL
PROJECT MANAGEMENT:									
PROJECT EXECUTIVE		WKS	0		1400	0		0	0
PROJECT MANAGER	52	WKS	0		1300	67,600		0	67,600
ASSISTANT PROJ. MANAGER		WKS	0		1200	0		0	0
PROJECT ENGINEER	52	WKS	0		700	36,400		0	36,400
SAFETY ENGINEER		WKS	0		700	0		0	0
TIMEKEEPER / CLERK	52	WKS	0		450	23,400		0	23,400
SECRETARY		WKS	0		450	0		0	0
MECH/ELECT COORDINATOR		WKS	0		1000	0		0	0
EXPEDITER / DETAILER		WKS	0		750	0		0	0
PROJECT ESTIMATOR		WKS	0		900	0		0	0
PROJECT SUPERINTENDENT	52	WKS	0		1300	67,600		0	67,600
ASSISTANT SUPERINTENDENT	30	WKS	0		1000	30,000		0	30,000
FIELD ENGINEER / FORM DETAILER		WKS	0		700	0		0	0
WATCHMAN/GUARD SERVICE-PROJECT		WKS	0			0		0	0
FLAGMAN	10	WKS	0		700	7,000		0	7,000
DOUBLE SHIFT / OVERTIME		LS	0			0		0	0
SURVEY, LAYOUT & ENGINEERING:			0			0		0	0
FIELD ENGINEER		WKS	0		900	0		0	0
LICENSED SURVEYOR	1	LS	0			0	30000	30,000	30,000
PRIMARY LAYOUT-SITE SURVEY		DAY	0			0	1220	0	0
ROADS & STREETS		DAY	0			0	1220	0	0
ELEC. & UTILITY LINES		DAY	0			0	1220	0	0
BUILDING GRIDS		DAY	0			0	1220	0	0
FDN. LAYOUT & BOLT ELEV.		DAY	0			0	920	0	0
ELEVATION TARGETS		DAY	0			0	920	0	0
FLOOR BASE LINE & ELEV.		DAY	0			0	920	0	0
CURBS AND WALKS		DAY	0			0	1220	0	0
EARTH SHORING MONITORING		WKS	0			0		0	0
CARPENTERS		WKS	0		850	0		0	0
LABORERS		WKS	0		750	0		0	0

APPENDIX A3-A

LKJ MEDICAL BUILDING

SWINERTON & WALBERG
GENERAL CONDITIONS
DATE: 02/26/92

PROJECT :   0
LOCATION :   0
OWNER   :   0   PRICED BY: 0

DESCRIPTION	QTY	UN	MATERIAL UNIT	MATERIAL TOTAL	LABOR UNIT	LABOR TOTAL	EQUIP. / SUBCONTRAC UNIT	EQUIP. / SUBCONTRAC TOTAL	GRAND TOTAL
TRANSPORTATION, TRAVEL & MANHAUL:									
MANAGEMENT TRAVEL		MOS		0		0	250	0	0
JOB PERSONNEL TRAVEL		MOS		0		0		0	0
AUTOMOBILES -MAINTENANCE/FUEL		MOS		0		0		0	0
PICKUP TRUCKS -MAINTENANCE/FUEL	12	MOS		0		0	400	4,800	4,800
FLAT BED TRUCKS -MAINTENANCE/FUEL		MOS		0		0		0	0
OTHER VEHICLES -MAINTENANCE/FUEL		MOS		0		0		0	0
PERMITS - LICENSES:				0		0		0	0
PLAN CHECK FEE		LS		0		0		0	0
BUILDING PERMIT		LS		0		0		0	0
CITY BUSINESS LICENSE	1	LS		0		0	400	400	400
DEMOLITION FEES		LS		0		0		0	0
CAL OSHA FEES		LS		0		0		0	0
INSPECTION FEES		LS		0		0		0	0
SEWER / WATER FEES		LS		0		0		0	0
STREET, WALK & CURB INSPECTION FEE		LS		0		0		0	0
STREET & WALK USE PERMIT		LS		0		0	4500	0	0
OFFICE AND ENGINEERING EXPENSE:				0		0		0	0
OFFICE TRAILERS	12	MOS		0		0	450	5,400	5,400
MOVE ON & OFF	1	LS	500	500	1000	1,000	1000	1,000	2,500
OFFICE EQUIP. & SUPPLIES	12	MOS	450	5,400		0		0	5,400
OFFICE COPIER	12	MOS	350	4,200		0		0	4,200
ONSITE COMPUTERS	1	LS	2500	2,500		0		0	2,500
TELEPHONE EQUIPMENT & INSTRUMENTS	12	MOS		0		0	50	600	600
TELEPHONE CONNECTION & INSTALL	1	EA		0		0	100	100	100
TELEPHONE CONSUMPTION	12	MOS		0		0	750	9,000	9,000
CHEMICAL TOILETS - 5 EA/MO.	12	MOS		0		0	750	9,000	9,000
TOILETS WITH SEWER CONNECTION		EA		0		0		0	0
PHOTOS		LS		0		0	2500	0	0
BLUE PRINTS	12	MOS		0		0	500	6,000	6,000
SAFETY & FIRST AID	1	LS		0		0	1000	1,000	1,000
RAIN GEAR	1	LS		0		0	750	750	750
HARD HATS	1	LS		0		0	750	750	750
HEAT, LIGHT, WATER & JAN. SERVICE		MOS		0		0	450	0	0
COFFEE, DRINKING WATER, CUPS, ETC.	12	MOS	75	900		0		0	900
SCHEDULES / COMPUTER	1	LS		0		0	10000	10,000	10,000
MISC OFFICE EQUIPMENT RENTAL	12	MOS		0		0	350	4,200	4,200
PAYROLL COMPUTER SERVICES	12	MOS		0		0	1000	12,000	12,000
JOB SIGNS	1	LS		0		0	750	750	750
CONCRETE MIX DESIGN		LS		0		0		0	0
TESTING & INSPECTION COSTS		LS		0		0		0	0
DESIGN COSTS		LS		0		0		0	0
CONSULTANTS FEES		LS		0		0		0	0
ENT., DONATIONS, CONTRIBUTIONS		LS		0		0		0	0
FAX MACHINE	1	LS	1000	1,000		0		0	1,000

APPENDIX A3-A

LKJ MEDICAL BUILDING

SWINERTON & WALBERG   PROJECT : 0
GENERAL CONDITIONS   LOCATION : 0
DATE: 02/26/92   OWNER   : 0   PRICED BY: 0

DESCRIPTION	QTY	UN	MATERIAL		LABOR		EQUIP. / SUBCONTRAC		GRAND
			UNIT	TOTAL	UNIT	TOTAL	UNIT	TOTAL	TOTAL
TEMPORARY BUILDING AND SERVICES:									
TOOL SHEDS / STORAGE FACILITIES		MOS	150	0		0		0	0
BASIC POWER INSTALLATION	1	LS		0		0	5000	5,000	5,000
POWER DIST(INCL HOISTS & CRANES)	1	LS		0		0	20000	20,000	20,000
TEMPORARY POWER CONSUMPTION	12	MOS		0		0	1500	18,000	18,000
TEMP WATER SERVICE CONNECTION	1	LS		0		0	200	200	200
TEMPORARY WATER CONSUMPTION	12	MOS		0		0	150	1,800	1,800
DRINKING WATER	30	WKS	50	1,500	350	10,500		0	12,000
TEMP SEWER LINES & SEPTIC TANKS		LS		0		0		0	0
TEMPORARY PARKING FOR EMPLOYEES		LS		0		0		0	0
TEMPORARY ELEVATOR RENTAL CHARGE		LS		0		0		0	0
TEMPORARY ELEVATOR OPERATOR	12	WKS		0	1200	14,400		0	14,400
TEMPORARY PROTECTION & CLEANUP:				0		0		0	0
CONSTRUCTION FENCE - RENTED	1600	LF		0	3	4,800		0	4,800
COVERED CANOPIES		LF	30	0	50	0		0	0
COMPOUND FENCING		LF		0		0		0	0
SAFETY ROPES/RAILINGS	8000	LF	0.50	4,000	2.00	16,000		0	20,000
BARRICADES (SHORING)		LF	1	0	3.50	0		0	0
FLOOR OPENING PROTECTION	50	LF	25	1,250	10.00	500		0	1,750
TEMPORARY CLOSURES		LF		0		0		0	0
SCAFFOLDING		LS		0		0		0	0
WEATHER PROTECTION	1	LS	500	500	2000	2,000	500	500	3,000
DUST CONTROL	1	LS	750	750	2000	2,000		0	2,750
DEWATERING		LS		0		0		0	0
FIRE PROTECTION	1	LS	1000	1,000	2500	2,500		0	3,500
TEMPORARY STAIRS & LADDERS		LS	1500	0	5000	0		0	0
GENERAL CLEANUP:				0		0		0	0
EXCAVATION	8	WKS		0	700	5,600		0	5,600
BLDG. ROUGH-IN	20	WKS		0	1400	28,000		0	28,000
BLDG. FINISH	24	WKS		0	1400	33,600		0	33,600
PARKING STR.		WKS		0	700	0		0	0
FINAL CLEANUP	1	LS		0		0	25000	25,000	25,000
CLEAN GLASS & FRAMES		LS		0		0		0	0
MISC. FIXTURES, ETC.		LS		0		0	1500	0	0
MAINTENANCE OF ROADS & FENCES		LS		0		0	225	0	0
DISPOSAL BINS & DUMP CHARGES	40	EA		0		0	150	6,000	6,000
PUNCH LIST	1	LS		0	5000	5,000		0	5,000

APPENDIX A3-A

LKJ MEDICAL BUILDING

SWINERTON & WALBERG PROJECT : 0
GENERAL CONDITIONS LOCATION : 0
DATE: 02/26/92 OWNER : 0 PRICED BY: 0

DESCRIPTION	QTY	UN	MATERIAL		LABOR		EQUIP. / SUBCONTRAC		GRAND
			UNIT	TOTAL	UNIT	TOTAL	UNIT	TOTAL	TOTAL
EQUIPMENT-OWNED & OPERATED / RENTED:									
AUTOMOBILES		MOS		0		0	450	0	0
PICK-UP TRUCKS	12	MOS		0		0	700	8,400	8,400
FLAT BED TRUCKS		MOS		0		0		0	0
OTHER VEHICLES		MOS		0		0		0	0
COMPRESSOR & TOOLS	2	MOS		0		0	600	1,200	1,200
GENERATOR	2	MOS		0		0	600	1,200	1,200
TRANSIT	10	MOS		0		0	125	1,250	1,250
LEVEL	10	MOS		0		0	100	1,000	1,000
RADIO COMMUNICATION		LS		0		0		0	0
TRUCKING FROM YARD		LS		0		0		0	0
TRUCKING - HIRED		LS		0		0		0	0
MISC EQUIPMENT RENTAL	12	MOS		0		0	750	9,000	9,000
MISC CRANE RENTAL		MOS		0		0		0	0
MISC SMALL TOOLS	12	MOS		0		0	750	9,000	9,000
INSURANCE & TAXES:				0		0		0	0
FRINGE BENEFITS - PROJ. MGT.	42	%				28,392			28,392
SUPERINTENDENTS	33	%				32,208		0	32,208
OTHER SUPERVISION	48	%				26,910		0	26,910
CRAFT & PUNCH	55	%		0		73,095		0	73,095
SALES TAX ON MATERIAL	8.25	%		1,939		0		0	1,939
LABOR ESCALATION	3	%		0		15,555		0	15,555
LEGAL & AUDIT		LS		0		0		0	0
ROOFING / MEMBRANE INSPECTION		LS		0		0		0	0
OTHER TAXES & INSURANCE		LS		0		0		0	0

	PERCENT OF TOTAL								
SUMMARY OF G.C. DIVISIONS:									
PROJECT MANAGEMENT	30.4 %			0		232,000		0	232,000
SURVEY, LAYOUT, & ENG.	3.9 %			0		0		30,000	30,000
TRANS., TRAVEL, & MANHAUL	0.6 %			0		0		4,800	4,800
PERMITS / LICENSES	0.1 %			0		0		400	400
OFFICE & ENG. EXPENSES	10.0 %			14,500		1,000		60,550	76,050
TEMP. BLDGS. & SERVICES	9.4 %			1,500		24,900		45,000	71,400
TEMP. PROT. & CLEANUP	18.2 %			7,500		100,000		31,500	139,000
EQUIP. OWNED & RENTED	4.1 %			0		0		31,050	31,050
INSURANCE, TAXES, & BENEFIT	23.3 %			1,939		176,160		0	178,099

GENERAL CONDITIONS GRAND TOTAL:	100 %			$25,439		$534,060		$203,300	$762,799
GENERAL CONDITIONS PER MONTH:	12 MOS		@	$63,567	PER MONTH				
GENERAL CONDITIONS PER CENT OF TOTAL PROJECT:				ERR					

SUMMARY

LKJ is in a perfect position to enter into the largest growing sector of the construction industry—healthcare. Though most companies do not or cannot afford to do marketing research during a recession, conventional wisdom suggests that this is the correct time. By preparing a plan of action to bring the company out of the recession, LKJ can catch other companies off-guard by either increasing its current market share or finding a niche in a new market.

The inevitable aging of America will lead to persons 65 years and older making up 20 percent of the population by the year 2000. The healthcare industry is almost recession-proof and is expected to grow at least 5 percent over the next few years.

Though hampered by its lack of experience in healthcare construction, LKJ has a solid reputation within the industry of completing prospects on time. It has high name recognition within the industry and should have no major problems transferring that strength into a new market. However, LKJ will have to become more knowledgeable about UBCs and the OSHPD regulations regarding healthcare facilities. LKJ will also have to do networking to get on the "inside track" with developers and architects to break into this tightly-knit sector.

A projected volume of $2.4 billion in healthcare construction by 1994 means that there will be more than ample opportunity for LKJ get on board. Anticipating a conservative market share and fee at 1 and 2.5 percent respectively, translates into a projected profit of $600,000. Compared to the rest of LKJ's fee potential this might not seem like much now, but the writer has no doubt that this figure will be much higher by the time LKJ starts building its first hospital.

There is no doubt that LKJ faces competition from the six major contractors in this sector, and is at a disadvantage when it comes to healthcare experience. However, LKJ has the advantage having its own Interiors and Industrial divisions, as well as a track record that is beyond reproach. LKJ can also take comfort in the fact that these six major contractors control only 38 percent of the market. Small regional players control the remaining 62 percent, none of which are larger than LKJ. The writer sees no reason why the 1 percent market share by 1994 cannot be achieved given these facts.

No new marketing plan can succeed without the commitment of top management. In the past, LKJ's top managers have been leery of new markets and so have basically confined themselves to the same segment for the last two decades. LKJ needs to get away from this conservative approach to marketing, and capitalize now on the potential money-making opportunity in healthcare construction. With the minimum projections stipulated in this marketing plan, LKJ's good standing in the industry, and the exploding growth of healthcare construction, there is no reason why LKJ will not exceed expectations.

BIBLIOGRAPHY

"California Construction Review," Construction Industry Research Board, January 9, 1992, p. 10.

Cole, Benjamin N. "County Med" Still Dwarfs Other Hospitals," *Los Angeles Business Journal,* April 29, 1991, p. 25.

Fay, James S., Editor. *California Almanac,* 5th edition. Santa Barbara, CA: Pacific Data Resources, 1991.

Gardner, Elizabeth. "Healthcare Construction Survives Ailing Economy," *Modern Healthcare,* March 11, 1991, p. 28.

Hoffman, Terry, Architect and Vice President. HNC Group, Ontario, CA. Personal interview, February, 28, 1992.

Marshall Valuation Service. Marshall & Swift, June 1989, Section 15, p. 21.

National Medical Enterprises, Inc. Consolidated Balance Sheet, 1991 Annual Report, p. 29.

Shiver Jr., Jube. "Developers Find a Cure in Health Care." Los Angeles Times, September 7, 1991, Section D, p. 4.

A4

A FARMER'S MARKET

Developed by
KRISTEN KUNISHIMA

Contents

EXECUTIVE SUMMARY

More and more, Americans are shopping at "Farmers' Markets." A Farmers' Market in the city of Cypress has great potential to become the largest supplier of fresh produce to the community. There are no other Farmers' Markets in the city or surrounding areas. This opportunity has been fully researched and is ready to be implemented.

The required investment for this project will be $9,000. This fee will pay for all of the market's expenses for the first year. Much of this money will be spent on fees and licenses required to run the market, insurance, rent, and other miscellaneous expenses.

The time needed to run the market is about five hours a week. The market will be open every Sunday in the parking lot of Cypress Community College from 9 A.M. to 1 P.M. The person running the market will need to be at the site one hour before the opening of the market, while the market is in progress, and one hour after the market closes.

The net income has been predicted for the first three years of operation. The first year is $19,111.75, the second year is $27,065.85, and the third year is $33,676.30.

The demand for fresh produce has increased over the years. This is important because there is a need for these products in everyday life. People enjoy shopping at Farmers' Markets for many reasons. They enjoy spending time with their families outdoors, talking with the growers of the produce, and buying good quality merchandise at low prices.

Due to the high cost of living, consumers today are watching their budgets. The Farmers' Market will not only bring fresh produce to the residents of Cypress, it will save them money.

There are many competitive advantages the Farmers' Market has over its competitors. The products will be fresher and sold at substantially lower prices than grocery stores. A variety of items will be available, including both traditional and hard-to-find items. All of the growers will be able to share their knowledge about the produce, how it is grown, how to prepare them, and any pesticides or chemicals that may be used on the produce.

The plans for this market include eventual expansion and inclusion of other types of vendors such as arts and crafts and food vendors. The sales will increase and the profits will rise.

Advertising and promotions have been set up to publicize the market. Yearly anniversary events will occur, advertising will be placed in newspapers, and flyers will be distributed.

The market will provide a great service to the community of Cypress. This Farmers' Market is an excellent opportunity to make a profit and have fun while doing so. The work is minimal but the rewards are great.

INTRODUCTION

Fruits and vegetables are an important factor in every person's life. They are foods needed to live a long healthy life. Because they are so vital, consumers deserve the best that money can buy.

Today's consumer is able to purchase fruits and vegetables of superior quality at a nearby Farmers' Market. Farmers' Markets are appearing all over the country due to the high demand for better goods. They are usually open-air markets located in parking lots, downtown areas, or on roadsides. They are filled with growers selling their fresh items at substantially lower prices than the local supermarkets. Although Farmers' Markets are best known for the fresh produce they provide, many also sell items such as homemade breads, jams and jellies, flowers, arts and crafts, honey, and many other items.

Farmers will bring their freshly picked produce to the market for the consumer to purchase. They provide their own tables or stands, chairs, coverings, and any other equipment they may need to sell their products.

Many consumers enjoy shopping at these markets because they allow the buyer and the actual grower to meet face to face. This allows the consumer to ask the grower questions about the products they are buying. Pesticides and other chemicals are of great concern to today's shoppers. By talking to a grower they are able to find out what may be used on the products before they purchase it.

All of the produce sold is very fresh. Most of the goods have been harvested that very same day or the previous week. They are guaranteed to be fresh and of good quality.

These markets have been around for many years, but they have only started becoming more popular within the past 40 years. Many people still do not know about the benefits they can receive by shopping at a Farmers' Market. Fresh produce has become increasingly important to consumers during these recent years.

Farmers' Markets not only benefit consumers, they also benefit farmers. Farmers sell their produce at the markets to subsidize their income. Commercial farmers make about 25 cents' profit on every dollar's worth of produce they sell to a supermarket. At a Farmer's Market, they are able to make a profit of almost the full dollar. Also, when the produce is grown and purchased locally, the money remains in the community and stimulates the local economy.[1]

The market being proposed will be located in the city of Cypress, California. There are no other markets of this type in the local area. Both population and housing have been increasing dramatically as can be seen in Figures A4-1 and A4-2. The site which has been chosen is the parking lot of Cypress Community College. This is a very good location because the college is located on a main street with a heavy traffic flow. Another reason this is a prime location is because the college is accessible from many different types of public transportation.

[1]Anonymous, "Find The Best At Your Farmers' Markets," *Glamour,* July 1991, p. 175.

Figure A4-1.   Population Increase in Cypress.

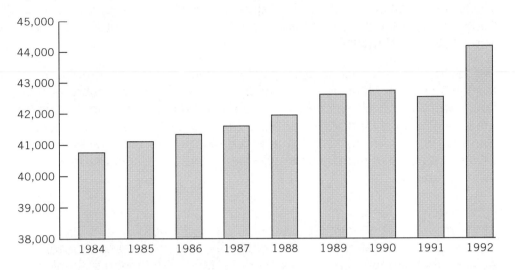

Orange County Progress Report—1991-92.

Figure A4-2.   Housing Increase in Cypress.

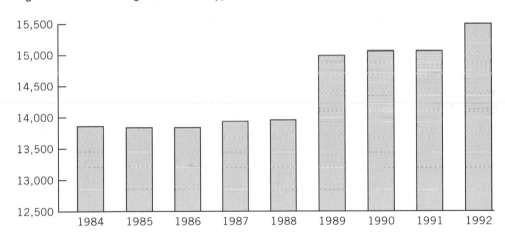

Orange County Progress Report—1991-92.

SITUATIONAL ANALYSIS

DEMAND. The demand for fresh produce has increased greatly over the past few years. Consumers are becoming more and more conscious about what types of foods they eat. In a survey of 20 Farmers' Markets, there is an increase in the total amount of sales from 1992 to 1993 of about 15 percent.[2] According to the California Department of Food and Agriculture, California only had a total of 8 markets in 1977. Since then, more than 120 markets have appeared.[3]

---

[2]Katie O'Kennedy, "The Best: Farmers' Markets," *Bon Appetit,* April 1993, p. 26.
[3]Anonymous, "Until The Revolution Comes: Where to Get Clean Food Now," *California,* June 1990., p. 104.

Across the country there are at least 2,000 Farmers' Markets in operation. Many of the largest markets, such as in Detroit and San Francisco, can attract as many as 20,000 people a day. These markets sell a wide variety of items and are known to be popular tourist attractions.[4]

TECHNOLOGY. Technology has no drastic effect upon the Farmers' Market. Although technology has increased the delivery time and the freshness of produce in the supermarkets, it can't compete with the social benefits one can receive by shopping at the local Farmers' Market. Shoppers seem to enjoy the old way of sealing a deal. They are able to bargain, sample the produce, and talk to the growers about the produce being offered. Many consumers who have their own small gardens enjoy getting tips from the experts.

Families enjoy coming to these markets as family outings. They are able to spend time together outdoors and enjoy the atmosphere. Many senior citizens enjoy coming to the markets as a weekly place to meet their friends.

The produce that one purchases from the supermarket cannot compete with these benefits that can be received at a Farmers' Market. Although technology is helping the supermarkets, the produce at the Farmers' Market is usually cheaper and the atmosphere is a lot more fun. Technology cannot compete with the benefits that the Farmers' Market can give the consumer.[5]

ECONOMY. Due to the higher costs of living, consumers are becoming more conscious of their budgets, and thus they no longer purchase frivolous items. If a consumer purchases an item, he or she wishes to receive the best quality possible at the best price. Farmers' Markets enable the consumer to purchase more items than they might at a grocery store. Many times the prices are lower, which is helpful for those on a limited budget.

Neutral Environ

Farmers' Markets are highly regulated by the government. This is important because it keeps consumers from getting taken advantage of. The reputation of the markets is very important because they advertise that the quality of the produce is much better than that sold at the supermarket, and consumers feel that they are receiving the best quality available.

U.S. Department of Agriculture. Growers need certification to sell their goods at the market. Anything that is sold must be grown, baked, or in the case of seafood, caught by the seller. Produce cannot be bought from a wholesale outlet and resold. Before a certificate is issued, an investigation is conducted by the department to make sure the seller is the actual producer.[6] The Department of Agriculture also makes unannounced visits to the markets to inspect the goods sold by the vendors. Each vendor must have his or her certificate displayed somewhere so that the inspector can see it. Anything that is being sold must be listed on the certificate; otherwise the inspector has the authority to close the vendor down until he or she is able to produce the correct papers. The market is responsible for making sure that the growers have all of the proper papers before they are able to sell.

---

[4]Cathy, Dold, "Green City Markets," *Amicus Journal* Summer 1992, p. 34.
[5]Anne Michaud, "OC Enterprise: Home-Produced Wares, Farmer's Market a Modern Day Bazaar for Small Vendors," *LA Times—OC Edition,* April 4, 1994, sec. D, p. 1.
[6]Anne Michaud, "OC Enterprise: Home-Produced Wares, Farmers' Market a Modern-Day Bazaar for Small Vendors," *LA Times—OC Edition,* April 4, 1994, sec. D, p. 1.

If any type of scales are used to weigh the products, a seal from the Department of Agriculture must be displayed to let the consumer know that the scale has been regulated by the department and the weight is accurate.

These types of procedures help to regulate how and what the vendors bring to the market. The presence of the representatives usually put the consumer's mind at ease. This way they are assured of receiving the best quality possible.

U.S. Department of Health. A Department of Health certificate is also needed. This certificate is needed by all of the growers who participate in the market. Sellers of fresh fish, and baked and canned goods are required to undergo additional inspection of their equipment and production premises and must obtain an individual permit.[7]

These certificates help to ensure that all the produce is grown in accordance with the health laws of the United States.

Special Interest Groups. There are a few interest groups that may be concerned with the welfare of the Farmers' Markets. Some groups of farmers let the consumers know that by patronizing city-based Farmers' Markets they are helping to preserve dwindling farmlands across the country.[8] These markets also help to eliminate waste, because farmers are able to sell their excess produce at the markets. Farmers concerned with this waste are very supportive of the markets.

Media. The local media helps to advertise for the Farmers' Markets. There are many articles written about the benefits a consumer can receive by shopping at them. Some of these articles can be found in health magazines.

Cookbooks and recipes in magazines also highlight the Farmers' Markets. They praise them due to the wide variety of items available and the good quality of the produce.

This type of publicity helps to make consumers more aware of their local markets. Many of the articles written about the markets contain some type of listing on the markets in the surrounding areas or where the consumer can receive more information about where to find one.

Competitor Environ

Every business has some type of competition. Each competitor has its own strengths and weaknesses. They vary depending upon what type of business the competitor is.

Supermarkets. Supermarkets will be the Farmers' Markets largest competitor. The prices at the Farmers' Market will be in direct competition with the supermarket. Supermarket prices are usually higher, but they are able to slash prices and take a loss on the produce so that the consumers will buy from their stores.

One large advantage that the supermarket has over the Farmers' Market is the availability of hours it is open and the number of locations in the local area. The Farmers' Market will only be open for four hours on Sundays, whereas most supermarkets are open 7 days a week, 24 hours a day. Some people will not be able to wait until Sunday to purchase certain items, and will be forced to buy their produce at the supermarket.

---

[7]Anne Michaud, "OC Enterprise: Home-Produced Wares, Farmers' Market a Modern Day Bazaar for Small Vendors," *LA Times—OC Edition* April 4, 1994, sec. D, p. 1.
[8]Cathy Dold, "Green City Markets," *Amicus Journal,* Summer 1992, p. 34.

The freshness of the produce available at the supermarket cannot compete with the products sold at the Farmers' Market. The selection of unusual goods is also more limited than in the supermarket.

Local Stands. Local produce stands will also compete with the Farmers' Market. These stands are usually found in small lots where many potential customers will be able to see them. They are usually limited in the amount of items which they sell, because the stands are basically run by one farmer and they only sell what is growing in their fields. The stands will offer only the traditional items that consumers buy on a regular basis. They do not offer the hard-to-find items which many people are interested in purchasing.

These local stands, like supermarkets, have the advantage of availability of time. They are usually open 7 days a week, 8 hours a day. Fresh produce can be purchased on a daily basis from these stands.

Other Farmers' Markets. Although there are no Farmers' Markets which are held in the surrounding areas, there are markets farther away. Many people are often reluctant to drive 20 miles to buy fresh produce. They prefer to purchase these items locally.

On the other hand, if the market has a good reputation or if consumers know that they will be able to purchase specific items, many are willing to drive the far distances to buy their produce and other goods. Sometimes people will make the trip into a family outing and drive to the Farmers' Market that is farther away.

Company Environ

The Farmers' Market has many strengths which will help to make it successful. This market will provide the best quality produce available to the local community. This is important because consumers always want to buy the very best that money can buy.

The market will be held every Sunday (with the exception of Easter Sunday) from 9 A.M. to 1 P.M., rain or shine. It will be held in the Cypress Community College parking lot every week. It is very important that the day, time, and location of the market remain the same every week because most of the shoppers will be repeat customers. They will be local residents who are doing their weekly grocery shopping and may become irritated if there are constant changes in any of these factors.

The shoppers will be able to bring their families and enjoy the outdoors because the market is open-air. It is necessary to emphasize a family atmosphere because many people want to spend time with their families on the weekends.

Farmers' Markets are on a cash-only basis, which is very popular with many of the vendors and consumers. Consumers like this policy because they do not have to wait in long lines and the service is faster because there are no checks or credit card transactions to deal with. Vendors also like this policy because they do not have to worry about bad checks or credit cards. The consumer buys what he or she is able to afford.

Along with many strengths, the Farmers' Market also has a few weaknesses. One weakness is that the market is only open once a week. This may be inconvenient for some shoppers. If they are unable to shop on a certain Sunday, they will have to wait until the next week or make their purchases somewhere else.

Another weakness of the market may be the dependency upon farmers who are selling the goods. It is important that the farmers are dependable and make a commitment to sell on a weekly basis. If the farmer does not sell much produce on a certain day, it will be a wasted trip for him and no profit for the market. Since the market makes its profit by charging 5 percent of the farmer's gross daily sales as space fee, the market will not make any money.

Competitive Advantage

This Farmers' Market has many advantages over the competitors. There are many benefits that make the Farmers' Market a better place to shop.

Product. This market will be able to provide produce which is fresher than other retailers, such as supermarkets. The produce is usually picked the morning it is sold or on the previous day. Much of the produce available in the supermarket is harvested at least 7 to 10 days before it is actually purchased and consumed.[9] It has been documented that vitamin C and other nutrients may deteriorate quickly in certain vegetables once they have been picked. Buying produce that has been harvested more recently is more nutritional.[10]

Sometimes the produce in the Farmers' Market may be sold early in the season. Supermarkets and other stores may not receive the "first of the season produce" as quickly as the Farmers' Market. If consumers want to purchase these items in the supermarket, they will have to wait until the season progresses.

Availability of Items. Hard-to-find or difficult to grow items may be found in the Farmers' Market. The farmers bring their produce from many different locations, which is why there is usually a wide variety of items available in the market. The growers bring produce which may not be as abundant in the local area. This increases the demand for this product, and the farmer will be able to sell the item quickly.

Some farmers may also bring certain ethnic foods to the market. Often this type of produce will only be found in ethnic stores. Farmers will bring this type of produce because the prices are usually lower than the stores and people of other nationalities enjoy trying different things.

Information About Produce and How It Is Grown Available. By shopping at the Farmers' Market the buyer is able to talk to the person who is actually growing the produce. There are no middlemen involved so consumers are able to receive firsthand information about the produce they are purchasing.

Many consumers today are interested in pesticides and other chemicals that may be used on the products. They do not want to purchase items that are heavily sprayed. This is important in today's health-conscious society.

People are always interested in knowing where their produce is being grown, and they usually want to know a little about the farms. Farmers enjoy talking about their produce and will gladly answer almost any question the consumer asks.

Farmers are usually the best people to ask for help in picking out the best produce. They are knowledgeable about which vegetables are riper and of better quality. The farmers and the consumers also trade recipes on how to prepare certain vegetables. Consumers seem to enjoy hearing about new ways of preparing certain vegetables.

Many times the shoppers who patronize Farmers' Markets have their own small gardens. They feel confident in asking growers for some firsthand advice since they are usually the experts.

---

[9]John Dodge, "Fresh from the Farm," *Farm Journal,* October 1993, p. 47.
[10]Anonymous, "Is Farm Stand Produce Better?" *USA Today,* June 1991, p. 12.0.

TARGET MARKET

Demographics

Gender. The target market for the Farmers' Market consists of both males and females. As long as the farmer grows or makes his or her own products, being male or female makes no difference.

Age. The age group targeted is 25 and older. This is the average age of a person who will be able to sell his or her produce at the market. The person needs to be knowledgeable about the product and be able to perform simple math calculations. Younger people are usually not as experienced in dealing with many customers at one time.

Income. The income level ranges from low to high, because many farmers use the markets to make extra income on the side. They do not need to sell their produce at the markets because they make a substantial living selling their produce to wholesalers. Many of them sell at the markets because they enjoy it.

On the other hand, other people whose income is not as high sell their produce here to make a living. Their farm or ranch may not be large enough to sell to a wholesaler. In order to make a profit from their goods, they take their produce to Farmers' Markets to sell.

Lifestyle

The lifestyle of the target market is people who are farmers. This is important because only producers who grow or make their goods are able to sell their products at a Farmers' Market. These are also people who do not mind spending time in the sun or rain and enjoy interacting with others.

Psychographics

The target market are farmers who are interested in making the most from their produce. They want to help to preserve the farmlands and do not want any of their produce to go to waste. They are concerned with helping people receive the best quality produce for their money.

PROBLEMS, THREATS, AND OPPORTUNITIES

Problems

Market Geared Toward One Ethnic Group. A problem may occur in the marketplace if consumers feel that the market is geared toward only one ethnic group. Some of the shoppers may feel uncomfortable or unwelcome if the market is perceived in this manner. This can occur if there is no diversity in the ethnic produce sold and it is focused upon only one ethnic group rather than a variety of ethnicities.

This potential problem may be resolved by having the marketing manager regulate the produce sold in the market. Before a grower participates in a market he or she must provide a list of the items they are going to sell. The market manager is then able to decide which items the grower can or cannot sell in the market. This will also prevent an overabundance of certain items and a shortage of others. If the manager feels that there may be too much produce being sold for only one particular ethnic group, he or she may prohibit other sellers from selling more products in this category.

Change in Location. Another problem may occur if Cypress Community College changes its mind about allowing the market to remain on their parking lot. This will always be a potential problem due to circumstances beyond the control of the market. The only way to eliminate this problem would be to purchase land for the market. However, this investment may be too expensive.

The way to prepare in advance for this problem is to have an alternate site picked out. There is a large parking lot a few miles down the street from the college, that has been chosen as the alternate site. The owner has agreed to offer this as the alternative site of the market, and the city has already zoned this area for business. The flow of traffic is still heavy and the new location is near the old site.

Threats

Bad Weather. Bad weather may become a threat for the Farmers' Market. Business is likely to become slower during the rainy season, because this is an open-air market.

The way to handle this is to remain optimistic. When the weather is bleak remind the vendors to bring coverings to protect themselves and their produce. It is also important that the vendors have ropes or weights to tie the coverings down in case of high winds.

Also, remind customers to bring umbrellas. Many regulars will come to the market regardless of the weather. If the weather begins to clear up toward the end of the day, the market hours can be extended.

More Small Produce Stands Emerge. Another threat may be the emergence of more small produce stands. These small businesses may appear in small lots around the city. They may take some of the customers who will be shopping at the Farmers' Market.

A way to deal with this problem may be to ask the owner of the stand if he or she would like to join the Farmers' Market. Emphasize the advantages of joining the market. They would be able to benefit from the high volume of consumers who will be shopping in the market.

Another way to deal with this may be to increase advertising in the local area. This will let the consumers know of the benefits they can receive by shopping at the market. The advertising may also bring in new customers who may not have heard of the market.

Other Farmers' Markets. Other Farmers' Markets that are held on the same day pose a threat to the market.

Markets with better reputations, or that are larger, have a tendency to draw more farmers to their markets. There may be waiting lists for the farmers to come in and sell their products. This is why the growth potential and the expansion of the market is very important. Farmers rely heavily on word of mouth to find the best markets.

The low space fee will also make the Cypress market more attractive. Along with its many potentials, farmers will be able to make higher profits because they will be paying a lower fee for their space.

Opportunities

Only Farmers' Market in Local Area. There are many opportunities for starting this market in the city of Cypress. This Farmers' Market will be the first to open in the local area. There are other markets available in Orange County, but the closest one is about 20 miles away. People in the area will benefit from the fresh produce that will be offered. This will help the market to expand quickly in sales and size. Once the market opens, residents in the local community will not have to drive far for their produce.

Community Population and Housing Increasing. Another advantage of beginning the market in Cypress is the increase in the community's population and housing. Since 1984 the population has increased from 40,850 to 44,218 in 1992.[11] Each year more people are moving into the city of Cypress.

Due to the increase in population, the number of housing units has also increased. Housing has increased from 13,650 units in 1984 to 15,082 in 1992.[12] This increase shows great potential for the market in the future. There is a possibility of gaining new shoppers each year.

MARKETING OBJECTIVES AND GOALS

Objective

The main objective of opening the Farmers' Market in the city of Cypress is to become the largest local supplier of fresh produce and other home-produced goods. This market will be the only one in the local area. There are other stands in the area that provide fresh produce to the community, but this market has the largest growth potential. Once the residents see the difference in the quality and prices over the supermarkets they will become dedicated customers. This will enhance the reputation of the market and sales will increase.

Goals

Expand Size of Market by 10 Percent Each Year. Each year there will be an increase in the size of the market. This will include expansion of the number of vendors selling their products. Once the market begins to grow, other produce vendors will want to sell their produce in this market, and current vendors will be able to bring and sell more items. The space available will accommodate the amount of produce available to the consumer. Once the market grows, there is a strong possibility that the reputation of the market will also be enhanced.

The parking lot of Cypress College is large enough to allow expansion of the market. There will be enough room for the vendors to sell their goods and the consumers to park their vehicles.

Include Arts and Crafts and Food Vendors. This goal is closely linked with the first goal. The Farmers' Market will expand its produce vendors and eventually include arts and crafts and food vendors. This will add to the variety of items available in the

---

[11] *Orange County Progress Report—1991–92* [United States]: n.p.
[12] *Orange County Progress Report—1991–92* [United States]: n.p.

market. Some people enjoy browsing around the market just looking at items. By including these new groups, there will be more for the consumer to see. Many of their purchases will be impulse buying.

The market will set up a nonagricultural area where the consumer will be able to purchase such items. Consumers enjoy buying arts and crafts because they're unlikely to make these items themselves.

Selling prepared food may keep the consumer at the market longer. They may decide to eat the food as they walk around. They may also come to eat certain foods for breakfast or lunch, and make a few purchases during the time they are at the market.

Increase Sales. By expanding the market to include new vendors and adding to the variety of vendors, sales should increase. The goal of the market is to increase sales by at least 50 percent within the next three years. This is very realistic because of the high potential of the area and the planning of the market.

Emphasize Low Prices and High Quality. It is important that the consumer be aware that he or she will receive the best quality available at the best possible prices. The Farmers' Market will implement this through advertising and by making sure that the market offers the best values.

If consumers know that they are receiving the best produce available, they will continue to shop at the Farmers' Market, and will keep returning to the market.

MARKETING STRATEGY

In order to become a successful business, a marketing strategy must be formulated. There are many different ways in which to become successful.

We will be using a niche strategy by selling both hard-to-find and traditional items. This is important because the market is offering hard-to-find items to consumers. Once shoppers know that they will be able to find these items at the Farmers' Market, they will continue to patronize the market. This will also boost the reputation of the market. When someone is in search of a hard-to-find item, they will look at the Farmers' Market first.

Along with selling the hard-to-find items it is important to continue selling traditional items. These items are what most people will shop for. They will buy their weekly items for meals throughout the week. Without these items the market would become a speciality place to shop. This market is geared toward the average consumer.

The life cycle for the market is still in its early stages. Although there are many Farmers' Markets throughout the country they have only recently grown in popularity. Being the first Farmers' Market in the local area is advantageous because consumers will become familiar with the market and will not want to shop elsewhere even if a new market should appear.

The market will be new to the community and should arouse people's curiosity. Shoppers may visit the market just to see what it is. Once they are drawn to the market, they will be able to see firsthand the benefits of shopping at the Farmers' Market.

When advertising, it is important to emphasize high quality and low prices. Stressing these benefits will ensure that consumers will not want to purchase their produce anywhere else.

Another strategy may be to include arts and crafts. As mentioned previously, this will increase the variety of goods available to the consumer in the market, and will help to make the market a more diverse place to shop. It will add to the uniqueness of the market, because these types of items cannot be found elsewhere. Many of the arts and crafts' vendors create items with their own style and creativity and only sell their products at these Farmers' Markets.

MARKETING TACTICS

Product

This Farmers' Market will be the first to be introduced in the community. Many consumers may not know what a Farmers' Market is, so it is imperative to introduce the product correctly because first impressions are very important. This way they are able to see the benefits they can receive.

After the market is initially introduced, it will slowly be modified once its sales increase. To modify the market there will be an increase of both produce and other vendors, including arts and crafts and food vendors. This will increase the variety of the items being sold, and loyal consumers will be able to receive a better selection. The modification will help to make the market larger and more interesting.

The market needs to be positioned in the consumer's mind as a place to receive lower prices and higher quality. People do not wish to spend money on produce they are not happy with. Satisfaction of the shopper is very important to the market. Keeping customers happy will make them return and will maintain the good reputation of the market.

Pricing

The space fees for the Farmers' Market will be 5 percent of the total net sales for each day. This fee is very competitive with other markets that are held on the same day.

Many other markets charge 6 percent for their space fees. The Cypress Farmers' Market will keep its fees at 5 percent when the market begins to grow. This will help to draw more farmers to the market.

The market will be able to continue to profit although the space fees will remain at 5 percent. This is because the market has plans for growth. The new farmers and the increase in sales will make up for the extra 1 percent that will not be charged to the farmer.

Farmers do not have a high risk with the space fee at 5 percent. If the farmer does not sell many goods that day, the 5 percent space fee will still leave him or her some profit. On the other hand, if the farmer does well that day, the 5 percent is enough for the market to make a profit.

Promotion

Promotion of the market is very important, because it will make consumers aware of the market. Advertising will also help the market become successful. Advertising in local newspapers on a weekly basis will help to keep the market in the consumer's mind.

Prior to the market's opening, flyers will be posted in places of high visibility. It is important to emphasize the opening day of the market. The advertising in the newspapers will let consumers know where and when the market will be open.

Publicity in newspapers and magazines is free to the market. Keeping in contact with the local newspapers and TV stations will help to increase visibility when special events occur at the market. This will be very beneficial because the market plans to hold special anniversary events that will involve increased advertising.

All of these promotions will help the market to become more prosperous. The better the market's business, the more farmers will want to sell their produce at this market.

Farmers' Markets are dependent upon word of mouth for their business from the farmers. By using promotion, new farmers will be able to get information on how they can contact someone to sell their produce. They will also be able to see how aggressive the market is in attracting customers.

Distribution

Direct channels of distribution will be used. The market emphasizes the avoidance of middlemen, and it is important to maintain this one-on-one policy. The farmers sell their goods directly to the public. The success of the market depends upon this.

Regulations of Farmers' Markets also keep the markets using this type of distribution. It is against the law for a seller to buy his or her products at a wholesale outlet; the seller must be the actual grower of the products.

CONTROL AND IMPLEMENTATION

The project will be controlled during implementation by using and adjusting the following charts and financial calculations included as a part of this plan: Project Development Schedule, Break-even Analysis, cash-flow estimates and net income estimates for a three-year period, and balance sheets calculated for three years (see Tables A4-1 to A4-12).

Table A4-1 Project Development Schedule

	Jan.	Feb.	March	April	May	June	July	Aug.	Sept.	Oct.	Nov.	Dec.
Apply For:				O								
Health License		——→		P								
Dept. of Agriculture Certificate		——→		E N								
Business License			——→									
Market Certificate		——————→		M								
Market Insurance			——→	A								
				R								
Advertising:				K								
Newspapers				E								——→
Flyers			——→	T								
Expansion of Market										——————→		

Table A4-2 Break-even Analysis

Break Even	=	Fixed Exp.	+	$\dfrac{\text{Variable Exp}}{\text{Net Sales}}$

$$\textbf{\$16,379.58} \quad = \quad 16,379.50 \quad + \quad \frac{4,097.00}{47,599.00}$$

$$\frac{16,379.58}{27 \text{ Vendors}} \quad = \quad \frac{606.65}{5\%} \quad = \quad \textbf{\$12,133.00}$$

For the market to break-even each farmer must sell $12,133.00 worth of produce in the first year because the market makes 5% of farmers' total sales. Five percent of $12,133.00 is $606.65. By multiplying $606.65 by the 27 vendors participating, the total is $16,379.58, which will cover the market's expenses.

Table A4-3 Cash Flow: Year 1

Cash	
Cash on hand	9,000.00
Total Cash	9,000.00
Income	
Net Sales	47,599.00
Total Income	47,599.00
Total Cash and Income	56,599.00
Expenses	
General and Fixed Exp.	20,296.50
Taxes	8,190.75
Total Expenses	28,487.25
Year End Cash Balance	28,111.75

Table A4-4 Cash Flow: Year 2

Cash	
Cash on hand	28,111.75
Total Cash	28,111.75
Income	
Net Sales	60,911.00
Total Income	60,911.00
Total Cash and Income	89,022.75
Expenses	
General Expenses	22,245.50
Taxes	11,599.65
Total Expenses	33,845.15
Year End Cash Balance	55,177.60

Table A4-5 Cash Flow: Year 3

Cash	
Cash on hand	55,177.60
Total Cash	55,177.60
Income	
Net Sales	71,349.00
Total Income	71,349.00
Total Cash and Income	126,526.60
Expenses	
General Expenses	23,240.00
Taxes	14,432.70
Total Expenses	37,672.70
Year End Cash Balance	88,853.90

Table A4-6 Net Income: Years 1, 2, and 3

	Year 1	Year 2	Year 3
Income			
Net Sales	47,599.00	60,911.00	71,349.00
General and Admin. Expenses			
Advertising	4,097.00	2,500.00	2,650.00
Total	4,097.00	2,500.00	2,650.00
Fixed Expenses			
Operating Expenses	15,430.00	18,890.00	19,690.00
Misc. Expenses	949.50	855.50	900.00
Total	16,379.50	19,745.50	20,590.00
Total Expenses	20,296.50	22,245.50	23,240.00
Net Income Before Taxes	27,302.50	38,665.50	48,109.00
Less Income Tax	8,190.75	11,599.65	14,432.70
Net Income	19,111.75	27,065.85	33,676.30

Table A4-7 Net Income: Year 1

	April	May	June	July	August	Sept.	Oct.	Nov.	Dec.	Jan.	Feb.	March
Income												
Net Sales	4234.50	3468.00	3567.50	4193.00	5168.50	4033.50	5210.00	4443.00	3677.00	2684.00	2953.00	3967.00
Gen. and Admin. Exp.												
Advertising	1056.00	678.00	563.00	200.00	200.00	200.00	200.00	150.00	250.00	200.00	200.00	200.00
Total	1056.00	678.00	563.00	200.00	200.00	200.00	200.00	150.00	250.00	200.00	200.00	200.00
Fixed Expenses												
Operating Exp.	2736.00	1154.00	1154.00	1154.00	1154.00	1154.00	1154.00	1154.00	1154.00	1154.00	1154.00	1154.00
Misc. Exp.	103.00	98.50	148.00	89.50	74.00	36.50	55.50	63.00	81.50	49.00	64.00	87.00
Total	2839.00	1252.50	1302.00	1243.50	1228.00	1190.50	1209.50	1217.00	1235.50	1203.00	1218.00	1241.00
Total Expenses	3895.00	1930.50	1865.00	1263.50	1428.00	1390.50	1409.50	1367.00	1485.50	1403.00	1418.00	1441.00
Net Income Before Tax	339.50	1537.50	1702.50	2929.50	3740.50	2643.00	3800.50	3076.00	2191.50	1281.00	1535.00	2526.00
Less Income Tax	101.85	461.25	510.75	878.85	1122.15	792.90	1140.15	922.80	657.45	384.30	460.50	757.80
Net Income	237.65	1076.25	1191.75	2050.65	2618.35	1850.10	2660.35	2153.20	1534.05	896.70	1074.50	1768.20

Table A4-8 Net Income: Year 2

	April	May	June	July	August	Sept.	Oct.	Nov.	Dec.	Jan.	Feb.	March
Income												
Net Sales	7254.00	5346.50	5528.00	5873.00	6472.00	4707.50	5124.00	4965.00	4741.00	3175.00	3428.00	4297.00
Gen. and Admin. Exp.												
Advertising	750.00	125.00	125.00	131.00	169.00	200.00	150.00	150.00	200.00	165.00	165.00	170.00
Total	750.00	125.00	125.00	131.00	169.00	200.00	150.00	150.00	200.00	165.00	165.00	170.00
Fixed Expenses												
Operating Exp.	6196.00	1154.00	1154.00	1154.00	1154.00	1154.00	1154.00	1154.00	1154.00	1154.00	1154.00	1154.00
Misc. Exp.	111.00	74.50	74.50	72.00	64.00	64.00	55.50	68.00	72.00	54.00	68.00	78.00
Total	6307.00	1228.50	1228.50	1226.00	1218.00	1218.00	1209.50	1222.00	1226.00	1208.00	1222.00	1232.00
Total Expenses	7057.00	1353.50	1353.50	1357.00	1387.00	1418.00	1359.50	1372.00	1426.00	1373.00	1387.00	1402.00
Net Income Before Tax	197.00	3993.00	4174.50	4516.00	5085.00	3289.50	3764.50	3593.00	3315.00	1802.00	2041.00	2895.00
Less Income Tax	59.10	1197.90	1252.35	1354.80	1525.50	986.85	1129.35	1077.90	994.50	540.60	612.30	868.50
Net Income	137.90	2795.10	2922.15	3161.20	3559.50	2302.65	2635.15	2515.10	2320.50	1261.40	1428.70	2026.50

Table A4-9 Net Income: Year 3

	April	May	June	July	August	Sept.	Oct.	Nov.	Dec.	Jan.	Feb.	March
Income												
Net Sales	8211.00	5643.00	6235.00	8013.00	7526.00	6421.00	5847.00	5342.00	5211.00	3600.00	4326.00	4974.00
Gen. and Admin. Exp.												
Advertising	725.00	130.00	145.00	185.00	162.00	203.00	165.00	189.00	196.00	155.00	200.00	195.00
Total	725.00	130.00	145.00	185.00	162.00	203.00	165.00	189.00	196.00	155.00	200.00	195.00
Fixed Expenses												
Operating Exp.	6996.00	1154.00	1154.00	1154.00	1154.00	1154.00	1154.00	1154.00	1154.00	1154.00	1154.00	1154.00
Misc. Exp.	185.00	78.00	37.00	68.00	52.00	80.00	83.00	65.00	52.00	50.00	85.00	65.00
Total	7181.00	1232.00	1191.00	1222.00	1206.00	1234.00	1237.00	1219.00	1206.00	1204.00	1239.00	1219.00
Total Expenses	7906.00	1362.00	1336.00	1407.00	1368.00	1437.00	1402.00	1408.00	1402.00	1359.00	1439.00	1414.00
Net Income Before Tax	305.00	4281.00	4899.00	6606.00	6158.00	4984.00	4445.00	3934.00	3809.00	2241.00	2887.00	3560.00
Less Income Tax	91.50	1284.30	1469.70	1981.80	1847.40	1495.20	1333.50	1180.20	1142.70	672.30	866.10	1068.00
Net Income	213.50	2996.70	3429.30	4624.20	4310.60	3488.80	3111.50	2753.80	2666.30	1568.70	2020.90	2492.00

Table A4-10 Balance Sheet: Year 1

Assets	
Cash	28,111.75
Accounts Receivable	0.00
Inventory	0.00
Land	0.00
Total Assets	28,111.75
Liabilities	
Accounts Payable	0.00
Total Liabilities	0.00
Net Worth	
Proprietorship	28,111.75
Total Net Worth	28,111.75

Table A4-11 Balance Sheet: Year 2

Assets	
Cash	55,177.60
Accounts Receivable	0.00
Inventory	0.00
Land	0.00
Total Assets	55,177.60
Liabilities	
Accounts Payable	0.00
Total Liabilities	0.00
Net Worth	
Proprietorship	55,177.60
Total Net Worth	55,177.60

Table A4-12 Balance Sheet: Year 3

Assets	
Cash	88,853.90
Accounts Receivable	0.00
Inventory	0.00
Land	0.00
Total Assets	88,853.90
Liabilities	
Accounts Payable	0.00
Total Liabilities	0.00
Net Worth	
Proprietorship	88,853.90
Total Net Worth	88,853.90

APPENDIX A4-A

Certified Farmers' Market Stall Sheet for Cypress Certified Farmers' Market

Producer's Name: _____

Date: _____

Items   Selling Unit Price

_____

_____

_____

_____

_____

_____

_____

_____

Total Collected Today Sales $ _____

Space Fee 5% $ _____

* *

I hereby certify that this produce is brought to this market in full accord with the direct marketing regulations of the California Department of Food and Agriculture, this market and all other pertinent regulations.

Signed: _____

Phone: _____

* *

Certified Farmers' Market receipt from Cypress Certified Farmers' Market.

Producer: _____

Date: _____ Location: _____

Total Sales: $ _____   Received by:

5% Space Fee: $ _____   _____

Southland Certified Farmers' Markets

Friendly Farmers

At a Southland Certified Farmers' Market, you buy directly from the farmer. In fact, the person handling your purchase is usually the person who grew it.

Most of our farms are family owned and operated and farmers come from all over California to sell their fresh-picked produce every week at your local farmers' market.

Our friendly farmers are committed to selling you the freshest food at competitive prices. Plus, they can help you select the juiciest fruit or ripest tomato while offering tips on cooking and canning.

Outdoor Markets

Rain or shine, our markets are open year-round. You can expect a shopping day like no other - a warm and friendly atmosphere combined with a festive

Shopping at a farmers' market is fun and you can feel confident that you are buying fresh, quality produce. A "certified" market means that our farmers meet the standards and conditions set forth by the California Department of Food and Agriculture.

Fresh Produce

At a Southland Certified Farmers' Market, we sell the freshest produce in town and freshness means good nutrition.

Vegetables, fruit, eggs, nuts, and honey are available at most markets and each season brings new crops-berries in Spring, melons in Summer, apples in Fall, and oranges in Winter.

Cut flowers, herbs, and garden plants are also sold at our farmers' markets along with a variety of specialty items including jams, baked goods, and fish.

farmers' markets come from a variety of cultural backgrounds. Americans, Asians, Mexicans, and Europeans all coming together to enjoy the freshness and fun. Plus many markets feature exotic fruits and vegetables that are used to prepare international recipes.

For many of our regulars, shopping at a certified farmers' market has replaced their weekly visit to the supermarket. Buying produce at your local farmers' market is the next best thing to growing it yourself!

Bringing It All Together

Dedicated to bringing farmers and consumers together, the Southland Farmers' Market Association is a non-profit tax exempt organization that serves over twenty markets in Southern California and our markets accept food stamps.

If you would like information about membership, markets, farmers or

SUMMARY

Although Farmers' Markets have been in existence for many years, they have not become popular until recently. They are open-air markets which sell a variety of home-produced and locally produced products. These items include fruits and vegetables, jams and jellies, arts and crafts, beef jerky, fresh fish, baked bread, and many other wonderful items.

This proposal has been made to start a market in the city of Cypress. The market will be located in the parking lot of Cypress Community College, from 9 A.M. to 1 P.M. every Sunday. This is a prime location due to the high visibility and easy accessibility.

Over the years the demand for fresh produce has increased, which may be why Farmers' Markets are becoming more popular. They have also increased in popularity because many people enjoy shopping the old-fashioned way. Customers are able to interact and bargain with the growers of the produce. This shows that technology has not had a large effect upon the market.

The economy has also caused consumers to watch how much they spend on their purchases. At a Farmers' Market they are able to receive high quality produce at lower prices.

The Farmers' Markets are highly regulated by the government. Certificates are needed from both the U.S. Departments of Agriculture and Health. These agencies both help to regulate the growers and make sure that goods are sold in accordance with the law.

There are also special interest groups that are interested in Farmers' Markets. Farmers want to make sure that consumers know how important these markets are to their occupation. The media also helps to promote the market. Many articles on Farmers' Markets include lists on where to find local markets and how they benefit the community.

Like every other business the Farmers' Market has many competitors. Some of them include local supermarkets, fresh produce stands, and other Farmers' Markets. All of them have many strengths as well as weaknesses. Supermarkets and fresh produce stands are usually more accessible for the consumer, but they do not provide the variety, freshness, and low prices that a Farmers' Market can.

The market has many strengths and weaknesses. People are able to shop in the open-air market with their families and talk to the growers. The produce is fresh and the atmosphere is very friendly. All markets are on a cash-only basis and do not accept checks or credit cards.

A disadvantage of the Farmers' Market is that it is only open once a week for four hours. Consumers will have to be available on that day in order to shop at the market.

Farmers' Markets have many competitive advantages. Consumers are able to talk with the actual growers of the produce. They can ask questions about pesticides or about the produce itself. The produce is much fresher because it is picked either that morning or the previous day. There is also a wide variety of items available, including traditional and hard-to-find items.

The market targets both male and female farmers who are interested in selling their goods. The average age of the farmer is usually 25 and above. Both high- and low-income farmers are targeted because both are interested in selling their produce. Most want to earn some extra money or to sell any surplus produce they may have grown on their farm.

Some problems may occur if consumers feel that the market is focusing on only one ethnic group or if Cypress College changes its mind about the use of the site. These problems are considered before the market is even opened. An alternate site has already been picked out in case the market needs to move. To solve the ethnicity problem, the manager of the market will regulate what types of produce are sold.

There are also some threats to the market. Bad weather, the emergence of more produce stands, and other Farmers' Markets pose a threat. The markets are open rain or shine. The Farmers' Market has more produce available than small produce stands, and this market has growth potential. This will keep the farmers and consumers coming to the market in Cypress.

This market will be the only Farmers' Market in the local area. The population and housing of the city of Cypress are also increasing; both offer great opportunities to the market.

The objective of this market is to become the largest supplier of fresh produce and homemade goods in the local area. This will be accomplished through the goals that have been set for the market. These goals include expansion of the market through more vendors, increasing the size of the market by 10 percent each year, vendors selling different types of goods, and emphasizing the higher quality and lower prices.

This Farmers' Market will use a niche strategy by offering both hard-to-find and traditional items. Consumers will not have to search the area for different types of produce, because they will be able to find everything at the Farmers' Market.

The life cycle for the market is still in its early stages. This market will be new to the community.

The product being offered to the community is fresh produce and other goods at fair prices. Promotion will be used to help advertise to both the consumers in the local community and to farmers who wish to sell their produce at the market. Distribution will be done through direct channels. The market will be conducted in a face-to-face manner; no middlemen will be allowed to sell produce that they have purchased from a wholesaler.

A Farmers' Market in the city of Cypress has great potential to become the largest supplier of fresh produce to the community, because there are no other Farmers' Markets in the city or surrounding areas. This opportunity has been fully researched and is ready to be implemented.

The required investment for this project will be $9,000. This fee will cover all of the market's expenses for the first year. Much of this money will be spent on fees and licenses required to run the market, insurance, rent, and other miscellaneous expenses.

The time needed to run the market is about five hours a week. The market will be held every Sunday in the parking lot of Cypress Community College from 9 A.M. to 1 P.M. The person running the market will need to be at the site one hour before the opening of the market, and one hour after the market closes.

The net income has been estimated for the first three years of operation. The first-year estimate is $19,111.75, the second year $27,065.85, and the third year $33,676.30.

The demand for fresh produce has increased over the years. This is important because there is a need for these products in everyday life. People enjoy shopping at Farmers' Markets for many reasons: They enjoy spending time with their families outdoors, talking with the growers of the produce, and receiving good quality merchandise at low prices.

Due to the high cost of living, today's consumers are watching their budgets. The Farmers' Market will not only bring fresh produce to the residents of Cypress, it will also save them money.

There are many competitive advantages the Farmers' Market has over its competitors. Products will be fresher and sold at substantially lower prices than at grocery stores. There will be a variety of items available, including both traditional and hard-to-find items. Growers will be able to share their knowledge about the produce, how it is grown, how to prepare it, and any pesticides or chemicals that may be used on the produce.

The plans for this market include eventual expansion and inclusion of other types of vendors such as arts and crafts and food vendors. In turn, sales will increase and profits will rise.

Advertising and promotions have been set up to publicize the market. Yearly anniversary events will be held, advertising will be placed in newspapers, and flyers will be distributed.

The market will provide a valuable service to the community of Cypress. This Farmers' Market provides an excellent opportunity to make a profit and to have fun while doing so. The work is minimal but the rewards are great.

Bibliography

Anonymous. "Until The Revolution Comes: Where to Get Clean Food Now." *California,* June 1990, pp. 102–137.

Anonymous. "Is Farm Stand Produce Better?" *USA Today Magazine,* June 1991, pp. 12–31.

Anonymous. "Find the Best at Your Farmers' Markets," *Glamour,* July 1991, pp. 176–179.

Braun, Dick. "Markets without Middlemen." *Farm Journal,* March 1990, pp. 46–47.

Davis, Shelly. "Fresh Off the Farm," *Washingtonian,* August 1990, pp. 131–135.

Dodge, Tom. "Fresh from the Farm," *Farm Journal,* October 1993, p. 24.

Dold, Cathy. "Green City Markets," *Amicus Journal,* Summer 1992, pp. 34–35.

Grubinger, Vern. "Sell Your Produce at a Roadside Stand," *Country Journal,* July 1992, pp. 31–32.

Michaud, Anne. "OC Enterprise: Home-Produced Wares, Farmers' Market—A Modern Day Bazaar for Small Vendors," *LA Times–OC Edition,* April 4, 1994, sec. D, p. 1.

Millman, Joel. "Zen and the Art of Fresh Produce," *Forbes,* February 15, 1993, p. 220.

O'Kennedy, Katie. "The Best: Farmers' Markets," *Bon Appetit,* April 1993, p. 26.

O'Neill, Molly. "Roadside Attractions," *New York Times Magazine,* August 30, 1992, p. 69.

Orange County Progress Report—1991–92. [United States]: n.p.

Shindler, Merrill. "The Farmers' Market," *Bon Appetit,* April 1991, p. 102–105.

Tunbridge, John E. "Farmers'/Festival Markets," *Canadian Geographer,* Fall 1992, pp. 280–285.

A5

PLAYLAND PRESCHOOL

Developed by
CANDY COSING

EXECUTIVE SUMMARY

Playland Preschool is a day care service that is situated in the vicinity of San Gabriel. Playland will offer half-day and full-day sessions to its potential clients.

Playland's objectives and goals are to gain name recognition and enough customer attendance and profits. Our goal for Playland's first year of operation is to gain profits of $8,066. We want an attendance of 70 children, which is 24 children over our break-even analysis.

In addition, we need some capital investment for advertising our start-up business. We need approximately $1,016.42 a month for the three successive years. We plan to advertise in the yellow pages, local newspaper, and distribute flyers to accomplish our goals. Our advertisements will emphasize our strengths/competitive edge among our competitors, including good customer service, uniqueness, nice location, and many more.

Through this marketing plan, we want to make Playland Preschool a well-known day care service in the selected neighborhood communities, to bring in clients, and to achieve our main objectives and goals.

Contents

INTRODUCTION

According to the U.S. Department of Labor, in the near future two out of three new employers will be women who are not presently in the out-of-home work force, primarily women outside the home for economic reasons. Given the coming worker shortage (due to different size of age cohorts), employers will need women employees as badly as women will need jobs. Today, most families need two incomes to achieve a decent standard of family life (Zigler, 1993:175). Therefore, both employers and women will be demanding more child care in the market.

We have thought about this, and, we are proposing to open a preschool in the San Gabriel area that will supply or accommodate these increasing needs. Basically, preschool can serve any one of several purposes, including education, parental free time, or as one of a variety of daily activities scheduled for the child.

Today, day care in the United States is a $20 billion industry. Parents pay thousands of dollars yearly for such care, which is about 10 percent of the average family's earnings. According to one child care analyst, single mothers on average pay more than 21 percent of their earnings in child care (Maynard, 1993:43).

We hope that with this business venture in mind, the preschool will be a huge success and profitable at the same time. We have several plans to meet this goal. The purpose of this marketing plan is to identify situational, neutral, competitor, and company environs; name our target market; identify and turn problems into opportunities; implement marketing strategies and tactics; and create evaluation charts and sheets. With these elements identified, we are looking forward to our marketing plan serving as an important means of marketing that will be able to accommodate the rising needs of the child care services.

SITUATIONAL ANALYSIS

The Situation Environ

Demand and Demand Trends. The Bureau of Labor Statistics estimates "that 64% of all families with children include a working mother, and mothers of pre-school children are the fastest growing segment of the workforce (Zampetti, 1991:54). Also, working-class parents face some of the worst preschool shortages in the country according to a study made public by the Harvard Graduate School of Education (Chira, 1993:A20).

In the day care service industry, we found that day care is a fact of life for more and more parents. Thus, there is an increasing demand for the day care service (see Appendix A5-A).

The demand trend is also not stable every month of the year. Demand rises during the opening of school starting in the month of September and it continues until June. At the end of June, demand begins to fall to its lowest during the months of July and August. This is because children spend their summer vacations with their relatives, go on out-of-the-country vacations, and other related reasons. The demand rises once again by the time September arrives (see Appendix A5-B).

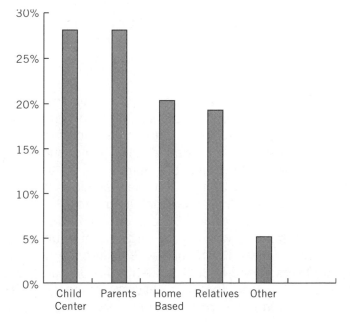

Appendix A5-A

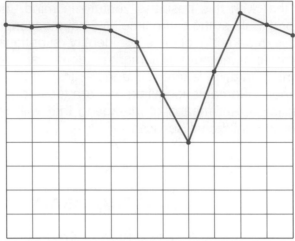

Jan. Feb. Mar. Apr. May Jun. Jul. Aug. Sept. Oct. Nov. Dec.

Appendix A5-B

Social and Cultural Factors. There are several factors to consider in the marketing plan for our selected geographic areas. Child care needs vary widely, depending on the specific circumstances of each family. In many families, both parents are employed, mostly full-time. In others, single parents must juggle the responsibilities of work and family essentials alone. Still other families must deal with work shift or unusual work hours. Thus, parents with preschool children must arrange for care during the entire day while they are away from home. Basically, people from many different occupations such as nurses, mail carriers, janitors, business executives, teachers, doctors, secretaries, chefs, janitors, and such need day care services for their children. Also, all nationalities regardless of culture need day care services, whether the parents are out of work or want their children to receive some basic learning skills before going to kindergarten.

Furthermore, the day care services are subdivided into various facilities, including for-profit facilities run by independent businesses and not-for-profit facilities run by state and federal government agencies, religious institutions, or community organizations. For instance, some parents might prefer to send their child to an affiliated religious institution preschool instead of other available facilities. Some with religious denominations might try still other available day care.

Demographics. With more parents trying to balance child-raising and work, child care is riding a demographic wave. It is interesting to note the factors that might relate to the distribution of preschools. One major factor influencing the location of the preschool is the existence of a market. This is measured by the actual population of preschool-age children and also the number of single parents, families, or female householders (presumably living in San Gabriel, Alhambra, and Rosemead) who would want or need this service. In San Gabriel, there are 23.6 percent, or 6,187 families with children under age 6; Alhambra, 26.5 percent, or 11,540 families; and Rosemead 24.9 percent, or 7,566 families with children 6 years or younger, (see Appendix A5-C).

The number of families with children between the ages of 3 and 4 in San Gabriel, Alhambra, and Rosemead is 38.4 percent (or 1,563 children), 34.0 percent (or 2,675 children), and 38.1 percent (or 2,224 children), respectively. The numbers and percentages are based on the 0-4 year-old-population categories (see Appendix A5-D).

Family Type by Presence of Own Children
Families, Married Couple Families, Female Householder
(with own children under 6 years)

Categories	#s	%s
San Gabriel city	6,187	23.6%
Alhambra city	11,540	26.5%
Rosemead city	7,566	24.9%

Source: Social and Economic Characteristics, U.S. Government
Printing Office, Washington, DC, 1993: 1469

Appendix A5-C

Age (numbers and percentages of 3 & 4 years old among 0–4 years of age)

Categories	#s	%s
San Gabriel city	1,563	38.4%
Alhambra city	2,675	34.0%
Rosemead city	2,224	38.1%

Source: Social and Economic Characteristics, U.S. Government
Printing Office, Washington, DC, 1993: 1469

Appendix A5-D

Labor Force Status (population 16+ —% in labor force)

Categories	#s	%s
San Gabriel city	37,582	64.8%
Alhambra city	53,475	63.2%
Rosemead city	38,157	61.8%

Source: The Sourcebook of Zip Code Demographics, CACI Marketing
Systems, La Jolla, CA, 1993: 25-D

Appendix A5-E

Finally, the labor force status for the population 16+ within the three geographic communities is as follows: San Gabriel city consists of 64.8 percent, or 37,582 out of the total population. Alhambra has 63.2 percent, or 53,475 workers or employees, while Rosemead consists of 61.8 percent, or 38,157 out of the total population (see Appendix A5-E).

Economic and Business Conditions. As we face the realities of a changing workplace, child care is a growing aspect of businesses. Moreover, the business conditions of child care services at this time in the San Gabriel, Alhambra, and Rosemead areas are normal. So far, several small businesses are opening, some are closing, and some are going strong. By keeping their (for-profit facilities) operating costs low and by providing the types of learning programs that many parents want for their children, many of the for-profit child care services enjoyed marked success in the 1980s.

As of now, our economy is in a recession. This creates problems for our country's productivity and international economic competitiveness. Due to growing acceptance of the benefits of adequate child care for the productivity of working parents, involvement in providing day care should continue. In addition, with concerns about tightening labor markets in the future, employers should increasingly recognize that the lack of child care is a major barrier to the entry of women to the labor force (Wash and Brand, 1990:23).

Politics, Laws, and Regulations. Questions have been raised about the role of government in the provision of day care services and about the advisability of having someone other than a parent raise the nation's children. Regulatory bodies are responsible for providing applicable laws, rules, regulations, and guidelines to the day care industry.

State government is an important player in the child care services industry. The state government is responsible for the licensing regulations that set staff qualifications and standards and mandate child/staff ratios. Most states have established maximum child/staff ratios, which vary by state and by the age of the children involved. In California, a 12 to 1 ratio is required for preschool age children. Minimum educational or training requirements for staffs also are established by most states. Some states require that day care directors have a college degree, often with specific training in early childhood development (ECE), as well as years of experience in the child care field. In addition, teachers must have a high school diploma. In many cases, a combination of related college education and experience is a must. A minimum age of 18 is required for teachers, and a minimum age of 21 for day care directors (Wash and Brand, 1990:19).

Furthermore, the implementation of a National Accreditation System is influenced by local and state licensing standards, which are mandatory government regulations that establish protection of health and safety for children. This is regulated by the National Association for the Education of Young Children (NAEYC). Accreditation and licensing standards are influenced by model standards such as the Health and Safety Standards of the American Academy of Pediatrics and the American Public Health Association. Standards have important functions of basic protection and education in health and safety (Bredekamp, 1993:234).

The Neutral Environ

Financial Environs. Even though we have low capital, there are various options that are offered to start-up businesses such as ours. The funds offered are community initiatives, bank reinvestment strategies, employer partnerships, small business loans and grants, bonds, pension funds, and such. However, borrowing unnecessary funds should be avoided whenever possible to prevent the rising debt of the business.

Government Environs. Federal, state, and local governments are actively involved in expanding the availability of child care. The federal government and 29 states subsidize child care through tax credits or deductions for parents. Also, eight states and the federal government allow tax credits or deductions for employers that provide child care assistance to their employees (Wash and Brand, 1990:19).

Furthermore, all states now offer various child care services such as training child care providers and resource and referral systems for parents seeking child care services. In addition, Federal Social Services Block Grants provide state assistance funding to low-income families, enabling states to help meet child care needs of low-income working parents, children receiving other protective services, and such.

Finally, the Child Care and Development Block Grant, which took effect in November 1990, provides additional grant money to the states to increase the availability, reduce the cost, and improve the quality of child care. The legislation also guarantees federal income tax credits for child care expenses for low-income families (Wash and Brand, 1990:19). Basically, the government is taking positive steps to help the day care industry as a whole.

Media Environs. The media are a powerful force that can influence society as a whole. The media might praise or criticize a particular situation. For instance, the media publicize child abuse by caregivers, and focus on situations or events that might cause or create it.

Furthermore, the media show confidence in the day care system (Chisholm, 1993:36), which helps people recognize the day care service industry as a valuable, reliable resource.

Special Interest Environs. There are several influential organizations that can be helpful and can serve as good resources for child care businesses. One of them is the Child Care Action Campaign, which is a national nonprofit organization that provides informative literature on the needs of families. The Children's Defense Fund monitors federal and state policies related to children. The Center for Policy Alternatives provides child care finance policy models. The Families and Work Institute is a research and planning organization that studies business, government, community work, and family efforts. The National Association of Child Care Resource and Referral Agencies is an association of about 400 nonprofit referral agencies that help parents explore child care alternatives. These agencies offer information about child care providers and contract with local businesses to provide child care services (Maynard, 1993:43).

The Competitor Environ

The indirect competitors to Playland Preschool, our proposed preschool, are Valley Blvd. Preschool and Wonder World Preschool. Valley Blvd. Preschool is a privately owned child care center that is open to any child between two and eight years of age. It was founded in 1950 and is licensed by the state and the city. It offers several programs for parents. Wonder World Preschool has several branches—in Rosemead, Alhambra, and Arcadia. Wonder World Preschool accepts children between two and six years of age. It offers preschool, kindergarten, and after-school programs.

One of Valley Blvd. Preschool's strengths is being the longest running day care school in the area. They have been in the business for more than 44 years. Most of their customers are from other past customers' recommendations. This gives them high name recognition among other day care services. Teachers' loyalty and longevity are also a strength for them. Valley Blvd.'s teachers have been on the job from 3 to 30 years, and they are very familiar with the individual needs of each child.

Valley Blvd. Preschool's major weakness is its location; it is located in a commercial area and on a busy street. This is a place of heavy traffic every day. The noise disturbs the children and makes it difficult for them to concentrate on their activities. This also prevents them from having restful naps after lunch. The saying, "you cannot have everything" is true. This is also a weakness for Valley Blvd. Preschool. Although they might have the reputation for being the longest running day care in the San Gabriel area, sooner or later they might have to renovate their place. This preschool has been in existence for quite a while, and the cost of renovation and other repairs might cause it to increase its asking price. This will make it less competitive among other day care services in the area. Parents also look at price as one of the variables for qualified child care for their kids.

Wonder World Preschool's strength is its visibility. They have several branches in the vicinity of San Gabriel, which enables them to accommodate more kids. Another strength of Wonder World Preschool is their name recognition. They have big ads in the yellow pages and in newspapers, advertising their service.

However, Wonder World has a weakness, too. Wonder World offers too many programs, which causes them to focus on different things. This makes them less effective when it comes to offering the best quality service to their customers.

The Company Environ. Playland Preschool specializes only in a preschool day care program. It is unlike other day care services in the area, which offer preschool, as well as after-school and kindergarten programs. Playland Preschool will evolve on its high standard and specialized preschool program environment and policies.

Playland Preschool is located at 122 E. Wells St., San Gabriel City. It will offer two types of preschool services to its customers. First, it will offer full-day sessions, which will be the majority of Playland's customers. The first type is a morning preschool of enriched educational program and an afternoon of custodial care and child maintenance. The morning is more structured with planned activities, whereas the afternoon is a time when children are supervised and allowed to do activities of their choice. Basically, the morning activities are preschool and the afternoon activities are day care. Second, Playland will offer a half-day preschool program, in which the children follow a structured schedule. This is a preschool program only, with no day care. Children leave the center at about 11:30 A.M. They just come in for the preschool program. The program schedules usually include reading, math, biology, geography, communication skill learning, and many more. Parents or family members are billed weekly. Parents pay $55.00 for half-day sessions and $105.00 for full-day sessions. The full-day kids are provided with hot lunches, and mid-morning and afternoon snacks.

Playground Preschool's strength will be its expertise and specialization on preschool kids between the ages of three and four. Being a specialty preschool, our policies are more concentrated on our specialized program instead of subdivided between an after-school program or kindergarten program like other services in the community. Also, Playland's resources will focus only on the preschool program. Therefore, consumers can expect what we offer as the best preschool program. In addition, Playland will be located in a quiet area in San Gabriel. This enables the kids to concentrate on their activities with less disturbance from the outside street noises. Also, Playland will be located near such facilities as neighborhood parks, library, elementary school, and many others. These outside resources allow kids to explore their surroundings and learn from each other as well.

Playland's major weakness is its lack of name recognition. This is because the preschool is a new business in the neighborhood. People do not know how much we can benefit them as yet. The second weakness is its size. Due to its small size, it may not be able to afford to buy bigger play equipment, and such. Also, Playland's advertisements will have to be limited to certain mediums during its first few years of operations.

The current strategies that Playland Preschool is aiming for are to get name recognition, to have knowledgeable teachers, and to offer a high cognitive learning standard. We want consumers to remember Playland Preschool whenever they want/need some type of day care services. Playland wants consumers to know that they can rely on Playland if they want their children to learn from and be supervised by knowledgeable teachers. In addition, we want people to realize that when it comes to educational programs, we maintain the best standard in the community. Playland should be remembered for its reputation of providing the best quality care and a good learning environment for the children as well.

The major future strategy that Playland Preschool wants to offer is to open another day care service that will provide joint programming of children and the elderly. There are several ways in which children and seniors can interact and get the services they need. One of them is that children who do not live near their grandparents get an opportunity to interact with senior citizens and learn that "growing old is not frightening at all" (Ogintz, 1993: p. 82). Second, children and the elderly will also benefit from the extra one-on-one attention they will receive from each other. Finally, more parents are now facing the dual responsibility of caring for their parents and their kids. We believe the concept of putting the two generations together is an idea whose time has come.

Calling All Preschoolers !!!!

Full day and half sessions preschool

Ages 3-4/state licensed   ***Open Year Round**

Hot Lunches and Mid-morning and Afternoon Snacks

☺ Enriched Standard Learning Environment

☺ Reading & Communication, Math, Biology, Geography and much more

☺ Fully Qualified Teachers

☺ Reasonable Rates . . .

☺ Open 7 – 6 p.m.

122 E. Wells Street
San Gabriel, CA 91776
(near McKinley Elementary School)

(818) 288-8744

CALL NOW !!!

> **Introductory Offer**
>
> **Attention:**
>
> **Parents/Family Members**
>
> Save **15% off**
>
> **By recommending 2 or more kids to us.**
>
> **Good through 5/31/95**
>
> Limit 1 coupon per customer
> Subject to change without
> prior notice

PLAYLAND PRESCHOOL

Appendix A5-F

TARGET MARKET

Based on the information presented in the Situational Analysis, we identified the following target market segment as potential clients: families, married couples, and single parents with preschool kids between three and four years of age who are working full- or part-time, and at the same time, living or working within the vicinity of San Gabriel, Alhambra, and Rosemead.

Also, the potential clients are employed in various occupations, including managerial positions and technical positions, as the demand for such day care services are widespread and unlimited.

San Gabriel, Alhambra, and Rosemead are good target market areas due to their closeness to Playland Preschool. Potential target markets do not have to travel far from their work or home to transport their children. Also, whenever emergency situations occur (child gets sick and needs hospitalization), parents or family members would be able to come right away and be able to attend to their child's needs. This provides security for parents and safety for children.

Our first target market brings us to our second target market: families, married couples, and single parents with preschool kids of three and four years of age, who are working full-time and/or part-time. This is an important target market because these people are the most likely to demand such day care services. This is the target market that is always out in the workforce trying to earn a decent living for their families, and at the same time wants reliable adults to teach and care for their children while they are at work. Our target markets' lifestyles are lives that are centered on their kids. Also, they have strong beliefs in good education.

PROBLEMS AND OPPORTUNITIES

Our marketing plan has encountered some unavoidable problems just like any other marketing plan, no matter how hard we tried to prevent them. The problems related to this marketing plan are limited capital resources, name recognition, and service comparisons.

First of all, we have limited capital resources available. With this capital restraint present, Playland Preschool would be unable to compete with full potential against its competitors. This lack of funding would hinder us in buying some necessary learning instruments, playing equipment, and other basic start-up equipment. Advertising costs money; therefore, we need some funds for advertisements too. We feel that we can overcome this problem by advertising in the places where our target market can be reached. By doing this, we should be able to minimize our costs and thereby use the leftover money to buy such items as learning instruments and other equipment.

In addition, name recognition is also a hindrance. Because Playland Preschool is a new business in the area, people are not yet aware of what our preschool can offer them. To solve this, we need to develop bright, eye-catching, and attractive ads and flyers that would make people remember us. Also, we will hire salespeople to drive around the area to sell our service. Our salespeople will serve as goodwill builders, and at the same time, recruit preschoolers for our day care service. Service comparisons between our facility and those of our other competitors will be made. There is no doubt that potential clients will compare our day care service with others, based on customer service, location, and additional benefits. We feel that by emphasizing a good, quiet location, and offering an enriched educational program, we will be able to outmatch our competitors.

As we gain extra capital resources, name recognition, and good customer feedback, we will be able to buy needed equipment for kids, advertise in more places (presumably with full-page ads), hire more salespeople to promote our service, and increase the number of clients and our positive image in the community. As we receive more funds, we will be able to place full-page advertisements in papers and yellow pages and buy other materials to be used in our preschool. Furthermore, we should be able to increase our clientele and make our preschool more widely recognized. Finally, we can project a positive image to the community based on customer feedback and word of mouth.

MARKETING OBJECTIVES AND GOALS

Our main objectives and goals are to acquire name recognition, increase customers, and raise profits as well. We want to become the leading supplier of day care service within the community. We want our potential customers to think of the Playland Preschool whenever they are searching for qualified day care for their children. We want them to perceive our high preschool educational standard and knowledgeable teachers. We feel that when we reach our objective of becoming a popular child service provider among the chosen surrounding communities, the numbers of customers should grow as well.

We estimate that we should be able to attain our goal profits by $8,066 in the first year, and 33 percent of our goal in the second year. We are aiming for an increase in profits up to 41 percent in the third year.

MARKETING STRATEGY

Our marketing strategies will apply positioning and product differentiation. Positioning strategy can help us distinguish our service from competitors in the minds of targeted consumers. Also, we strongly believe that the number of service differences in day care that can be promoted to the consumer is unlimited.

The reasons why we decided to apply these strategies are as follows. As mentioned in the demographic section, there is a potential market size for preschool-age kids. Day care is a distinct type of service. The preschool service is different from kindergarten, after-school, or infant care. Thus, the service can be modified to be desirable and advantageous to the target segment. This differentiation reduces the extent to which consumers will view our service as interchangeable with other services. In addition, consumers are very sensitive to service differences for preschools, because this involves their loved ones (children). Day care service is also in the growth stage of the product life cycle. Because there are few competitors in the targeted areas, it is much easier to differentiate our service.

Our marketing strategies, which are the actions we take to achieve our objectives, are fairly simple. We want to emphasize that Playland is a specialty preschool, emphasize knowledgeable teachers, and emphasize a high cognitive learning standard.

We want to emphasize that Playland Preschool is a specialty school, a unique small business, like no other preschool in the area. This means that we are the only facility in the area that specializes in preschool programs without offering any after-school and kindergarten services. Conversely, our competitors in the area may

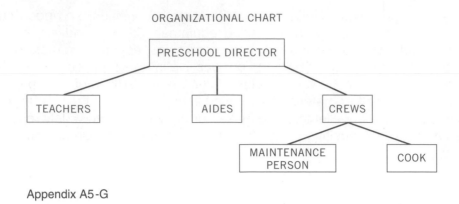

ORGANIZATIONAL CHART

Appendix A5-G

provide preschool services but also provide other services as well. They offer uniform services as any other preschool. This makes us one step ahead of our competition due to our uniqueness.

In addition, we want to emphasize our knowledgeable teachers. This is because we require our teachers to have AA degrees in Child Development (or equivalent), with 20 units or more in ECE (Early Child Education) courses taken in universities, and at least four or more years of background experience in preschool. They are expert in handling preschool-age children based on past experience.

Furthermore, we want to stress cognitive learning development to our students. We emphasize specific areas of learning, including science, math, computer literacy, reading & communication, and geography, aside from the usual activities (crafts, songs, etc.). In doing so, we provide the necessary background they need to enter kindergarten.

MARKETING TACTICS

Our marketing tactics describe how we will have to carry out our strategy. We strongly believe that to attain name recognition, to let other people know that we are experts and specialists, our tactics must support our strategies.

Product

Our emphasis is on service. Therefore, we must do all we can to ensure consistent quality. To implement this effectively, we must portray the service benefits rather than emphasizing the service itself. We decided to associate our service with tangible goods such as computer hardware and class textbooks to suggest educational attainment. Also, we portray our knowledgeable teachers to project stability and security.

Price

Consumers rely heavily on price as an indicator of a product's quality. Playland decided to use the meet-the-competition pricing as its pricing tactic. This tactic is particularly suitable for the service we offer. We believe that with our service priced approximately the same as our competitors, by offering more added value to our service by being a specialty (unique) preschool, and having an enriched educational program, we should be able to attract potential customers. Playland will charge $105.00 for a full day and $55.00 for a half day, which is close to the fees charged by other competitors.

Promotion

Advertising is one of the best ways to communicate and to achieve our strategies, objectives, and goals. We plan to advertise in the yellow pages, local newspapers, and flyers. We plan to place a large sign outside our center to attract passersby. Furthermore, we will hire salespeople to sell our service.

First, we will place an ad in the yellow pages. We believe that the yellow pages are one of the best and cheapest forms of advertisement. We plan to place ads in the Donnelley Directory and Pacific Bell yellow pages. Second, we will advertise in local newspapers. We will place ads in local neighborhood papers, including the *Alhambra Post Advocate, Pasadena Star News, San Gabriel Valley Tribune,* and *Whittier Daily News.* These ads will be placed under the child care section. They will reach our targeted customers. In local papers and flyers we will advertise a coupon special as an introductory incentive to attract potential clients. The coupon special will specify certain fee percentage discounts to mothers or family members who can recommend two or more children to the center. We will have flyers printed, too. This is one way to use our investment capital wisely. These flyers will be handed out and posted in nearby supermarkets, churches, community bulletin boards, pediatricians' offices, universities/ colleges, and wherever our target market congregate.

Furthermore, we plan to put a large sign in front of our center. This sign will be visible to passing motorists and pedestrians. The large sign will be a large piece of plywood that says, WELCOME TO PLAYLAND PRESCHOOL. The sign will also include our business telephone number and the hours of operation.

Appendix F, is a sample advertisement for local papers and flyers. This sample is the one to be advertised, handed out, and posted.

We decided to design colorful flyers and newspapers decorated with pictures of happy children playing together as they enjoy some activity. We feel this will be effective, because families with young children are attracted to signs that are bright and creative. In addition, these ads emphasize our strengths or the competitive edge we offer, such as enriched learning environment, preschool specialization, knowledgeable teachers, nice locations, and others. The ads also include a special coupon offering to initiate business activity with target customers. Business telephone number and address are also listed so parents will know general vicinity of our center, and can call us with questions or for additional information.

Basically, the yellow pages are somewhat similar to flyers and newspaper ads except the coupon is not visible. This information can be found in the yellow pages of San Gabriel Valley West and Alhambra, under day care or child care services.

We strongly believe that by using these advertising mediums, the amount of interest generated will be enormous. In addition, we will hire salespeople to promote our service. These people will drive around the San Gabriel, Alhambra, and Rosemead areas. They will be paid on a commission basis, through recruiting as many children as they can and building goodwill at the same time. Because Playland is a small business, we must relate our compensation expenses directly to sales.

Place

The physical distribution can also affect our marketing mix. Because a service is intangible, it requires personal contact between teachers and preschool kids. Thus, a direct channel of distribution is used. We decided to place our preschool in a quiet location in San Gabriel. We strongly believe that this will help our business to achieve its goals. This service is near neighborhood parks, a public library, and an elementary school. This enables the kids to explore the inside and outside worlds of learning. Also, a nice location adds another advantage to our potential customers; it helps each child to maximize concentration on his or her activities with less outside disturbance.

Task	1	2	3	4	5	6	7	8	9	10	11	12
Initiate Advertising	1016	1016	1016	1016	1016	1016	1016	1016	1016	1016	1016	1016
Purchase Start-up Equip. and Textbooks	3400	0	0	0	0	0	0	0	0	0	0	0
Purchase School and Office Sup.	150	159	160	150	155	140	130	70	110	135	140	145
Salespeople Commissions	1075	875	750	675	650	625	450	350	1200	1400	1025	975
Salespeople's Transporation Costs	100	110	120	130	120	100	90	80	150	160	130	110
Monthly Totals ($)	5741	2176	2046	1971	1941	1881	1686	1516	2476	2711	2311	2246
Advertising	1016	1016	1016	1016	1016	1016	1016	1016	1016	1016	1016	1016
Purchase Equip. and Textbooks	150	0	0	0	0	0	0	0	0	0	0	0
Purchase School and Office Supp.	160	170	170	175	175	165	165	95	170	250	175	175
Salespeople Commissions	1025	875	825	750	775	725	650	450	1750	2000	1000	950
Salespeople's Transporation Costs	110	120	130	130	110	100	95	85	150	160	140	150
Monthly Totals ($)	2461	2181	2141	2071	2076	2006	1926	1646	3886	3426	2331	2291
Advertising	1016	1016	1016	1016	1016	1016	1016	1016	1016	1016	1016	1016
Buy Fixtures and Computers	800	0	0	0	250	0	0	0	150	0	800	0
Buy Office and School Supplies	180	185	200	200	175	180	150	135	150	250	230	250
Salespeople's Commissions	1250	1100	1050	950	1000	825	550	450	1350	1500	1250	1050
Salespeople's Transporation Costs	125	135	120	115	125	130	110	95	160	170	180	170
Monthly Total ($)	3371	2436	2386	2281	2566	2151	1826	1696	2826	2936	3476	2486

Appendix A5-H Product/Project Development Schedule

CONTROL AND IMPLEMENTATION

Project Development Schedule

Our project development schedule for 36 months consists of advertising costs, equipment and fixture purchases, school and office supplies, salespeople commissions, and transportation costs. Our advertising costs will be the same every month. However, the other project development expenses will have a slight increase or decrease in costs as the months proceed (see Appendix A5-H).

Advertising Expenses

We are planning to advertise in local newspapers, yellow pages, and to distribute flyers. Our advertising expenses for one year are shown in Appendix A5-I. We plan to advertise in the four local papers. The *Alhambra Post Advocate* will cost $4,752 for each 2 × 3 size advertisement per year. The *San Gabriel Valley Tribune, Pasadena Star News,* and *Whittier Daily News* will serve as a package deal for $4,752 for each two lines of advertisement per year. The advertisement can be found in the business and service section of the three newspapers.

In addition, we plan to advertise in the yellow pages. The Donnelley Directory and Pacific Bell Smart Yellow Pages, will cost $1,710 and $828 for each advertisement per year. The ads can be found in yellow pages of San Gabriel Valley West and Alhambra division under day care services.

We plan to post and distribute the 8 1/2 × 11 flyers in nearby grocery stores, churches, elementary schools, junior highs, and community bulletin boards. Papers for the flyers will cost $60. Printing expenses for the flyers are $95. This includes printing 2,500 papers twice a year at a cost of $0.019 per page.

ADVERTISING EXPENSES

Newspapers:

	Monthly	Yearly
Alhambra Post Advocate	$396	$ 4,752
San Gabriel Valley Tribune		
Pasadena Star News	396	4,752
Whittier Daily News		
Yellow Pages:		
The Donnelley Directory	142.50	1,710
Pacific Bell Smart Yellow Pages	69	828
Flyers:		
Papers		60
Printing (.019 × 2,500 × 2 times a year)		95
Total:		$12,197

Average per month $\dfrac{\$12,197}{12} = \$1,016.42$

Appendix A5-I

BREAK-EVEN ANALYSIS

$$BE = \frac{\text{Fixed Costs}}{\text{Selling Price} - \text{Variable Costs}}$$

$$= \frac{6,372}{362.25 - 240.94}$$

$$= 52.5 \text{ kids}$$

Appendix A5-J

The total advertising expenditure is $12,197 per year, which averages out to $1,016 per month.

Break-Even Analysis

The break-even analysis is shown in Appendix A5-J. We calculate our break-even point in number of customers by dividing fixed costs by the average selling price minus the variable cost.

The fixed costs are obtained from our advertising expense, director's salary, rent, maintenance, license, and insurance, which is $6,372. We achieve our selling price by averaging the fees we charge at Playland. We placed weighting factors for our full- and half-day services. We project that 75 percent of our clients are attending full-day and 25 percent are attending half-day sessions. Based on this, we reach our average selling price at $362.25. Our variable cost for the service is $240.94. Our break-even point comes to 52.5 kids. Hence, we must have approximately 53 kids a month in order for our marketing plan to break even.

Cash-Flow Projections

Our monthly cash-flow projection is shown in Appendix A5-K. Playland's total cash revenues will consist of charge fees from customers plus other cash income from registration and other material fees.

The operating expenses consist of advertising, rent, maintenance, director's salary, wages, commission, transportation, supplies, utilities, equipment expenses, food, taxes, licenses, and insurance. During the slow season (July and August), cash revenues are lower than usual, which causes the total cash flow to decrease. However, during the other months of the year, cash revenues are stable or increasing at a certain dollar amount.

Income Statement

Our three-year projected income statement under our plan is shown in Appendix A5-L. In the first year of operation, we plan to increase net sales to $214,077, which leads us to a profit of $8,066. In the second year, we plan to increase net sales to about 33 percent, which would add $32,767 to the second-year profit. In the third year of operation, we plan to increase net sales to about 8 percent, leading to profits of about $48,629.

The total operating expenses for the projected income statement are the same amount that can be found in the cash-flow projections.

Cash Flow Projections (Monthly)

	Jan.	Feb.	Mar.	Apr.	May	June	July	Aug.	Sept.	Oct.	Nov.	Dec.
Total Cash	5000	-757	-260	-780	-332	804	1574	1745	1	5643	8855	12277
Income:												
Cash Sales	0	17050	17501	18404	19092	18641	15910	10686	21823	23865	23865	23865
Other Cash Income	0	180	45	90	90	45	45	0	2475	225	90	90
Total Cash & Income	5000	16473	17286	17714	18850	19490	17529	12431	24299	29733	32810	36232
Operating Expense:												
Advertising	1016	1016	1016	1016	1016	1016	1016	1016	1016	1016	1016	1016
Direct. Salary	0	2250	2250	2250	2250	2250	2250	2250	2250	2250	2250	2250
Rent	0	2600	2600	2600	2600	2600	2600	2600	2600	2600	2600	2600
Maintenance	0	430	430	430	430	430	430	430	430	430	430	430
License	16	16	16	16	16	16	16	16	16	16	16	16
Insurance	0	1000	500	500	500	500	500	500	500	500	500	500
Transportation	100	110	120	130	120	100	90	80	150	160	130	110
Food	0	500	550	600	620	550	520	450	700	750	800	780
Utilities	0	115	120	125	135	135	120	80	130	175	180	185
Equip. Expense	3400	0	0	0	0	0	0	0	0	0	0	0
Supplies	150	159	160	150	155	140	130	70	110	135	140	145
Wages	0	7662	9554	9554	9554	9554	7662	4588	9554	11446	11446	11446
Commission	1075	875	750	675	650	625	450	350	1200	1400	1025	975
Taxes	0	0	0	0	0	0	0	0	0	0	0	0
Total Operating Expenses:	5757	16733	18066	18046	18046	17916	15784	12430	18656	20878	20533	20453
Cash Flow Excess	-757	-260	-780	-332	804	1574	1745	1	5643	8855	12277	15779

Appendix A5-K

Cash Flow Projections (Monthly)

	Jan.	Feb.	Mar.	Apr.	May	June	July	Aug.	Sept.	Oct.	Nov.	Dec.
Total Cash	15779	16889	19272	22101	24990	27493	29996	33386	32016	36413	42945	49826
Income:												
Cash Sales	24317	22726	23177	23177	22726	22726	21586	14139	23865	27950	27499	27499
Other Cash Income	135	90	90	45	90	45	0	0	2700	450	90	180
Total Cash & Income	40231	39705	42539	45323	47806	50264	51582	47705	58581	64813	70534	77505
Operating Expense:												
Advertising	1016	1016	1016	1016	1016	1016	1016	1016	1016	1016	1016	1016
Direct. Salary	2250	2250	2250	2250	2250	2250	2250	2250	2250	2250	2250	2250
Rent	2600	2600	2600	2600	2600	2600	2600	2600	2600	2600	2600	2600
Maintenance	430	430	430	430	430	430	430	430	430	430	430	430
License	16	16	16	16	16	16	16	16	16	16	16	16
Insurance	500	500	500	500	500	500	500	500	500	500	500	500
Transportation	110	120	130	130	110	100	95	85	150	160	140	150
Food	800	850	880	870	840	875	800	500	900	1000	950	1000
Utilities	150	160	175	150	155	145	120	85	140	200	185	185
Equip. Expense	150	0	0	0	0	0	0	0	800	0	0	0
Supplies	160	170	170	175	175	165	165	95	170	250	175	175
Wages	11446	11446	11446	11446	11446	11446	9554	7662	11446	11446	11446	11446
Commission	1025	875	825	750	775	725	650	450	1750	2000	1000	950
Taxes	2689	0	0	0	0	0	0	0	0	0	0	0
Total Operating Expenses:	23342	20433	20438	20333	20313	20268	18196	15689	22168	21868	20708	20718
Cash Flow Excess	16889	19272	22101	24990	27493	29996	33386	32016	36413	42945	49826	56787

Appendix A5-K   Continued

Cash Flow Projections (Monthly)

	Jan.	Feb.	Mar.	Apr.	May	June	July	Aug.	Sept.	Oct.	Nov.	Dec.
Total Cash Income:	56787	51344	57232	63215	69066	74814	81192	85279	85385	88197	97919	103635
Cash Sales	27047	26596	26596	26359	26596	26596	23865	15910	21823	27950	27499	27950
Other Cash Income	180	135	135	90	45	90	90	45	180	3150	90	90
Total Cash & Income	84014	78075	83936	89664	95707	101500	105147	101234	107388	119297	125508	131675
Operating Expense:												
Advertising	1016	1016	1016	1016	1016	1016	1016	1016	1016	1016	1016	1016
Direct. Salary	2250	2250	2250	2250	2250	2250	2250	2250	2250	2250	2250	2250
Rent	2600	2600	2600	2600	2600	2600	2600	2600	2600	2600	2600	2600
Maintenance	430	430	430	430	430	430	430	430	430	430	430	430
License	16	16	16	16	16	16	16	16	16	16	16	16
Insurance	500	500	500	500	500	500	500	500	500	500	500	500
Transportation	125	135	120	115	125	130	110	95	160	170	180	170
Food	950	975	950	900	925	750	650	575	870	1000	975	1000
Utilities	185	190	170	175	160	165	150	120	145	200	180	190
Equip. Expense	800	0	0	0	250	0	0	0	150	0	800	0
Supplies	180	185	200	200	175	180	150	135	150	250	230	250
Wages	11446	11446	11446	11446	11446	11446	11446	7662	9554	11446	11446	11446
Commission	1250	1100	1050	950	1000	825	550	450	1350	1500	1250	1050
Taxes	10922	0	0	0	0	0	0	0	0	0	0	0
Total Operating Expenses:	32670	20843	20748	20598	20893	20308	19868	15849	19191	21378	21873	20918
Cash Flow Excess	51344	57232	63215	69066	74814	81192	85279	85385	88197	97919	103635	110757

Appendix A5-K Continued

Projected Income Statement (Yearly)

	Year 1	Year 2	Year 3
Net sales	214077	285482	309062
Operating Expenses:			
Selling Expense:			
Advertising	12192	12192	12192
Commission	10050	11775	12325
Transportation	1400	1480	1635
Total Selling Expense	23642	25447	26152
Admin. & Gen Expense:			
Director salary	24750	27000	27000
Rent	28600	31200	31200
Maintenance	4730	5160	5160
Wages	102020	131676	131676
Food	6820	10265	10520
Utilities	1500	1850	2030
Equip. Expense	3400	950	2000
Supplies	1660	2045	2285
License	200	200	200
Insurance	6000	6000	6000
Total Admin. & Gen. Exp.:	179680	216346	218071
Tot. Operating Exp.:	203322	241793	244223
Operating Profit	10755	43689	64839
Less Income Tax	-2689	-10922	-16210
Net Profit	8066	32767	48629

Appendix A5-L

Projected Balance Sheets (Yearly)

	12/31/95	12/31/96	12/31/97
Current Assets			
Cash	15779	49826	110757
Fixed assets			
Fixtures and Equipment	3400	950	2000
Other assets			
License	200	200	200
Insurance	6000	6000	6000
Total Assets	25379	56976	118957
Current Liabilities			
Accounts Payable	9800	8850	8200
Accrued expenses	5500	8500	11000
Taxes Owed	2689	10922	16210
Total Liabilities	17989	28272	35410
Net Worth	7390	28704	83547

Appendix A5-M

Balance Sheet

Our three-year projected balance sheet is shown in Appendix A5-M. In year one, we have a cash balance of $15,779. The fixed assets include fixtures and equipment. The other assets consist of license and insurance, which is the same amount for the three-year period. On the liabilities side, there are accounts and accrued payable for purchases of planned fixtures and equipment, and taxes payable.

In the second year, the cash balance has increased. The rise in the cash position implies that customers' attendance rose. We plan to spend about $950 to add additional fixtures to the business. The liabilities have also risen to compensate for the increasing assets of the business.

In year three, we want to purchase some more equipment to provide our customers with the necessary learning instruments. There are also some changes in the cash balance over the last year. In addition, the liabilities for accrued expenses should go up as more assets are being added to the business.

SUMMARY

In conclusion, "expectations of future tight labor markets, skill shortages, and lagging international economic competitiveness have provoked a dialogue on the relationship between the availability of suitable child care and a parent's productivity in the workplace" (Wash and Brand, 1990:17). In other words, there is a growing concern about the welfare of America's children, worker attitudes and values are changing, and evidence shows that inflexibility in the workplace regarding family responsibilities has an adverse effect on productivity. Indeed, day care service demands are growing and will continue to do so.

By properly identifying our target market in our selected geographic areas, we should be able to successfully attain our goals and get off to a good start. The marketing mix effects should also be considered as one of the major reasons for reaching our objectives and goals. In our 4 P's, we emphasize Playland Preschool's strengths or competitive edge among its competitors. This should enable us to attain our target sales and profits percentage goals as we meet our customers' needs. In addition, we should be able to achieve our main objective, which is to gain name recognition.

We strongly believe that with our marketing plan guiding us through the coming years, we will be successful with our start-up business and later enable us to pursue other future strategies.

BIBLIOGRAPHY

Bredekamp, Sue. "Day-Care Standards: Need and Impact," *Pediatrics,* January 1993:234– 236.

Chira, Susan. "Working-Class Parents Face Shortage of Day Care Centers, A Study Finds," *The New York Times,* 14 September 1993:A20.

Chisholm, Patricia. "Kids, Careers and the Day Care Debate," *Maclean's,* May 31, 1993:36.

Darnay, Arsen and Marlita Reddy. *SIC 83 - Social Services,* Michigan: Gale Research Inc., 1993.

Maynard, Roberta. "Child-Care Options for Small Firms, Includes related articles on Child Care," *Nation's Business,* February 1993:43.

Ogintz, Eileen. "The Young and Old Can Be Perfect Playmates," *Parents Magazine,* May 1993:82.

Social and Economic Characteristics. Washington DC: Government Printing Office, 1993.

The Sourcebook of Zip Code Demographics. La Jolla, CA.: CACI Marketing Systems, 1993.

Wash, Darrel and Liesel Brand. "Child Day Care Services: An Industry at a Crossroads," *Monthly Labor Review,* December 1990:17–23.

Zampetti, James. "Building ABCs for an On-site Childcare Center," *Management Review,* March 1991:54–56.

Zigler, Edward and Elizabeth Gilman. "Day Care in America: What Is Needed?"*Pediatrics,* January 1993:175.

A6

COMPUWARE, INC.

Developed by
KAM KUEN FAN

EXECUTIVE SUMMARY

This report presents a detailed marketing plan for opening a store for personal computers in Santa Barbara, California. On the basis of information gathered during the course of my research, I have determined that there is a potential market for personal computers beyond that already existing in Santa Barbara. The existence of one university and two colleges, as well as a large professional and entrepreneurial population in the area makes the area receptive to a personal computer store such as ours.

Our primary marketing strategy consists of offering a high-quality personal computer at a lower price than the competition now asks. We will do this by assembling the computer in our store. We will sell by direct mail as well as through a showroom, especially to college and university students. Promotion will be done through flyers, on-campus demonstrations and exhibits, classified ads, trade shows, and personal sales.

Contents

INTRODUCTION

Today all kinds of people use personal computers for a great variety of reasons. And as the technology improves, growing numbers use computers both at work and at home. Since the early 1980s the increase in computer usage has been phenomenal.

Statistics show that Americans have come to depend on computers both at home and in the office, and also that in the years ahead a wide range of computers will play increasingly important roles in our daily lives.

The Microcomputer Arrives

In 1965, there was only 1 computer for every 10,000 Americans. Even in the mid-1970s, when the microcomputer first appeared on the scene, there was only 1 computer per 1,000 Americans.

Then throughout the 1970s and 1980s, computer acceptance grew rapidly. In the 10 years following the microcomputer's arrival in 1975, computer density grew at a 140-fold pace. The number of computers zoomed to 99 per 1,000 people. Over the past seven years, computer density has grown at a comparably modest rate of 168 percent, so that by the end of 1992, personal computers accounted for 250 of the 265 computers per 1,000 people.

MORE GROWTH AHEAD

The *Computer Industry Almanac* predicts that computer density will continue to grow at a rapid rate throughout the 1990s. The company points out that the computer density per 1,000 people increases by about 25 units each year in the United States, indicating that it should reach approximately 335 to 345 per 1,000 people by the end of 1995.

If multimedia and personal digital assistant (PDA) computers are moderately successful, forecasts the firm, the number of computers could hit the 500 to 1,000-person range by the turn of the century.

THE MULTIMEDIA-PDA FACTOR

On the other hand, if multimedia and PDA computers really take off, and speech recognition and virtual reality live up to our expectations, computer density could approach 600 to 700 per 1,000 people by the beginning of the twenty-first century.

The purpose of this marketing plan is to analyze the environmental situation and the market opportunity for starting a computer store, *CompuWare,* in Santa Barbara, California. This plan also intends to develop marketing objectives and formulate a marketing strategy for the entire Santa Barbara region.

SITUATIONAL ANALYSIS

Situational Environ

Business Conditions. According to a new study conducted by the Software Publishers Association, 27 percent of U.S. households and 50 percent of U.S. businesses now own personal computers.

In the past two years, falling prices for smarter and faster high performance multimedia machines capable of cruising the "information superhighway" have, according to an SPA study, attracted droves of new buyers from among a decidedly educated and affluent segment of the U.S. population. Fully 60 percent of the computer-using households in 1994 had members who attended or graduated from college. That figure compares with 51 percent of computer-using households in 1993.

Household income levels of personal computer owners remain high and steady. In both 1993 and early 1994, about one-quarter of computer households had incomes over $75,000. About half of computer households had incomes over $50,000, versus 25 percent of U.S. households as a whole.

Multimedia machines (those equipped with CD-ROM drives) accounted for 37 percent of the home computers purchased in 1993 and early 1994, versus 19 percent in 1991 and earlier. Computers with modems accounted for 62 percent of sales in 1993 and early 1994, versus 39 percent in 1991. Sales of computers equipped with fax boards more than doubled to 35 percent from 17 percent in that same time period.

Among PC compatibles, which account for 70 percent of the total market, Intel 486 chips power 40 percent of the computers bought in 1993 and early 1994, versus 18 percent in 1992 and 3 percent in 1991 and earlier.

More than three-quarters (76 percent) of newly purchased PC compatibles use Windows, versus 63 percent in 1992 and only 14 percent in 1991 and earlier.

Word processing, spreadsheets, and entertainment games remained the top three applications for home use. Personal finance packages replaced graphics-drawing programs in four.

Economic Conditions. The South Coast region of Santa Barbara County includes the entire commercial, industrial, and residential area along the southernmost strip of the county. From Goleta in the west to Carpinteria in the east, the South Coast area includes 199,300 residents, more than 100,000 jobs, and is the principal center of retail and commercial activity in Santa Barbara County.

The county seat is located in downtown Santa Barbara, and together with the University of California, the two state organizations represent the largest employers in the region. High-technology manufacturing, tourism, and many professional services are the principal sectors of the South Coast economy.

The population of the city of Santa Barbara was 88,921 in 1993, and the greater South Coast now has nearly 200,000 residents. Since 1990, the population of the South Coast area has been expanding at a 1.1 percent per year rate.

Although retail sales during 1992 in Santa Barbara declined 1.6 percent from sales levels recorded in 1991, the city's largest and newest shopping mall, Paseo Nuevo, which opened in August of 1990, has helped general merchandise retail sales remain comparatively strong. Other retail sales sectors have shown sharp declines, particularly automobile and building material sales. The recession that began in the last half of 1990 continues to hamper retail businesses in downtown Santa Barbara. The Economic Forecast Project now expects retail growth in Santa Barbara to turn positive by the spring of 1994.

Neutral Environ

January 11, 1994, was an important day for those people who follow computers and communications. That was the day Vice-President Albert Gore, Jr., outlined the Clinton administration's goals, objectives, and plans for helping to implement the "national information superhighway." This plan means that the government is encouraging industry to provide affordable information services that will be accessible to all Americans. In the future, voice, video, and data will be transmitted over cable television lines, fiber-optic lines, or even low-capacity copper telephone lines to the personal computer. Many communication companies are now spending billions of dollars on the information superhighway project. The trend can provide unlimited opportunities.

Competitor Environ

The computer industry is a fast-growing industry in the United States. In 1993, the computer industry was the fourth largest business in the country. Because of the profitable nature of the business with its low overhead and unlimited opportunities, more and more competitors have entered the personal computer retail market. Compared to Los Angeles County, however, there are not many computer retail stores in the Santa Barbara area, so most of the Santa Barbara PC retail stores mark up their product prices 15 percent higher than those in the Los Angeles area.

The three major competitors in the Santa Barbara area are CompUSA, Computer Land, and Data Net.

CompUSA is a nationally franchised computer sales organization. For the most part they sell IBM-PC compatibles and Apple Macintosh personal computers. Their major customers are household individuals. Usually they sell the high-end models and, because of their high overhead advertising, the prices of the products they sell are generally higher than those of the average computer store. In addition to personal computers, they also sell computer accessories such as printers, monitors, hard disks, CD-ROMs, mice, fax/modem cards, floppy disk drives, etc.

Computer Land is a chain-owned computer company whose major business lies in selling Apple Macintosh and IBM-PC compatible personal computers. However, their main customers are from business offices, and the prices of the products they sell are usually high.

Data Net is an individually owned computer store whose major business is selling only IBM-PC compatible personal computers. Data Net can sell personal computers at a lower price because of their low overhead and because most of the computers they sell are assembled by the store itself, as opposed to the factory.

Company Environ

To establish a successful business we first need to evaluate the strengths and weaknesses of our major competitors. Since our company is a start-up company, we need to emulate the good things done by our major competitors and eliminate the weaknesses. For example, CompUSA has such a large advertising overhead that the price of the computers they sell must be very high. Because of the financial difficulty this approach presents, we definitely will not follow this trend. Instead we will use a less expensive and more cost-effective way to advertise our products.

TARGET MARKET

Demographics

On the basis of the information gained in our Situational Analysis, we identified the following target market segment as potential product users:

1. College students or graduates

2. Member of households where household income exceeds $50,000 annually

3. Professionals or managers

Psychographic

Life Style. Our target market will also include the following target segments:

1. People who seek computers to solve their problems or to help themselves get things done efficiently

2. People who enjoy or are involved with a multimedia environment

3. People who like to invest in the stock market and would like to obtain primary stock market information by computer at home

Loyalty/Status. Because computer technologies are improving so rapidly, more and more new and powerful computer software and hardware are reaching the market every year, and so personal-computer users will eventually upgrade to a new, more powerful computer. Ideally, when we develop a brand loyalty on the part of our customers, they will purchase their computers from our store.

PROBLEMS AND OPPORTUNITIES

Market Characteristic

Problem. The actual demand for personal computers in Santa Barbara is unknown.

Opportunities. Because of the limited number of existing computer retail stores and the large number of potential customers from the University of California at Santa Barbara, Santa Barbara City College, Westmont College, as well as professionals from the industrial sector and the high-technology sector, a potentially profitable market for personal computers exists in Santa Barbara.

Competition

Problem. Personal computers are at the mature state of the product life cycle.

Opportunities. A rapid growth market for and changing technology of personal computers can provide a new variety of software and hardware options for the potential buyer.

Product Comparisons

Problem. Personal computers are less powerful compared to mini computers and network stations.

Opportunities. Since personal computers are less expensive than mini computers and network stations, the demand for personal computers is increasing.

Environmental Climate

Problem. Computer technology is changing so rapidly that many new kinds of computer technology have come onto the market. Many people are finding it difficult to catch up.

Opportunities. Because of changing computer technology, many new product lines have developed, with the result that profits should increase.

Internal Resources

Problem. CompuWare requires $60,000 in start-up and introduction costs.

Opportunities. In an area such as Santa Barbara where computer sales are not yet highly competitive, the expected return on the investment is high.

MARKETING OBJECTIVE AND GOALS

The Company Objective

Our company's objective is, over a 10-year period, to establish a "CompuWare" retail network around the state of California.

The Company Goals

Our goals include the following:

Short-Term Goals

1. Annual sales of 500 personal computers and $130,000 of net profit in the first business year

2. Provision of on-line customer services within 2 years

3. To provide the extension of warranty services in 2 years

4. Expansion of services of related products such as wireless phones, computer notebooks, other hardware and software products within 3 years

Long-Term Goals

1. An increase in the number of CompuWare stores to 15 different California locations within 10 years

2. An increase in sales through international trade within 5 years

MARKETING STRATEGY

Product Strategy

The key to success inherent in our product strategy comes out of three essential values: high quality, product flexibility, and reliability. In our store we will only sell a high quality of personal computers. All the computer components are distributed by reliable manufacturers with high quality control. Our excellent product will build up a good image to the customers and develop their brand loyalty.

The second key success factor of our product strategy, our product flexibility, aims to encourage customers to add on additional hardware and accessories from our store. Basically we will provide the optional products for customers so that they can extend their requirements for the personal computer. This should bring convenience to the customers as well as profit to us.

The third key success factor, reliability, ensures the confidence we have in our products. We will offer a one-year warranty with free 48-hour expedited repair. A highly reliable product is one of the factors that ensures user-oriented word-of-mouth recommendation of our store.

Pricing Strategy

Price is one of the major factors encouraging customers to buy our products. Since we assemble the computers ourselves, we have a low overhead. The result is that we can offer our products at lower prices than our competitors can.

Positioning

Our positioning strategy will be achieved by using our effective strategic methods with lower cost.

Since personal computers are consumer-service oriented products, we will be selling directly to the end users. Therefore a successful positioning strategy for our products should include the following tactics to implement our overall strategies of creating purchasing incentive for customers:

1. *Direct Mail*

    A mailing list will be purchased to distribute the following information:
    - Flyers
    - Product catalog
    - Discount information

2. *Publicity*

    Publicity is free advertising. The tactics to be implemented will be:
    - Press releases
    - Exhibits and demonstrations in the university, the colleges, and public areas

3. *Word of Mouth*

    Word-of-mouth advertising is a powerful means of spreading the word. Most people trust their friends' recommendations. A referral plan will be in place to encourage this kind of communication.

4. *Personal Selling*

    Personal selling will be heavily used to establish corporate accounts.

5. *College & University Newspapers*

    College and university newspapers are targeting students for whom we will emphasize both the quality and price of our products.

6. *Computer Magazine*

    Since the personal computer is a complex product requiring an important and often difficult decision, customers will need to obtain information and evaluate their choice of product through computer magazines in order to make the final decision to purchase.

7. *Trade Shows*

    One of the best ways to introduce our product to the market is through major trade shows. Every weekend computer trade shows are open to the public in Santa Barbara.

8. *Holiday Discounts, Cumulative Discounts, and Coupons*

Offering holiday discounts, cumulative discounts, and coupons are effective ways of attracting customers to buy our products. We will use these as sales promotions.

The details for implementing these strategies are listed under Promotional Tactics.

Production/Distribution Strategy

Our production strategy will focus on the quality of the computer components. Since we build our own computers, we can save a tremendous amount of manufacture cost from the supplier.

Moreover, our product production will be based on the just-in-time (JIT) philosophy, whose expectation is to reduce or eliminate inventories, thereby saving financing and storage costs.

Location Strategy

We expect the economy in the city of Santa Barbara to turn positive in fall 1994. Therefore, we are planning to begin our business in September 1994. CompuWare will be located inside the Paseo Nuevo shopping mall on State Street in downtown Santa Barbara. The reasons we have chosen this location are as follows:

Easy Access. Paseo Nuevo, which opened in August of 1990, is the city's largest and newest shopping mall. For people who drive, the mall is easy to access by freeway 101. Parking space is ample. For the people who don't drive, public transportation is also available.

One-Stop Shopping Center. There are a variety of stores in the Paseo Nuevo shopping mall, such as Broadway, restaurants, a bakery, gift shops, fashion shops, a theater, and so on. Thus this plaza provides customers the convenience of one-stop shopping.

Reasonable Leasing Rate. We found out that the rent in Paseo Nuevo is reasonable. We plan to rent a 600-square-foot store in Paseo Nuevo shopping mall for $648 per month.

Marketing Strategy—A Recoup and a Projection

Our overall strategies can be applied to the market segment of our operation. However, we will use our strategies to concentrate on the following target markets:

1. College students

2. Professionals

3. Entrepreneurs

Since 60 percent of the computer-using households in 1994 had members who attended or graduated from college, our primary target market will be college students. However, based on the fact that in both 1993 and early 1994 about one-quarter of computer households' income levels remain high and steady (incomes of over $75,000) and we presume those high-income computer owners are professionals or entrepreneurs, we therefore will be targeting professionals and entrepreneurs as potential customers.

MARKETING TACTICS

Product

1. In order to build up brand loyalty on the part of the customers, in May 1994 we will design a logo for our products

2. In August 1994 our company will begin to assemble and display three different 80486 models and a Pentium PC compatible for our showroom. We will also display some of the components and computer accessories in our showroom. Showrooms are one of the important marketing strategies for the computer market, and a nicer showroom will mean more customers will come to our store and purchase a computer.

Promotion

1. Direct mail is one of the powerful methods of increasing sales volume. Customers find it convenient to shop by mail-order catalog. Therefore we will design an effective mail-order catalog beginning in June 1994.

2. Since college students are our primary target market, in June 1994 we will begin to design flyers to put on bulletin boards at the college, the university, and in the public area.

3. In September 1994 we will begin to contact Santa Barbara City College and University of California, Santa Barbara for permission to set up exhibits to demonstrate the performance of the personal computer.

4. Classified advertising is one of the most effective and popular ways of advertising products. In August 1994 we will place ads for computers in the Channel newspaper at Santa Barbara City College and the University Post newspaper at the University of California, Santa Barbara.

5. Personal selling is one of the powerful methods to increase sales. A commission-based personal selling system will be developed beginning in June 1994.

6. As mentioned earlier, buying a computer is an important decision requiring extensive research. Many computer users rely on computer magazines for information and purchase. In August 1994, we will begin to contact the local computer-magazine agent for the computer ad.

7. Trade shows can provide an opportunity to introduce our product and services as well as help our company generate revenue. We will begin to contact the computer trade-show organization in August 1994 to arrange a place to exhibit our products.

Price

Since the price of computer components varies daily, our price for each computer will be set according to the total cost of each computer plus 30 percent profit. However, our product price may vary slightly from that formula because it will also depend on the average price of the local computer market.

Production/Distribution

1. We will arrange a contractual supply agreement for computer components with different companies. Our ordering method will be based on the just-in-time (JIT) manufacturing system, to be finalized within one month from now (May 1994) with purchasing to begin in late August 1994.

2. In August 1994 we will purchase tools for assembling the personal computers.

3. In August 1994 we will order the computer stickers for company logo.

ORGANIZATION, EVALUATION, CONTROL, AND IMPLEMENTATION

Break-Even Analysis

CompuWare will begin by offering the following PC models:

1. 486 DX 33 MHz

2. 486 DX2 50 MHz

3. 486 DX2 66 MHz

4. Pentium PM 66 MHz

Our break-even analyses are calculated by average products. We are confident that by following our marketing plan, we should be able to reach our break-even point easily, and from there, make our desirable profit.

The break-even point for CompuWare will be reached at 83 personal computers sold at an average price of $2,000.58 for each unit model sold at an average of seven units each month. The break-even point should be reached within 12 months after our marketing plan has been activated.

SUMMARY

- The computer industries are booming in the 1990s; the demand for computers is increasing every year, which creates great opportunities for the computer retail market. Because of this, *CompuWare* will be born in September 1994.

- Falling prices for smarter and faster high-performance personal computers have attracted many new buyers from among a decidedly educated and affluent segment of the U.S. population.

- The computer retail market is not highly competitive in Santa Barbara; a potential market for personal computers exists. The one university and two colleges, as well as large professional and entrepreneurial population in the area, makes the area receptive to a personal computer store such as *CompuWare.*

- The U.S. government is beginning to help implement the "national information superhighway," and to encourage industry to provide affordable information services that will be accessible to all Americans. This can provide unlimited opportunities to the computer industry.

- There are three major competitors in Santa Barbara area: CompUSA, Computer Land, and Data Net. *CompuWare* will copy the successful strategies from these competitors, but eliminate the weaknesses.

- The primary target market segments for *CompuWare* will be college or graduate students, members of households where income exceeds $50,000 annually, and professionals or managers. However, the target market will also include those people who seek computers to solve their problems or to help them get things done efficiently, those who enjoy or are involved with a multimedia environment, and people who like to invest in the stock market and wish to obtain primary stock market information by computer at home. Furthermore, *CompuWare* will develop a brand loyalty on the part of the customers.

- The actual demand for computer purchase in Santa Barbara is unknown, but because of less competition and the existence of potential market segments, a profitable market for the personal computers exists in Santa Barbara. Another problem is that *CompuWare* requires $60,000 in start-up and introduction costs. Again, in an area such as Santa Barbara where computer sales are not yet highly competitive, the expected return on investment is high.

- *CompuWare's* objective over a 10-year period is to establish a retail network throughout the state of California.

- The goal for *CompuWare* is to make 500 personal computer sales and $130,000 of net profit in the first business year, and increase the store to locations in California within 10 years, expansion of services of related products, provision of on-line services within 2 years, an increase in sales through international trade within 5 years, and to provide the extension of warranty services in 2 years.

- The key to success inherent in *CompuWare* product strategy comes out of three essential values: high quality, product flexibility, and reliability.

- Price is one of the major factors encouraging customers to buy *CompuWare* products. Since *CompuWare* has a low overhead, it can offer products at lower prices.

- *CompuWare's* positioning strategy will be to use effective strategic methods with lower cost, such as use of direct mail, publicity, word of mouth, personal selling, college and university newspapers, computer magazines, trade show, holiday discounts, cumulative discounts, and coupons.

- *CompuWare's* production strategy will focus on the quality of the computer components. The product production will be based on the just-in-time (JIT) philosophy, because it can reduce or eliminate inventories, thereby saving financing and storage costs.

- The economy in the city of Santa Barbara is expected to turn positive in the fall of 1994. *CompuWare* is planning to begin business in September 1994. *CompuWare* will be located inside the Paseo Nuevo shopping mall on State Street in downtown Santa Barbara.

- In order to build up brand loyalty on the part of the customers, a logo designed for *CompuWare* is a must. However, a showroom is also important to attract customers. *CompuWare* will have four different models of personal computers displayed in the showroom. The showroom will also display some of the components and computer accessories.

- College students are the primary target market for *CompuWare,* so flyers will be put on bulletin boards at the college, the university, and in public areas. *CompuWare* will also begin to contact the city college and university for permission to put on exhibits to demonstrate the performance of the personal computer. Further, classified advertising in college and university newspapers will also be used for *CompuWare's* products.

- Personal selling is one of the most effective methods to increase sales. A commission-based personal selling system will be developed after the business has been established.

- Personal computers are a high decision-making product, and many computer users rely on computer magazines for information about the products they purchase. A computer ad will be placed in the local computer magazine before the business begins.

- Trade shows can provide an opportunity to introduce *CompuWare's* products and services to the customers. An arrangement will be made for a place to exhibit the *CompuWare's* personal computers.

- Since computer component prices vary daily, the price for *CompuWare's* computer will be set according to the total cost of each computer plus 30 percent profit.

- A contractual supply agreement for computer components will begin with different companies. The ordering method will be based on the just-in-time (JIT) manufacturing system.

- The break-even point for CompuWare will be reached at 83 personal computers sold at an average price of $2,000.58 for each unit model sold at an average of seven units each month.

- The expectation of the first-year business for *CompuWare* is to generate $982,660 in net sales and to earn $131,019.10 in net profit. However, second-year business is expected to increase by 50 percent of sales revenue and to earn $194,098.70 in net income. Moreover, third-year business is expected to be excellent, and net sales are expected to increase 100 percent and generate $388,197 in net income.

BIBLIOGRAPHY

"PC Multimedia Is Here and Growing," Prodigy Service, Feb. 28, 1994.
"Computer Buyer," Prodigy Service, Feb. 14, 1994.
"The Personal Computer," Prodigy Service, April 8, 1994.
"Fax Technology," Prodigy Service, Dec. 13, 1994.
Economic Profile 1993, Santa Barbara County Chamber of Commerce.
California Dept. of Finance, Population Research Unit, 508.
Census of Retail Trade, (Geographic Area Series California), 1987.
"The Latest Laptop Program Is TV's," Washington Post, Tuesday, Sept. 9, 1993.
"Bad News for Dell Computer," The New York Times, Tuesday, July 15, 1993.
"In PC Big Blue Is Red Hot," Washington Post, Monday, Nov. 18, 1993.
"Big Blue Is Reclaiming Market Share," The New York Times, Thursday, Nov. 12, 1993.
Statistical Abstract of the United States, Computer Shipments and Revenue: 1989–92, 761.
Forbes Annual Report on American Industry, Forbes Inc., New York, NY.
"Workstations Have Their Work Cut Out," Business Week, Nov. 17, 1993.
"Future Phone," Business Week, Jan. 24, 1994.
"Intel Steers the PC onto the Info Highway," Business Week, Jan. 31, 1994.

APPENDIX A6-A

Break-even = Total Fixed Cost ÷ Unit Contribution Margin

Total Fixed Cost = $40,608.00

Total Average Variable Cost = $1,511.25

Total Average Product Price = $2,000.58

Total Average Unit Contribution Margin = 489.33

Break-even = $40,608.00 ÷ (489.33) = 83 units

APPENDIX A6-B

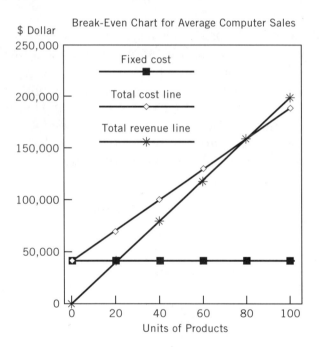

Break-Even Chart for Average Computer Sales

APPENDIX A6-C

Break-Even Point Analysis In One Year Period

Fix Cost	Amount
Rent	$7,776.00
Phone Bill	360.00
Car Leasing Fee	3,000.00
Gas Expenses	800.00
Advertising	2,400.00
Car Insurance Exp	1,500.00
Insurance Expenses	1,500.00
Trade Show Expenses	4,800.00
Sales Salaries	17,472.00
Misc	1,000.00
Total	40,608.00

Motherboard Model	Amount
486 DX 33 MHz	$247.00
486 DX2 50 MHz	278.00
486 DX2 66 MHz	427.00
Pentiums PM 66 Mz	1,049.00

Other Components	Amount
Computer Case	$35.00
8 RAM Memory	32.00
Hard Disc 500 MB	100.00
Window 3.1	54.00
Dos 6.2	40.00
Mouse	8.00
1.2/1.44 MB FDD	78.50
Color Mont	249.00
Color Card	56.00
HD controller Card	30.00
Key Board	24.50
Total	1,007.00

Sticker/Other Expenses	Amount
Computer Sticker	$4.00

Product Total Cost	Amount
486 DX 33 MHz	$1,258.00
486 DX 50 MHz	1,289.00
486 DX2 66 MHz	1,438.00
Pentiums PM 66 MHz	2,060.00
Total	4,045.00

Product Total Price	Amount
486 DX 33 MHz	$1,635.40
486 DX2 50 MHz	1,675.70
486 DX2 66 MHz	2,013.20
Pentiums PM 66 MHz	2,678.00
Total	8,002.30

APPENDIX A6-D

Cost and Price Analysis

Cost and Price analysis/ 486 DX 33 MHZ	Amount
Product Cost	$1,254.00
Computer Sticker/Other	4.00
Fix Cost	82.00
Subtotal	1,340.00
Markup 22%	295.40
Product Price	1,635.40
Unit Cost	1,340.00
Unit Profit	295.40

Cost and Price analysis/ 486 DX 50 MHZ	Amount
Product Cost	$1,285.00
Computer Sticker/Other	4.00
Fix Cost	82.00
Subtotal	1,371.00
Markup 22%	304.70
Product Price	1,675.70
Unit Cost	1,371.00
Unit Profit	304.70

Cost and Price analysis/ 486 DX2 66 MHZ	Amount
Product Cost	$1,434.00
Computer Sticker/Other	4.00
Fix Cost	82.00
Subtotal	1,520.00
Markup 32%	493.20
Product Price	2,013.20
Unit Cost	1,520.00
Unit Profit	493.20

Cost and Price analysis/ Pentium P5-66 MHZ	Amount
Product Cost	$2,056.00
Computer Sticker/Other	4.00
Fix Cost	82.00
Subtotal	2,142.00
Markup 22%	536.00
Product Price	2,678.00
Unit Cost	2,142.00
Unit Profit	536.00

APPENDIX A6-E

Price List for Compuware Computers

PC 80486 System	Pentium PM System

Intel 80486 DX CPU.
3 VESA Slots.
CPU Heat Sink w/ Cooling fan.
256K Cache Memory on board.
8MB SIMMS expandable to 32MB.
500MB Hard Drive.
TEAC 1.44MB Floppy drive.
Orchild 1MB Windows Accelerator.
- 32 Bits VESA Local Bus
- 24 Bits colors, 16 Million Color
- Window Accelerator 33 Chip
- expandable to 2MB Rams.
32-bit VESA BUS IDE controller.
14" Super VGA NI Monitor
- Resolution: 1024 × 768, 28 dot pitch.
Mini Tower Case
Focus 101 Keys Keyboard.
Logitech Mouse

Intel Pentium PM CPU
3 EISA, 2 VESA and Sisa Slots
CPU Heat Sink w/ Cooling fan.
256K Cache Memory on board.
8MB SIMMS expandable to 32MB.
500MB Hard Drive.
TEAC 1.44MB Floppy drive.
Dimond Viper Window Accelerator
  - 2MB RAM
  - 32 Bits VESA Local Bus
  - 24 Bits colors, 16 Million Color
  - Window Accelerator 33 Chip
32-bit VESA BUS IDE controller.
14" Super VGA NI Monitor
- Resolution: 1024 × 768, 28 dot pitch.
Medium Tower Case
Focus 101 Keys Keyboard.
Logitech Mouse

486DX 33 Mhz	$1,635.40	Pentium PM 66 Mhz	$2,678.00
486DX2 50 Mhz	$1,750.70		
486DX2 66 Mhz	$2,013.20		

Parts

CD-ROM

Sony CD ROM 31A IDE	$239
Sony CD ROM 541 SCSI	$379
NEC MultiSpin 84	$579

Sound Card

Sound Blaster Compatible	$65
Sound Blaster	$79
Sound Blaster Pro	$139
Pro-Audio Spectrum 16	$169

Type Drive

120MB Colorado Drive (external)	$159
250MB Colorado Drive (external)	$189

Modem

2400bps Modem	$40
9600/2400 Fax/Modem	$60
14.4/9600 Fax/Modem	$120
14.4/14.4 Fax/Modem	$140

Monitor

14' Areus int Monitor	$245
14' Areus NI Monitor	$279
15' CTX NI Monitor 1561	$389
15' MAG MX15F	$530
17' MAG MX17F	$940

Video Card

Dimond Stleath 24VLB 1 MB DRAM	$179
Dimond Stleath Pro 1MB VRAM	$179
Dimond Viper 2MB VLB	$395

Printer

Panasonic KPX 23	$190
HP Deskjet 500	$389
HP Laser 4L	$649
HP Laserjet 4	$1349
Dos 6.0 & Windows 3.1	$85

APPENDIX A6-F

CASH FLOW

	Start-up	Month 1	Month 2	Month 3	Month 4	Month 5	Month 6	Month 7	Month 8	Month 9	Month 10	Month 11	Month 12
Cash	60,000.00	60,000.00	70,408.50	80,817.00	92,214.50	103,612.00	128,826.00	154,040.00	179,254.00	204,468.00	232,539.00	260,610.00	288,681.00
Income (Computers)		48,188.50	48,188.50	50,077.50	50,077.50	98,266.00	98,266.00	98,266.00	98,266.00	98,266.00	98,266.00	98,266.00	98,266.00
Income (Components)		3,000.00	3,000.00	3,000.00	3,000.00	5,000.00	5,000.00	5,000.00	5,000.00	7,000.00	7,000.00	7,000.00	7,000.00
Income (Accessory)		2,000.00	2,000.00	2,000.00	2,000.00	3,000.00	3,000.00	3,000.00	3,000.00	5,000.00	5,000.00	5,000.00	5,000.00
Total Income		53,188.50	53,188.50	55,077.50	55,077.50	106,266.00	106,266.00	106,266.00	106,266.00	110,266.00	110,266.00	110,266.00	110,266.00
Total Cash & Income		113,188.50	123,597.00	135,894.50	147,292.00	209,878.00	235,092.00	260,306.00	285,520.00	314,734.00	342,805.00	370,876.00	398,947.00
Expenses													
Purchase		37,943.00	37,943.00	38,843.00	38,843.00	76,215.00	76,215.00	76,215.00	76,215.00	77,358.00	77,358.00	77,358.00	77,358.00
Overhead		1,403.00	1,403.00	1,403.00	1,403.00	1,403.00	1,403.00	1,403.00	1,403.00	1,403.00	1,403.00	1,403.00	1,403.00
Transportation		442.00	442.00	442.00	442.00	442.00	442.00	442.00	442.00	442.00	442.00	442.00	442.00
Wages		2,912.00	2,912.00	2,912.00	2,912.00	2,912.00	2,912.00	2,912.00	2,912.00	2,912.00	2,912.00	2,912.00	2,912.00
Other		80.00	80.00	80.00	80.00	80.00	80.00	80.00	80.00	80.00	80.00	80.00	80.00
Total Expenses		42,780.00	42,780.00	43,680.00	43,680.00	81,052.00	81,052.00	81,052.00	81,052.00	82,195.00	82,195.00	82,195.00	82,195.00
Total Cash Flow		70,408.50	80,817.00	92,214.50	103,612.00	128,826.00	154,040.00	179,254.00	204,468.00	232,539.00	260,610.00	288,681.00	316,752.00

APPENDIX A6-G

MARKETING PLAN SCHEDULE

MONTHS AFTER STRATEGY INITIATION/$ ALLOCATED

Task	1	2	3	4	5	6	7	8	9	10	11	12	Total
Initial Production	38,915	38,915	38,915	38,915	77,830	77,830	77,830	77,830	77,830	77,830	77,830	77,830	$778,300
Advertising	200	200	200	200	200	200	200	200	200	200	200	200	$2,400
Trade Show	400	400	400	400	400	400	400	400	400	400	400	400	$4,800
Special Publicity				100	100	100	100						$400
Sales Promotion			500	500	500								$1,500
Transportation	442	442	442	442	442	442	442	442	442	442	442	442	$5,304
Misc.			100	100	100	100	100	100	100	100	100	100	$1,000
Monthly Total	$39,957	39,957	40,557	40,657	79,572	79,072	79,072	78,972	78,972	78,972	78,972	78,972	$793,704

APPENDIX A6-H

CompuWare Inc.
Profit and Loss Statement
For the Year Ended September 30, 1995

Revenues		
Net Sales	$982,660.00	
Total Revenue		$982,660.00
Cost and Expenses		
Cost of Goods Sold	$778,300.00	
Selling Expenses	2,000.00	
General and Administrative Expenses	40,608.00	
Income Taxes Expense	30,732.88	
Total Costs and Expenses		851,640.00
Net Income		$131,019.10

APPENDIX A6-I

CompuWare Inc.
Profit and Loss Statement
For the Year Ended September 30, 1996

Revenues		
Net Sales	$1,473,990.00	
Total Revenue		$1,473,990.00
Cost and Expenses		
Cost of Goods Sold	$1,170,450.00	
Selling Expenses	3,000.00	
General and Administrative Expenses	60,912.00	
Income Taxes Expense	45,529.32	
Total Costs and Expenses		1,279,891.00
Net Income		$ 194,098.70

APPENDIX A6-J

CompuWare Inc.
Profit and Loss Statement
For the Year Ended September 30, 1997

Revenues		
Net Sales	$2,947,980.00	
Total Revenue		$2,947,980.00
Cost and Expenses		
Cost of Goods Sold	$2,340,900.00	
Selling Expenses	6,000.00	
General and Administrative Expenses	121,824.00	
Income Taxes Expense	91,058.64	
Total Costs and Expenses		2,559,783.00
Net Income		$ 388,197.40

APPENDIX A6-K

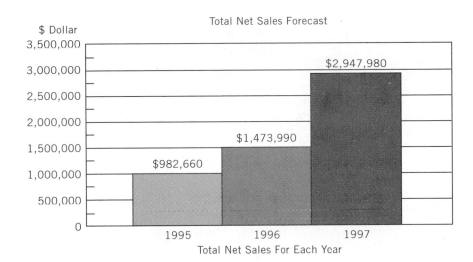

Total Net Sales Forecast

APPENDIX A6-L

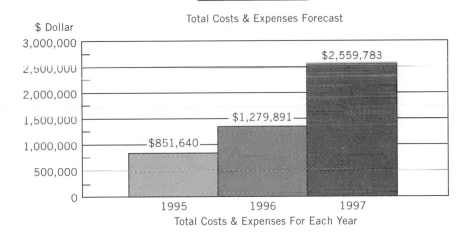

Total Costs & Expenses Forecast

APPENDIX A6-M

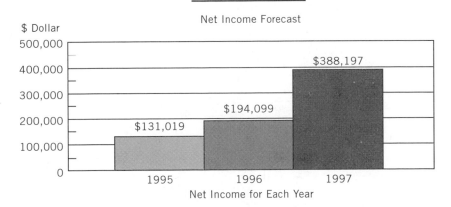

Net Income Forecast

APPENDIX A6-N

CompuWare Inc.
Balance Sheet
September 30, 1994

Assets

Cash		$49,972.00
Account Receivable		0.00
Prepaid Rent		648.00
Prepaid Insurance		375.00
Prepaid Car Insurance		375.00
Office Equipment	$8,630.00	
Less Accumulated Depreciation	0	8,630.00
Total Assets		$60,000.00

Liabilities

Accounts Payable	0	
Salaries Payable	0	
Income Taxes Payable	0	0
Total Liability		

Owner's Equity

Common Stock	60,000.00	
Retained Earnings	0	
Total Owner's Equity		
Total Liability and Owners' Equity		$60,000.00

APPENDIX A6-O

CompuWare Inc.
Balance Sheet
September 30, 1995

Assets

Cash		$165,663.98
Account Receivable		0.00
Prepaid Rent		648.00
Prepaid Insurance		375.00
Prepaid Car Insurance		375.00
Office Equipment	$8,630.00	
Less Accumulated Depreciation	3,452.00	12,082.00
Total Assets		$179,143.98

Liabilities

Accounts Payable	0	
Salaries Payable	0	
Income Taxes Payable	30,732.88	$30,732.88
Total Liability		

Owner's Equity

Common Stock	17,392.00	
Retained Earnings	$131,019.10	
Total Owner's Equity		148,411.10
Total Liability and Owners' Equity		$179,143.98

A7

SNEAK PEEK: A STUDENT'S GUIDE TO UNIVERSITY COURSES

Developed by
TONETTE DOVE
DAVID GRAJEDA
ANTHONY B. LUJAN
DONNA TOM
HUEI MING TSAI
CAROLINE WANG

EXECUTIVE SUMMARY

This marketing plan was developed to study the economic feasibility of distributing a campus publication. *Sneak Peek: A Student's Guide* serves as a detailed brochure for students about courses offered at the California State University at Los Angeles (CSULA) campus. Preliminary research indicates there exists a strong demand for this product and a stable target market. As of fall 1989 the student population of CSULA was 20,804 and has remained fairly constant at the 20,000–21,000 range for the past four years (see Appendix A7-A). Primary research data have established that 70 percent of the target market would be willing to purchase this product at a price range of under $10 (Appendix A7-B). Of this market, 50 percent will be captured the first year (i.e., 35 percent of the total market) and sales are expected to increase by at least 50 percent per year thereafter. Further appeal is that the brochure has very low overhead, minimal competition, and benefits both students and the quality of CSULA's education.

This venture would require an initial capital investment of $18,000 (6 shares at $3,000 each). This initial capital investment will be paid back the first year. Furthermore, a first-year return on investment of 44 percent is expected. The sales projection for the initial year is $128,055.53. Of the first year's revenue, 12.8 percent will be from local business advertising sales. Throughout the five-year projection sales are projected to grow tremendously.

INTRODUCTION

The objective of this marketing plan is to study the feasibility of publishing a student's inside guide to courses and instructors at CSULA. Based upon a preliminary survey of 450 currently enrolled CSULA students, an 88 percent favorable response rate for this product and a 70 percent buy rate from students who wished to purchase this product was established. This survey represents a cross-section of all students currently attending CSULA. Surveys were purposely done at random times during the day and evenings throughout campus. This gave a representative mix of undergraduate and graduate students as well as dormitory and commuter students (see Appendix A7-C).

Demand for the product will be strong because CSULA has a high percentage of commuter students (97 percent) with limited access to "word-of-mouth" recommendations on class and instructor information. Primary research data on 450 randomly selected CSULA students indicate only 62 percent had access to "word-of-mouth" recommendations from friends for classes they were planning to take the next quarter. This information gap is further compounded by the fact that many CSULA students have less time for social interactions than traditional college students. Many CSULA students are trying to balance full-time jobs and family responsibilities in conjunction with school demands (see Appendix A7-A). This guidebook will provide a reasonable alternative to traditional "word-of-mouth" recommendations college students of the past utilized when they had the time and opportunity to develop a social network with fellow dorm residents and classmates.

Promotion and advertising of this publication will be directed along CSULA's mass communication channels (CSULA *University Times* ads, quarterly *Schedule of Classes* ads, campus flyers, and advertising/sales booths during new student orientation days). Students will be offered discount coupons for the publication or free advertising of their used books on a selected basis. This will be a means of generating increased awareness and interest in the guidebook.

Printing and advertising costs will constitute the major expense. To maintain production costs at a minimum and keep the final product at a reasonable price to cost-conscious students, the guidebook will be limited to 160 pages for the initial printing. The guidebook will consist of five sections:

1. Information on courses and instructors.

2. Business advertising space (encourage free or discount coupon offers).

3. Invitation for students to participate in the next publication as a respondent.

4. Invitation to advertise in the recycler section for free.

5. Recycler section (will need to limit this section since it is being used as a promotion technique—i.e., lost leader).

One method that will be employed to offset publishing costs is to entice local businesses (fast-food, laundry, printing or photocopying establishments, bookstores, apartment managers, or other student-oriented services) to advertise in the guidebook for a fee. This additional advertising revenue will make it feasible to keep the price charged for the publication under $10. This should aid greatly in overcoming student price resistance.

Based on the results of a random survey of 450 CSULA students, sales and market share projections will be forecasted for the initial year. This will be followed by a complete analysis of capital expenses, promotion and distribution costs, start-up costs, and a quarter-to-quarter cash-flow projection for a five-year period.

SITUATIONAL ANALYSIS

In this section various factors that affect the marketability of the product will be discussed. Customer profile, relevant social and cultural factors, prevailing economic and business conditions, legal and political aspects, and other environmental factors impacting the product will be examined.

Customer Profile

Sneak Peek's target market is comprised of CSULA's student body. Of the total quarterly 20,000 plus enrollment, the specific target marketing will be directed toward the freshman, sophomore, and junior class levels. It is this 45.2 percent of total students, who enroll in the general and lower division courses, that have been selected for the student guide's first edition. Currently totaling 12,407, this undergraduate segment population will be the primary focus, but not to the exclusion of the 54.8 percent senior class level. It is believed the intended target market will actively seek this product. *Sneak Peek* enhances the opportunity to effectively choose classes which otherwise would require informational networking that may not be easily accessible.

Location Profile

Realistically, the two most visible and therefore most ideal sites to sell the product would be the University Square Bookstore and the Student Book Mart located at 1689 N. Eastern Avenue. These two locations have established themselves as CSULA student-oriented outlets and generate tremendous student traffic. Secondary methods of generating sales would be to employ direct marketing techniques to solicit sales through advertising in the CSULA quarterly *Schedule of Classes,* the CSULA *University Times,* and flyers distributed throughout campus. Another ideal site location would be to set up a booth during new student orientation days and distribute sales information on the guidebook.

The fact that this venture does not require a permanent storefront as a prerequisite to doing business is a definite advantage. By avoiding this major fixed overhead expense this business can be initiated on a shoestring budget.

Sales Projections

The average student at CSULA spends approximately $40 to $50 on textbooks per course. The guidebook will be priced at under $10.

Most students would perceive this as a bargain. Insights obtained from the publication are valuable if they allow one to avoid the ordeal of registration's drop-and-add. Also, there is the added "hook" of the recycler section to aid in increasing sales. Students will have the opportunity to contact other students and purchase used books at a savings. Thus, all or a significant portion of the cost of the guidebook can be recouped. Another positive selling feature of the guidebook is the discount or free coupons offered by local merchants in the business advertising section.

Based on the CSULA student survey a conservative sell rate of 35 percent of the 20,804 total student population is anticipated. This represents 50 percent of the students who said they would buy based upon a selling price of less than $10. Therefore, the first-year sales projection on guidebooks is approximately $111,602 based upon an introductory direct mail price of $5 and a wholesale price of $4 for the publication. The calculation used was a 70 percent buy response × 50 percent sales rate × total CSULA student population × selling price of guidebook × 4 issues per year (with the added stipulation that direct mailing will account for 20 percent of total sales for the first year). Sales are targeted to increase by 50 percent per year since 88 percent of the respondents saw a need for the publication, but only 70 percent said they would actually buy. Through "word-of-mouth" customer recommendations and additional product features, the remaining market population will be captured within a three-year period.

Additional revenue will be attained through advertising sales to local businesses: $175 per quarter, $330 for two quarters, $435 for three quarters, and $540 for four quarters for a 1/4-page advertisement in the guidebook. This represents 50 percent less than rates charged by the CSULA *Schedule of Classes* publication. Revenues generated from this source will add a minimum of $10,000 to $15,000 in yearly profits using a conservative target of 20 advertisers per issue. Therefore, total sales projections for the first year from sales of guidebooks and sales of advertising space is $128,055.53.

Additionally, if the option to charge $2 per used book ad is utilized in the Recycler Section, profits will increase once again.

Competition

As with any business, competition is always a critical factor. Currently, CSULA does not have a publication similar to the guidebook available for its students. Thus, one significant advantage to be enjoyed at the introduction of this publication is a monopoly on the market. To capitalize on this advantage, the first year will be used to refine the publication through soliciting suggestions for improvement in the product's format from customers, and revising to meet these new standards as quickly as possible. Thus, competition strategy will be to keep the publication price low and the product quality high in order to discourage competitors from entering the marketplace.

Technological Factors

Production involves no new technology. Essentially, the final product is a quarterly periodical. The majority of efforts will be directed at the time-consuming process of gathering class and instructor information, compiling and organizing it, then sending the completed manuscript for printing. To save time on processing information, a computer word processor would be advantageous although not absolutely necessary to accomplish the required objectives.

Political and Legal Factors

The business community, as with any other group that must work in harmony for the common good, needs rules and regulations concerning the conduct of its members. *Sneak Peek* is owned and operated by a six-member partnership. Each partner has an equal investment in the organization. In this partnership, rules and regulations established by federal, state, and local government, as well as the California State University system must be adhered to.

The federal government has authorized the freedom to publish *Sneak Peek* when it guaranteed freedom of the press. The right of freedom of the press has been one of the basic rights granted by the U.S. Constitution. In other words, the owners of *Sneak Peek* can print any material as long as it does not infringe on the rights of the administrators, teachers, and the student population. If published material is dishonest in any way, the authors can be subject to libel lawsuit by the individual who was libeled. To prevent this from happening, all of the questions in the guidebook are objective. Also, all responses will be based on collective students' answers, not an individual. To ensure the sincerity of the guidebook, all material will be available to the professors before publication. At that time, any problems concerning the content of the publication can be addressed before printing. The brochure will be based solely on the opinion of contributing students. It is expected that the publication may generate some unpopular criticism from students or instructors. Of the students surveyed, 12 percent believed students did not have the right to have prior knowledge of course or instructor requirements. Also, there may be times when professors will say that the information written about them is not true. In these cases, legal counsel will be available for resolving this type of miscommunication. To be prudent, a disclaimer to the effect that this publication does not represent the viewpoint of the editors, but rather the result of opinion polls of CSULA students will be prominently displayed. Additionally, it will be made clear that the information included in the publication is updated quarterly to be as accurate as possible. There is, however, no guarantee that a course will be conducted exactly as described in the publication. Instructors have complete freedom to change their course requirements from quarter to quarter.

This publication will be protected by copyright. This is accomplished through the Copyright Office in Washington, D.C., for a fee of $10 per issue.

In regard to federal taxes, provisions change almost yearly. As a partnership, Form 1065 (only the signature of one of the partners is required) must be filed. The Partnership Income Tax Return is filed for information purposes only since the partnership is not taxable as an entity. The purpose of the Form 1065 is merely to report the business income that should be included on each partners' individual tax returns. Individual proprietors and partners are required to pay their federal income tax and self-employment tax liability on a "pay-as-you-go" basis. This requires filing the Declaration of Estimate Tax, which is Form 1040ES. Payments on the estimate are made over a period of nine months; the first payment is due on April 15. Additional payments are due June 15, September 15, and January 15. Adjustments to the estimate will be made at the time of each payment. Other than the risk of a libel suit and payment of taxes, there are no other basic regulations at the federal level that must be complied with.

At the state level, according to Jamie Green of the State Board of Equalizations, quarterly periodicals are not subject to state taxes. Therefore, the price charged for the guidebook is the price that must be charged to retail customers. State sales tax will not be collected at the wholesale or the retail level. By registering *Sneak Peek* at the office of the State Board of Equalization, a resale number can be obtained through which sales can be made to vendors. No business license is required at the state level. This type of licensing is done only at the municipal level.

Obtaining a normal business license to fulfill city level requirements involves filing and paying license fees at the county clerk's office. Two licenses are required: the Consumer Retail Sales License (CRS) and the Wholesale Sale License (WSL). The CRS has an initial cost of $100.78, and the WSL has a first-time cost of $107.50. Every January thereafter, the CRS requires a payment of $1.25 per $1,000 worth of units sold. Similarly, every subsequent January the WSL requires a payment of $1.25 per $1,000 worth of units sold. Once these two licenses are obtained, it is legal to operate this business in the city.

However, this does not mean that *Sneak Peek* automatically receives the approval of the California State University at Los Angeles. According to Ruth Goldway, Director of Public Affairs–CSULA, the first step in getting the school to approve this project is through the Office of Student Life, Student Union 425. Vera Perez, Office of Student Life, stated that printing the guidebook could be approved by the university. However, final approval must be obtained from Central Reservations, Student Union 410. Any item that is circulated throughout the university must have a university stamp of approval.

Once *Sneak Peek* has this stamp, total freedom is allowed in marketing it to students. Setting up a table in front of the Student Union would cost $25 per day and promote high visibility of the product. On the other hand, selling this guidebook through the University Book Store would require the approval of Catherine Rembol, CSULA Book Store Manager. Ms. Rembol claims that the retail cost to students for each guidebook would be the product's wholesale price plus a 25 percent markup.

PROBLEMS AND OPPORTUNITIES

A primary survey of 450 CSULA students yielded encouraging statistics. Seldom does a company have the opportunity to market a new product to a target group where 88 percent of the market believes there is a need for that product, 63 percent of the target market is willing to participate in the production of that product, and 70 percent of the market is also willing to buy the finished product when it becomes available (see Appendix A7-C, Table 2). It was interesting to note that 97 percent of the freshman class (the best indicator of future sales) believes there is a need for this product and 76 percent are willing to buy the guide if it is priced at less than $10. Once again, this reinforces the belief that even with access to "word-of-mouth" recommendations (52 percent for freshmen), students are still eager to find out more about classes and instructors, especially from a reasonably priced source.

It is expected that the demand for this product will continue to grow until the full market share of 70 percent is attained and then remain constant because customers will be encouraged to repeat buy each quarter. Some students may choose to photocopy sections of the guide rather than purchase it, but this will be a relatively low number due to the low price ($5) of the product. To encourage repeat buyers, the courses selected for the guide will vary slightly each quarter to correspond to courses offered by the university. Additionally, emphasis will be placed on obtaining business advertisers that will offer discount coupons on goods and services in their advertisement through the guidebook. Finally, the possible savings on purchasing used books through the guide's Recycler Section will spur sales and encourage repeat buyers.

Perhaps the primary obstacle to the success of this venture will be compiling the required data quickly enough to update the publication every quarter. This requires being totally dependent upon the input of students responding to invitations to be part of the student panel. Therefore, the incentives offered (discount coupon or free advertising space) must be compelling enough to entice students to participate. Based on the students surveyed, 63 percent of the respondents said they were willing to participate for these incentives. Of this group, 60 percent preferred receiving the discount coupon, 25 percent the free advertising, and 15 percent had no preference (see Appendix A7-C, Table 3). It is anticipated that one person using the telephone to collect all required information should be able to update the publication each quarter.

Due to the quarterly publication of the product, inventory levels must be monitored very carefully. With experience, the ability to accurately judge demand for the product will be gained. Strict inventory control will increase profits by reducing the amount of outdated merchandise created by the quarterly turnover of this product. To address this problem, the "Just-in-Time" method of inventory control will be utilized.

FINANCIAL ANALYSIS

In order to determine start-up and operational costs the following financial analysis was compiled:

1. *Initial Investment.*   The initial investment for the proposed business is for capital equipment (typewriter, telephone, answering machine) and miscellaneous expenses (stationery, phone line, optional P.O. box). This business is designed to be run out of one's home. As stated earlier, the major expense will be printing and postage costs for the respondents.

2. *First-Year Operations.*   From the target sales of $111,602 for the first year, the net income of $38,320 is derived after deducting cost of sales and all other operating expenses. (See Appendix A7-N, Table 2, Projected Profit and Loss Statement—Year 1.) This represents a return of 30 percent on sales and 44 percent on investment. A positive cash flow of $33,450 is projected at the end of the first year of which $30,000 is available for distribution to the partners ($5,000 per partner). The break-even sales for the first year are based on a total fixed cost of $6934.28.

3. *Five-Year Projection.*   In the five-year projection, sales are estimated to grow at 50 percent for year 2, 75 percent for year 3, 40 percent for year 4, 25 percent for year 5. This growth objective is realistic based upon the sales strategy not only of the guidebook but of increasing sales from local business advertising and student used-books advertising in subsequent years.

OPERATIONAL ASPECTS

This section will describe the actual product to be published and the process utilized to gather and coordinate course/instructor information from fellow students.

Product

The publication will consist of six sections:

1. Course/instructor information

2. Local business advertising

3. Invitation to be a student respondent

4. Invitation to advertise in Recycler Section for free

5. Recycler Section

6. Invitation to place an advance order

The largest section of the guidebook (70–90 pages) will be the information on course requirements and instructors. The criteria for segmenting courses were based on identifying those courses needed by students to fulfill their undergraduate degree requirements. General Education courses form the foundation for every undergraduate student. Selecting these courses will result in the greatest demand for this guidebook and promote active sales. For the first edition of the guidebook, General Education courses that attract the most enrollment will be selected. Essentially, courses offering more than two choices of instructors will be included in the guidebook. This translates into surveying approximately 128 classes for course requirements and instructor information to be published in the first edition of the guidebook.

Future issues will utilize the same basic strategy as above. Each quarter, courses will be analyzed and those with the highest enrollment selected for publication. Future expansion and marketing strategy would call for plans to produce a separate guidebook for graduate students and select majors with high enrollment. For example, analyzing the core requirements of Business and Economics majors would yield a marketable product as well as examining Child Development and Nursing coursework (see Appendix A7-A).

Once the courses for inclusion into the publication are selected, responses from students who wish to participate in the publication (Appendix A7-F) will be culled to select those who are currently taking the courses to be evaluated. These students will be contacted by phone and the appropriate information collected (see Appendix A7-I). A minimum of three to five students will be polled for each course in order to gain a representative overview of students' opinions on course and instructor requirements (see Appendix A7-I and Appendix A7-D). This information will be compiled, collated, and organized for final publication. By updating course requirements each quarter, any recent changes in course requirements will be noted. This action does not obviate the necessity of including a disclaimer stating in effect that up-to-date information on courses and instructors has been compiled, but there is no guarantee that future courses taught by this instructor will follow the described format. Although course requirements may vary slightly from quarter to quarter, the information presented on instructors' teaching and grading methods is still applicable and will be valuable to customers.

The final product is envisioned to be approximately 160 pages and will be printed by Art's Press, 4727 E. Olympic Blvd., Los Angeles, CA 90020 (213) 262-0431. The guidebook will consist of 40 pages of 11 × 17 inch standard stock white paper saddle-stitched down the middle (160 total pages of 8½ × 11 inch paper printed on both sides) with a goldenrod cover of slightly heavier stock paper and done in one-color print. Total printing time for 2,000 copies is seven days, plus an additional seven days to typeset the first edition. Total printing cost for the first batch of 2,000 copies is $2,500, including typesetting. Additional runs of 2,000 copies will take 7 days' printing time and cost $1,900 per batch as quoted by Paul Go, owner of Art's Press.

The Just-In-Time method of inventory control will be utilized and the appropriate number of copies reordered when available stock drops below 500 copies. Since this publication is updated quarterly, outdated merchandise from overestimating demand is a concern. It is anticipated that after the first two quarters of publication, data on product demand will become accurate.

MARKETING STRATEGY

Basically, the guidebook will consist of the six sections mentioned previously. Each section will play a distinct role in the marketing of the product.

PRODUCT STRATEGY

Overall product strategy was to develop a product that was of universal appeal to CSULA students. A guidebook on course and instructor information seemed the most logical product to market to students. To separate this publication from the CSULA General Catalogue, which also gives course information, the guidebook will include information on grading methods and student insights. Also, a more free-flowing, entertaining style of writing will be employed to make the publication enjoyable to read. Therefore, initial product strategy was threefold:

1. Offer course information from a student's perspective with student tips on how to do well.

2. Keep the price of the publication low to fit students' tight budgets.

3. Offer free services or discounts on merchandise to create the feeling that the buyer was getting his money's worth.

To accomplish these objectives, six sections to the guidebook were devised.

Section 1: Course/Instructor Information (70–90 pages). This section will contain a brief description of course content to lend substance and credibility to the product. This description will be kept short so as to not cover the same information presented in the CSULA General Catalogue. Students' insights on how to prepare for tests and helpful hints will be included. Student comments on instructors will be carefully reviewed to ascertain if they are appropriate for inclusion in the guidebook. There is no wish to threaten or antagonize instructors by becoming too personal or subjective in instructor evaluations. Each course will receive a half-page write-up in the guidebook.

Section 2: Local Business Advertising (10–20 pages maximum). This section was designed as a means of offering free or discount goods to students from local merchants while serving as an important source of revenue for the guidebook through paid advertising fees. Local merchants will be strongly encouraged to offer student discounts when placing their advertisements.

Section 3: Invitation to Be a Student Respondent (2 pages). This will save the cost of advertising in other publications to recruit student participants (see Appendix A7-F). A copy of the student Participant Questionnaire (see Appendix A7-I) will be included in the guidebook so interested students will know what information will be needed in evaluating courses for the guidebook. The invitation will include a postcard size prepaid reply card for interested students to mail in to the guidebook's P.O. box.

Section 5: Recycler Section (40–50 pages). This section contains brief ads for used books (see Appendix A7-H). Students will call each other based on information contained in the ad. The staff of the guidebook will not be involved with these used-book sales. Depending on student response, there are plans to turn the recycler into a third avenue of income in the future through sale of used-book advertising.

Section 6: Order Form for Advance Book Sale (1 page). This form will allow students to order the next issue of the guidebook in advance (see Appendix A7-J). By selling at a retail price ($5/copy) instead of a wholesale price ($4/copy), an additional $1/copy of sales revenue is obtained at the expense of $0.35/copy in mailing costs. More important, advance sales will help in maintaining adequate inventory levels.

It is projected that direct mail sales will constitute 20 percent of total sales the first year and increase slightly each year as students become familiar with the content and quality of the product.

PRICE STRATEGY

Marketing strategy dictates setting the price of this publication below $10 per copy. In fact the price for the first edition is only $5 by direct mail (postage and handling included), or $5 through the university bookstore or the Student Book Mart. This will allow the publication to be perceived as a bargain. It offers students a range of desirable features as well as the opportunity to recoup their investment through the recycler section and merchant discount coupons. This low price will lend an initial price advantage over future competitors and hopefully discourage them from entering the market. It will also make it easier to repeat sell the publication each quarter to the same clientele.

As a means of keeping production costs low and therefore product price low, local businesses will be actively solicited to advertise in the publication and offer free services or goods. Advertisements in *Sneak Peek* can be done on a quarterly or yearly basis for fees far lower than conventional advertising rates. The CSULA *Schedule of Classes* is published quarterly and charges for a quarter-page ad: $350 for 1 quarter, $660 for 2 quarters, $870 for 3 quarters, and $1,080 for 4 quarters. Businesses in the CSULA local area will be approached to solicit advertisements at a rate 50 percent lower than those charged by the publishers of the CSULA quarterly *Schedule of Classes.* This additional revenue will be used to keep the price charged for the guidebook low. It is anticipated that 10 to 20 business ads will be placed in the guidebook each quarter the first year. Business advertising revenue is targeted to increase by 50 percent each year.

PROMOTION STRATEGY

The promotion for this product will concentrate on mass advertising through campus publications and activities. Direct mail solicitation through the CSULA *Schedule of Classes,* the CSULA *University Times,* and flyer distribution throughout campus will be utilized. Also, information and sales booths will be set up on campus during new student orientation days.

Advertising costs for the above mentioned publications are as follows: CSULA *University Times* has a flat fee of $337 per year for an advertisement that is placed in the classified section of the campus newspaper in a two-column, 3-inch deep, boxed enclosure. It will run for 30 consecutive issues. The *University Times* is printed three days a week, Monday, Wednesday, and Thursday, with a circulation of 8,000 copies each quarter; 6,000 copies are printed each Monday and Thursday; and 12,000 copies are printed for registration, welcome back, and special issues. The *University Times* has a daily readership over 23,500 of which 20,000 are students, 1,500 are faculty, and 2,000 are campus employees (see Appendix A7-J). The *University Times* is distributed free on campus from circulation boxes located at high traffic points and also at the student housing complexes.

The CSULA *Schedule of Classes* is issued on a quarterly basis. The advertising fee for a quarter-page ad depends upon the frequency: $350 for 1 quarter $660 for 2 quarters, $870 for 3 quarters, $1,080 for 4 quarters. The University Square Bookstore orders 23,000 to 25,000 *Schedule of Classes* per quarter according to Katherine Rembold, general manager of the bookstore.

Posters will also be utilized on campus to inform potential customers of this publication. The posters will be placed in high traffic points, such as the Student Union, the cafeterias, in and around the library, kiosks, and housing complexes. The size of the poster mentioned will be 11 × 17 inches.

Flyer distribution promoting the features of the publication and how to obtain a copy will be hand placed on car windshields during the period of class registration. The size of the flyers mentioned will be 8½ × 11 inches.

DISTRIBUTION STRATEGY

This product will be available for in-person sales through the University Square Bookstore and the Student Book Mart. Rates these establishments charge for their services are as follows: the University Square Bookstore will mark up the wholesale price charged them by 25 percent to obtain the retail price. The Student Book Mart will discount the retail selling price of the University Square Bookstore by 10 to 15 percent to obtain their selling price.

Alternatively, the publication can be purchased at the booth set up during new student orientation days provided this does not conflict with sales at the University Square Bookstore. Permission to operate a booth outside the Student Union can be obtained through the Student Union management.

Another source for obtaining the publication will be through the direct mail ads run in the *Schedule of Classes* and the *University Times.* Purchases can be made by calling the listed telephone number to request an order form or by sending in an order form and a check to a P.O. box or dropping it off at a campus mailbox. Approval from the university as a legitimate business is required before a campus mailbox can be obtained from the Associated Student Office, Student Union 424. One of the incentives for students to use direct mail purchase is the opportunity to order the publication in advance to obtain the guidebook before it is released through the bookstores. Advance sales give students first opportunity to purchase the used books offered. In terms of product distribution, advance sales are beneficial in maintaining adequate product inventory levels. It decreases demand peaks and reduces unplanned shortages due to insufficient supply.

Statistics will be followed for each of the above mentioned distribution methods to determine which avenues generate the most sales. Future advertising budget and distribution efforts will be concentrated on the most effective mediums.

IMPLEMENTATION SCHEDULE

The advertising period of *Sneak Peek* will extend throughout CSULA's school year. Advertising will be heavy beginning the fifth week of spring 1990. This is *Sneak Peek's* introduction period. Promotion continues through the summer quarter with emphasis on the third through eighth week coinciding with student registration. Special emphasis will be placed on promotion for new student orientation and the fall 1990 quarter.

1. ***Immediate.*** Collecting data will begin the first week of the spring 1990 quarter. Class schedule data will be continuously accumulated throughout the school year. Information such as the instructors' curriculum data and students' input will be gathered until the second week of the fall 1990 quarter.

2. ***Spring 1990 Quarter.*** During this period, *Sneak Peek's* advertising and promotion begins as follows:

   University Times ads: Submit ad for year-round circulation.

   Flyers and posters: Print up and distribute. Announce arriving campus product.

   Schedule of Classes: Submit ad to directory of classes for each upcoming quarter scheduled publication.

   In this quarter, students will be invited to participate in a survey in exchange for free advertising of a used book or for a $2 discount coupon off the purchase price of the publication.

3. ***Summer 1990 Quarter.*** All scheduled objectives, except product distribution, implemented. Advertising, data collection, editing, and promotion will continue through the span of this quarter. Accumulated data are edited and revised. Organization of collected information is prepared for the fall 1990 quarter's second week.

4. ***Fall 1990 Quarter.*** Advertising, promotion, printing, and distribution are the main emphasis of this scheduled section. By the end of week 1, all required editing will be completed and the finished draft sent to the printer. The final product will be made available by the fourth week. This is the optimum time for release of this publication since it coincides with peak demand for the product.

   Distribution (direct mailing and bookstore circulation) will begin the fifth week. This will correspond with CSULA's winter 1991 *Schedule of Classes* and winter registration period. Promotional activities will be carried through as indicated under the Promotion heading of the Implementation Schedule (Appendix A7-M).

FINANCIAL DATA

The initial investment is a relatively low amount of $3,000 for each person with a total of $18,000. The reason for this low initial investment is the low cost of expenses. For example, a retail outlet is not needed, personnel is limited, and the distribution is solely through the bookstores or through mail order. These advantages greatly reduce costs. The initial fiscal year will start from fall 1990. The financial data used are in a conservative form so all projections of expenses and costs will not be less than actual cost. Also, the expected sales will not be less than the actual sales. Sales of $128,055.53 are expected for the first year from both guidebook and advertising sales. Total sales will grow by 50 percent for year 2, 75 percent for year 3, 40 percent for year 4, and 25 percent for year 5. Total sales of $588,255.07 are expected by year 5. The best selling season is the fall quarter (see Appendix A7-N, Profit and Loss Statement). The seasonal factors used were: fall 1.35, winter 1.1, spring 0.9, and summer 0.65. These factors are based on the enrollment of students each quarter on campus. For example, the fall quarter is the highest selling quarter because it has the largest enrollment, and summer will be our lowest quarter in sales because it has the smallest enrollment. *Sneak Peek* is so profitable that the return on investment is 44 percent, which is 10 percent more than normal in the industry. This is due to high student demand for this item. Each investor will receive a $5,000 distribution for the first year. This will increase by 15 percent for year 2, 50 percent for year 3, 75 percent for year 4, 50 percent for year 5. The distribution for each investor will increase fivefold by the end of year 5.

CONCLUSION

In conclusion, this marketing plan has clearly outlined why this product will be successful. High student demand for this product (88 percent), as exhibited by willingness of students to participate in the production of the guidebook (63 percent) and in their desire to purchase the finished product (70 percent), has conclusively been established. Thus, the first caveat of marketing has been accomplished, namely, "Produce or obtain a product that sells itself." Another positive feature is the variety of ways this publication generates revenue: through direct mail sales, wholesale sales, business advertising sales, and student advertising sales. Besides being highly profitable with a 44 percent first return on investment and first-year sales of $128,055.53, required initial start-up capital is minimal ($18,000) due to low overhead and very low product costs. This, coupled with the flexibility of being able to quickly adapt the publication to respond to student needs or to branch off into more specialized guidebooks for specific degree majors, ensures both the present and future viability of this product.

Bibliography

Cohen, William, *Building a Mail Order Business.* John Wiley & Sons, New York, 1982.

Office of Public Affairs and Analytical Studies, *Facts #2: Fall 1989 Enrollment Information.* California State University at Los Angeles, January 1990, p. 2.

Office of Public Affairs and Analytical Studies, *Facts #1: Fall 1988 Enrollment Information,* California State University at Los Angeles, January 1989, p. 2.

Office of Public Affairs and Analytical Studies, *Facts Sheet: Fall 1987,* Enrollment Information, California State University at Los Angeles, January 1988, p. 1.

References

Ruth Goldway, Public Affairs Director (213) 343-3050.
Katherine F. Rembold, General Manager of Student Bookstore (213) 343-2500.
Terrance Timmins, J. D., Coordinator, Legal Information CSULA (213) 343-3110 or (213) 343-3414; State Board of Equalization, County Clerk's Office.

Appendix A7-A

CALIFORNIA STATE UNIVERSITY, LOS ANGELES TARGET POPULATION STATISTICS

Apportioned by class level, part-time, and full-time status
Years 1987, 1988, and 1989

	Fall 1987		Fall 1988		Fall 1989	
Total	21,189	100.00%	21,150	100.00%	20,804	100.00%
Freshmen	2,903	13.70	3,363	15.90	3,375	16.22
Sophomores	2,373	11.20	1,967	9.30	2,144	10.31
Juniors	4,047	19.10	3,997	18.90	3,888	18.69
Seniors	5,827	27.50	5,901	27.90	5,976	28.73
Grad-PB	6,039	29.50	5,922	28.00	5,421	26.05
Part-time	10,806	51.00%	10,617	50.00%	10,358	49.80%
Full-time	10,383	49.00	10,300	49.00	10,446	50.20
Comprehensive exams			233	1.00		

Fall 1989 Population Statistics

Commuter students	20,217	97.18%
Campus residents	587	2.82

Sources:
Office of Public Affairs and Analytical Studies, *Facts Sheet: Fall 1987 Enrollment Information,* California State University, Los Angeles, January 1988, p. 1.
Office of Public Affairs and Analytical Studies, *Facts #2: Fall 1988 Enrollment Information,* California State University, Los Angeles, January 1990, p. 2.
Office of Public Affairs and Analytical Studies, *Facts #3: Fall 1989 Enrollment Information,* California State University, Los Angeles, January 1990, p. 2.

Appendix A7-B

GUIDE TO CLASSES AND INSTRUCTORS OF CSULA SURVEY

1. Male _____ Female _____

2. Freshman _____ Sophomore _____ Junior _____ Senior _____

   Graduate student _____ Instructor _____

3. Do you think there is a need for a student guide to classes and instructors of CSULA?

   Yes _____ No _____

4. Do you think students have a right to know each instructor's course requirements and grading personality habits before signing up for their course?

   Yes _____ No _____

5. Do you have access to word-of-mouth recommendations from friends for the classes you intend to take next quarter?

   Yes _____ No _____

6. Would you be willing to participate anonymously as one of the students we polled to gain information on courses and instructors in exchange for a $2.00 discount coupon on our publication or an opportunity for free advertising of a used book you wish to sell?

   Yes _____ No _____

   I prefer: Discount coupon _____ Free advertising _____

7. Would you be willing to pay less than $10.00/copy for this publication?

   Yes _____ No _____   Thank you for your participation in this survey.

Appendix A7-C

STATISTICAL ANALYSIS OF CSULA COURSE/INSTRUCTOR GUIDE SURVEY

Table 1: CSULA Student Sample Population Breakdown by Class Levels

	Freshman	Sophomore	Junior	Senior	Grad.	Total
No. of students	64	92	119	132	40	450
% of total	14	21	27	29	9	100

Table 2: Percentage of "Yes" Response to Survey Questions*

	Freshman	Sophomore	Junior	Senior	Grad.	Total
Need for guide	97	85	86	92	79	88
Right to know	96	83	88	91	83	88
Access to word-of-mouth recommendations	52	65	60	73	40	62
Willingness to participate	67	71	60	59	43	63
Will buy guide	76	76	73	66	54	70

*Also polled 1 instructor who voted "yes" on "Need for Guide" and "Right of Students to Know" course and instructor information before signing up for a class.

Table 3: Analysis of Incentive Offering for Student Participation (in %)

	Freshman	Sophomore	Junior	Senior	Grad.	Total
Willingness to participate	67	71	60	59	43	63
Discount coupon	58	72	56	54	47	60
Free ad	33	20	20	29	29	25
Either	9	8	24	17	24	15

Appendix A7-D

SAMPLE FORMAT OF COURSE/INSTRUCTOR INFORMATION

Course number/section:

Instructor:

Course requirements:	Tests (number of tests)
	(Comprehensive or non-comprehensive final exam)
	(Multiple choice, essay, true/false format)
	(covers lectures only, textbook only, or both)
	Papers
	Projects
	Presentations
	(What percentage do each of the above contribute to the final grade)?

Course Information: (Obtained from students who have taken this course previously)

1. Plan to spend _____hours outside of school studying for this course each week.

2. On a scale of 1 to 5, to what degree does this class give you practical knowledge you could apply immediately to improve your job or personal life? (Use: Not at all = 1. A great deal = 5)

This course received a _____ rating

3. Students felt that this class (_____did _____did not _____not sure) offer them more than they originally expected when they enrolled for the class.

4. Students (_____would _____would not) recommend this course to their friends.

5. Students felt it (_____was _____was not) necessary to do well in prerequisite requirements to handle the class load of this course.

6. Students gave this class an average difficulty rating of _____(using a scale of 1 to 5 with Easy = 1, Average = 3, Extremely difficult = 5)

Additional student comments:_____

_____

_____

APPENDIX A7-E

SAMPLE FORMAT OF LOCAL BUSINESS ADVERTISING

C·H·O·I·C·E·S

Located next to Eagles' Landing

Choices has an all-you-can-eat buffet and salad bar with courteous waiters to serve you. So why not keep those lunch dates on campus and let us serve you in a quiet relaxing atmosphere.

Mon. - Fri. 11:30 a.m. - 1:45 p.m.   (Fri. soup & salad bar only)

PJ's

Located next to King Hall, for those people who have to eat on the run. We have a nice selection of grab-and-go-items

Mon. - Thurs. 7:30 a.m. - 8:00 p.m.

THE PUB

Second Floor Student Union
J.Newbauer's has a large menu to choose from including a variety of hot sandwiches, Itza-pizza, beer and wine.

45" GIANT screen TV

Mon. - Thurs. 11:00 a.m. - 8:30 p.m.
So come by and check us out

PumperKnikles deli FIRST FLOOR STUDENT UNION

Pumperknikles offers a wide variety of fresh sandwiches and salads.
Fast friendly courteous service. Custom line of non-dairy frozen yogurt.

Mon. - Thurs.	10:30 a.m. - 8:00 p.m.
Fri. & Sat.	10:00 a.m. - 1:30 p.m.

Eagles' Landing offers a large selection of food for all tastes

Including Mexican cuisine, deli, Itza-pizza, grille, and a large selection of hot entrees. Try our garden fresh salad bar.

Mon. - Thurs.   7:00 a.m. - 6:30 p.m.
Friday   7:00 a.m. - 1:30 p.m.

EAGLE EXPRESS

Our modular food service trailer located in Lot C
Beverages, Sadwiches, Snacks and other grab & go items
Open Mon. - Thurs. 9:00 a.m. - 8:30 p.m.

THE SPOT

Our Convenience Store Located in Housing Phase I

From self-serve drinks and snacks to microwavable dinners. Also, most of your household items to stock up the apartment.
Open Sun. - Fri. 5:00 p.m. - 10:30 p.m.

Appendix A7-F

SAMPLE FORMAT OF INVITATION TO BE A STUDENT RESPONDENT

Join the Crowd!

Be a participant in our next issue. Fill in the application below and we'll send you a $2.00 discount coupon good for our next issue if you're selected to be a student participant.

Name:_____

Phone: (   ) _____ Best time to call me is _____ A.M. _____12–6 P.M. _____ P.M.

Classes I'm taking Fall quarter 1990:

   Course No.   Section   Instructor   Time

_____

_____

_____

_____

_____

Mail to: Sneak Peek
          P.O. Box 109
          Monterey Park, CA 91754

Appendix A7-G

SAMPLE FORMAT OF INVITATION TO ADVERTISE IN RECYCLER

Do You Have a Used Book You'd Like to Sell?

Put an ad in our recycler section. **It's Free!**

Hurry, though—we only have a limited number of ads we can run.

Name of book: _____

Course/Instructor: _____

Your first name: _____

Phone number: _____

Best time for buyer to call you is: _____ A.M. _____ Afternoons _____ P.M.

Selling Price: _____ (Optional)

Mail to: Sneak Peek
          P.O. Box 109
          Monterey Park, CA 91754

Appendix A7-H

SAMPLE FORMAT OF RECYCLER SECTION FOR USED-BOOK ADVERTISING

USED BOOKS FOR SALE . . . . . BUY NOW!

Principles of Accounting
Accounting 200A
Prof. M. Davidson
$18.00
Contact: Tim
(818) 388-9276
Leave message on machine

Fundamentals of Astronomy
ASTR 151
Prof. R. Carpenter
$22.00
Contact: Jonathan Riley
(213) 728-3535
Call anytime between 2 P.M. and 5 P.M.

Basic Spanish
SPAN 100A
Prof. G. McCurdy
$20.00
Contact: Juli McNamara
(213) 555-3667
Call between 3:30 P.M. and 4:30 P.M.

Extemporaneous Speaking
SPCH 150
Prof. Robert Powell
$26.00
Contact: Ann Markell
(818) 377-8799
Call between 10 A.M. and Noon

Modern Man
ANTH 250
Prof. E. Oring
$27.00
Contact: Reanna
(213) 377-5988
Leave message on machine

Principles of Biology
BIOL 101
Prof. Wayne P. Alley
$32.00
Contact: Anthony
(213) 666-5667
Leave Message

Principles of Biology
BIOL 101
Prof. Wayne P. Alley
$32.00
Contact: Donna
(818) 322-2633
Call between 10 A.M. and 2 P.M.

The World of Plants
BIOL 155
Prof. B. Capon
$34.00
Contact: Caroline
(213) 585-2356
Leave message on machine

Appendix A7-I

SAMPLE FORMAT OF STUDENT TELEPHONE SURVEY

Instructions: Please call in all information to our telephone answering machine operating 24 hours a day. Start at the top of the page with your *name, ID number, phone,* and *address.* Then proceed to the questions and give your responses in order using complete sentences (Example: Say "Question 1: I spend 5 to 10 hours outside of school studying per week," etc.). You must call in your responses before the following date _____. We will send your $2.00 discount coupon to your address as soon as your telephone survey is received. Thank you for your participation in this survey.

Name _____ Phone _____

Address _____ Zip Code _____

Student respondent number _____(Stamped in right upper corner of this form)
(Students, please be completely honest in answering all questions. Remember, other students will be relying on your answers for the selection of their classes. Furthermore, feel free to make additional comments at the end of this questionnaire.)

1. How many hours outside of school did you have to study per week?
   _____ 0–5 _____ 6–10 _____ 11–20 _____ more than 20 hours.

2. To what degree did your class give you knowledge you could apply immediately to improve your job or personal life?
   On a scale of 1 to 5, I would rate this class a _____.
   (Use Not at all = 1, Average = 3, and Helped a great deal = 5)

3. Do you feel that the class offered more than you originally expected?
   _____ Yes _____ No _____ Not sure

4. Would you recommend this course to your friends? _____ Yes _____ No

5. Does doing well in the prerequisites for this course come in handy for handling the class load?
   _____ Yes _____ No

6. How do you rate the difficulty of this course on a scale of 1 to 5? _____
   (Use Easy = 1, Average = 3, and Extremely difficult = 5)

Any additional comments concerning course or instructors are welcome. If you have suggestions on questions to ask in the future issue please let us know. This publication is for your benefit, so let us help you get the information you need to pick your classes!

Appendix A7-J

SAMPLE FORMAT OF INVITATION TO PLACE ADVANCE ORDER
(to be run in the *University Times* 4 weeks prior to release of our guide)

Order Your Next Issue of Sneak Peek in Advance!
Be the first to buy your books through our recycler section.
Give yourself the time to plan your classes next quarter.
Get the inside scoop on courses and instructors with Sneak Peek as your guide.

Send a check or money order for $5.00 (includes tax, postage, and handling charge) to:
   Sneak Peek
   P.O. Box 109
   Monterey Park, CA 91754
(If you have a discount coupon, take $2.00 off above price and mail in check and coupon.)
Yes, I'd like to order the Winter quarter of Sneak Peek now.

Send to: Name _____

         Address _____

Appendix A7-K

CSULA UNIVERSITY TIMES ADVERTISING RATES

OUR READERS

- Cal State L.A. has the most culturally rich and distinctly varied student body of any university in the nation.
- Located in the heart of the San Gabriel Valley, it is within 5 miles of most major communities.
- The average student is 28 years old, financially independent and active in the purchasing process.
- The *University Times* has a captive audience of more than 20,000 students, 1,500 faculty and 2,000 additional campus employees. Our daily readership is over 23,500.

DISTRIBUTION

The *University Times* is distributed free on campus from circulation boxes located at high traffic points, at the Student Housing complexes and local businesses.

CIRCULATION

8000—Monday, Wednesday and Thursday—Fall, Winter and Spring quarters
6000—Monday and Thursday—Summer quarter
12,000—Registration, Welcome back and Special issues

DISPLAY ADVERTISING RATE

LOCAL OPEN RATE—$6.60 per column inch. Pickup rate—$6.30 (Same ad must appear without changes twice in a week).

BUSINESS RATE—$5.60
(On-campus businesses)

CAMPUS RATE—$4.60

ASSOCIATED STUDENTS RATE—$4.30
(CSLA recognized student organizations)

FREQUENCY DISCOUNT

3x to 6x per month $5.94
7x to 10x per month. $5.61
11x more per month $5.28
Frequency discounts DO NOT apply to Annual Contracts.

ANNUAL BULK CONTRACT RATES

75″ to 100″. $5.60
100″ to 300″. $5.30
301″ to 500″. $5.00
501″ to 700″. $4.60

Terms

All local rates are NET. Any commissions or charges by representing agencies are additional.

Annual bulk space must be contracted in advance of insertions and publication date. If total inches do not run as contracted, the next higher rate will be charged retroactively. Frequency ads should be the same ad with minimal or no copy changes and must run regularly throughout the quarter. If frequency of insertions is not maintained as contracted, the next higher frequency rate will be retroactively charged.

COLOR CHARGES

Spot color ROP. $100.00
Color specified $130.00
Four color process ask Advertising Manager

Appendix A7-K. Continued

INSERTS

$55 /M single sheet
$75 /M multiple sheet

All prices are net. Advertising Manager must receive sample copy one week prior to insertion for review. Inserts must be delivered to printer one week prior to publication. 8,000 minimum or complete run.

Commissionable $11.00

Representatives

American Passage Media Corp.	(800) 426-5537
CASS Communications, Inc.	(800) 888-4044
College Media Placement Service, Ltd.	(818) 848-8799

CLASSIFIED RATES

15 words or less 10 cents for each additional word. Quarterly contact rates available.

1–3 consecutive insertions. $4.00/day
4–6 consecutive insertions. $3.75/day
7–9 consecutive insertions. $3.50/day
10–12 consecutive insertions $3.25/day

CLASSIFIED DISPLAY

Local classified display rate. . . . .$6.60 pc (2 inch minimum)

Classified ads are payable in advance. A check must accompany all mailed ads. For billing information contact Business Manager.

COPY DEADLINES

Monday. . . . . .Noon previous Wednesday
Wednesday . . . . .Noon previous Friday
Thursday. . . . . .Noon previous Monday

Makegood Policy: The advertising manager must be notified within seven working days after publication of the advertisement for a makegood. The original copy and instructions must be clear and legible. The *University Times'* liability shall not exceed the cost of the advertisement in which the error occurred, and credit will be for the first incorrect insertion only. The *University Times* will not be responsible for copy changes made by phone. Minor spelling errors will not qualify for makegood. We reserve the right to cancel any advertisement at any time.

Cancellations: All cancellations of previously submitted advertisements must be made in writing. Cancellations must be made before ad copy deadline. They will not be accepted after that time.

Proofs are furnished upon request. Copy and art must be received 7 working days prior to publication for a proof.

Camera charges will be made for screening halftones, reductions, enlargements, reverses, veloxes and extra prints. Charges range from $5 to $10 depending on the size of the art and amount of work required.

Excessive typesetting: Rates quoted include normal typesetting. Ads requiring excessive typesetting (as determined by the Art Department) will be charged $25/hour above normal space cost.

MECHANICAL REQUIREMENTS

Column width: 1½ inches (9½ picas)
Six columns per page × 16 inches deep
Minimum display space: 4 column inches
Screen: 85% printed offset
Advertisements more than 14 inches deep will be billed for full column depth.
All fractions of an inch in display advertising will be increased to the next half inch.

APPENDIX A7-K(A)

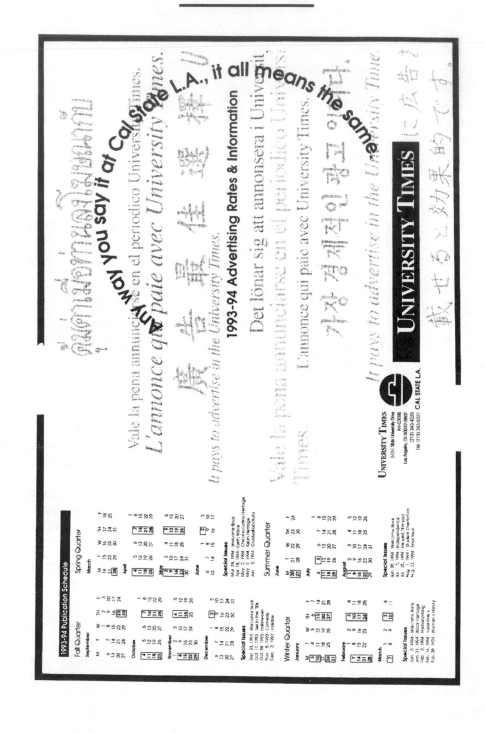

APPENDIX A7-L

UNIVERSITY PRESS RATES FOR FLYERS AND POSTERS

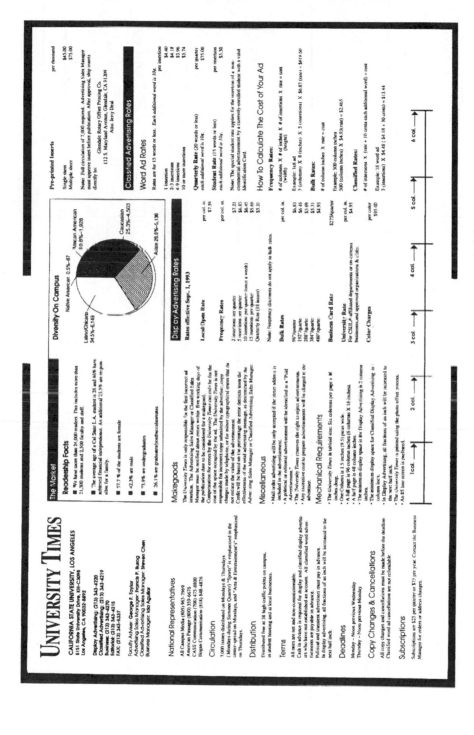

SNEAK PEEK MARKETING IMPLEMENTATION SCHEDULE

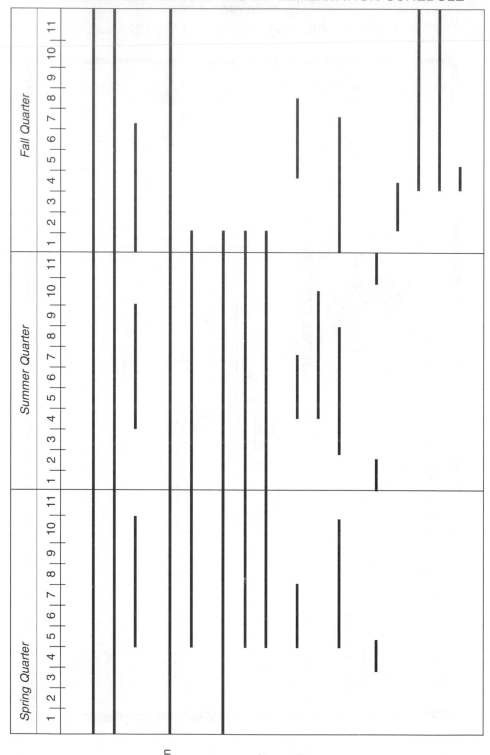

APPENDIX A7-N

FINANCIAL DATA

Table 1 Sneak Peek: break-even analysis

Fixed Cost per Year	Amount
Post office box	$28.00
Business license	$101.78
Wholesale license	$107.50
Ad in *University Times*	$337.00
Ad in *Schedule of Classes*	$1,080.00
Bulk rate postage permit	$60.00
Bulk rate postage fee	$60.00
Postage paid address permit	$60.00
Copyright on publication	$40.00
Answering machine	$60.00
Telephone	$30.00
Telephone/Utilities	$840.00
Typewriter	$130.00
Legal/Accounting	$2,080.00
Insurance	$1,500.00
Orientation booth	$200.00
Fliers	$140.00
Posters	$80.00
Total	$6,934.28

Variable Cost per Year	Amount
Wholesale License	$116.48
Business License	$36.40
Postage for response	$14,414.40
Transportation cost	$291.20
Postage for mail orders	$2,038.40
Printing cost	$36,400.00
Total	$1.83
$P =$	$10,317.50
$U =$	2,926

$P = (U*p) - (U*V) - F$

$U = F/(p - V)$

P = profits

p = price

U = break-even quantities

V = variable cost

F = fixed cost

Table 2 Sneak Peek: five-year projected profit and loss statement

	QUARTERS AFTER STARTING BUSINESS				
	1 (Fall)	2 (Winter)	3 (Spring)	4 (Summer)	Year 1
Sales	$29,192.80	$28,100.80	$27,227.20	$27,081.60	$111,602.40
Advertising Sales	$2,025.00	$3,037.50	$4,556.25	$6,834.38	$16,453.13
Cost of sales	$12,481.56	$10,170.16	$8,321.04	$6,009.64	$36,982.40
Gross profit	$18,736.24	$20,968.14	$23,462.41	$27,903.64	$91,073.13
Operating Expenses					
Advertising	$619.99	$505.18	$413.33	$298.51	$1,837.00
Postage	$5,552.82	$4,524.52	$3,701.88	$2,673.58	$16,452.80
Payroll	$6,952.50	$5,665.00	$4,635.00	$3,347.50	$20,600.00
Office Supplies	$624.36	$622.77	$635.67	$678.32	$2,561.11
Permit and Fee	$70.20	$57.20	$46.80	$33.80	$208.00
Legal and accounting	$520.00	$520.00	$520.00	$520.00	$2,080.00
Telephone/Utilities	$200.00	$170.00	$170.00	$170.00	$710.00
Licenses and taxes	$103.67	$94.11	$86.47	$76.91	$361.16
Copyright	$10.00	$10.00	$10.00	$10.00	$40.00
Insurance	$375.00	$375.00	$375.00	$375.00	$1,500.00
Other administrative and selling expenses	$1,560.89	$1,556.92	$1,589.17	$1,695.80	$6,402.78
Total operating expenses	$16,589.42	$14,100.69	$12,183.31	$9,879.42	$52,752.85
Profit	$2,146.82	$6,867.45	$11,279.10	$18,026.91	$38,320.28

	QUARTERS AFTER STARTING BUSINESS				
	5 (Fall)	6 (Winter)	7 (Spring)	8 (Summer)	Year 2
Sales	$43,789.20	$42,151.20	$40,840.80	$40,622.40	$167,403.60
Advertising sales	$3,037.50	$4,556.25	$6,834.38	$10,251.56	$24,679.69
Cost of sales	$18,722.34	$15,255.24	$12,481.56	$9,014.46	$55,473.60
Gross profit	$29,104.36	$31,452.21	$35,193.62	$41,859.50	$136,609.69
Operating expenses					
Advertising	$929.98	$757.76	$619.99	$447.77	$2,755.50
Postage	$8,329.23	$6,786.78	$5,552.82	$4,010.37	$24,679.20
Payroll	$10,428.75	$8,497.50	$6,952.50	$5,021.25	$30,900.00
Office supplies	$936.53	$934.15	$953.50	$1,017.48	$3,841.67
Permit and fee	$105.30	$85.80	$70.20	$50.70	$312.00
Legal and accounting	$780.00	$780.00	$780.00	$780.00	$3,120.00
Telephone/utilities	$300.00	$255.00	$255.00	$255.00	$1,065.00
Licenses and taxes	$155.50	$141.17	$129.70	$115.37	$541.74
Copyright	$15.00	$15.00	$15.00	$15.00	$60.00
Insurance	$562.50	$562.50	$562.50	$562.50	$2,250.00
Other administrative and selling expenses	$2,341.34	$2,335.37	$2,383.76	$2,543.70	$9,604.16
Total operating expenses	$24,884.13	$21,151.03	$18,274.97	$14,819.14	$79,129.27
Profit	$3,220.23	$10,301.18	$16,918.64	$27,040.37	$57,480.42

Table 2 continued

	QUARTERS AFTER STARTING BUSINESS				
	9 (Fall)	**10 (Winter)**	**11 (Spring)**	**12 (Summer)**	**Year 3**
Sales	$76,631.10	$73,764.60	$71,471.40	$71,089.20	$292,956.30
Advertising sales	$5,315.63	$7,973.44	$11,960.16	$17,940.23	$43,189.45
Cost of sales	$32,764.10	$26,696.67	$21,842.73	$15,775.31	$97,078.80
Gross profit	$49,182.63	$55,041.37	$61,588.83	$73,254.13	$239,066.95
Operating expenses					
Advertising	$1,627.47	$1,326.08	$1,084.98	$783.60	$4,822.13
Postage	$14,576.15	$11,876.87	$9,717.44	$7,018.15	$43,188.60
Payroll	$18,250.31	$14,870.63	$12,166.88	$8,787.19	$54,075.00
Office supplies	$1,638.93	$1,634.76	$1,668.63	$1,780.59	$6,722.92
Permit and fee	$184.28	$150.15	$122.85	$88.73	$546.00
Legal and accounting	$1,365.00	$1,365.00	$1,365.00	$1,365.00	$5,460.00
Telephone/utilities	$525.00	$446.25	$446.25	$446.25	$1,863.75
Licenses and taxes	$272.13	$247.04	$226.98	$201.90	$948.05
Copyright	$26.25	$26.25	$26.25	$26.25	$105.00
Insurance	$984.38	$984.38	$984.38	$984.38	$3,937.50
Other administrative and selling expenses	$4,097.34	$4,086.90	$4,171.58	$4,451.47	$16,807.29
Total operating expenses	$43,547.23	$37,014.31	$31,981.20	$25,933.49	$138,476.22
Profit	$5,635.40	$18,027.06	$29,607.63	$47,320.64	$100,590.73

	QUARTERS AFTER STARTING BUSINESS				
	13 (Fall)	**14 (Winter)**	**15 (Spring)**	**16 (Summer)**	**Year 4**
Sales	$107,283.54	$103,270.44	$100,059.96	$99,524.88	$410,138.92
Advertising sales	$7,441.88	$11,162.81	$16,744.22	$25,116.33	$60,465.23
Cost of sales	$45,869.73	$37,375.34	$30,579.82	$22,085.43	$135,910.32
Gross profit	$68,355.68	$77,057.91	$86,224.36	$102,555.78	$334,693.73
Operating expenses					
Advertising	$2,278.45	$1,856.52	$1,518.97	$1,097.03	$6,750.98
Postage	$15,304.96	$12,470.71	$10,203.31	$7,369.05	$45,348.03
Payroll	$25,550.44	$20,818.88	$17,033.63	$12,302.06	$75,705.00
Office supplies	$2,294.51	$2,288.67	$2,336.08	$2,492.82	$9,412.08
Permit and fee	$257.99	$210.21	$171.99	$124.22	$764.40
Legal and accounting	$1,911.00	$1,911.00	$1,911.00	$1,911.00	$7,644.00
Telephone/utilities	$735.00	$624.75	$624.75	$624.74	$2,609.25
Licenses and taxes	$380.98	$345.86	$317.77	$282.66	$1,327.26
Copyright	$36.75	$36.75	$36.75	$36.75	$147.00
Insurance	$1,378.13	$1,378.13	$1,378.13	$1,378.13	$5,512.50
Other administrative and selling expenses	$5,736.27	$5,721.66	$5,840.21	$6,232.06	$23,530.20
Total operating expenses	$55,864.47	$47,663.13	$41,372.58	$33,850.53	$178,750.70
Profit	$12,991.22	$29,394.79	$44,851.78	$68,705.25	$155,943.03

Table 2 continued

	QUARTERS AFTER STARTING BUSINESS				
	17 (Fall)	**18 (Winter)**	**19 (Spring)**	**20 (Summer)**	**Year 5**
Sales	$124,104.43	$129,088.05	$125,074.95	$124,406.10	$512,673.53
Advertising sales	$9,302.34	$13,953.52	$20,930.27	$31,395.41	$75,581.54
Cost of sales	$57,337.17	$46,719.17	$38,224.78	$27,606.78	$169,887.90
Gross profit	$96,069.60	$96,322.39	$107,780.45	$128,194.73	$418,357.17
Operating expenses					
Advertising	$2,848.07	$2,320.65	$1,898.71	$1,371.29	$8,438.72
Postage	$12,435.29	$10,132.45	$8,290.19	$5,987.36	$36,845.27
Payroll	$31,338.05	$26,023.59	$21,292.03	$15,377.58	$94,631.25
Office supplies	$2,363.14	$2,860.83	$2,920.10	$3,116.03	$11,765.10
Permit and fee	$322.48	$262.76	$214.99	$155.27	$955.50
Legal and accounting	$2,388.75	$2,388.75	$2,388.75	$2,388.75	$9,555.00
Telephone/utilities	$918.75	$780.94	$780.94	$780.94	$3,261.56
Licenses and taxes	$476.22	$432.33	$397.21	$353.32	$1,659.08
Copyright	$45.94	$45.94	$45.94	$45.94	$183.75
Insurance	$1,722.66	$1,722.66	$1,722.66	$1,722.66	$6,890.63
Other administrative and selling expenses	$7,170.34	$7,152.08	$7,300.26	$7,790.08	$29,412.75
Total operating expenses	$63,134.56	$54,122.97	$47,251.78	$39,089.20	$203,598.61
Profit	$22,934.94	$42,199.42	$60,528.67	$89,105.52	$214,768.55

Table 3 Sneak Peek: five-year cash flow projections

	Year 1	**Year 2**	**Year 3**	**Year 4**	**Year 5**
Cash Balance (beginning of year)	$8,775.14	$3,451.40	$5,966.90	$18,992.08	$34,231.84
Receipts: Sales	$111,602.40	$167,403.60	$292,956.30	$410,138.82	$512,673.53
Ad sales	$16,453.13	$24,679.69	$43,189.45	$60,465.23	$75,581.54
Total cash available	$120,377.54	$170,855.00	$298,923.20	$429,130.90	$546,905.37
Disbursements:					
Printing cost	$36,982.40	$55,473.00	$97,078.80	$135,910.32	$169,887.90
Payroll cost	$20,600.00	$30,900.00	$54,075.00	$75,705.00	$94,631.25
Advertising cost	$1,837.00	$2,755.00	$4,822.13	$6,750.00	$8,438.72
License and taxes	$361.16	$541.74	$948.05	$1,327.26	$1,659.08
Postage	$16,452.80	$24,679.20	$43,188.60	$45,348.03	$36,845.27
Insurance	$1,500.00	$2,250.00	$3,937.50	$5,512.50	$6,890.63
Legal/accounting	$2,080.00	$3,120.00	$5,460.00	$7,644.00	$9,555.00
Telephone/utilities	$710.00	$1,065.00	$1,863.75	$2,609.25	$3,261.56
Office supplies	$2,561.11	$3,841.67	$6,722.92	$9,412.08	$11,765.10
Other administrative expenses	$3,841.67	$5,762.49	$10,084.38	$14,118.12	$17,647.65
Total disbursements	$86,926.14	$130,388.10	$228,181.12	$304,336.56	$360,582.16
Cash before distribution	$33,451.40	$40,466.90	$70,742.08	$124,794.34	$186,323.21
Distribution	$30,000.00	$34,500.00	$51,750.00	$90,562.50	$135,843.75
Cash balance (end of year)	$3,451.40	$5,966.90	$18,992.08	$34,231.84	$50,479.46

Table 4 Sneak Peek: initial investment cost $18,000.00

Initial investment		
Less:		
Answering machine	$60.00	
Phone	$30.00	
Typewriter	$130.00	
Copyright	$10.00	
Telephone and utilities	$70.00	
Post office box	$28.00	
Postage permit	$120.00	
Office supplies	$270.00	
License	$208.28	
Legal/accounting	$520.00	
Insurance	$375.00	
		$ 1,821.28
Preopening expenses		$16,178.72
Postage for response	$3,603.60	
Postage paid permit	$60.00	
Advertising	$619.99	
Printing cost	$2,500.00	
Promotions	$619.99	
		$7,403.58
Cash balance—beginning of operations		$8,775.14

Table 5 Sneak Peek: balance sheet (pro forma)

	Year 1	Year 2	Year 3	Year 4	Year 5
Assets					
Current assets					
Cash	$3,451.40	$5,966.90	$18,992.08	$34,231.84	$50,479.46
Inventory	$2,500.00	$3,750.00	$6,562.50	$9,187.50	$11,484.38
Account receivables	$22,422.40	$50,450.40	$103,002.90	$127,921.41	$192,337.45
Fixed assets					
Furniture/fixture	$3,000.00	$4,500.00	$7,875.00	$7,875.00	$7,875.00
Telephone	$30.00	$60.00	$90.00	$120.00	$120.00
Typewriter	$130.00	$260.00	$520.00	$520.00	$520.00
Answering machine	$60.00	$60.00	$60.00	$60.00	
Office Supplies	$138.76	$208.14	$364.24	$509.93	$637.42
Less: Accumulated					
depreciation	($335.88)	($844.69)	($1,735.61)	($2,644.11)	($4,576.21)
Other asset					
Copyright	$40.00	$40.00	$40.00	$40.00	$40.00
Total Assets	$31,436.68	$64,450.75	$135,771.10	$177,821.58	$258,917.49
Liabilities and Capital					
Liabilities					
Account payable	$5,116.40	$15,150.05	$37,629.67	$14,299.62	$16,470.73
Capital					
Capital—beginning	$18,000.00	$26,320.28	$49,300.70	$98,141.43	$163,521.96
Add: Earnings	$38,320.28	$57,480.42	$100,590.73	$155,943.03	$214,768.55
Less: Distributions	($30,000.00)	($34,500.00)	($51,750.00)	($90,562.50)	($135,843.75)
Capital—ending	$26,320.28	$49,300.70	$98,141.43	$163,521.96	$242,446.76
Total liabilities and					
capital	$31,436.68	$64,450.75	$135,771.10	$177,821.58	$258,917.49

Table 6 Sneak Peek: selections on criteria

Accounting		No. Sec.	Instructor	Faculty
200A		13	6	1
200B		13	6	1
202		1		1
300		12	3	3
320A		7	2	1
320B		5	2	
320C		5	2	
321		3	2	
322		4	1	1
398		4		
420		3	1	
421A		2	1	
424A		3	2	
427		1	1	
433		1		1
503		1		
520		2	1	
524		1	1	
587		1		
598		4		
Total	20	86	31	9
Assuming ½ for each instructor			16	5
Assuming ¼ for each instructor			8	2

General Education	No. Sec.	Instructor	Faculty
ANTHO 250	5	2	2
ANTHO 260	4	1	3
ANTHO 265	1	1	
ARAB 100A			
ARAB 100B			
ARAB 100C			
ART 101A	2	2	
ART 101B	1	1	
ART 101C	1	1	
ART 151	1	1	
ART 152	4	2	2
ART 153	2	1	
ART 154			
ART 155	1		1
ART 156			
ART 157	1	1	
ART 158			
ART 159	3	3	
ASTRO 151	10	9	
ASTRO 152			
BIOL 155	14	2	12
BIOL 156	15	3	12
BIOL 165	2	1	1
CHEM 158	1	1	
CHEM 159	1	1	

Table 6 continued

General Education	No. Sec.	Instructor	Faculty
CHEM 160	1	1	
CHIN 100A			
CHIN 100B	1		1
CHIN 100C	1	1	
CHIN 101A			
CHIN 101B			
CHIN 101C	1	1	
CHIN 200A			
CHIN 200B			
CHIN 200C	1	1	
CHIN 201A			
CHIN 201B			
CHIN 201C			
CH S 111	4	2	2
DANC 157	4	2	2
ECON 150	2	1	1
ENGL 190	20	9	11
ENGL 225	1	1	
ENGL 250	9	4	
ENGL 258	1	1	
ENGR 250	1		1
FREN 100A	4	3	1
FREN 100B	2	1	
FREN 100C	1	1	
FREN 200A			
FREN 200B	1	1	
FREN 230			
FSCS 120	3	1	1
FSCS 250	2		2
GEOG 150	10	4	5
GEOL 150	2	2	
GEOL 151	2	2	
GEOL 152	4	2	2
GEOL 155	3	2	1
GEOL 156	3	1	2
GEOL 158	1	1	
GEOL 160			
GERM 100A			
GERM 100B	1	1	
GERM 100C	1	1	
H S 150	7	5	1
HIST 110A	1	1	
HIST 110B	1	1	
HIST 110C	1	1	
HIST 202A	10	4	3
HIST 202B	10	6	4
ITAL 100A			
ITAL 100B			
ITAL 100C	1	1	
JAPN 100A	2		2
JAPN 100B	1		1
JAPN 100C	2		2
JAPN 130			
JAPN 200A			
JAPN 200B			
JAPN 200C	1		1
LAS 150	1	1	

Table 6 continued

General Education	No. Sec.	Instructor	Faculty
LATN 100A			
LATN 100B			
LATN 100C			
LATN 222			
MICR 151	5	4	2
MUS 150	3		3
MUS 160	3	1	1
MUS 264			
PAS 101	1	1	
PAS 125	1		1
PAS 260	1	1	
PHIL 151	6	3	
PHIL 152	4	2	
PHIL 160	17	2	14
PHIL 238	1	1	
PHIL 250	4	2	2
P E 150	4	1	2
PHYS 150	3	2	
PHYS 155	1	1	
POLS 150	15	5	7
POLS 155	7	2	3
POLS 200			
POLS 250	1	1	
PSY 150	6	2	3
PSY 160	2	2	
PSY 270	1	1	
RELS 200	5	2	2
RUSS 101A			
RUSS 101B			
SOC 201	12	5	5
SOC 202	6	3	2
SOC 263	1	1	
SPAN 100A	10	7	3
SPAN 100B	2	2	
SPAN 100C	2	1	1
SPAN 105	2	2	
SPAN 130			
SPAN 200A	1	1	
SPAN 200B	1	1	
SPAN 200C	1	1	
SPAN 205A	1	1	
SPAN 205B			
SPAN 230			
SPCH 150	26	4	17
SPCH 176	3	2	
T.A. 152	1	1	
URBA 101	2		2
Total	128	357	168	149
Assuming ½ for each instructor		84	75
Assuming ¼ for each instructor		42	37

Table 6 continued

Business core requirements	No. Sec.	Instructor	Faculty
ACCT 200 A	13	7	1
ACCT 200 B	13	7	1
ACCT 300	12	5	3
CIS 294	15	4	5
CIS 301	10	6	
ECON 201	7	3	3
ECON 202	8	4	3
ECON 209	10	5	4
ECON 303	9	2	4
ECON 309	9	4	4
ECON 310	8	2	5
ECON 391	9	2	5
FIN 205	8	4	
FIN 303	10	8	
MATH 242	7	3	3
MGMT 306	11	4	4
MGMT 307	9	3	2
MGMT 308	9	7	
MGMT 497	10	10	
MKT 304	7	4	
OSBE 301	13	8	2

		No. Sec.	Instructor	Faculty
Total	21	207	102	49
Assuming ½ for each instructor			51	25
Assuming ¼ for each instructor			28	12

Biology	No. Sec.	Instructor	Faculty
BIOL 101	5	1	4
BIOL 102	2	2	
BIOL 103	2	2	
BIOL 302	3	1	
BIOL 315	3	1	
BIOL 330	3	1	2
BIOL 357	1	1	
BIOL 360	2	1	
C S 290	3		3
CHEM 101	9	3	
CHEM 102	8	3	3
CHEM 103	8	2	3
CHEM 122	3	1	
CHEM 123	3	1	
CHEM 201	1	1	
CHEM 301A	1	1	
CHEM 301B	1		1
CHEM 301C	2	2	
CHEM 302A	2		1
CHEM 302B	3	1	1
CHEM 302C	1	1	
CHEM 319	1	1	
CHEM 360	1	1	
CHEM 401	1	1	

Table 6 continued

Biology		No. Sec.	Instructor	Faculty
CHEM 402		1	1	
CHEM 403		1	1	
CHEM 412A		1	1	
CHEM 412B		1	1	
CHEM 419		1	1	
CHEM 462		1	1	
MATH 206		4	1	3
MATH 207		4	3	1
MATH 208		5	3	2
MATH 209		4	4	
MATH 215		4	4	
MATH 225		1	1	
MATH 230		1	1	
MATH 401		1	1	
PHYS 101		4	2	
PHYS 102		4	2	
PHYS 103		4	2	
PHYS 121		1	1	
PHYS 122		1	1	
PHYS 123		1	1	
PHYS 201		7	7	
PHYS 202		8	5	
PHYS 203		11	7	
PHYS 204		4	2	
PHYS 205		1	1	
PHYS 206		2	1	
Total	49	147	86	24
Assuming ½ for each instructor			43	12
Assuming ¼ for each instructor			22	6

Upper Division Themes	No. Sec.	Instructor	Faculty
ANTH 350	1	1	
ANTH 400	1	1	
ANTH 444	6	2	2
ANTH 450	1	1	
ANTH 438	1	1	
ART 341	1	1	
ART 350	1	1	
ART 357	3	1	
ART 381	1	1	
ART 455	1	1	
ART 456	1	1	
ART 485	1	1	
BCST 466	1	1	
BIOL 319	1	1	
BIOL 321	1	1	
BIOL 350	1	1	
BIOL 353	1	1	
BIOL 361	1	1	
BIOL 484	1	1	

Table 6 continued

Upper Division Themes	No. Sec.	Instructor	Faculty
BIOL 486	1	1	
CHEM 350	1	1	
CHEM 358	1	1	
CHEM 380	1		1
DANC 357	3	2	
ECON 460	1	1	
EDAD 480	1	1	
ENGL 350	1	1	
ENGL 358	1	1	
ENGL 381	1	1	
ENGL 383	1	1	
ENGL 385	1	1	
ENGL 387	1	1	
ENGL 392	1	1	
ENGL 399	1	1	
ENGR 352	2		2
FSCS 300	4	1	3
FSCS 450	6	2	4
FSCS 451	1		1
FL 389	1	1	
GEOG 421	1	1	
GEOG 433	1	1	
GEOG 476	1	1	
GEOL 350	1	1	
GEOL 420	2	2	
HIST 311	1	1	
HIST 350	1	1	
HIST 380	1		1
HIST 456	1	1	
HIST 459	1	1	
LAS 435	1	1	
LAS 442	1	1	
LAS 460	1	1	
LBS 300A	1	1	
LBS 300B	1	1	
LBS 300C	1	1	
MICR 363	1	1	
MUS 355	1	1	
MUS 357	3	1	2
MUS 455	1	1	
MUS 456	1	1	
NUR 307	1	1	
NUR 455	1	1	
PAS 427	1		1
PAS 442	1	1	
PAS 460	1	1	
P E 300	4	3	
PHIL 321	1	1	
PHIL 350	1	1	
PHIL 412	1	1	
PHIL 418	1	1	
PHIL 461	1	1	
PHIL 491	1	1	
PHYS 350	1	1	
PHYS 358	1	1	
PHYS 363	1	1	
PHYS 452	1	1	

Table 6 continued

Upper Division Themes	No. Sec.	Instructor	Faculty
PSY 307	1	1	
PSY 323	1	1	
PSY 462	1	1	
PSY 488	1	1	
POLS 458	1	1	
POLS 459	1	1	
REL 425	1	1	
SOC 400	1	1	
SOC 425	1	1	
SOC 430	1	1	
SOC 441	1	1	
SOC 442	1	1	
SOC 450	1	1	
SOC 483	1	1	
SPCH 385	1	1	
SPCH 489	2	1	1
SW 455	1	1	
SW 462	1	1	
T A 357	3	3	
T A 457	2	2	
Total	96	125	101	18
Assuming ½ for each instructor		51	9
Assuming ¼ for each instructor		25	5

Table 7 Sneak Peek: ratio analysis

	Year 1	Year 2	Year 3	Year 4	Year 5
Return on investment	44%	45%	47%	52%	61%
Profit margin	30%	30%	17%	12%	10%
Debit equity ratio	19%	31%	28%	9%	7%
Working capital ratio	6	4	3	12	15

RDI   = Net profit/total investment
PM   = Net profit/net sales
DER   = Total liabilities/total asset
WCR = Current asset/current liabilities

APPENDIX

B

SOURCES OF SECONDARY RESEARCH

Following are more than 100 sources based on bibliographies put together by Lloyd M. DeBoer, Dean of the School of Business Administration at George Mason University, Fairfax, Virginia, and the Office of Management and Training of the SBA and published by the Small Business Administration as a part of two booklets, *Marketing Research Procedure, SBB 9,* and *National Directories for Use in Marketing SSB 13.*

U.S. GOVERNMENT PUBLICATIONS

The publications in this section are books and pamphlets issued by federal agencies and listed under the issuing agency. Where availability of an individual listing is indicated by the Government Printing Office (GPO), the publication may be ordered from the Superintendent of Documents, U.S. Government Printing Office, Washington, DC 20402. When ordering a GPO publication, give the title and series number of the publication, and name of agency. You can also order by phone by calling (202) 783-3238. Contact GPO for current prices.

Publications should be requested by the title and any number given from the issuing agency. Most libraries have some listings to identify currently available federal publications. Some keep a number of selected government publications for ready reference through the Federal Depository Library System.

American Statistics Index: A Comprehensive Guide and Index to the Statistical Publications of the United States Government. Washington, DC: Congressional. Information Service, 1973–. Monthly, with annual cumulations. This is the most comprehensive index to statistical information generated by the federal agencies, committees of Congress, and special programs of the government. Approximately 7,400 titles of 500 government sources are indexed each year. The two main volumes are arranged by issuing breakdown, technical notes, and time period covered by publication. Separate index volume is arranged by subject and title and also includes the SIC code, the Standard Occupation Classification, and a list of SMSAs (standard metropolitan statistical areas).

Bureau of the Census, Department of Commerce, Washington, DC 20233

Contact the Public Information Office for a more complete listing of publications. The following is a sample.

Catalog of United States Census Publications. Published monthly with quarterly and annual cumulations. A guide to census data and reports. This catalog contains descriptive lists of publications, data files, and special tabulations.

Census of Agriculture. Performed in years ending in 4 and 9. Volumes include information on statistics of county; size of farm; characteristics of farm operations; farm income; farm sales; farm expenses; and agricultural services.

Census of Business. Compiled every five years (in years ending in 2 and 7).

Census of Construction Industries. Information from industries based on SIC codes. Included is information about number of construction firms; employees; receipts; payrolls; payments for materials; components; work supplies; payments for machinery and equipment; and depreciable assets.

Census of Governments. Done in years ending 2 and 7. This is the most detailed source for statistics on government finance.

Census of Housing. Provides information on plumbing facilities, whether a unit is owned or rented, value of home, when built, number of bedrooms, telephones, and more.

Census of Manufacturers. Compiled every five years (in years ending in 2 and 7). Reports on 450 different classes of manufacturing industries. Data for each industry include: information on capital expenditures, value added, number of establishments employment data, material costs, assets, rent, and inventories. Updated yearly by the *Annual Survey of Manufacturers.*

Census of Mineral Industries. Covers areas of extraction of minerals. Information on employees, payroll, work hours, cost of materials, capital expenditures, and quantity and value of materials consumed and products shipped.

Census of Population. Compiled every 10 years (in years ending in zero). Presents detailed data on population characteristics of states, counties, SMSAs, and census tracts. Demographics data reported include: age, sex, race, marital status, family composition, employment income, level of education, and occupation. Updated annually by the *Current Population Report.*

Census of Retail Trade. This report presents statistics for more than 100 different types of retail establishments by state, SMSAs, counties, and cities with populations over 2,500. It includes data on the number of outlets, total sales, employment, and payroll. Updated each month by *Monthly Retail Trade.*

Census of Selected Services. Provides statistics similar to those reported by the *Census of Retail Trade* for retail service organizations such as auto repair centers and hotels. Does not include information on real estate, insurance, or the professions. Updated monthly by *Monthly Selected Service Receipts.*

Census of Transportation. Information on four major phases of U.S. travel. (1) National Travel Survey, (2) Truck Inventory and Use of Survey, (3) Commodity Transportation Survey, and (4) Survey of Motor Carriers and Public Warehousing.

Census of Wholesale Trade. Statistics for over 150 types of wholesaler categories. The data detail the number of establishments, payroll, warehouse space, expenses, end-of-year inventories, legal form of organization, and payroll. Updated each month by *Monthly Wholesale Trade.*

Statistical Abstract of the United States. Published annually. This is a useful source for finding current and historical statistics about various aspects of American life. Contents include statistics on income, prices, education, population, law enforcement, environmental conditions, local government, labor force, manufacturing, and many other topics.

State and Metropolitan Area Data Book. A *Statistical Abstract* supplement. Presents a variety of information on states and metropolitan areas in the United States on subjects such as area, population, housing, income, manufacturers, retail trade, and wholesale trade.

Country and City Databook. Published every five years, this supplements the *Statistical Abstract.* Contains 144 statistical items for each county and 148 items for cities with a population of 25,000 or more. Data are organized by region, division, states, and SMSAs. Standard demographics are contained in addition to other harder-to-find data.

County Business Patterns. Annual. Contains a summary of data on number and type (by SIC number) of business establishments as well as their employment and taxable payroll. Data are presented by industry and county.

Bureau of Economic Analysis, Department of Commerce, Washington, DC 20230

Business Statistics. This is the biennial supplement to the *Survey of Current Business* and contains data on 2,500 series arranged annually for early years, quarterly for the last decade, and monthly for the most recent five years.

Bureau of Industrial Economics, Department of Commerce, Washington, DC 20230

United States Industrial Outlook. Projections of sales trends for major sectors of the U.S. economy, including business services; consumer services; transportation; consumer goods; and distribution.

Domestic and International Business Administration, Department of Commerce, Washington, DC 20230

County and City Data Book. Published every other year, supplements the *Statistical Abstract.* Using data taken from censuses and other government publications, it provides breakdowns by city and county for income, population, education, employment, housing, banking, manufacturing, capital expenditures, retail and wholesale sales, and other factors.

Measuring Markets: A Guide to the Use of Federal and State Statistical Data. Government Planning Office. Provides federal and state government data on population, income, employment, sales, and selected taxes. Explains how to interpret the data to measure markets and evaluate opportunities.

Selected Publications to Aid Business and Industry. Listing of federal statistical sources useful to business and industry.

Statistics of Income. Annual. Published by the Internal Revenue Service of the Treasury Department. This publication consists of data collected from tax returns filed by corporations, sole proprietorships and partnerships, and individuals.

State Statistical Abstract. Every state publishes a statistical abstract, almanac, or economic data book covering statistics for the state, its counties and cities. A complete list of these abstracts is in the back of each volume of the *Statistical Abstract* and *Measuring Markets*.

International Trade Administration, Department of Commerce, Washington, DC 20230

Country Market Survey. These reports describe market sectors and the markets for producer goods, consumer goods, and industrial material.

Global Market Surveys. Provides market research to verify the existence and vitality of foreign markets for specific goods as well as Department of Commerce assistance to U.S. business to help in market penetration.

Foreign Economic Trends. Prepared by U.S. embassies abroad. Each volume has a table of "Key Economic Indicators" and other data on the current economic situation and trends for the country under discussion.

Overseas Business Reports. Analysis of trade opportunities, marketing conditions, distribution channels, industry trends, trade regulations, and market prospects are provided.

Trade Opportunity Program (TOP). On a weekly basis indexes trade opportunities by product as well as type of opportunity.

U.S. Small Business Administration, Washington, DC 20416

The SBA issues a wide range of management and technical publications designed to help owner–managers and prospective owners of small business. For general information about the SBA office, its policies and assistance programs, contact your nearest SBA office.

A listing of currently available publications can be obtained free from the Small Business Administration, Office of Public Communications, 409 Third St., SW, Washington, DC 20416 or call 1-800-U-ASK-SBA toll free. The SBA offers 51 publications currently. One particular publication, *Basis Library Reference Sources,* contains a section on marketing information and guides to research. Get the latest *Directory of Publications* by writing or calling the 800 number. You can also obtain a free booklet, *Your Business and the SBA,* which gives you an overview of all SBA services and programs.

Management Aids (3- to 24-page pamphlet). This series of pamphlets is organized by a broad range of management principles. Each pamphlet in this series discusses a specific management practice to help the owner–manager of a small firm with management problems and business operations. A section on marketing covers a wide variety of topics from advertising guidelines to marketing research to pricing.

PERIODICALS

Business America: The Magazine of International Trade. United States. International Trade Administration. Biweekly. Activities relating to private sector or the Department of Commerce are covered, including exports and other international business activities.

Business Conditions Digest. United States. Department of Commerce. Bureau of Economic Analysis. Washington, DC: Government Printing Office. Monthly. Title includes estimates on forecasts for recent months. Very useful for data not yet published elsewhere.

Economic Indicators. United States. Council of Economic Advisors. Washington, DC: Government Printing Office. Monthly. Statistical tables for major economics indicators are included. Section on credit is useful for marketers. Statistics quoted annually for about six years and monthly for the past year.

Federal Reserve Bulletin. United States. Board of Governors of the Federal Reserve System. Washington, DC: Government Printing Office. Monthly. Contains official statistics on national banking, international banking, and business.

Monthly Labor Review. United States. Bureau of Labor Statistics. Washington, DC: Government Printing Office. Monthly. This publication covers all aspects of labor including wages, productivity, collective bargaining, new legislation, and consumer prices.

Survey of Current Business. United States. Department of Commerce. Bureau of Economic Analysis. Washington, DC: Government Printing Office. Monthly, with weekly supplements. The most useful source for current business statistics. Each issue is divided into two sections. The first covers general business topics; the second, "Current Business Statistics," gives current data for 2,500 statistical series or topics. Also, indexed in *Business Periodicals Index.*

Treasury Bulletin. United States. Department of the Treasury. Washington, DC: Government Printing Office. Monthly. Statistical tables are provided on all aspects of fiscal operations of government as well as money-related activities of the private sector. Useful for consumer background or from a monetary view.

DIRECTORIES

The selected national directories are listed under categories of specific business or general marketing areas in an alphabetical subject index.

When the type of directory is not easily found under the alphabetical listing of a general marketing category, such as "jewelry," look for a specific type of industry or outlet, for example, "department stores."

Apparel

Hat Life Directory. Annual. Includes renovators, importers, classified list of manufacturers, and wholesalers of men's headwear. Hat Life Directory, 66 York St., Jersey City, NJ 07302.

Knitting Times—Buyer's Guide Issue. Annual. Lists manufacturers and suppliers of knitted products, knit goods, materials, supplies services, etc. National Knitwear and Sportswear Association, 386 Park Ave. South, New York, NY 10016.

Men's & Boys' Wear Buyers, Nation-Wide Directory of (exclusive of New York metropolitan area). Annually in August. More than 20,000 buyers and merchandise managers for 6,100 top department, family clothing, and men's and boys' wear specialty stores. Telephone number, buying office, and postal zip code given for each firm. Also available in individual state editions. The Salesman's Guide, Inc., Reed Reference Publishing, 121 Chanlon Rd. New Providence, NJ 07974. Also publishes *Metropolitan New York Directory of Men's and Boys' Wear Buyers.* Semiannually in May and November. (Lists same information for the metropolitan New York area as the nationwide directory.)

Women's & Children's Wear & Accessories Buyers, Nationwide Directory (exclusive of New York metropolitan area). Annually in October. Lists more than 25,000 buyers and divisional merchandise managers for about 6,100 leading department, family clothing, and specialty stores. Telephone number and mail zip code given for each store. Also available in individual state editions. The Salesman's Guide, Inc., Reed Reference Publishing, 121 Chanlon Rd. New Providence, NJ 07974.

Appliances Household

Appliance Dealers—Major Household Directory. Annual. Lists manufacturers and distributors in home electronics, appliances, kitchens. Gives complete addresses and phone. Compiled from Yellow Pages. American Business Directories, Inc., 5711 S. 86th Circle, Omaha, NE 68127.

Automatic Merchandising (Vending)

NAMA Directory of Members. Annually in June. Organized by state and by city, lists vending service companies that are NAMA members. Gives mailing address, telephone number, and products vended. Also includes machine manufacturers and suppliers. National Automatic Merchandising Association, 20 N. Wacker, Dr., Chicago, IL 60606.

Automotive

Manufacturer's Representatives Division. Irregular. A geographical listing of about 300 representatives, including name, address, telephone number, territories covered, and lines carried. Automotive Service Industrial Association, 444 N. Michigan Ave., Chicago, IL 60611.

Automotive Warehouse Distributors Association Membership Directory. Annually in April. Includes listing of manufacturers, warehouse distributors, their products, personnel, and territories. Automotive Warehouse Distributors Association, 9140 Ward Parkway, Kansas City, MO 64114.

Aviation

World Aviation Directory. Published twice a year in March and September. Gives administrative and operating personnel of airlines, aircraft, and engine manufacturers and component manufacturers and distributors, organizations, and schools. Indexed by companies, activities, products, and individuals. Aviation Week Group, 1200 G. St. NW, Washington, DC 20005.

Bookstores

Book Trade Directory, American. Annually in June. Lists more than 25,000 retail and wholesale booksellers in the United States and Canada. Entries alphabetized by state (or province), and then by city and business name. Each listing gives address, telephone numbers, key personnel, types of books sold, subject specialties carried, sidelines and services offered, and general characteristics. For wholesale entries gives types of accounts, import–export information and territory limitations. R. R. Bowker Company, Reed Referencing 121 Chanlon Rd., New Providence, NJ 07974

Building Supplies

Building Supply and Home Centers Giant Issue. Annually in February. Classified directory of manufacturers of lumber, building materials, equipment, and supplies. Cahners Publishing Co., 1350 E. Touhy Ave., Des Plaines, IL 60018.

Business Firms

Million Dollar Directory Series—Top 50,000 Companies. Annually in March. Lists about 50,000 top corporations. Arranged alphabetically. Gives business name, state of incorporation, address, telephone number, SIC numbers, function, sales volume, number of employees, and name of officers and directors, principal bank, accounting firm, and legal counsel. D & B Information Service, D & B Corporation, 3 Sylvan Way, Parsippany, NJ 07054-3896.

China and Glassware

American Glass Review. Glass Factory Directory Issue. Annually in March. Issued as part of subscription (thirteenth issue) to *American Glass Reviews.* Lists companies manufacturing flat glass, tableware glass, and fiberglass, giving corporate and plant addresses, executives, type of equipment used. Doctorow Communications, Inc., 1011 Clifton Ave., Clifton, NJ 07013.

China Glass & Tableware Red Book Directory Issue. Annually in September. Issued as part of subscription (thirteenth issue) to *China Glass & Tableware.* Lists about 1,000 manufacturers, importers, and national distributors of china, glass, and other table appointments, giving corporate addresses and executives. Doctorow Publications, Inc., 1011 Clifton Ave., Clifton, NJ 07013.

City Directories Catalog

Municipal Year Book. Annual. Contains a review of municipal events of the year, analyses of city operations, and a directory of city officials in each state. International City Management Association, 777 N. Capitol St. NE, Washington, DC 20002-4201.

College Stores

College Stores, Directory of. Annual. Published every two years. Lists about 3,000 college stores, geographically with manager's name, type of goods sold, college name, number of students, whether men, women, or both, whether the store is college owned or privately owned. B. Klein Publications, P.O. Box 8503, Coral Springs, FL 33075.

Confectionery

Candy Buyer's Directory. Annually in January. Lists candy manufacturers, importers and U.S. representatives, and confectionery brokers. The Manufacturing Confectionery Publishing Co., 175 Rock Rd., Glen Rock, NJ 07452.

Construction Equipment

Construction Equipment Buyer's Guide. Annually in November. Lists 1,500 construction equipment distributors and manufacturers; includes company names, names of key personnel, addresses, telephone numbers, branch locations, and lines handled or type of equipment produced. Cahners Publishing Co., 1350 E. Touhy Ave., Des Plaines, IL 60018.

Conventions and Trade Shows

Directory of Conventions. Annually in January. Contains over 18,000 cross-indexed listings of annual events; gives dates, locations, names and addresses of executives in charge, scope, expected attendance. Bill Communications, Inc., 355 Park Ave. S., New York, NY 10010-1789.

Trade Show and Exhibits Schedule. Annually in November. Lists over 10,000 exhibits, trade shows, expositions, and fairs held throughout the world with dates given two years in advance. Listings run according to industrial classification covering all industries and professions; full information on dates, city, sponsoring organization, number of exhibits, attendance, gives title and address of executive in charge. Bill Communications, Inc., 355 Park Ave. South, New York, NY 10010-1789.

Dental Supply

Dental Supply Houses, Hayes Directory of. Annually in August. Lists wholesalers of dental supplies and equipment with addresses, telephone numbers, financial standing, and credit rating. Edward N. Hayes, Publisher, 4229 Birch St., Newport Beach, CA 92660.

Department Stores

Sheldon's Retail. Annual. Lists 1,500 large independent department stores, 600 major department store chains, 150 large independent and chain home-furnishing stores, 700 large independent women's specialty stores, and 450 large women's specialty store chains alphabetically by states. Gives all department buyers with lines bought by each buyer, and addresses and telephone numbers of merchandise executives. Also lists all New York, Chicago, Dallas, Atlanta, and Los Angeles buying offices, the number and locations of branch stores, and an index of all store/chain headquarters. Phelon, Sheldon & Marsar, Inc., 15 Industrial Ave., Fairview, NJ 07022.

Discount Stores

Discount Department Stores, Directory of. Annual. Lists headquarters address, telephone number, location, square footage of each store, lines carried, leased operators, names of executives and buyers (includes Canada). Also special section on leased department operators. Chain Store Guide Information Services, 3922 Coconut Palm Dr., Tampa, FL 33619.

Drug Outlets—Retail and Wholesale

Chain Drug Stores Guide, Hayes. Annually in September. Lists headquarters address, telephone numbers, number and location of units, names of executives and buyers, wholesale drug distributors. Edward N. Hayes, 4229 Birch St., Newport Beach, CA 92660.

Druggist Directory, Hayes. Annually in March. Lists about 53,000 retail and 700 wholesale druggists in the United States, giving addresses, financial standing, and credit rating. Also publishes regional editions for one or more states. Computerized mailing labels available. Edward N. Hayes, 4229 Birch St., Newport Beach, CA 92660.

Drug Topics Red Book. Annually in March. Gives information on wholesale drug companies, chain drugstores headquarters, department stores maintaining toilet goods or drug departments, manufacturers' sales agents, and discount houses operating toilet goods, cosmetic, proprietary medicine or prescription departments. Medical Economics, 5 Paragon Dr., Montvale, NJ 07645-1742.

National Wholesale Druggists' Association Membership and Executive Directory. Annually in January. Lists 800 American and foreign wholesalers and manufacturers of drugs and allied products. National Wholesale Druggists' Association, Box 2219, Reston, VA 22090-0219.

Electrical and Electronics

Electronic Industry Telephone Directory. Annually in August. Contains over 22,890 listings of manufacturers, representatives, distributors, government agencies, contracting agencies, and others. Hams Publishing Co., 2057-2 Aurora Rd., Twinsburg, OH 44087.

Electrical Wholesale Distributors, Directory of. Detailed information on 3,400 companies with over 7,630 locations in the United States and Canada, including name, address, telephone number, branch and affiliated houses, products handled, etc. Intertec Publishing Corp, 9800 Metcalf Ave., Shawnee Mission, KS 66212-2215.

Who's Who in Electronics, Regional/National Source Directory. Annually in January. Detailed information (name, address, telephone number, products handled, territories, etc.) on 12,500 electronics manufacturers, and 4,800 industrial electronic distributors and branch outlets. Purchasing index with 1,600 product breakdowns for buyers and purchasing agents. Harris Publishing Co., 2057-2 Aurora Rd., Twinsburg, OH 44087.

Electrical Utilities

Electrical Power Producers, Electrical World, Directory of. Annually in November. Complete listings of electric utilities (investor-owned, municipal, and government agencies in the United States and Canada) giving their addresses and personnel and selected data on operations. Publications Division, McGraw-Hill, Inc., 11 W. 19th St., New York, NY 10011.

Embroidery

Embroidery Directory. Annually in November. Alphabetical listing with addresses and telephone numbers of manufacturers, merchandisers, designers, cutters, bleacheries, yarn dealers, machine suppliers, and other suppliers to the Schiffli lace and embroidery industry. Schiffli Lace and Embroidery Manufacturers Association, Inc., 8555 Tonnelle Ave., North Bergen, NJ 07047-4738.

Export and Import

American Export Register. Annually in September. Includes over 30,000 importers and exporters and products handled. Thomas International Publishing Co., Inc., 5 Penn Plaza, New York, NY 10001.

Canadian Trade Directory, Fraser's. Annually in May. Contains more than 42,000 Canadian companies. Also lists over 14,000 foreign companies that have Canadian representatives. Fraser's Trade Directories, Maclean Hunter Ltd., 777 Bay St., Toronto, Ontario, Canada, M5W 1A7.

Flooring

Flooring Directory and Resource Guide Issue. Annually in October. Reference to sources of supply, giving their products and brand names, leading distributors, manufacturers' representatives, and associations. Leo Douglas Publications Inc., 9609 Gayton Rd., Ste. 100 Richmond, VA 23233.

Food Dealers—Retail and Wholesale

Food Brokers Association, National Directory of Members. Annually in July. Arranged by states and cities, lists member food brokers in the United States and Europe, giving names and addresses, products they handle, and services they perform. National Food Brokers Association, 2100 Reston Parkway #400, Reston, VA 22091.

National Frozen Food Association Directory. Annually in January. Lists packers, distributors, supplies, refrigerated warehouses, wholesalers, and brokers; includes names and addresses of each firm and their key officials. Contains statistical marketing data. National Frozen Food Association, 4755 Linglestown Rd., Ste. 300, Harrisburg, PA 17112.

Food Industry Register, Thomas'. Annually in May. *Volume 1*: Lists supermarket chains, wholesalers, brokers, frozen food brokers, exporters, warehouses. *Volume 2*: Contains information on products and services; manufacturers, sources of supplies, importers. *Volume 3*: A–Z index of 48,000 companies. Also, a brand name/trademark index. Thomas Publishing Co., 5 Penn Plaza, New York, NY 10001.

Tea and Coffee Buyers' Guide, UKers' International. Annual. Includes revised and updated lists of participants in the tea and coffee and allied trades. The Tea and Coffee Trade Journal, Lockwood Trade Journal, Inc., 130 W. 42nd St., 22nd floor, New York, NY 10036.

Gas Companies

Gas Companies, Brown's Directory of. North American and International. Annually in November. Includes information on every known gas utility company and holding company worldwide. Energy Publications Division, Advanstar Communications Inc., 7500 Old Oak Blvd., Cleveland, OH 44130.

LP/Gas. Annually in March. Lists suppliers, supplies, and distributors. Advanstar Communications Inc., 131 W. 1st St. Duluth, MN 55802.

Gift and Art

Gift, Housewares and Home Textile Buyers, Nationwide Directory of. Annually with semiannual supplement. For 7,000 types of retail firms lists store name, address, type of store, number of stores, names of president, merchandise managers, and buyers, etc., for giftwares and housewares. State editions also available. The Salesman's Guide, Inc., Reed Reference Publishing, 121 Chanlon Rd., New Providence, NJ 07974.

Gift Shops Directory. 66,291 listings. American Business Directories, Inc., 571 1 S. 86th Circle, Omaha, NE 68127.

Home Furnishings

The Antique Dealers Directory. Annual. Lists 35,636 dealers with name, address, and phone number as well as size of advertisement and first year advertised in Yellow Pages. American Business Directories, Inc. 571 1 S. 86th Circle, Omaha, NE 68127.

Home Fashions—Buyer's Guide Issue. Annually in December. Lists names and addresses of manufacturers, importers, and regional sales representatives. Fairchild Publications, Capital Cities Media, Inc., 7 W. 34th St., New York, NY 10003.

Interior Decorator's and Designer Supplies. Semiannually in spring and fall. Published expressly for decorators and designers, interior decorating staff of department and furniture stores. Lists firms handling items used in interior decoration. American Business Information, 5711 S. 86th Circle, Omaha, NE 68127.

Hospitals

Hospitals, Directory of. Annually in January. Lists 12,173 hospitals, with selected data. American Business Directories, American Business Information, 5711 S. 86th Circle, Omaha, NE 68127.

Hotels and Motels

Hotels and Motels Directory. Annually. Lists more than 62,465 hotels and motels. American Business Directories, Inc. 571 1 S. 86th Circle, Omaha, NE 68127.

OAG Travel Planner and Hotel Redbook. Quarterly. Lists over 26,000 hotels in the United States. Also lists 14,500 destination cities, etc. Official Airline Guide Inc., 2000 Clearwater Dr., Oak Brook, IL 60521.

Housewares

NHMA Membership Directory and Buyers Desk-Top Guide to Houseware Manufacturers. Annually in June. Compilation of resources of the housewares trade, includes listing of their products, trade names, and a registry of manufacturers' representatives. National Housewares Manufacturers Association, 6400 Shafer Ct. Ste 600, Rosemont, IL 60608.

Jewelry

Jewelers' Circular/Keystone—Jewelers' Directory Issue. Annual in June. Lists manufacturers, importers, distributors, and retailers of jewelry; diamonds; precious, semiprecious, and imitation stones; watches, silverware; and kindred articles. Includes credit ratings. Chilton Co., Chilton Way, Radnor, PA 19098.

Liquor

Wine and Spirits Wholesalers of America—Member Roster and Industry Directory. Annually in January. Lists names of 700 member companies; includes parent house and branches, addresses, and names of managers. Also, has register of 2,200 suppliers, and gives state liquor control administrators, national associations, and trade press directory Wine and Spirits Wholesalers of America, Inc., 1023 15th St. NW, 4th fl., Washington, DC 20005.

Mailing List Houses

Mailing List, Directory of. Lists 1,800 firms, brokers, compilers, and firms offering their own lists for rent; includes the specialties of each firm. Arranged geographically. American Business Directories, Inc., American Business Information, 5711 S. 86th Circle, Omaha, NE 68127.

Order Businesses

Mail Order Business Directory. Lists 10,000 names of mail order firms with buyers' names, and lines carried. Arranged geographically. B. Klein Publications, P.O. Box 8503, Coral Springs, FL 33075.

Manufacturers

MacRae's Blue Book. Annually in March. In three volumes: Volume 1 Corporate Index lists company names and addresses alphabetically, with 40,000 branch and/or sales office telephone numbers. Volumes 2 and 3 list companies by product classifications. MacRae's Blue Book, Business Research Publications, 65 Bleecker St., New York, NY 10012.

Manufacturers, Thomas' Register of American. Annual. Volume 1–14 products and services; suppliers of each product category grouped by state and city. Vols. 15–16 contain company profiles. Vols. 17–23 manufacturers' catalogs. More than 150,000 firms are listed under 50,000 product headings. Thomas Publishing Co., 5 Penn Plaza, New York, NY 10001.

Manufacturer's Sales Representatives

Manufacturers & Agents National Association Directory of Members. Annually in May/June. Contains individual listings of manufacturers' agents throughout the United States, Canada, and several foreign countries. Listings cross-referenced by alphabetical, geographical, and product classification. Manufacturers' Agents National Association, Box 3467, Laguna Hills, CA 92654.

Metalworking

Metalworking Directory, Dun & Bradstreet. Annually in June. Lists about 78,000 metalworking and metal producing plants with 20 or more production employees. Arranged geographically. Dun and Bradstreet Information Service, Dun & Bradstreet Corporation, 3 Sylvan Way, Parsippany, NJ 07054-3896.

Military Market

Military Market Magazine—Buyer's Guide Issue. Annually in January. Lists manufacturers and suppliers of products sold in military commissaries. Also lists manufacturers' representatives and distributors. Army Times Publishing Co., Times Journal Co., 6883 Commercial Dr., Springfield, VA 22159.

Paper Products

Sources of Supply Buyers' Guide. Lists 1,700 mills and converters of paper, film, foil, and allied products, and paper merchants in the United States alphabetically with addresses, principal personnel, and products manufactured. Also lists trade associations, brand names, and manufacturers' representatives. Advertisers and Publishers Service, Inc., P.O. Box 795, Park Ridge, IL 60068.

Physicians Supply Houses

Physician and Hospital Supply Houses, Hayes' Director of. Annually in August. Listings of 1,850 U.S. wholesalers doing business in physician, hospital, and surgical supplies and equipment; includes addresses, telephone numbers, financial standing, and credit ratings. Edward N. Haves, Publisher, 4229 Birch St., Newport Beach, CA 92660.

Premium Sources

Incentive Resource Guide Issue. Annually in February. Contains classified directory of suppliers and list of manufacturers' representatives serving the premium field. Also lists associations, clubs, and trade shows. Bill Communications, 355 Park Ave., New York, NY 10010-7789.

Purchasing Government

U.S. Government Purchasing and Sales Directory. Irregularly issued. Booklet designed to help small business receive an equitable share of government contracts. Lists types of purchases for both military and civilian needs, catalogs procurement offices by state. Lists SBA regional and branch offices, Office of Government Contracting, Small Business Adm., 409 3rd St. SW, Washington, DC 20416.

Refrigeration and Air Conditioning

Air Conditioning, Heating & Refrigeration News—Directory Issue. Annually in January. Lists 1,900 manufacturers and 3,000 wholesalers and factory outlets in refrigeration, heating, and air-conditioning. Business News Publishing Co., 755 W. Big Beaver Rd., 10th fl., Troy, MI 48084.

Selling Direct

Direct Selling Companies, World Directory. Annually in April. About 40 direct selling associations and 750 associated member companies. Includes names of contact persons, company product line, method of distribution, etc. World Federation of Direct Selling Associations, 1776 K St. NW, Suite 600, Washington, DC 20006.

Shopping Centers

Shopping Center Directory. Annual. Alphabetical listing of 34,000 shopping centers, location, owner/developer, manager, physical plant (number of stores, square feet), and leasing agent. National Research Bureau, Division of Information, Product Group, Automated Marketing Systems, Inc., 150 N. Wacker Drive Ste. 222., Chicago, IL 60604.

Specialty Stores

Women's Apparel Stores, Phelon's. Lists over 7,000 women's apparel and accessory shops with store headquarters name and address, number of shops operated, New York City buying headquarters or representatives, lines of merchandise bought and sold, name of principal and buyers, store size, and price range. Phelon, Sheldon, Marsar, Inc., 15 Industrial Ave., Fairview, NJ 07022.

Sporting Goods

Sporting Goods Buyers, Nationwide Directory of. Including semiannual supplements. Lists over 7,500 top retail stores with names of buyers and executives, for all types of sporting goods, athletic apparel and athletic footwear, hunting, fishing, and outdoor equipment. The Salesman's Guide, Inc.,121 Chanlon Rd., New Providence, NJ 07974.

Textiles

Textile Blue Book, Davison's. Annually in March. Contains more than 8,400 separate company listings (name, address, etc.) for the United States and Canada. Firms included are cotton, wool, synthetic mills, knitting mills, cordage, twine, and duck manufacturers, dry goods commission merchants, converters, yam dealers, cordage manufacturers' agents, wool dealers and merchants, cotton merchants, exporters, brokers, and others. Davisons Textile Bluebook, Davisons Publishing Co., Box 477, Ridgewood, NJ 07451.

Toys and Novelties

Playthings—Who Makes It Issue. Annually in June. Lists manufacturers, products, trade names, suppliers to manufacturers, supplier products, licensors, manufacturers' representatives, toy trade associations, and trade show managements. Geyer-McAllister Publications, Inc., 51 Madison Ave., New York, NY 10010.

Small World—Directory Issue. Annually in December. Lists 200 wholesalers, manufacturers, manufacturers' representatives of toys, games, and hobbies for children and infants. Earnshaw Publications Inc., 225 West 34th St., Suite 1212, New York, NY 10122.

Trailer Parks

Campground Directory, Woodall's. Annual. Lists and star-rates public and private campgrounds in North American continent alphabetically by town with location and description of facilities. Also lists more than 800 RV service locations. Regional editions available. Woodall Publishing Company, 28167 North Keith Dr., Lake Forest, IL 60045.

Trucking

Trucksource: Sources of Trucking Industry Information. Annually in November. Includes over 700 sources of information on the trucking industry, classified by subject. American Trucking Association, 2200 Mill Road, Alexandria, VA 22314-4677.

Variety Stores

General Merchandise, Variety, and Specialty Stores, Directory of. Annually in March. Lists headquarters address, telephone number, number of units and locations, executives and buyers. Chain Store Guide Information Services, 3922 Coconut Palm Drive, Tampa, FL 33619.

Warehouses

Public Warehousing, Guide to. Annually in July. Lists leading public warehouses in the United States and Canada, as well as major truck lines, airlines, steamship lines, liquid and dry bulk terminals, material handling equipment suppliers, ports of the world and railroad piggyback services and routes. Chilton Co., Chilton Way, Radnor, PA 19089.

Members Associated Warehouses, Directory of. Irregularly. Listing of 90 members. Associated Warehouses, Inc., Box 471, Cedar Knolls, NJ 07927.

Other Important Directories

The following business directories are helpful to those persons doing marketing research. Most of these directories are available for reference at the larger libraries. For additional listings consult the *Guide to American Directories* at local libraries.

Bradford's Directory of Marketing Research Agencies and Management Consultants in the United States and the World. Gives names and addresses of over 2,400 marketing research agencies in the United States, Canada, and abroad. Lists service offered by agency, along with other pertinent data, such as date established, names of principal officers, and size of staff. Bradford's Directory of Marketing Research Agencies, 9991 Caitland Ct, Manassas, VA 22110.

Consultants and Consulting Organizations Directory. Contains 16,000 entries. Guides reader to appropriate organization for a given consulting assignment. Entries include names, addresses, phone numbers, and data on services performed. Gale Research Company, 835 Penobscot Bldg., Detroit, MI 48226-4094.

Research Centers Directory. Lists more than 11,000 nonprofit research organizations. Descriptive information provided for each center, including address, telephone number, name of director, data on staff, funds, publications, and a statement concerning its principal fields of research. Has special indexes. Gale Research Company, 835 Penobscot Bldg., Detroit, MI 48226-4094.

MacRae's Blue Book—Manufacturers. Annual. In three volumes: Volume 1 is an index by corporations; Volumes 2–3 are a classification by products showing under each classification manufacturers of that item. Business Research Publications, Inc., 65 Bleecker St., New York, NY 10012.

Thomas' Food Industry Register. Annually in May. Lists in two volumes wholesale grocers, chain store organizations, voluntary buying groups, food brokers, exporters and importers of food products, frozen food brokers, distributors and related products distributed through grocery chains. Thomas Publishing Company, 5 Penn Plaza, New York, NY 10001.

Thomas' Register of American Manufacturers. Annually in February. In 23 volumes. Volumes 1–14 contain manufacturers arranged geographically under each product, and capitalization or size rating for each manufacturer, under 50,000 product headings. Volumes 15 and 16 contain company profiles and a brand or trade name section with more than 112,000 listings. Volumes 17–23 are catalogs from more than 1,500 firms. Thomas Publishing Co., 5 Penn Plaza, New York, NY 10001.

APPENDIX

C

EXAMPLES OF SIMPLE RESEARCH AND A MARKETING RESEARCH CHECKLIST

The kind of marketing research you do is limited only by your imagination. Some research can be done, even of the primary type, at very little cost except for your time. Here are some examples of simple research done by small businesses which greatly increased sales. These ideas were suggested by J. Ford Laumer, Jr., James R. Hams, and Hugh J. Guffey, Jr., all professors of marketing at Auburn University of Auburn, Alabama, in their booklet *Learning about Your Market,* published by the Small Business Administration.

1. *License Plate Analysis.* In many states, license plates give you information about where car owners live. Therefore, simply by taking down the numbers of cars parked in your location and contacting the appropriate state agency, you can estimate the area from which you draw business. Knowing where your customers live can help you in your advertising or in targeting your approach to promotion. By the same method you can find who your competitors' customers are.

2. *Telephone Number Analysis.* Telephone numbers can also tell you the areas in which people live. You can obtain customers' telephone numbers from sales slips, credit card slips, or checks. Again, knowing where they live will give you excellent information about their life-styles.

3. *Coded Coupons.* The effectiveness of your advertising vehicle can easily be checked by coding coupons that can be used for discounts or inquiries about products. You can find out the areas that your customers come from, as well as which vehicle brought them your message.

4. *People Watching.*   Simply looking at your customers can tell you a great deal about them. How are they dressed? How old are they? Are they married or single? Do they have children or not? Many owners use this method intuitively to get a feel about their customers. However, a little sophistication with a tally sheet for a week can provide much more accurate information simply, easily, and without cost. It may confirm what you've known all along, or it may completely change your opinion of your typical customer.

Checklist for Appraisal of Your Research Study

1. Review of research objectives:
   a. In relation to the problem.
   b. In relation to previous research.
   c. In relation to developments subsequent to initiation of research.

2. Overall study design:
   a. Are the hypotheses relevant? Consistent?
   b. Is the terminology relevant and unambiguous?
   c. Is the design a logical bridge from problem to solution?
   d. Are there any biases in the design that may have influenced the results?
   e. Was care taken to preserve anonymity, if needed?
   f. Were proper ethical considerations taken into account?
   g. Was the study well administered?

3. Methods used:
   a. Were the right sources used (populations sampled)?
   b. Do any of the data collection methods appear to be biased?
   c. What precautions were taken to avoid errors or mistakes in data collection?
   d. If sampling was used, how representative is the sample? With what margin of error?
   e. Were the data processed with due care? What precautions were taken to assure good coding?
   f. Are the categories used in tabulation meaningful?
   g. Were any pertinent tabulations or cross classifications overlooked? On the other hand, are the tabulations so detailed as to obscure some of the main points?
   h. Do the analytical (statistical) methods appear to be appropriate?
   i. Is the report well executed in terms of organization, style, appearance, etc?

4. Review of interpretations and recommendations:
   a. Do they follow from the data? Are they well supported?
   b. Are they comprehensive? Do they relate to the whole problem or only part of it?
   c. Are they consistent with the data? With existing information, other studies, executives' experiences, etc?
   d. Were any relevant interpretations overlooked?

5. Responsibility for action and follow-up:
   a. Will information receive due consideration from all those concerned?
   b. What are the implications of the results for action? Will all action possibilities be considered? (How do the results affect aspects of total operation outside the scope of the report?)
   c. Is an action program necessary? Will it be formulated?
   d. Is further information needed? If so, along what lines?
   e. Is responsibility for follow-up clearly assigned?
   f. Should a time be set for reevaluation of the action program (e.g., to reevaluate an innovation, or test a new package after introduction)?

HOW TO LEAD A TEAM

One of the most important and difficult challenges in developing a marketing plan is working on a team. Teamwork is never easy. You must work with different personalities, having different work schedules, different priorities, different motivation, and different ways of approaching the project. Further, someone may or may not be assigned as team leader. You may think that teamwork is something that you only need to be concerned with as a student. You may be under the impression that once you graduate, you need never be concerned with teamwork again. You would be very much mistaken. Most companies of all sizes use teams to accomplish work to some extent or another. Over the last decade, there has been a dramatic increase in the use of team structures in companies due to the quality movement and the use of process action teams. Process action teams focus on improving the process of getting some type of work accomplished. But long before the quality movement, teams had already made important contributions in industry. In fact, back in 1987, management guru Tom Peters stated, ". . . the power of the team is so great that it is often wise to violate apparent common sense and force a team structure on almost anything."[1]

To understand just how powerful teams are, try to identify what kind of work has all of the following characteristics:

- The workers work very hard physically, including weekends, with little complaint.
- The workers receive no money and little material compensation for their services.
- The work is dangerous, and workers are frequently injured on the job.
- The work is strictly voluntary.
- The workers usually have very high morale.

---

[1] Tom Peters, *Thriving on Chaos* (New York: Knopf, 1987) p. 306.

- There are always more volunteers than can be used for the work.
- The workers are highly motivated to achieve the organization's goals.
- Not only is the work legal, but many community organizations encourage it.

Turn the page to identify this work. The work which has all of these characteristics is

. . . A HIGH SCHOOL FOOTBALL TEAM

WHAT'S SO GREAT ABOUT A TEAM?

Yes, all of the characteristics of the football team are true. The operative word here is TEAM. Can you see just how powerful and unique a team can be? Yet the basic concept of a team is very simple. A team is simply two or more individuals working together to reach a common goal.

Teams in industry have achieved incredible goals. One of General Electric's plants in Salisbury, North Carolina, increased its productivity by 250 percent compared with other General Electric plants making the same product, but without teams. General Mills' plants with teams are 40 percent more productive than plants without teams. Westinghouse Furniture Systems increased productivity 74 percent in three years with teams. Using teams, Volvo's Kalimar facility reduced manufacturing defects by 90 percent.

A number of scientists have observed that when geese flock in a V formation to reach a destination, they are operating as a team. Their common goal is their destination. And by teaming, they extend their range by as much as 71 percent! Flocking also illustrates some other important aspects of effective teaming. One goose doesn't lead all the time. The lead position at the point of the V varies. Note that this is also true in football. On different plays, the leadership role varies. Also, at different times in football, different individuals may assume important leadership roles. At any given time, the head coach, line coach, team captain, quarterback, or someone else may have the most important leadership role on the team.

Getting back to our flock of geese, should a single goose leave formation, it soon returns because of the difficulty in flying against the wind resistance alone. Should a goose fall out of formation because it is injured, other "team members" will drop out and attempt to assist their teammate. You may think that the honking noise made by geese in formation serves no useful purpose. But scientific investigation found that honking is all part of their teamwork. The honking is the cheering that encourages the leader to maintain the pace. Flocks of geese, football teams, and teams of students developing a marketing plan are effective if they share the following characteristics:

- They demonstrate coordinated interaction.
- They are more efficient working together than alone.
- They enjoy the process of working together.
- Responsibility rotates either formally or informally.
- There is mutual care, nurturing, and encouragement among team members and especially between leaders and followers.
- There is a high level of trust.
- Everyone is keenly interested in everyone else's success.

As you might expect, when a group acts together toward a common goal showing these characteristics, you see some very positive results. It becomes not just a team, but a winning team. The team members have a degree of understanding and acceptance not found outside the group. They come up with better ideas, and these ideas are more innovative than those suggested by individual members. Such a team has higher motivation and performance levels which offset individual biases, and cover each others' "blind spots."

If you saw the movie *Rocky,* you may remember the scene where Rocky's girlfriend's brother demands to know what Rocky sees in his sister. "She fills spaces," answers Stalone, playing the role of Rocky. "Spaces in me, spaces in her." With fewer "blind spots" and performing together so as to emphasize each member's strengths and make his or her weaknesses irrelevant, an effective team is more likely to take risks and innovative action that lead to success.

When a flock of geese becomes a winning team, it reaches its destination faster than other flocks. It gets the most protective nesting areas which are located near sources of food and water. The goslings are bigger, stronger, and healthier, and they have a much better chance of survival and procreation. We see the winning football teams in the Super Bowl. And a winning marketing planning team? In class, this is the team that gets the "A," and has a lot of fun doing it. In real life, the winning team developing a marketing plan gets the necessary resources, and goes on to build a multi-billion dollar success in the marketplace.

WHO GETS TO BE THE TEAM LEADER?

Sometimes you will be assigned the position of team leader. Sometimes not. Sometimes no team leader assignment will be made. However, you may be the only graduate student on a team with undergraduate students. Moreover, in your "other life," you are a company president. You are confident that your fellow team members will follow your lead. You attend several meetings and attempt to take charge. Guess what? Your teammates reject you in favor of someone who isn't one tenth as qualified. What do you do?

My advice is this. If you are assigned or selected as team leader by your teammates, do the job to the best of your ability. If you are not assigned or selected as team leader by your teammates, support whoever is team leader to the best of your ability. Never let your ego get in the way of your doing your best for your team. Not only will this help your team become a winner, but you will earn the respect of your teammates and maintain your own self respect as well. A good leader can both lead and follow. He or she doesn't need to be the leader in order to make a major contribution to the team.

HOW DO I LEAD IF I AM THE LEADER?

There is no way of telling you how to be a leader in 25 words or less. There are volumes written about leadership. I should know—I wrote one, a bestseller recommended by leaders including Mary Kay Ash, CEO Emeritus of Mary Kay Cosmetics and Senator Barry Goldwater, and I recommend it to you.[2] I will point out one critical fact. There is no question that as team leader, you have a major responsibility for the ultimate marketing plan that is produced. There is an old saying that it is better to have

---

[2] William A. Cohen, *The Art of the Leader* (Englewood Cliffs, NJ: Prentice-Hall, 1990).

an army of lambs led by a lion than an army of lions led by a lamb. This emphasizes the extreme importance of the leader in getting the job done. There is no such thing as an excuse that "all my team members were lambs." A leader who says this is really saying that "I am a lamb." We don't know what the team members were. They could have all been lions and still failed with a lamb as a leader.

Although I can't make you an expert leader in a few pages of suggestions, there are specific things I can tell you about being a *team* leader. Psychologists and researchers in leadership found that teams progress through four stages of development. Each stage not only has different characteristics, but team members tend to ask different questions in each stage. Because the concerns of the team tend to be different in each stage, the leader's focus, actions, and behavior must be different in each stage as well. This is extremely important because what might be the correct actions in one stage would be counterproductive and incorrect in another. For example, in the second stage of development members actually tend to be committed, and even obedient. The leader's focus during this stage must be on building relationships and facilitating tasks. But beware! In the next stage, members tend to challenge each other and even their leader. You've got to focus on conflict management and examining key work processes to make them better. If you are stuck in stage two while your team is in stage three, you may lose your moral authority as leader.

So, as a team leader, you must first identify what stage the team is in. Then, pay attention to your focus and attempt to answer the concerns of your team while you help move them toward completing the project. With this in mind, here are the four stages of team development:

- Stage 1: Getting Organized
- Stage 2: Getting Together and Making Nice-Nice
- Stage 3: Fighting It Out
- Stage 4: Getting the Job Done

Now let's look at each in turn.

STAGE 1: GETTING ORGANIZED

When you first get together as a team, you're going to find that many of your team members may tend to be quiet and self-conscious, unless they have known one another previously. This is because they are uncertain. They don't know what is going to happen, and they may be worried about what is expected of them. The questions that may occur to your fellow team members at this time include: Who are these other people? Are they going to be friendly or challenge me? What are they going to expect me to do? What's going to happen during this process? Where exactly will we be headed and why? What are our precise goals? Where do I fit in? How much work will this involve? Is this project going to require me to give up time that I need to put in elsewhere?

As the team leader, your primary focus during stage 1 is just as the stage is named: to organize the team. Your actions should include making introductions; stating the mission of the team; clarifying goals, procedures, rules, expectations; and answering questions. The idea is to establish a foundation of trust right from the start. You want an atmosphere of openness with no secrets. While members may disagree with each other or with you, everyone gets his or her say and everyone's opinion is listened to and considered.

To do this, you must model these expected behaviors yourself. If you aren't open, no one else will be. If you don't respect the opinions of others, neither will anyone else. If you listen carefully, so will everyone else. If you argue and try to shout down others, so will those you are attempting to lead.

You may be interested in characteristics of high performance teams as distinguished from those that performed less well.[3] Keep these in mind as you organize your team.

- Clear goals
- Goals known by all
- Goals achieved in small steps
- Standards of excellence
- Feedback of results
- Skills and knowledge of everyone used
- Continuous improvement expected
- Adequate resources provided

- Autonomy
- Performance-based rewards
- Competition
- Praise and recognition
- Team commitment
- Plans and tactics
- Rules and penalties
- Performance measures

Remember, in stage one, your principal focus is on getting organized. At the same time, you are laying the foundations of trust and openness for the stages that follow.

STAGE 2: GETTING TOGETHER AND MAKING NICE-NICE

Congratulations! You did a great job of getting your marketing planning team at the first meeting. Now you have a different challenge. Members tend to ignore disagreements and conform obediently to the group standards and expectations, as well as your directions as leader. There is heightened interpersonal attraction, and at the end, everyone will be committed to a team vision. All of this is desirable.

Of course, team members still wonder and ask themselves questions. What are the team's norms and expectations? How much should I really give up and conform to the group's ideas? What role can I perform on this team? Where can I make a contribution? Will my suggestions be supported, or will others "put me down"? Where are we headed? How much time and energy should I commit to this project?

During this stage, you have several major challenges:

- Facilitating role differentiation
- Showing support
- Providing feedback
- Articulating and motivating commitment to a vision

To facilitate role differentiation, you need to continue to build relationships among your team members. You want your team members to contribute according to their strengths where they are most needed. You also want to assist them in whatever tasks they are working on. You can do this by asking about their strengths and their preferences for tasks that need to be done. As they proceed, it is your responsibility to

---

[3] F. Petrock, "Team Dynamics: A Workshop for Effective Team Building." Presentation at the University of Michigan Michigan Management of Managers Program.

ensure they have the resources to do the job. When there are disagreements between team members, as leader it is your responsibility to resolve the situation. As a task facilitator, you yourself may function in a variety of roles. At times you may give direction, or at least suggestions. You are sometimes an information seeker and, at others, an information giver. You must monitor, coordinate, and oversee everything that is going on. Avoid blocking others from contributing, and don't let anyone else block either. People try to block others in a variety of ways, including fault-finding, overanalyzing, rejecting out of hand, dominating, stalling, and some others we might never anticipate. Don't let them do it!

Show support for others by building people up every chance you get. Build on their ideas, but give them credit for their ideas. And as indicated earlier, let everyone be heard. Don't let someone who is more articulate, powerful, or popular block the ideas of some less aggressive team member.

Providing effective feedback is not easy. You must indicate what is going to work, and what won't. To do this without offending, so this person maintains his or her self-respect and continues to contribute is the real challenge. To best accomplish this, talk about behavior, not about personalities. Make observations, not inferences. Be as specific as possible. Share ideas and information. Don't set yourself up as a "know-it-all" who gives advice. Learn the art of the possible. It is possible to give too much feedback at one time, especially if the feedback is more critical than congratulatory. In fact, critical feedback is always difficult. Look for ways of criticizing which remove the "sting." President Reagan gave a small statue of a foot with a hole in it to his Secretary of the Interior when the secretary made a major public gaffe. The statue was the "Shot Yourself in the Foot" Award. There was a lot of laughter and good humor as President Reagan presented it. Still, it was criticism. You might establish a pot where people have to put in a dollar if they show up late for a team meeting. The money could go toward a team party or for some other team purpose. Finally, remember you give feedback to help the team—not for personal emotional release. Not to show who's boss and not to show how clever you are.

Finally, you must focus on articulating and motivating commitment to a vision. A vision is a type of mental picture of the outcome of the mission. Maybe the vision is to submit the best marketing plan in the class. Maybe it is to win a prize with the plan. Maybe it is to develop a plan for someone who is actually going to implement it. In any case, you should sell the outcome, the good things that will happen as a result of the team's work in precise terms. Motivating your team means making your vision their vision as well. To do this, you must get them involved with it. Ask their opinions. Modify your vision, as necessary. Ground the vision in core values. Remember, people don't sacrifice to do small tasks. They sacrifice only for big tasks. So if you are preparing a marketing plan for a medical product that can benefit humanity, emphasize creating a better world more than profitability. If you can get people involved with suggestions and ideas about the vision and how to achieve it, you will have attained two essential elements—public commitment and ownership. Get those, and you've gone a long way to building a winning team.

STAGE 3: FIGHTING IT OUT

When you enter stage three, the good news is that you have a team fully committed to a vision, and fighting to get a first-class marketing plan developed, printed, and bound. Unfortunately, because individuals have so much of themselves invested, members in this stage can become polarized, may form cliques, become overly competitive, and may even challenge your authority as leader.

Clearly, you have your work cut out for you. Your focus during this stage must be on conflict management, continuing to ensure that everyone gets to express his or her ideas, examining key work processes to make them better, getting team members working together rather than against each other, and avoiding groupthink. All of these are fairly straightforward except for groupthink. What is groupthink?

Groupthink means adopting some idea or course of action simply because the group seems to want it, and not because it is a particularly good idea that has been thoroughly discussed and thought through. The most conspicuous example of groupthink has been popularized as a "Trip to Abilene." In a "Trip to Abilene," a family makes a miserable two-hour trip to Abilene and returns to a ranch in west Texas. The trip is made in a car without air-conditioning on a hot, humid summer day at the suggestion of one of the family members. All members agreed on the trip, although later it turns out that they did so simply "to be agreeable." Whereupon, the member who suggested the idea states that he didn't want to go either. He simply suggested the idea to make conversation.

To avoid groupthink, all ideas should be critically evaluated. You should encourage open discussion of all ideas on a routine basis. Some more sophisticated ideas can be better evaluated by calling in outside experts to listen or even rotating assignment of a devil's advocate to bring up all the reasons to oppose any proposed action. One idea that helps many teams avoid groupthink is a policy of second chance discussions. With this technique, all decisions made at a meeting have their implementations deferred until one additional confirmation discussion at a later date.

During this stage, the questions raised by your fellow team members will include: How will we handle disagreements? How do we communicate negative information? Can the composition of this team be changed? How can we make decisions even though there is a lot of disagreement? Do we really need this leader? You may wish that your fellow team members were not asking themselves these questions, especially the last. However, better to be forewarned so you can deal with these issues, than to be surprised.

There are a number of actions you can take to help your team during this stage. You can think up ways to reinforce and remotivate commitment to the vision. You can turn your fellow team members into teachers, helping others with their problems. In fact, you should know that using others as teachers, or leaders, for subareas in the project helps to generate their public commitment. You might devise ways of providing individual recognition, such as a small prize for the most accomplished during the previous week. As arguments arise, you can work on being a more effective mediator. You can look for win/win opportunities and foster win/win thinking, where both sides of an argument or an issue benefit. One way to increase feelings of cohesion in the group is to identify a common "enemy." Other class teams competing for "best marketing plan" might constitute one such "enemy."

There are plenty of challenges for you as a leader in this stage. You will learn a tremendous amount about leading groups. Do it right, and your team enters the final stage looking, acting, and performing like a real winner.

STAGE 4: GETTING THE JOB DONE

Of course your team is getting the job done during all four stages. But if you've done things right, when you get to stage four, you are really on a roll. How soon your team gets to this stage varies greatly. Clearly, it is to your advantage to get to this stage as soon as you can, and to spend the bulk of your time working on your marketing plan in this stage. During this stage, team members show high mutual trust and unconditional commitment to the team. Moreover, team members tend to be self-sufficient and display a good deal of initiative. The team looks like an entrepreneurial company. As team leader, your focus during this final stage should be on innovation, continuous improvement, and emphasizing and making most of what your team does best, its core competencies.

Team members' questions reflect this striving for high performance. How can we continuously improve? How can we promote innovativeness and creativity? How can we build on our core competencies? What additional improvements can be made to our processes? How can we maintain a high level of contribution to the team?

As team leader, your actions are in direct line with these questions. Do everything you can to encourage continuous improvement. Celebrate your team's successes. Keep providing feedback on performance on an ongoing basis. Sponsor and encourage new ideas and expanded roles for team members. And most important, help the team avoid reverting back to earlier stages.

WHEN GOOD TEAM MEMBERS DO BAD THINGS

As you progress through the four stages, you will occasionally be surprised by team members you considered first rate, doing things to hurt the team. When that happens, you will have to take some kind of action. You might also consider the root cause. Why did this productive team member go wrong? Here are some of the more common reasons that good team members err:

- Inequity of effort.
  When one or more members of the team fail to maintain a certain standard of effort, you will soon find that others will do the same. The erring team member thinks "If this other person isn't working up to this effort, why should I?" This is one reason why you cannot allow one member of the team to goof off and do less than his or her fair share. You must stop inequity of effort before it starts.

- No accountability.
  This occurs when members are allowed to "freewheel," and no feedback occurs. Since no one else seems to care, the member feels insignificant and unimportant. This can lead to general inequity of effort.

- Same reward to everyone.
  This, too is related to inequity of effort. The team member wonders why he or she should work harder than other team members when all get the same reward. You want each member to contribute to the maximum extent possible. Same reward can lead to everyone trying to do the minimum. The solution is to set up a reward system, even if the "reward" is a simple public recognition of an above-the-call-of-duty or a successful accomplishment.

- Coordination problems.
  There is no getting around it; the more people involved, the more coordination required. That can mean waiting for the work of others, having to get others' approval, and other delays. For someone who has always worked successfully alone, the inefficiencies are frustrating and painfully obvious. As already noted, however, the loss in efficiency of the individual can be more than made up by the synergistic effect. Team members can not only help one another, but cheer them on and rejoice in another individual's success. As team leader, you must make certain this happens. You must make it rewarding and fun to be part of the team. Do this, and members will see that they can accomplish more as a member of a group than they ever could individually.

SUMMARY

The focus of this book is how to put together a marketing plan. You will learn a lot from doing this. It is a skill that is valuable to any corporation. You may get to work on a team. If so, you are going to learn a great deal from this also. It is an invaluable experience. If you are really lucky, you will have the responsibility of team leader. You have achieved a triple whammy. You are going to learn more than anyone else. It's not going to be easy. You will face the stiffest challenges and the most difficult work. You will bear the heaviest responsibility. It can also be one of the most rewarding experiences you have ever had. This appendix can help you, but only you can determine how to apply the information. Your success is up to you. Good luck!

Index